CHILD FROM 2 TO 5

Molly Mason Jones

HARCOURT, BRACE & WORLD, INC.

NEW YORK

For W. T. J.

PREFACE

ONE OF THE topics discussed in this book concerns the difficulties—and the satisfactions—of being a working mother. One of the difficulties in my own case was finding time to finish the book. But this slow progress was not without its advantages. I have had the opportunity, over the years, of thinking about theories of learning and about the practice of child guidance; of utilizing these in the actual guidance of children; and then of revising theories and practice in the light of children's behavior in the nursery school and of parents' reports of life at home. And the fact that I am a working mother has been helpful, too, in the formulation of the content of the book.

Now, with the book finally completed, I have the great satisfaction of being able to thank some of the many people who have contributed in various ways to my ideas about child guidance:

—My colleagues in St. George's School for Child Study at the University of Toronto, from whom I learned so much: Miss Margaret I. Fletcher, Miss Dorothy A. Millichamp, and Mrs. Anne Harris Blatz. To the late Dr. W. E. Blatz I shall always be enormously grateful.

—My colleagues in the Mary B. Eyre Nursery School at Scripps College, especially Miss Jean Gillies, Mrs. Mary D. Westbrook, and Mrs. Helen S. Cunliffe, who has also most generously read the galleys; also the young women, many of them Scripps graduates, who have served as Assistants in the Nursery School whom I will not try to mention by name.

—The students at Scripps, Pomona, and the other Claremont Colleges, who have participated in the Nursery School and taken part in our staff discussions.

—The children whom I have known professionally, their parents, and my own children.

I am grateful to Radcliffe College for the Putnam Research Fellowship which enabled me to start on the book; to Scripps College for its generous sabbatical policy; and to Professor Jerome Kagan, of Harvard, for many helpful suggestions.

Most of all, I am grateful to my husband for his inestimable help and encouragement in all stages of the manuscript, without which it would never have been completed.

M. M. J.

Contents

Preface, vii
Introduction, 1

1: WHAT CHILDREN IN GENERAL ARE LIKE   6

2-year-olds
"Negativism" between 2 and 3
3-year-olds
4-year-olds

2: HOW PEOPLE LEARN   19

Conditioning
Learning by consequences
Applying learning by consequences to guidance

3: WHAT DO YOU WANT YOUR CHILD TO LEARN?   53

Long-range aims
Promoting long-range aims through everyday experiences
Things to take into account when setting aims for your
child's behavior

ix

4: ARRANGING YOUR CHILD'S SURROUNDINGS   74

What home should be for each person in the family
Safety measures
A place designed expressly for your child
Play materials
Books, music, television

5: TECHNIQUES OF GUIDANCE   113

Preparing yourself for direct guidance of your child
A record of children at "family" play
Guidance techniques for children of any age

6: SUPPLEMENTARY GUIDANCE TECHNIQUES FOR PARTIC-
ULAR STAGES OF DEVELOPMENT   142

Supplementary guidance techniques for 2-year-olds
Supplementary techniques for the child who is feeling
negativistic
Supplementary techniques for 3- and 4-year-olds
Further suggestions for 4-year-olds
Turnabout is fair play: children using these techniques

7: GUIDANCE IN PLAY   184

Your part in your child's play
Settling conflicts over play materials
Play with other children
Some further examples of guiding your child's play by
the way you phrase instructions

8: GUIDANCE IN BUSINESS ACTIVITIES   210

Motivating your child to perform business activities
Eating
Sleep
Elimination
Dressing, washing, baths, tidying up

9: GUIDING YOUR CHILD'S FEELINGS   262

   Anger and fear
   Guiding your child when he is angry
   Guiding your child when he is fearful
   Jealousy
   Tensional outlets
   Guidance of sexuality

10: GETTING ON WITH OTHER PEOPLE   314

   The immediate family
   Contemporaries outside the family
   Nursery school for your child
   Parties for children of preschool age
   Grandparents
   The sitter

11: WHAT DO YOU WANT YOUR LIFE TO BE LIKE?   341

References cited and readings suggested, 353
Index, 357

Guiding your child from 2 to 5

Introduction

THIS BOOK IS focussed on the years from 2 to 5—for several reasons. During a child's first five years, his behavior and attitudes are more easily influenced than they will be later on. Furthermore, early influences on feelings and actions profoundly affect the kind of person he becomes. And it is during this particularly impressionable period of his life that he is most closely and extensively involved in home life.

But why start with age 2? Why not include babyhood? Most important, because the 2-year-old stands on a threshold. Still a baby in many ways, his needs are changing rapidly. He is faced toward his next three years of active life, before he embarks on his school career as a kindergartener. Not only is he changing; his parents' attitudes toward him are changing, too. As one mother said to me, "For a long time, when a baby or toddler does something we don't like, we think it's our fault. But the time comes when we think it's his fault." Many parents find that this change in attitude occurs when a child is near 2. Therefore you need to give a new kind of thought to a 2-year-old's guidance. If you do, I believe you may go far in making it unnecessary for him to go through a ripsnorting stage of negativism, which some children do somewhere between 2 and 3. And, I suspect, your child

1

will be less of a rebel during adolescence if he has understanding guidance in the preschool years. As your child becomes 3 and 4, and moves on to kindergarten, you can help him and help yourself, through guiding him to develop his potentialities in many ways.

This book is designed for parents—both fathers and mothers. Effective guidance can help everyone at home. It results in children learning what they need to learn and so relieves them of nagging, which spells irritation for everyone; it promotes parents' feelings of adequacy, of relaxation, and enjoyment of life. This last is one of the main themes of this book.

This is in sharp contrast to what many books for parents have emphasized in recent years. They have concentrated so much upon satisfactions for children that sometimes conscientious parents overlook their own needs and interests. But parents' lives matter, not just children's, and actually, children themselves benefit when reasonable satisfactions for parents are woven into life. Home belongs to everybody.

Other books for parents frequently take the view that "what parents are matters more than what they do." There is a great deal to this point of view; the kind of people parents are and the basic feelings which they have toward each other and toward their children are of enormous importance. Probably no single factor can mean so much to a child as growing up in a home where his father and mother are fond of each other and of their children. But more is required than love if children are to learn to live with other people and to develop their own potentialities in other ways. They need guidance. As a matter of fact, they always receive it. Even the parent who "does nothing" is, in his very inaction, doing something to influence his child. Hence the importance of thinking through the consequences for a child of what is done or left undone.

Still other books underrate the importance of guidance; they almost suggest that a child in our culture will pass from one stage to another rather as a rose unfolds. Now, if parents have only one idea about the development of a child, this is a good one to have. This enables them to take behavior in their stride, as they comfort themselves by thinking, "This too will pass!" But child development is not as simple as this. What *happens* to a child is instrumental in shaping the changes that occur.

So this book will emphasize techniques of guidance—but not just techniques; enough theory will be included to provide an understanding of the underlying reasons for the guidance recommended.

If you want to concentrate on specific suggestions, skip the first three chapters and begin with Chapter 4, Arranging Your Child's Surroundings. However, I happen to think that the most helpful and interesting way to read this book is straight through from start to finish. But then, of course, I'm interested in both the practice and theory of child guidance. The application of techniques seems to me much more meaningful when seen in relation to the underlying theories. Even though I make concrete suggestions, this is not a book of recipes. You will see that I believe guidance needs to be tailor-made to the feelings and behavior of each particular child. Here is where the basic point of view which precedes my specific suggestions is useful; it will help you formulate guidance suited to your child. In a word, I believe many parents are thinking people who, some of the time at least, want to bring their intelligence to bear on what is going on at home.

To my mind, there are four considerations involved in effective guidance: 1) what children are like; 2) how people learn; 3) decisions as to what one is aiming for in guiding children; 4) techniques of guidance—that is, application of the theory of learning. Does this sound formidable? It shouldn't. You take it into account if you try to train a puppy. Suppose your puppy's behavior is causing you some concern. Whenever he is outdoors, he scampers off out of reach and eats mouthfuls of gravel, which later causes trouble for both of you. You consult a dog trainer, who tells you, "Get your puppy a training collar attached to a long rope. Be sure to put it on so that it is slack and comfortable when he stays close to you, but tightens uncomfortably if he goes running to the end of this rope. That way he'll find out that everything is fine when he is near you but quite unpleasant when he goes dashing off." These simple techniques of guidance presuppose a theory of learning—that dogs learn what you want them to learn when their "good" behavior has a pleasant outcome and their "bad" behavior has an unpleasant one. I'm not suggesting that children and dogs should receive the same kind of guidance. My point is simply that everyone uses these four components of guidance, though often unreflectively. Effective guidance depends upon understanding them and using them intelligently.

Effective guidance also reduces tension in home life. Sometimes, I believe, the intensity of conscientious parents' interest in their children has worked to the children's disadvantage. This conviction has grown from remarks made to me by parents about their children, often children older than the preschool years. Three points emerge fairly often in these conversations. First, parents tell me their children are often overdemanding, self-centered, inconsiderate, not just when they are little, which is a self-centered period, but later on, too, when other people's needs should figure in their thinking. Second, as they grow into school age, some children seem indifferent to wanting to do well in school. They may be buzzing with ideas, possibly when quiet concentration is the teacher's aim, but school learning has not captured their imagination or their energies. Learning is something that grown-ups are trying to impose on children, rather than something that comes from inside them, as it should. (If indifference to learning does occur in children, the causes for it must be complex. I am only suggesting that the kind of guidance children receive may be one of the contributing factors to such an attitude.) And lastly, parents sometimes say the flavor of home life is unpleasant and the atmosphere of harmony and affection that ought to exist is snowed under by daily irritations and frictions. This happens not only in families where children are allowed to do whatever they want, but also in families where constant instructions are given to unheeding children. It has been helpful for such parents, according to their own reports, to apply at home the techniques of guidance I have suggested.

Throughout the book, the points discussed will be illustrated—usually with records of the actual behavior of children in real-life situations, occasionally with hypothetical examples. Some of the actual records were made in homes; but many are drawn from the Mary B. Eyre Nursery School at Scripps College, where taking records is all in a day's work, and usually can be done without the children becoming aware that they are being scrutinized. Wherever the same name appears (though it is a fictitious one, of course), it refers to one particular child, whom you may encounter at different ages.

In discussing behavior and guidance, I use the pronoun "he" when referring to a child, except where girls are described in specific examples. To say "he or she" would be hopelessly cumbersome, but please bear in mind that "he" can apply equally to girls or boys.

And one last note: although the focus of the book is on the guidance of young children, the point of view may be applied to children of any age—school children, adolescents, even young adults who are still receiving some guidance from their parents. Occasionally you will find yourself looking back into babyhood or forward into the school years. Development, of course, is continuous, and a sound philosophy of guidance is needed at whatever age.

1

What Children in General Are Like

THE FIRST STEP in effective guidance is to figure out what the learner is like—and to bear it in mind. This would be true whether you were training seals, airplane pilots, or guiding juvenile delinquents. Since our concern here is child guidance during the early years, our question is, what are children from 2 to 5 like? You may feel that this is a ridiculous question to ask you. You are involved with a small child twenty-four hours a day. But the very fact that you are so deeply involved with a child may mean that you have neither the chance nor the inclination to try to figure out what children in general of his age are like. (What he in particular is like will come later.)

If you can visit a group of children of your child's age, adequately supervised, do so. (If you are looking for "young" 2-year-olds, that is, close to 24 months of age, perhaps you could watch two or three playing in the same place. A park is a good spot for this. At this age you are not likely to find them in a nursery school.) You need to be quite free of any supervising responsibilities so that you can sit back and ruminate about the children. Why watch a group? To give you a chance to see how children of about the same developmental stage act when they are together. They are likely to reveal more about themselves in a group of their own kind than in solitude or with children of differing ages.

6

You will notice that I said "children of the same developmental stage"—not of the same age; what matters in planning a child's guidance is his stage of development, not his age. But I will talk of 2-year-olds, 3-year-olds, and 4-year-olds because this is a convenient way of designating different developmental stages through which children tend to pass. While many children do show characteristics of a particular age at the time indicated, there are wide individual variations. As children assume characteristics of the next developmental stage, they do so gradually and unevenly, in various parts of their lives.

Before making some brief generalizations about developmental stages during the preschool years, let me urge you to keep an open, questioning attitude as you read what I—or anyone else—say about what children are like. While it is relatively easy to observe how children act, it is much more difficult to judge how they feel. It is all too easy to accept some theory of why children act as they do, and then to read into the observed behavior proof of the theory that is supposedly being tested. This may be done in either of two ways: through ignoring what does not substantiate the theory or, without even realizing it, by putting ideas into children's heads to which they respond, since they are highly suggestible.

This does not mean that it is useless to read what child psychologists have to say. It does mean that, whatever explanation is given, it is important to scrutinize the theory and measure it against the actual behavior of children. In short: read what is written here and elsewhere about what children in general are like; observe your own and other children. But, above all, maintain the open, objective, and questioning attitude that is important for effective guidance.

Now for my generalizations, which are not intended as the complete descriptions that many books aim to give. Mine are only sketches designed to suggest what to look for. I shall describe, in turn, 2-year-olds, 3-year-olds, and 4-year-olds. In addition, I shall say something about so-called "negativism" between 2 and 3.

2-year-olds (close to 24 months of age)

Two-year-olds are active with their whole bodies. They thrive, therefore, on so-called gross motor activities, like climbing, hoisting and lugging large blocks or cardboard cartons, running about in ample space. They enjoy quieter activities, too, such as digging in sand, looking at books, playing with fit-together toys, but need almost continual access to more strenuous activity. They enjoy playing at household activities, with sturdy equipment scaled to their size, dish arranging, ironing, bed making (layers of covers and sheets in unconventional order). They like to undress dolls, but usually cannot dress them.

They are in a manipulative stage. Watch a 2-year-old at an easel. He slathers on paint with an allover stroke. Watch him pasting. He smears paste on a page with a barn-door-painting technique; he is not yet interested in sticking papers together. Or watch a 2-year-old let loose in a kitchen. I know a child who took a butcher knife out of a kitchen drawer and thrust the point into an electric outlet. (It is not paint and paste and butcher knives that need constant supervision; it is 2-year-olds in general.)

Typically 2-year-olds play in a hither-thither way, now picking up a doll, now leaving it to go look out the window, now pushing a train, now back to the doll again. A typical 2-year-old in our nursery school changed her activity thirty-one times in thirty-four minutes.

Usually 2-year-olds play alone or alongside another child, with almost no give-and-take. This sometimes leads parents to ask worriedly, as they watch their own child in a group with other children, "But doesn't he ever play *with* anyone?" The answer is that young 2-year-olds just seem to get more pleasure out of playing alongside other children than by themselves, and this parallel play paves the way for real interaction later. But plenty of squabbles over play materials are likely to occur when 2-year-olds play alongside other children. For them, seeing an appealing object means wanting to possess it. The kind of guidance they receive about these conflicts is of great importance in helping them learn how to get on.

There is great variability in the language skill of 2-year-olds. Some use few words; some talk volubly most of the time.

The 2-year-old is rooted in the here and now. This shows itself in many ways. For instance, he wants what he wants right this minute. This does not mean, of course, that he has to have it, but that you need to bear this characteristic in mind in your dealings with him. He also tends to react at once to the spoken word, rather than storing it up for future action. If you say to him as you come toward him with a glass of orange juice, which he usually welcomes, "Bobby, after you've had your juice, you're going for a ride in the car," he is likely to be halfway out the door before you catch up with him.

He is literal. For example:

> A 2-year-old in his first days of nursery school has joined a group of children who are singing, with appropriate gestures, "This is the way we wash our hands." "Sandy," says the teacher, "can you wash your hands, too?" Smiling agreeably, Sandy trots to the washroom to prove his prowess.

The 2-year-old is capable of varied and complex emotions: anxiety, jealousy, curiosity, rollicking mirth, both liking and being annoyed with someone at the same time, to name only a few.

He is a conservative. From his accustomed way of life he derives security. For this reason he profits by a gradual introduction to any pronounced change that is geared to his ability to adjust. His security is centered in his parents, though this may not become obvious until he is put in a thoroughly new situation, where the familiar figures stand out because of the strangeness of everything else.

"Negativism" between 2 and 3

Children, like other human beings, sometimes have feeling of objection, protest, and refusal—feelings commonly termed "negativistic." The reason I have put the words "negativism" and "negativistic" in quotes is that some adults are too quick to apply these labels when a child shows signs of protest. These adults often think that negativism is as sure to occur between ages 2 and 3 as is midnight between evening and dawn. This is a misconception. Negativism is not inevitable. If parents think it is, they are likely to invite it by their very expectation. Nonetheless, most children of preschool age in our culture will show some signs of refusal and protest; typically they do so at 2½. But I believe that only when these feelings characterize a child's outlook do they warrant the term negativistic. (When the word is used in this sense, I remove the quotes.)

Since some children do go through a period which may be accurately called negativistic, here is a description of the kind of behavior which deserves such a characterization:

Sometimes negativism appears gradually. Sometimes it seems to arrive suddenly, transforming almost overnight an agreeable child into one who is a trial to parents, brothers and sisters, in fact to anyone who has dealings with him. "Balky," "ornery," "stubborn" are words that parents use in describing him when he tends to react immediately with "No!" by word or deed to grownup direction.

In extreme cases a child may respond with refusal to almost every approach to him. It is not even necessary to say or do anything, the harassed parent may find. The most trivial of household happenings can bring about a violent protest; let the family cat but disappear under the piano—the outraged child had other plans for it. In milder cases, the child may single out some part of daily life to object to—for example, going to the toilet. And sometimes he may suddenly refuse to get off the toilet that he reluctantly got on. Or there may be no set pattern of objection. His parents never know where a refusal will next appear. A child suddenly takes a stand on something about which he has felt quite agreeable up to this point. For instance, he refuses to put his hat on to go outdoors, although he has done it cheerfully before now. Subsequently, there may be no further trouble on this score, but he now makes it known that eggs are the last thing in the world he wants for supper. The next night, they are the only food he would like.

When there are older children in the family, the negativistic child may be always wanting precisely what an older child is busy with at a particular moment. A 6-year-old girl I know would give up a favorite and fragile doll to her clamoring 2½-year-old sister, knowing it would be ruined, just to have a little peace and quiet in the house.

Another child in this stage ran, with arms outstretched, to welcome a well-loved grandmother, then greeted her by a slap in the face.

A less dramatic but equally effective means of showing negativistic feelings consists in standing motionless and limp in response to grownup direction.

There often appears a drive for independence so strong that a child is determined to carry on activities by himself which he cannot adequately manage: for example, getting out of his shirt, which, to be sure, he can do by popping off the buttons, or trying vainly to climb into a difficult snowsuit.

Children who are feeling genuinely negativistic often seem to want to do impossibly contradictory things at the same time, like a child I know who wanted to ride both in the front and back seat of the family car simultaneously.

A truly negativistic phase is a trying time for everyone, including the child, a time when knowledge about children in general and the particular child involved may help immensely in guiding him toward more peaceful days.

3-year-olds (close to 36 months of age)

Happily, with sound guidance, even the kind of negativistic behavior I have been talking about does not last forever, although we all probably know some adults who seem never to have outgrown it. Characteristically it is over by the time a child is 3.

The 3-year-old has made great strides in his development since his second birthday. Perhaps one of the most striking changes is his tendency to stay with activities for a longer time than the typically hither-thither 2-year-old. However, he continues to need ample opportunity for change of occupation.

He is still keyed to gross motor activity, but less exclusively so than the 2-year-old. Finer coordination is apparent in almost everything he does.

For the sake of comparison with a 2-year-old, note 3-year-old easel painting and pasting. In painting, the 3-year-old often makes clearly defined strokes or shapes, characteristically not yet designs but the beginnings of them. In pasting, while he may achieve his results by spreading out paste on the large base sheet, he is definitely concerned with using paste to stick papers together.

His doll play more accurately resembles household activities. Bed making, for example, starts with a sheet on the bottom and ends with blankets on top.

Three-year-olds are definitely interested in play with other children. Their ability to handle the inevitable conflicts which occur depends considerably upon earlier opportunity for group play, upon wise handling of earlier disputes by grownups, as well as upon intelligent planning for harmonious play at the 3-year-old level.

The 3-year-old enjoys both parallel play and solitary occupation. He is, as a matter of fact, usually resourceful in playing by himself, provided his life includes sufficient opportunities to play with other children.

Though infantile articulation is often present in the speech of 3-year-olds, by and large it does not interfere with understanding what is said.

With sound guidance, the 3-year-old can understand that one activity comes before another—indeed, may well be the means to that other activity. "After you've had your juice, you're going for a ride in the car" will lead, then, to no such precipitation of events as is likely a year earlier. This is one of the reasons why the 3-year-old is typically easier to deal with than in the days of his 2-year-old desire for *immediate* gratification of his wants.

Three-year-olds seem to vary greatly in imaginativeness in their activities. Some display little, and appear to accept objects and happenings in their lives at face value. Most 3-year-olds, however, show a good deal of imagination in their play. The following behavior is typical:

> Tommy comes running outdoors, calling as he hurries to a bike, "I little baby." "Yes, you little baby," replies Alice, already riding. "George, Daddy, and I'm Mommy." "Go downtown," she commands, still cycling quickly, but stops while Tommy is mounting his bike. Then, "Ready, set, go," she calls. "You go with Mommy." Both she and "baby" pedal quickly away. Meanwhile, "Daddy" is cycling slowly and spasmodically, stopping to watch what is going on around him. "Hurry, hurry," calls Alice. Then, catching up with him, she puts her hand on the handle bar of his bike, and says affectionately in a soft voice, "Oh, that's a nice Daddy," and more, which cannot be heard beyond the words "pretty pie." "Daddy" does not respond further than looking at Alice affably. Then off she rides again, calling, "Baby, baby." She catches up with Tommy and says to him in a dramatically hushed voice, "Better hide."

For 3-year-olds, sand typically becomes pies, cakes, or the like, though many children seem to enjoy manipulating it without giving it "pretend" qualities. Block constructions are often named.

Three-year-olds are likely to mix up the real and the unreal, which may lead adults to a too hasty conclusion that they are purposely fabricating. Sometimes vivid imaginative play of 3-year-olds may be disturbing, because pretense for one is reality for another. Danny's behavior, just two days before his third birthday, indicates this:

> When an almost-3½-year-old tells him, "I'm a wolf, and I'm going to eat you up," Danny screams and bursts into tears.

Both Alice's and Danny's play also give us clues to the emotional life of 3-year-olds. Alice's soft, affectionate, "Oh, that's a nice Daddy," reflects the warm closeness which 3-year-olds tend to experience with their parents. At the same time, they are usually not so dependent upon their parents in adjusting to a new situation as they were at 2. Danny's fear of the "wolf" illustrates a tendency of the children in our school for 3-year-olds to be more fearful than either 2- or 4-year-olds. While the parents of young 2-year-olds seldom report that their children seem fearful, the picture is quite different when the children are near 3. At this age fears are often mentioned. In ten consecutive years in our nursery school, the ones most commonly reported for children of this age were fear of the dark, of dogs, and of cars or trucks. In two instances, injudicious suggestion had resulted in nighttime fears: of a "boogieman"—attributed to the conversation of a sister—for a boy of 2 years, 8 months; of bears for a girl of 2 years, 11 months who had been told by a person looking after her that bears would get her if she was not good.

Three-year-olds are often interested in anatomical differences between boys and girls (an interest which usually begins earlier than this). Here is an example of a little boy (with two brothers, but no sisters) who was clearly taking advantage of an opportunity to satisfy his curiosity.

> A 3-year-old boy in his early days at nursery school lingers by the door of the bathroom, although he has finished there. Usually he is quick to return to his play. When a little girl gets up from the toilet, there is a chance to see what she is shaped like. He looks, thoughtfully and intently, then swings through the doorway into the playroom.

I shall not try to describe further the emotional life of 3-year-olds. It is far too complex to be dealt with in a cursory fashion.

4-year-olds (close to 48 months of age)

The 4-year-old still greatly enjoys physically active play. He often takes pride in physical feats, such as hanging upside down by his knees, using a slide at different heights, climbing high, performing on swings. But he has a greater capacity for interesting, quiet occupation than the 3-year-old. When he paints, he holds his brush between thumb and forefinger, and often gives a running commentary on what he is depicting. There is often symmetry in his paintings, which may be designs or crude representations. Symmetry is also shown in his pasting, which is likely to be a much neater performance than earlier, with paste put directly on the to-be-pasted papers rather than on the base sheet. If he does not finish a paper construction, he may work on it the next day, provided, of course, he has a place to store unfinished products in which he is likely to look and so be reminded of his unfinished work.

Four-year-olds are very sociable. When, side by side, they are busy at individual play, they are likely to converse extensively. The sociability of groups of 4-year-olds is so pronounced that it is likely to run away with them unless grownups are alert to maintain a relaxed tempo and to redirect activities when sociability tends to get out of hand and dominate the scene. For example:

> In groups of twos and threes sit half a dozen 4-year-olds, busy at adjacent tables. Sammy, age 4 years and 2 months, stops drawing with crayons and says, "When I saw my Daddy this morning, I said, 'Hi table.'" An instantaneous gleeful response from his nearest neighbor: "When I saw my Daddy this morning, I said, 'Hi, chair.'" Another child picks it up: "When I saw my Daddy this morning, I said, 'Hi, poo poo.'" (This may be a bathroom word; 4-year-olds sometimes introduce bathroom terms into word-play.) "When I saw . . ." continues as other children stop their activities. It is time for redirection.

Here, on the other hand, is an instance in which the sociability did not spread:

> Again in a playroom sit an almost-4-year-old and a slightly older companion, working individually with clay. "Do you know what I

saw?" one of them asks. Then, in an invitation-to-laugh tone, "Windows walking. Isn't that funnee?" Arthur, his companion, engrossed in his construction, gives him a stare but keeps on with his clay without comment.

If a typical 3-year-old declines this kind of invitation, it is likely to be simply because his sociability is not easily triggered off by such remarks. When a typical 4-year-old, on the other hand, fails to respond, it is likely that interest in what he is doing overshadows the attractions of sociability. As a matter of fact, Arthur is an unusually sociable little boy, who recently regaled his dining-room table of 4-year-olds with the statement "My dog is named Potato," which caused such hilarity that a grownup had to redirect the conversation to keep it from taking the place of dinner.

Three 4-year-olds playing together may have difficulties, for two tend to gang together against the third. (They have no monopoly on this well-known characteristic of a threesome.) Or exclusion and unhappiness may result when a third child wishes to join in the play of two others, as in the following episode:

Two little girls, having just decided to "make a house," are providing themselves with a "baby" (doll) and baby carriage. A third approaches. She has been excluded in recent days by these two. "Can I play?" she asks rather wistfully. "No," they answer firmly. "Couldn't I even be the grandmother?" she pleads, but even this does not melt their hearts. "No," one of them replies, "and besides, your underwear is showing."

This last remark is apt. It refers to a border of undershirt showing beneath the child's dress sleeves, and reminds me of another characteristic of 4-year-olds. They are often quite clothes conscious. (I would like to add that the excluded little girl appeared in a new dress the next day, and, incidentally, had a happier time, though with different companions.)

Usually 4-year-olds, if they are used to group play and if they have had consistent guidance in learning how to handle disputes, can effectively settle most of their controversies. But this does not mean that supervision and informed adult guidance are not still necessary. Indeed, a 4-year-old who has mastered a customary procedure can use it to settle a conflict between two younger children:

Two 3-year-olds are pushing each other with increasing vigor at the base of a tree, each wanting to climb. Peter, a young 4-year-old (with a year of nursery school behind him) approaches, and asks authoritatively, "Who got here first?" The pushing stops. "I did," says one. "Then go up," says Peter, and that is the end of that.

Four-year-olds may enjoy companionship so much that they are reluctant to play alone in the afternoon, even when they play regularly with other children in the morning.

They are usually quite capable of efficient performance in such business activities as washing, going to the toilet, dressing with little help; yet often they are uninterested in performing them, or, particularly in groups, become involved in play in the process, and so need guidance. There are several probable reasons for this 4-year-old lack of interest in business activities. One is that at an earlier age, interest is lent to routine tasks because real achievement is involved in efficient performance. Witness an almost-3-year-old's exclamation, "I did it myself," after managing to undo buttons before going to the toilet. At 4, the performance is relatively easy, and inherently tedious, since it no longer involves developing skills. Furthermore, the fact that sociability is so attractive often serves to sidetrack 4-year-olds from the task at hand through the substitution of either social play or conversation for the activity in question. Such conversation is likely to slow progress because many 4-year-olds cannot both talk and carry on a routine performance at the same time. In short, in performance of these common business activities, though capability is high, motivation is low.

Four-year-olds are great talkers, as has just been suggested. They are also sometimes endless questioners, but it seems hardly necessary to document this by citing a flow of "whys?"

Their play is highly imaginative. This may sometimes create difficulties in play with younger children whose imaginations are not so fully developed:

Gordon, getting on toward 4½, is bent upon having an organized birthday celebration. He has made a "table" of large outdoor blocks, set "chairs" (smaller blocks) around it, and, with no other 4-year-olds available, has induced four 2¾- and young 3-year-olds to "come to the party." A "cake," a handsome creation of dirt smoothed into a tin pan, decorated with "candles" (twigs), is out of sight at a distance of about 20 feet. Gordon's plan is to have the "guests" sing "Happy Birthday" as he brings in the cake. He shepherds them to their places, enthusiastically tells them to sing, dashes for his cake. But the group begins to wander off before he appears. Returning the cake to "the kitchen," he patiently reassembles the guests, recommends "Happy Birthday," disappears to once more produce his cake. The same thing happens.

Or, here is 4-year-old imaginativeness causing trouble at home for mother:

Danny (whom you saw at 3, disturbed when an older child said he was a wolf and was going to eat him up), now 4, builds a boat out of blocks and asks his mother to come see it. In doing so, she inadvertently steps into the "captain's cabin" instead of remaining "on deck" as she should, an easy mistake, since no inner partitions and no prior explanation from Danny suggest what is what. This is no light matter to Danny, intent on his imaginative plans; he is upset.

Four-year-olds still confuse the real and the unreal. They sometimes concoct extremely convincing tall tales. It is a puzzle to know how much they convince themselves.

They have widening interests; they enjoy seeing things they have heard about and finding out more about familiar objects. Excursions to such places as a bakery, a dairy, a kennel, an airport are likely to give them a lot of pleasure.

The 4-year-old in a familiar environment may appear to be more self-sufficient and assured than he really is. His tendency to assertiveness helps to create this impression. Typical remarks are: "I can make a bigger one." "I'm quicker than you." "That's no good" (of another child's efforts at construction. This may become epidemic in a group). But at night, awakening from sleep upset with some fear, as 4-year-olds may be, he seems a little child.

As regards fears, the 4-year-old's are likely to be more imaginative than those of younger children. For instance, David at 4 is worried about poisonous things, about sticks on the playground, for example, that might poison him if he puts them in his mouth, and is greatly concerned about the sudden death from tetanus of a man who had lived nearby. And Donna, after having seen a man without arms, is greatly upset by a blister on her foot. Donna's and David's fears illustrate how 4-year-olds may relate to themselves what is seen and heard, a tendency which may lead to worries and fears about such matters as death or injury.

Without sufficient guidance, 4-year-olds may investigate anatomical differences between boys and girls. This reflects, of course, their interest in such matters and need for guidance.

The 4-year-old's humor is crude by adult standards. He enjoys wordplay. When two 4-year-olds are batting a phrase back and forth, it is often hard to tell whether they are amused at the phrase or just responding to the other child's laughter.

To sum up some of these points, the 4-year-old is likely to be noisier, more boisterous, more assertive, more sociable, more imaginative (in play, in concerns, in fears), less interested in efficient performance of routine tasks than he was at 3. He is likely to seem more assured than he really is.

As you have been reading these descriptions of behavior, if you are like the parents I know (including myself) you have been noting to yourself, "Johnny doesn't do that," or "Margaret would react quite differently," and you may have been forgetting how much variability there is likely to be in children of the same ages. Suppose your child behaves quite differently from the picture of his age level. Remember, one of the main themes in this book is that what happens to children influences them greatly. In any case, so far we have merely considered the question "What are children in general like?" You still have to ask, "What is my particular child like?" but you need to do some more thinking first.

2

How People Learn

YOU HAVE JUST CONSIDERED the first step in effective guidance: what children are like. The next step is how people learn. There are many different theories of learning. I shall talk about only two of them—two ways of thinking about learning which seem to be particularly useful for parents to bear in mind when guiding children.

Conditioning

EXAMPLES OF CONDITIONING AND A
DESCRIPTION IN GENERAL TERMS

A 7-month-old baby who enjoys his bath and is quite accustomed to hearing the water gush from the faucet is brought into the bathroom one day where a portable heater has just been placed for the first time. It is turned on, giving off a whirring sound as its fan goes round. The faucet is turned on as usual; the water gushes out with its usual sound. The baby, looking intently at the heater, starts to cry and clutches his mother, who, judging he is afraid of the new heater, takes him out of the room, finishes warming the bathroom, and removes the heater before taking him back there. He gives

19

every sign of his usual good spirits on his return and throughout his bath.

The next day, his mother warms the bathroom and removes the heater before she takes him into the bathroom. He does not see the heater at all. She carries him in as usual (he seems cheerful), and turns on the faucet. As the water gushes out, he begins to cry, and clutches his mother as he did the day before.

What we have here, which "just happened" in this baby's home, is exactly the kind of situation which the psychologist John B. Watson once carried out in a conditioning experiment. (This and all subsequent references cited or readings suggested are listed alphabetically on pp. 353–55.) He made an 11-month-old baby afraid of a white rat by making a loud noise behind the boy's head when he was watching the rat. The experiment went like this: The first day, when the rat was put down in front of him, the baby reached out his hand and touched it, just as the noise was made behind him. The rat was removed, then placed in front of him again; the same thing happened. A week later, when the boy was brought back, the rat was placed in front of him; he reached out to touch it, but instead, withdrew his hand. Then, three times, the rat was placed in front of him as the noise was made behind his back. When, a fourth time, the rat was presented, but now without the accompanying noise, the baby puckered up his face and began to cry.

Learning is called conditioning when, in circumstances such as these, a response associated with one stimulus comes to be associated with another stimulus. For instance, in Watson's experimental case, fear was a response originally associated with noise, not with the rat; interest was initially aroused by the rat, for at first the child reached out his hand and touched the animal. But after Watson had presented rat and noise simultaneously, the child became afraid of the rat. To put this in technical language, the rat had become a substitute stimulus which called forth the response originally associated with the noise. Or in ordinary language, the child had learned something new— to be afraid of the rat in addition to being afraid of the noise; and he had learned this by "conditioning"—by simultaneous presentation of the two stimuli. Several simultaneous presentations of rat and noise were necessary in this case to build up the new association.

In the case of the 7-month-old baby and the heater, one simultaneous presentation of whirring heater plus usual water-gushing-from-faucet had resulted in the fear response, originally called forth by the heater, becoming attached to the stimulus of the familiar running water.

Here is another example from home life:

A 2-year-old is taken by his parents to a railroad station to have a chance to see a train, just for the fun of it. They know when a local is due, and all stand close to the tracks to watch it come in. Instead, to everyone's surprise, a fast express train comes roaring by, thoroughly startling them all. Thereafter, for months when this little boy hears a train, he is uneasy.

This is essentially the same situation as the earlier examples: trains were originally associated with the response of interested watching, but because of the intense noise that accompanied the express, they came to be associated with a feeling of fright.

And here is a more complicated example, which occurred in our nursery school:

Carl, a 4-year-old, takes readily to his first two weeks at nursery school, without tears at any time. Then, one day in his third week, the children who up till now have been singing outdoors unaccompanied by a piano, sing indoors to piano accompaniment. As the singing starts, one of the grownups notices that Carl's eyes are filled with tears. Taking him aside, she asks him what is the matter. He just shakes his head, eyes still brimming with tears. When she asks him if he would rather look at a book in an adjoining room than be with the other children, he brightens up and chooses to "read." The next day the children have a story instead of music; Carl seems to enjoy it. On following days, he happily takes part in music outdoors, but again becomes teary whenever singing is accompanied by a piano. Subsequently, his mother clears up the mystery to our satisfaction. The year before, she had played the piano for the children's singing in Carl's Sunday school.

This can be put in conditioning terms. Watson, for instance, would say that the "original stimulus" is Carl's mother. But in this case, as in most other real-life situations, the learning is much more complicated than in the case of Watson's 11-month-old baby. For one thing, people outside of laboratories live in a world where many varied stimuli are acting on them at the same time, not like a baby in an experimental room, where there is carefully controlled stimulation. How does it happen then, if there are many stimuli, that certain ones come to be singled out to take part in a conditioning process? Carl, for example, was in a complex situation in Sunday school, yet somehow he singled out his mother and piano accompaniment to children's singing as the stimuli involved in conditioning. How? The answer is that these two parts of the situation had particular significance for him. An individual's interests, his motives, determine what parts of a situation he responds to—and, therefore, what stimuli and responses are occurring at the same time—and so take part in the process of learning. These complications do not show that the learning in question is not conditioned. They do show, however, that it is necessary to be careful in accounting for real-life learning in purely conditioning terms.

It is easy to see that as a result of conditioning, feelings often get attached to particular stimuli "by accident." Suppose your 4-year-old says, in a drugstore, "How does a baby get inside a mommy before it is born?" A group of teen-agers snicker. You have a lot of thoughts going around in your head. Perhaps you are surprised that this question is coming so early, perhaps you are wondering what prompted it. If it has taken you quite by surprise, you are probably reaching for words. You may want to tell your child that you will talk about this at home, without sounding as if the delay is embarrassed evasion, which, indeed, it may not be at all. But what the child may associate with his question is the snicker, the delayed answer, the emotional overtone, perhaps misjudged, but nonetheless there.

Or, suppose your small child is playing outdoors and calls to you to come out. Squatting close to a flower bed, he points with interest to something concealed in a plant. You bend closer to look, suddenly realize you are peering at a snake. With an involuntary shriek, you step back quickly. The next time a snake appears your child shows unmistakable signs of fear.

Many parents make use of the conditioning process in dealing with babies and little children. If, for example, you are introducing a new food to the baby, you do not choose a day when he is out of sorts. The out-of-sorts feeling might get attached to the new food. You make sure it is the right temperature, perhaps even much the same consistency as what he is used to, so that only the taste is new. You make sure he is comfortable. You do not cram too much into his mouth at once. Or, later on, when he starts to use a little toilet seat, you make sure it is not too cold and that he does not feel physically insecure as he sits there. Probably you keep him company and see that he sits on the seat for only a short time.

But parents tend to forget conditioning as children get older. I know a man who for years came home at the end of the day, sank exhausted into the nearest chair, and let out the elegant expression, "I'm pooped." He wondered why his teen-age son seemed so uninterested in going into the family business. Granted, it is much too facile to conclude that only conditioning is at work here, but nonetheless, the possibility of its influence should not be discounted.

Conditioning is often involved in building up a heedless, even antagonistic attitude to what grownups say. How so? For one thing, many grownups launch such a flow of instructions that children form a habit of retiring into their own thoughts when adults begin to talk, a conditioned reaction. Also, unfortunately, much of what parents say is likely to make children feel antagonistic. When you get a chance, listen to the daily barrage directed at a 7- or 8-year-old boy (who is likely to be in a harum-scarum developmental period, I grant you). "Tuck your shirt in," "Zip up your fly," "Tie your shoes," "Don't slam the door," "Keep your dirty hands off the wall," "That's too big a bite," and so forth. Small wonder that he may feel like shrugging his shoulders with indifference or irritation when parents start to talk. (If he does, he will be in for more talk.) Now I am not saying that parents should not be concerned with their child's behavior; nor am I saying that they should not try to guide him. I *am* saying, first, that many parents do not get the results they want, and, second, that at least some of the indifference to school learning which many children show may carry over from attitudes engendered (conditioned) by the grownups' attempts at guidance. Parents will do well to bear the conditioning process in mind when trying to guide their children.

APPLYING CONDITIONING TO GUIDANCE

The timing of what you say to your child is important. If you have to say something that is likely to make him react with irritation, do not couple it with some other matter that has no connection. Watch for a good time to talk over the second matter, when your child is more likely to have a receptive attitude. You will have a better chance of getting the hoped-for results.

"Unlearning" as a conditioning process. Suppose you want to have a child "unlearn" a fear response. How can you make use of conditioning? (Please note, this kind of "unlearning" is not the treatment I necessarily advise for children's fears, though it might well be part of suggested guidance in a particular case. I am simply illustrating "unlearning" as a conditioning process.)

What is needed is to have a new (nonfearful) response come to be associated with the stimulus which calls forth fear. There is an experiment by the psychologist Mary Cover Jones in which this was accomplished. A little boy named Peter was afraid of a rabbit. The experimenter arranged that while Peter was enjoying a mid-morning lunch, the rabbit would be brought into the room and placed on a table 4 feet away from him. At later lunches, the rabbit was gradually brought closer until finally it was right beside him. By then, Peter showed no signs of fear. We see that this "unlearning" is a positive process in which the rabbit (formerly associated with a fear response) has become the "substitute stimulus" that now calls forth an enjoyment response, originally associated with Peter's lunch. Clearly, this kind of "unlearning" is just another case of the conditioning process.

Some further examples of applying conditioning to guidance. Here is a case in which a mother failed in her efforts. It serves to remind us that in real-life situations various stimuli are always present.

A mother decides to teach her 20-month-old son to call her Mommy. He has been calling his father Daddy for months and she is tired of being a nameless creature, even though Gesell's writings assure her that this is not uncommon with boy children of her son's age. She chooses, one day when he is washing his hands in the bathroom, to point to the mirror where she looms, saying, "Mommy, see Mommy," making quite a point of this, with gesticulations.

Later that afternoon, when it is time to wash for supper, the child begins washing, saying agreeably, as his mother helps him soap his hands, "Mommy, mommy." It becomes all too clear on later occasions that the word "Mommy" has become attached to soap and water.

In the following cases, conditioning worked better:

A father and mother I know made a point of seeing to it that their child never climbed into his crib directly from the floor, but always used a chair, which was put in position for climbing, then removed to a more distant spot. This was to help build up the attitude that staying in bed was the thing to do. The chair was always put in place again when it was time to climb out. The system seemed to work well in their family, both with this child and, later, with a younger brother.

A mother in another family saw to it that when her small child was ill and had to stay in bed during the day, his bed was put in a new position in his room while he played. This gave added pleasure, too, by enabling him to see out of the window. Then, when naptime came in the afternoon, the bed was restored to its usual place, the room tidied up, and curtains drawn, to help create the atmosphere of time for sleep.

Still another family, in telling their child for the first time that he was adopted, chose a particularly cozy occasion, in front of a grate fire (in itself, a treat for this child), when father, mother, and child were already having a nice time together.

Knowledge of conditioning can be useful when a young child has formed a habit of refusal in a particular situation, without strong feelings being involved. Suppose that lately when you say, "Time for dinner," your 2-year-old has taken to running into a far corner of the yard and hiding behind a bush. Your remark seems to trigger off this behavior. Then do not say it. Get up close to him; take him by the hand. Perhaps one of you has collected some flowers or leaves. You might say, "Let's get a vase for these," as you lead your child indoors.

Conditioning is a process to be borne in mind in child guidance. Can we, as some psychologists do, explain all learning in conditioning terms and so rely on it as the basis for guidance? As I have already indicated, I think we cannot. In some cases, conditioning is a wholly adequate account of learning; in others, it is a factor involved; in still others, it is not present at all. When it is involved in learning, when it can help you, try to be aware of it and put it to good use.

Learning by consequences

EXAMPLES OF LEARNING BY CONSEQUENCES
AND A DESCRIPTION IN GENERAL TERMS

> Four-year-old Stephen is taken to the doctor, a doctor whom he knows and seems to like. He greets the doctor pleasantly, but when he is given a shot becomes very much upset, cries, and protests. On a second trip for a booster, once inside the doctor's office he flies at him, kicks the doctor's legs, hits him with his fists, and cries.

It is obvious how this would be described in conditioning terms. The "original stimulus" was the shot which called forth a response of crying and protest. The "substitute stimulus" was the doctor, to whom up to this point there had been a friendly response. But after simultaneous occurrence of these two stimuli, the doctor called forth the response (crying and protest) originally associated with the shot.

But there is another way of talking about what happened. Stephen has come to feel very strongly about not wanting shots; he has learned that the doctor gives them; when he sees the doctor, he vents his feelings on him. Perhaps he thinks he can avoid having a shot by his attack. This implies something quite different from a description in terms of conditioning. So let us work out a second description of learning which will account for this kind of case. First, take a look at a 2-year-old at home:

Michael pulls open a drawer in a storage cupboard which he has not opened before, spies a new truck (put away to give him something to do on a rainy day), pulls it out, and plays with it.

We can analyze this in the following way:

An individual is motivated. Like other 2-year-olds, Michael liked to be active. He did not yet want the truck specifically because he knew nothing about it. A closed drawer was inviting. When Michael noticed it, he wanted to open it.

He acts to satisfy the motive. He opened the drawer.

The consequence to his act brings him satisfaction. He found the truck, took it out, and enjoyed playing with it.

The next day here is what happened:

Saying "Duh" (truck), Michael goes purposefully to the cupboard, opens the right drawer, and again takes out the truck.

Since on this second day we know more about Michael's motive, we can now say:

An individual is motivated toward a goal. Michael had the truck in mind before he opened the drawer; or, if his goal was not this specific, we can at least say that he wanted something to play with. In any case, he was motivated toward a goal.

He acts to attain it. He opened the drawer.

The consequence to what he does brings him satisfaction. Michael was successful in finding the truck.

Much learning on the part of babies and children and adults can be analyzed like this. We learn to act in particular ways, just as Michael did, because we discover they bring us satisfaction. Unfortunately for those of us who want to guide children, it is not always easy to find out what brings them satisfaction. A lot of guidance goes astray in this respect. Here is an example:

Four-year-old Sandra, at the start of her nursery-school career, is most determined in wanting her own way, regardless of other children's rights. She tends to single out Jane as her victim, who has not yet begun to learn how to defend herself.

Jane is swinging. Sandra comes up, grabs the swing rope, bringing the swing to a lurching stop. Jane, on the verge of tears, protests ineffectually. As Mrs. A arrives on the scene, Sandra yanks the swing rope again. Then she is told, "Sandra, Jane had the swing first. *I'll help you see when there's a swing to use.*" Sandra still hangs on to the rope. Mrs. A tells her, "Leave the swing alone." "I won't," replies Sandra, and gives another yank. "You do need to take your hands off the rope," says Mrs. A. "Either you do it by yourself, or I'll help you." Still another determined yank. Mrs. A then pries Sandra's hands away and as Sandra, very angry, turns on her and tries to kick her shins, Mrs. A picks her up and carries her indoors away from the other children.

Now this certainly seemed to be an unsatisfactory consequence for Sandra. She did not get the swing. Removal from the play yard was also unsatisfactory, for Sandra liked being with the other children. But, on the other hand, in this particular instance, it was Mrs. A's later guess that Sandra derived satisfaction from the drama of the skirmish with the grownup and from the attention of being carried inside. The net result for Sandra in this case? It might well be satisfaction. If so, the net effect of this particular episode was probably to make Sandra feel like repeating this kind of behavior.

Because it is often hard to figure out whether consequences are satisfactory or unsatisfactory for a child, one of your most important jobs in guidance is to know enough about how your child feels to guess correctly whether the net effect of consequences to his various acts are satisfactory or not.

Bearing in mind the importance of figuring out what the consequences of a child's behavior mean to him, let us get back to Michael. Suppose, when he pulls out the drawer the second morning, the truck is no longer there. If he still wants it, he will be faced with a problem. He looks in the other drawers. Still no truck. He peers around on the floor without success. Then he sees it, high on the shelves of a bookcase. He reaches as high as he can, but this is not high enough. He tries to climb up, but he can find no foothold. Then he picks up a nearby chair, moves it close to the shelf, climbs on it, and gets the truck.

This time,

An individual is motivated toward a goal. Michael wanted the truck.

He acts to attain it. He opened the drawer.

The consequence to his act is unsatisfactory. It was not effective in getting the truck, nor in giving Michael satisfaction in some other way.

Since Michael still wanted the truck, the unsatisfactory consequence to his attempt to get it was an obstacle to what he wanted. We can, therefore, sum up this problem situation by saying:

An individual is motivated toward a goal.

He acts to attain it.

An obstacle prevents him from attaining it.

He acts further to attain it.

Michael now did a number of different things to find the truck. He looked for it in various places, each time with an unsatisfactory consequence until he saw it on a bookshelf. Seeing it was satisfactory up to a point, but he still had to reach it. After two unsuccessful attempts (two acts followed by unsatisfactory consequences) Michael solved his problem. When he put a chair by the bookcase and climbed on it, he was tall enough to reach it. At last,

The consequence to one of his acts is effective. Getting the truck was a thoroughly satisfactory consequence.

In this problem situation, since no other people were involved, the consequences to Michael's actions depended entirely on his relation to the physical environment. The only way of getting what he wanted, by himself, was to bridge the space between his hand and the truck. The act which produced the effective consequence would always be effective when the truck was this same distance away on the shelf.

CONSISTENT CONSEQUENCES IN THE
PHYSICAL ENVIRONMENT

It is a great help in learning situations if consequences are consistent. In fact, learning may be impossible if consequences are not consistent. What do I mean by "consistent consequences in the physical environment"? Here is an example.

Suppose a small child touches a hot oven door with his finger.

The heat he feels is a consistent consequence: it happens *at once* (not, for example, "when Father comes home"); it *always* happens (remember, I am saying he is involved with a hot oven door); it is *the same*—a feeling of heat (not a mellow musical note every once in a while); it is *proportional* in its duration to his behavior (the longer he keeps his finger on the oven door, the longer he feels the heat). So Michael, once he had bridged the gap between his hand and the truck, would *always*, *at once*, have the *same consequence* to his behavior. And this consequence would be *proportional* to what he did in the sense that once he had hold of the truck, it would stay in his possession until he let it go.

Now, let us suppose that when Michael found the drawer empty, instead of searching for the truck, he called his mother. And suppose she called back, "Michael, I'll help you as soon as I finish giving the baby his bath." Or suppose she came at once, showed him the truck, and said, "It's too bad. It has a very sharp place on it so it's not safe to play with. That's why it's way up high." Or suppose she did not hear him at all, and only came to his rescue when, frustrated in his search, he burst into tears. Clearly, when other people are involved in the consequences to a person's actions, these consequences are likely to be much less consistent than those in the physical environment. If you want your child to learn something, you must see to it that the consequences to his actions are sufficiently consistent so that he can learn what you want him to.

CONSISTENT CONSEQUENCES IN GUIDANCE

There is no doubt that it helps a child in learning if the consequences to his behavior *always* happen *at once* and if they are *proportional* to what he has done. These three conditions for learning are well worth bearing in mind in child guidance. But parents should not try to ape the invariability of the laws of nature. It is not the sameness of an event which can be felt or seen or heard that is desired (like always saying "No" when a child reaches toward a hot oven door). Rather it is a sameness in terms of the child's feelings that is important.

Suppose you ignored his motives and cared only about his behavior. To induce him to be kind to the baby, you gave him a dime whenever he did something nice. This ten-cent reward would not continue to bring him satisfaction for his behavior, I am convinced. He would come to expect a larger or different reward. And so, in the long run, this mechanically consistent consequence would not even be effective in promoting the behavior you desired.

And now, suppose, on the other hand, you *do* care how your child feels. You want to cultivate in him not only behavior but kind feelings toward the baby. The sort of invariability to aim at in guidance is having satisfactory consequences relevant to the situation for behavior you want to encourage. To see what I mean by "relevant to the situation," contrast the difference between giving your child a dime and saying when he does something kind, "That was a real help. And since it has saved me time in looking after the baby, how about a story? If you'd like one, I'll read to you." This one little incident will help the older child on his way, I hope, toward an attitude which will lead to more kindness: that babies need care; that it is the job of the family to give it; that when *he* helps, there is time left over for other things, including things he likes to do (which would, of course, be varied over a period of time to continue to give him satisfaction). I also hope, of course, that he will enjoy his kindness and the baby's reaction to it.

Consistency in guidance is not, then, a mechanical consistency; it is a consistency adjusted to a child's motives and behavior in order to promote his learning to *want* to behave in ways which will help him get along well in the various situations that make up his life. You can see his behavior. But you can only speculate about his motivation, which is one of the reasons a parent's job is a difficult and fascinating one.

When I said a moment ago that the kind of invariability to aim at in guidance is having satisfactory consequences relevant to the situation for behavior you want to encourage, I told only half the story, but I did this by intent. Many parents, unfortunately, overlook the importance of satisfactory consequences for desirable behavior, and only step in when their children do something objectionable. To discourage undesirable behavior, you need to cultivate consequences that are not only invariably unsatisfactory, but that also motivate a child to want to behave as you would like him to.

Of course, you cannot always achieve the kind of invariability I am recommending. To do it, you would have to be omniscient in figuring out your child's motives. But the closer you come to it, the more easily will he learn.

FURTHER DESCRIPTION AND EXAMPLES OF LEARNING BY CONSEQUENCES

Let me sum up what has been said so far about learning by consequences, and go on from there. When a person is motivated, and acts to satisfy his motive, there is always a consequence to his action. If the consequence is immediately satisfactory, there is no problem. When the individual is again motivated in the same way, he is likely to repeat the behavior which brought him satisfaction earlier.

If, however, the consequence to his action is unsatisfactory, he is faced with a problem. This unsatisfactory consequence is then an obstacle to the satisfaction of his motive. If he is going to overcome the obstacle, he has to keep wanting to do so. In other words, the motive has to persist until he is successful. Otherwise, the whole situation will be at an end. But when an individual is faced with a problem and does persist until he solves it, there are, as I have said, four factors involved:

An individual is motivated toward a goal.
An obstacle prevents him from attaining it.
He acts to attain it.
The consequence to one of his acts is effective.

Awareness as a factor. There is one more factor which is sometimes involved in learning by consequences. This is *awareness of the various components in the learning.* Awareness, when it occurs, is an extremely important factor in learning. Here is an example:

Stephen, almost 3, has been pulling a wagon outdoors on the nursery-school track. One of the rear wheels has slipped down off the track and is caught at an angle against the track edge. Stephen tries to pull; the wagon does not move. Though he keeps on tugging, he is beginning to look upset. A grownup helps with, "Take a look, Stephen. Can you see what the trouble is?" He looks back, vaguely, over his shoulder, rather baffled. So the grownup says, "Take a look at the other end of your wagon." Stephen lets go of the handle and walks around to the back, but he still does not see what the matter is. The grownup spells it out for him. "Can you see what makes it stick? It's that wheel. I'll help you push it back on the track." Stephen pushes, though not hard enough to be effective. The grownup lends a helping hand, and off he goes again.

Stephen realized he could not move the wagon, but not what was holding it back. The grownup's guidance was designed to help him see this, not to simply bail him out of his difficulty. He was encouraged, once he saw what made the wagon stick, to go through the motions which would easily solve this kind of problem when he was a little older and stronger. In this case, the nature of the problem was immediately apparent to the grownup. Helping Stephen to realize it was also a relatively simple matter. It is not always as easy for adults to see what is involved in a child's problem. Here is a much more complex situation:

In the playroom in the mornings, 3½-year-old Barbara has hit on a fine technique for leaving the next move up to the grownups. When told, "Time to have a try at the toilet," she starts out toward the washroom, but then, part way there, stands stock still.

At first, the nursery-school staff thinks that Barbara may feel resistant to going to the toilet. But this theory does not hold, for she shortly transfers this kind of behavior to other situations and willingly goes to the washroom. What is it all about? It certainly seems like a bid for attention. Efforts are made to give her a lot of attention for behavior which the grownups feel merits it. She seems to enjoy the attention she gets, but the difficult behavior keeps on.

Unfortunately, her parents are too busy to come for a conference, but Barbara herself throws light on her feelings. One morning, she remarks, "I hope my mother comes and gets me" (that is, calls for her when it is time to go home from school). "She's only come once." And about three weeks later, in talking to another *child about the toy dog which she has brought to school to play with, she says, "He just loves his mother. He slept with his mother once. It was a long time ago."*

In a conference at last with Barbara's mother, it turns out that Barbara is being extremely difficult at home. She seems to be going out of her way to be unreasonable. For example, she will point to a box high on a kitchen shelf, without knowing what is in it, saying that is what she wants for supper. She then cries intensely when she cannot have it.

Thus it seems clear that Barbara needed to feel assured of her parents' affection, especially of her mother's, and she had hit upon making scenes as a way of getting the attention she craved. How much did Barbara realize about her feelings and her troublesome behavior at home and in nursery school? Her remarks show that she was aware of wanting more time with her mother. Beyond this, we have no clues about her realization in this problem situation.

I have chosen this example because there was no particular event in Barbara's life which called her parents' attention to her feelings. She had seemed to take in her stride the baby's arrival over half a year before. There was no family crisis, like a critical illness, to upset this little girl. It took quite a while to figure out what seemed to be the motives behind her difficult behavior. Sometimes grownups overlook what is happening to children's feelings when they develop (as Barbara's did) in the pattern of everyday living.

The only way Barbara could gain the assurance she needed was from day-to-day happenings and the emotional color which surrounded them. Along with such reassuring daily experiences, it might well be beneficial, in addition, if her mother or father talked with her to help her realize the factors in the whole situation: how life had been going along so busily at home that she had been feeling left out; that this happened sometimes in families; how, now, there would be more time to do things with her; she did not need to make a fuss to get attention. But this kind of a talk would never serve as a substitute for assurance to be gained from satisfactions in home life itself.

Without multiplying examples, you can see that the learner's *awareness of the various factors in the problem-solving situation is* extremely variable. There may be awareness partially, wholly, or not at all, of any of the other four factors in learning. When awareness does enter the picture, it may be so illuminating to the learner that the whole situation is changed.

In guidance, what you the grownup do is often crucial in determining not only what your child learns, but also how much of the whole situation your child is aware of.

Applying learning by consequences to guidance: motivating your child to learn what you want him to learn

Many of the examples you have seen of learning by consequences were drawn from learning situations which involved guidance, because that, presumably, is what you are interested in. Now in this section we are going to concentrate on setting this kind of learning to work for you in guidance.

WATCH THE CONSEQUENCES OF YOUR CHILD'S BEHAVIOR

In order to set learning by consequences to work for you, you need to keep a weather eye on the consequences to your child's behavior. Lots of times these consequences will further the learning you hope for, without any intervention by you. Very good. The more this happens, the better. But stay alert to occasions on which you should intervene.

PLAN THE SURROUNDINGS FOR YOUR CHILD TO FOSTER THE LEARNING YOU WANT

You will see when I am talking about arrangement of your home setting and about play activities for your child that we are applying learning by consequences. In so far as possible, we shall try to plan the surroundings for your child so that the consequences of his behavior will both foster the kinds of learning you have in mind for him and bring him satisfaction. That is all I shall say about this now, because such an important matter needs a chapter to itself (see Chapter 4).

ARRANGING CONSEQUENCES FOR BEHAVIOR WHEN YOU APPROVE OF WHAT YOUR CHILD WANTS, BUT NOT OF HOW HE ACTS TO ATTAIN IT

Many times, of course, consequences to your child's actions need a helping hand from you to foster the kind of learning you are after. Many times you approve of the end result your child has in mind—you do not want to try to change that. But you are concerned with how he acts to attain it. It is at this point that you enter the picture. Here is a child in this kind of situation:

> Dinah, just over 3, is sitting at a table in nursery school working a puzzle. Paul comes along and holds a crayon upright on one of the pieces of the puzzle, which brings a protest from Dinah. "Don't," she says, in a very whining tone. Paul still holds the crayon in position; Dinah screws up her face as if to cry. At this point, Mrs. A says, "Could you tell him in a big voice? He's more likely to pay attention." Dinah does speak in a firm tone, whereupon a meaningful look from Mrs. A sends Paul about his business.

From Mrs. A's point of view, Dinah's wish to have Paul take his crayon away from her puzzle was quite reasonable. But her whining—her act to attain what she wanted—was undesirable. In the wish that Dinah would learn not to whine, Mrs. A preferred that whenever Dinah acted in a desirable way to get what she wanted, she would succeed in getting it, when this was reasonable. Whenever, however, she acted in an undesirable way (when she whined), Mrs. A hoped that Dinah's action would not only be ineffective in gaining what she wanted, but also that the unsatisfactory consequence would motivate her to act in a desirable way.

In the particular example above, luckily for Dinah's learning, her whine was ineffective in gaining her end. Paul kept his crayon on her puzzle. A second consequence to her whine (Mrs. A's suggestion to ". . . tell him in a big voice. He's more likely to pay attention") motivated her to talk in a non-whining tone. Mrs. A then saw to it that this desirable behavior was effective in attaining what Dinah wanted.

Luck was not always on the side of Dinah's learning. When necessary, the grownups were ready to step in to prevent whines from being effective (at the same time advising Dinah to "talk in a big voice"). Now, despite the grownups' efforts, the consequences to Dinah's behavior were not always consistent. Staff members did not hear every time Dinah whined, and sometimes, even when they did hear her, they were too busy to give her their attention. But over a period of months the consequences to Dinah's way of talking were sufficiently consistent to bring marked improvement.

WAIT TO TRY TO CHANGE YOUR CHILD'S BEHAVIOR
UNTIL YOU FEEL YOU CAN CARRY THROUGH EFFECTIVELY

You have to be realistic about taking life into account before you try to guide your child's behavior. There is an important reason for this. If you start a program to get your child not to whine, but the consequences to his behavior are so inconsistent that this learning program has little effect, much more has happened than just failure to discourage whining. Your child has learned that you do not mean what you say, at least about whining, and he probably feels nagged besides. Nagging makes him irritable. In fact, you may be conditioning him to feel nagged, irritated, and inattentive whenever you speak to him. You feel irritated, too, probably more so than would be the case if you had merely heard the whine and had not started trying to remedy it. Therefore, wait to try to modify your child's behavior until you feel you can carry through effectively—until you can manage to see to it that the consequences to his actions will be consistent enough so that he can learn what you want him to. Sometimes this means waiting while you try to figure out what a child's motivation is and how you plan to go about your attempts at guidance. Sometimes, although you have figured out what seems a good plan, it means waiting until life simmers down enough so that your plan is feasible for you to try.

ARRANGING CONSEQUENCES FOR BEHAVIOR WHEN
YOU DISAPPROVE OF WHAT YOUR CHILD WANTS

Dinah was an example of a child motivated, without grownup assistance, toward an approved goal. Guidance entered only to direct
her how to act in attaining this goal. But sometimes your child is
motivated toward a goal, on his own, without grownup suggestion,
and you disapprove of what he aims to do. Sandra (pp. 27–28) illustrated this kind of case when she was bent on taking over Jane's
swing. Let us look again at the consequences.

1. *Jane, on the verge of tears, protested ineffectually.*
2. *Mrs. A: "Sandra, Jane had the swing first. I'll help you see when
   there's a swing to use." (This was an attempt to get Sandra to
   realize the approved way to get a swing, but it did not work.)*
3. *Mrs. A: "Leave the swing alone."*
4. *Mrs. A: "You do need to take your hands off the rope. Either
   you do it by yourself, or I'll help you."*
5. *Mrs. A pried Sandra's hands away and carried her indoors when
   Sandra tried to kick her. (It was Mrs. A's guess that Sandra derived satisfaction from the drama of their skirmish.)*

Perhaps you are inclined to say, "If this little drama were going
on at home, the best thing to do would be to give Sandra a good
spanking. That would teach her." I disagree. Sometimes, of course,
spanking clears the air, though more often for the grownup than
for the child. The trouble with it as a consequence is that it is inconsistent. And, furthermore, it often engenders feelings in children
which get in the way of their learning what grownups want them
to learn. I think the guidance used with Sandra (separation from
the swing) when she refused to do as directed is a much sounder
consequence. Now, of course, if it turned out that Sandra enjoyed
the drama of this scene so much that she cultivated other dramatic
scenes, then her guidance would have to be shaped accordingly.
Guidance would need to involve not one ounce of drama. One way
to go about it would be to have a talk with Sandra when she arrrived
in the morning to this effect: "Sandra, you know how playing with
things works at nursery school. If you get something first, you may

use it till you are through with it. I'm always glad to help you see when you can get something you want to use. But you keep trying to take things away from other children. Now, if you don't manage to keep from doing that, you'll need to play by yourself. How about it? Do you think the best thing to do would be to have you play by yourself right now to help you remember?" Since Sandra enjoys playing with the other children, the chances are she would choose to join them. Then the adult response would be: "All right, but if you don't manage, you'll need to play by yourself." If it proved necessary during the day to remove Sandra from group play, then she would have to start off the next morning by playing alone for a while.

It is interesting that during the period of her learning to accept approved procedure for finding play materials, although once in a while she had a flare-up of temper, on the whole Sandra's attitude toward the grownups was warm and friendly. For example, she particularly liked, when the children were singing, to plump herself down in Mrs. A's lap. Yet it was Mrs. A who was most involved in guiding her.

Sandra's feelings for Mrs. A were not just accidental. I think children not only derive security from being helped and, when necessary, being made to behave reasonably and fairly; in the long run they often actually like it and become attached to the grownup most involved in their learning. This is a point that some parents seem to overlook when they let a child go too far in his behavior for fear of building up resentment or dislike toward themselves.

In the course of time, to all appearances, Sandra changed what she wanted to do. She really accepted a "first come, first served" policy for getting playthings and, as far as could be seen, ceased wanting to take things away from other children by force.

Often you can choose when to start guidance. In Sandra's case, the circumstances forced the grownup to step in to start guidance when she did. But there are many cases in which you can choose when your child starts learning. For instance, you can choose when he is introduced to a new food, or to toilet training. Or take the matter of his hopping out of bed instead of settling down to go to sleep.

You can choose whether or not you will try to change your child's behavior at this time.

If your child is getting out of bed, he has a motive which is directing him to do the opposite of what you would like (presuming that you want him to settle down quietly when he goes to bed). Since sleep is a physiological need, you hope his need for it will serve to motivate him to behave as you want him to.

It is certainly helpful, in these matters which involve physiological needs, to plan your child's day so that the times for eating, toileting, and sleeping are geared to your child's need for these activities. But, unfortunately, this is often not enough to motivate your child to behave as you want him to. He may keep bouncing out of bed, even though you are sure he is tired.

And as your child gets older, take such matters as doing chores at home, a reasonably good job of raking up leaves, for example, or tidying up his room so that it can be cleaned. At least some of the time, it is you, not he, who is the one who wants these chores done. But since your child is the learner, he is the one who has to have the motive inside him for the learning you want to take place. How are you going to bring this about?

Relevant, significant motives. For any learning situation, you must find in your child a motive to appeal to which is both really relevant to the situation and significant to him. You need to think carefully about the motive to which you appeal. I know a mother who, as each day began, put two big lumps of milk chocolate in her bureau drawer. Then, whenever either of her two children behaved in ways she did not like, she took a bite out of his piece of chocolate. The size of the piece which each got at the end of the day reflected, then, just how "good" each child had been. This system worked quite well for almost two weeks. Then the children became tired of chocolate and it failed altogether.

Now if all we cared about in children's learning was how they act, it would not matter how we got them to act as we want them to. Chocolate for two days, a spanking on the third, a trip to the zoo at the end of the week, and so forth. We would be likely to find, to be sure, that we had to keep increasing the allure of rewards and the severity of punishments as time went on, but if we were ingenious enough, always keeping one step ahead with our various inducements, we might be able to keep our children performing the actions we wanted. But there is a very good reason for not relying on a system of irrelevant rewards and punishments if we care to have children learn to *want* to behave in ways which will serve their own and other people's interests.

Such irrelevant consequences simply will not lead to the kinds of long-range attitudes that will motivate your child to *want* to act in ways which will further his adjustment to the world in which he lives. Such long-range attitudes include due consideration for other people. Suppose the children whose mother tried to induce "good" behavior with chocolate had not tired of it. Unless they were very stupid indeed, they would have found out after a while that the best way to get chocolate is to buy it. The brighter children are, the sooner irrelevant rewards and punishments fail to be effective.

This example of trying to promote "good" behavior by the prospect of a large piece of chocolate at the end of the day illustrates that when you appeal to a motive in order to guide your child's learning, what you are trying to do is to get him to think ahead to the consequences of his behavior. You hope that your child's thinking about the consequences of his actions will cause him to choose to act in an acceptable way. Many times such thinking ahead to consequences will bring about the behavior desired, when you have created a sound learning situation through your appeal to a relevant, significant motive. But lots of times your child will actually have to experience an unsatisfactory consequence in order to make the "right" choice on some future occasion.

I have said that *for any learning situation, you must find, in your child, a motive to appeal to which is both really relevant to the situation and significant to him*. Obviously, each learning situation has to be tailor-made to your particular child, in terms of his motivation. But, unique though he is, still he shares many characteristics with other children at his developmental level. This is why generalization about guidance is possible; this is why, earlier, I asked you to think about what children in general are like at 2 and 3 and 4.

Among other things, the chocolate-dispensing mother wanted her children to be on time to meals. In contrast with her system of trying to bring this about, let us see what happened with 4-year-old Tim when his mother appealed to a relevant, significant motive to get him to come in promptly for his midday dinner:

> Tim was usually playing outdoors near the house when it was time for his dinner. When his mother called him, he simply did not come. Why not? There were many possibilities, of course; among them, that he did not hear, that he did not want his dinner, or that he just wanted to keep on playing. It seemed likely that this last motive was the important one behind his failure to come. If this guess was right, then his desire to play was the relevant, significant motive to which to appeal. So here is the plan worked out.
>
> Tim was asked, "You would like to keep on playing as long as there is time before dinner, is that right?" "Yes," said Tim. "Then," said his mother, "if you want to keep playing until just dinnertime, that means that you have to manage to come right away when I call you. If you don't manage that, I am going to call you early the next day, so that you come in and get washed and are right there when dinner is ready. Now, do you understand? If you have to be fetched, then the next day you will have to come in early." Tim said he understood.
>
> "I'll do another thing," his mother added. "I'll tell you a few minutes before it is time to come in, so that you'll know you will be coming in soon and then I'll tell you too when the time comes." (This was to give him a chance to gear his activities to their approaching end.)

On several days, Tim did have to be fetched, and was therefore brought in early the next day. But in time this plan of guidance worked; he learned to come in when his mother called.

In this case the motive appealed to—Tim's desire to play—was relevant to the situation (through the way his mother made use of it) and significant to Tim. When he behaved as she wanted him to, when he came promptly when called, the consequence was satisfactory to him; he could play as long as possible before dinner. When he failed to come in, the consequence of having to come in early the next day was not only unsatisfactory to him, it also motivated him to want to be prompt in the future. (Of course, Tim was old enough to understand and keep in mind a consequence which carried over to the next day. Sufficient maturity for understanding and remembering is absolutely essential with this kind of carry-over consequence.)

ADEQUATE AND INADEQUATE MOTIVES: WHAT MAKES SOME MOTIVES INADEQUATE

Affection. Perhaps you are thinking, "Tim ought to have come in because he knew his mother wanted him to, because he was fond of her and should want to please her."

I know a number of parents who think along these lines. They do a lot of dull things for the good of the family. Their affection helps them. It is only reasonable, they feel, that their children should follow suit. My answer to this is that parents are grownup. Your child will be, too, someday, but he is not there yet.

In the long run, children's affection may well motivate them to be thoughtful of others. And often, of course, children do want to do what their parents tell them because they are fond of their parents. This is particularly likely when they are going through a phase of wanting to please grownups (as children characteristically do around 3). What about trying to utilize their affection as motivation for things that need doing around home, coming promptly to meals, chores for older children, and so forth? Parents who feel that this should work sometimes talk in this vein to a school-age child. "Now I do lots of things for you. And all I asked you to do this weekend was tidy up your room so that it could be cleaned tomorrow. And what have you done? Look at the mess under your bed. You ought to care more about other people in the family. You make it very hard . . ." and so forth. Is this an appeal to affection? Certainly. It is clearly an if-you-really-cared-about-me-you-would-do-thus-and-so approach. Granted, a school-age child should come to feel that he ought to do jobs efficiently around home for the benefit of other family members. But in the first place, the appeal to affection is coupled with irritation and indignation, which is unfortunate in the light of the conditioning process; and in the second place, appealing to his affection simply will not work to motivate him to do all the humdrum little jobs that are necessary for him. And it is not fair to either of you to expect such a motive—affection for you—to sustain him through chores. If he is a child with a number of interests, the chances are that this motive will not loom large enough in relation to the immediacy of his other interests to lead him to do household jobs. And if you try to link up affection with chores, he may come to conclude that if not tidying up his room means he is not fond of mother, then, alas, that is the case. Further, if you beat this tom-tom of affection frequently, which you are likely to have to do because it is ineffective as motivation, it is going to have a very irritating sound in his ears. Is this what you want affection to mean to him?

Contrast this appeal with reaching an understanding with your child about a deadline, which he has had a part in picking, for completing his tidying-up job. Then, if he does not meet the deadline, the room gets tidied at once, no matter what his other plans. This *will* work in the long run.

With younger children, I have heard the appeal to affection take the form of, "Johnny, if you don't keep out of the cookie jar, it means you don't love Mommy." If Johnny really wants a cookie, and he has a logical mind, this can lead him to the conclusion that he doesn't love Mommy.

Sometimes, instead of the if-you-do-so-and-so-it-means-you-don't-love-me appeal by parents, the handle is turned the other way, so the appeal becomes if-you-do-so-and-so-I-won't-love-you. This is equally disastrous. A child needs to feel that his parents' love is not conditional upon "good" behavior. This does not mean that his parents have to approve his every action, but there is a vast difference between disapproving of what he *does* and disapproving of what he *is*, with threats of withdrawing love. As he gets older, he needs to come to realize that what he *is*, the kind of person he comes to be, is made up of what he does. This, when he is ready for it, may help him see the significance of his actions. But children need to feel secure in their parents' love. As a matter of fact, often it is when they have misbehaved that they especially need this sense of security. In short, affection between parent and child is far too important to be used as a bartering tool to try to get children to perform tasks— and it does not work.

Please do not conclude that I underrate the importance in children's lives of their desire to please parents, their affection for them, often their wish to imitate them. Many times these are immensely strong motivating factors in children's behavior. There is something very moving, without involving sentimentality, about a child's, particularly a little child's, efforts to be like grownups. As we all know, there is a snag in this sometimes, because children imitate both our desirable and our less attractive traits. Nevertheless, cultivate your child's impulse to admire and copy his elders, but do not devalue it by trying to use it as motivation when it is irrelevant to the learning at hand.

Consideration. Consideration is an attitude which most of us would like children to have toward people in general, whether or not they are fond of these people. Frequently, parents use such an appeal.

> *Eleven-year-old Paul has been waiting while his mother has been involved in a consultation. They are leaving the consultation building, when a small pool catches Paul's eye and he starts over to have a look in it. At once, his mother calls to him in a complaining voice, "Paul, come on. Mrs. Smith is waiting to take us home. It was so nice of her to drive us down and she has so many things to do. You wouldn't want to inconvenience her, would you?"*

Now, when Paul's mother put it this way, he would be likely to feel, "If that inconveniences Mrs. Smith, let her be inconvenienced." This guidance not only deprived Paul of a chance to satisfy his curiosity, but also prohibition on the grounds of inconsideration had no significance for him. A splendid setup to teach Paul to pay no attention to his mother, and to convince him that, in his parents' eyes at least, he is inconsiderate! Of course, Paul should not have been allowed to loiter when a busy friend was waiting for him, but it would have been quite possible to have let him satisfy his curiosity about the pool, and then concentrate the guidance on speeding him on his way after a quick look, instead of attempting (unsuccessfully as it turned out) to keep him from looking at all.

Paul, like other children, needed understanding and consideration of his interests and drives. His parents needed to think through carefully what they could reasonably expect of him. And then they needed to find relevant motives to appeal to for each of the things they wanted him to learn, motives which had significance for him. Among the desired learnings was consideration for other people. How could he learn this? In the same way he learned everything else. One of the best ways to learn consideration is to live with considerate people. Conditioning plays no small part in developing this kind of attitude. Learning by consequences is necessary, too. It might well be the case that Paul would have to go through the kind of learning process that Sandra went through; it might be necessary for him to find out that inconsiderate behavior was not effective in getting what he wanted (as her swing grabbing was not effective in gaining a swing). He would have to discover too, of course, that it served his own interests to act considerately.

Perhaps you object to this, since you want your child to act considerately because he feels considerate. So do I, in the long run. But he is never going to learn consideration if you appeal to a motive which does not exist. How can that have significance for him?

What about appealing to consideration when it is relevant to the situation and when it is significant to the child concerned? Obviously, that is fine. Only do not overdo such an appeal by making too great demands on the kindly attitudes of a considerate child.

By all means, when your child acts spontaneously in considerate ways show your appreciation, for it is then a part of the consequences to his behavior. But, as always, only express genuine feelings, for children see through pretense with alacrity.

WHEN AND HOW TO EXPRESS APPROVAL AND
DISAPPROVAL OF YOUR CHILD'S BEHAVIOR

When and how you express approval and disapproval is important. Remember, whenever you show approval or disapproval (in words, or actions, or both) your expression is part of the consequence to your child's behavior. This means, of course, that anticipation of your approval or disapproval may motivate his actions.

How about using approval and disapproval as your regular means of trying to motivate your child to do what you want him to? This appeal to his desire for approval can boomerang. If desire for your approval is what motivates him to perform the jobs in his life which need doing, what will happen when he is feeling out of sorts? Clearly, he may choose not to perform them in order to annoy you. And some of the time he is bound to feel out of sorts. Growing up in our culture tends to produce hostility toward grownups, even when they are wise and understanding. Children need far better reasons than pleasing or not pleasing the grownups in their lives as motivation for doing the things that need doing. This is why it is unsound to thank or praise them for doing what they *ought* to do, unless their actions really merit these reactions. Have you ever heard a grownup say, for example, "What a good girl you are! You ate up all your dinner." Now what does this remark imply?—that, by eating, the child is doing the grownup a favor. Children should not feel that they are doing favors when they merely behave as they ought, in a reasonable way. Here again, effective guidance must find some other motive, one, needless to say, for each learning situation, which is relevant to it and significant to the learner.

In expressing approval or disapproval, remember that your child's feelings are part of the consequence to his actions. Suppose you are sick, and your child picks some flowers for you. Then, in getting a vase from a crowded shelf, as you have let him do before, he knocks over a favorite piece of china and breaks it. The chances are he feels bad. How will he feel if you blame him severely? He will probably react like most people who are censured: regret will change to defense or even antagonism.

Let me make it plain that I am not asking you to be super-human, not advising you to hold in and clamp down too hard on your own feelings. But I am making a plea that you try to look at the outcome of your child's behavior from his point of view, and take his motivation into account, before condemning what he does. Sometimes, like all people, you will be tired and out of sorts your-self, and you may react impulsively with annoyance. But you are likely to discover as time goes on that as you manage to think of the whole situation and not just the end result of your child's actions, it becomes easier to give him credit for his motives and the part his feelings play as consequences to his action; in short, that you find it easier to acquire a kind of perspective which helps you to reserve disapproval for behavior which merits it.

Suppose your child is doing something intentionally to annoy you, and you happen not to be annoyed. What is more, you do not feel that you have to check what he is doing. Fine, then do not manufacture disapproval. The very fact that you are not annoyed is an unsatisfactory consequence for your child, who wants to get a rise out of you. Here again, you are taking his feelings into account as you note the consequences of his behavior.

My point is that your approval and disapproval should be reserved for occasions that really merit it—real achievement, real misbehavior, as you take his motives and behavior into account.

Moving on now to the question of how you express these attitudes, voice your approval in terms of *how* your child acts, not what he *is*. When you do this, instead of giving blanket approval or disapproval (what a good child, or what a bad child), he will hear how nice it was of him to get the baby's squeak toy that fell out of the playpen, or what an interesting picture he has painted, with spaces around the colors he has used (or some other comment in terms of why his picture is of interest). Or, he will be told that knocking down someone else's block building is not the thing to do— if he wants to knock something down he must build it up first; or that another child got that pail first, he must let go—if he wants one, he should look in the box and get a pail that is not being used. What a different meaning these remarks carry from "Johnny, you good [or bad] boy!" Approval or disapproval expressed in terms of actions highlight for your child the behavior that matters; this sort of response helps him realize what he has achieved or how he should act differently. Here, incidentally, is an example of the kind of disapproval I disapprove of:

> Almost-3¾-year-old Andy, sitting at a table drawing, remarks, "We have an elephant in our back yard," and waits for interested comments. Five-year-old Ralph meets this conversational gambit with

"You're a liar and a thief and when you grow up you'll go to jail."
This is too much for poor Andy, who bursts into tears.

There is another reason for voicing your approval or lack of it in terms of your child's behavior. If you keep telling him he is bad, you may convince him he *is* bad, and he may come to feel it is no use trying to do better. Further, telling him he is bad, instead of talking about how he acts, may make him feel unsure of your affection. I have already stressed the importance for your child of being assured of your love; he should not be made to feel that it is conditional upon "good" behavior.

TAKE YOUR CHILD'S WHOLE LIFE INTO ACCOUNT
IN PLANNING HIS GUIDANCE

So far in this section about motivating your child to learn what you want him to learn, the illustrations have all been isolated learning situations. But in point of fact, before you can decide what are relevant, significant consequences for a particular situation, you have to look at the whole situation, that is, take your child's whole life into account. (For suggestions on how to go about this see pp. 114–16.)

Let us compare three guidance situations which vary in the extent to which a child's whole life seems to be involved in guidance.

Suppose your 2-year-old, who has given up thumb sucking, takes it up again with the arrival of a new baby in the family. You try to appraise his whole life, to figure out the satisfactions and dissatisfactions he is experiencing in being the particular 2-year-old he is. And suppose you conclude that he is feeling insecure; furthermore, that his feeling of insecurity prompts his thumb sucking, colors what he does and how he feels about everything that is happening to him.

Effective guidance will consist in changing his attitude of insecurity to one of security. To do this, you will need to take into account his whole life, and probably devise particular kinds of guidance in many different situations.

If instead of searching for the motive for this behavior and arranging satisfactions which, you hope, will change the attitude, you had concentrated on "getting him to stop sucking his thumb," you might have succeeded. But you might well have found that new behavior which you did not like arose from the still-existing unsatisfied motive, his seeking security.

Now suppose that your 4-year-old has taken to running away from home. After an over-all appraisal to try to figure out as much as you can about him, including why he wants to run off, suppose you decide that he is bored and lonely for companionship of his own age, but that the rest of his life is giving him the satisfactions he needs. Then your plan of guidance will not involve his whole life to the extent that your plan for your 2-year-old did. What you will aim to do is give him a chance to get the companionship he longs for. You may, at the same time, have to devise a consequence for his running off, if it happens again, designed to make him choose to stay home, but the emphasis in your guidance will be on satisfying in an acceptable way the motive which prompts his running away.

In both of the above cases, an over-all appraisal shows that it is the larger context of your child's life, rather than the undesirable behavior itself, that needs to be dealt with. In the next example, in contrast, over-all appraisal shows that only the immediate situation itself requires attention.

> Julie, just over 3½, an old hand at nursery school, has begun to be very restless in the sleeping room after lunch. She is obviously sleepy, but wiggles about and watches the grownup who has been very busy during the previous first month of school helping new children learn to settle down to go to sleep. In a staff meeting, after talking over the way life is going for Julie, it is decided that she is probably being restless to get adult attention. The rest of her life, as the staff knows it, does not need change at this time. Therefore, the staff members decide to give her attention in the sleeping room when she is lying quietly, but to ignore her restless behavior. For a number of days during the going-to-sleep period the staff member involved whispers to her, "That's the way, Julie. You certainly know how to settle down by yourself, don't you?" Her restless behavior stops.

In this particular case, guidance consists in arranging satisfactory consequences for desirable behavior, rather than (as is sometimes necessary) arranging unsatisfactory consequences for behavior that you disapprove of.

Do not conclude from this illustration that one of the satisfactory consequences I advise is indiscriminate praise for what you want a child to do. You know already that I believe approval and disapproval should be reserved for behavior which really merits it. Julie's quiet behavior does deserve praise because, as it happens, a number of children were receiving help from grownups in learning to "settle down so as not to disturb the other children." When a good deal of attention is needed by one child, it may be that extra attention should be given another in order to avoid placing a premium on being "bad." This should serve to remind us that in appraising a child's life, we need to take into account the total situation, which includes, of course, how grownups are acting toward other children.

SUMMARY: APPLYING LEARNING BY CONSEQUENCES TO GUIDANCE
In this long section, the main points I have made are these:

1. It is important to plan your child's surroundings so that when he is active in them, the consequences to his actions are likely to foster the learning you want to occur.

2. In some learning situations you will have to take a direct part in order that consequences will foster desired learning. I have given an example (Dinah and her whining) in which what your child wants, his goal, is approved by you, but in which you need to manipulate consequences so that he will learn to act in an acceptable way to get what he wants. Another example (Sandra and the swing) illustrates the more difficult and complicated case in which what your child wants has to change in order for the desired learning to occur; this example also illustrates the kinds of consequences which are necessary if change in motivation is to take place.

3. It is helpful when you are looking for a relevant, significant motive to remember that what you are trying to do is to get your child to think ahead to the consequences of his behavior and to act accordingly, with acceptable behavior, to gain an approved goal.

4. Especially in connection with a child's learning to do chores, you need to remember that some motives are inadequate: irrelevant rewards and punishments, affection between parent and child, consideration for people in general, desire for approval, anticipation of disapproval. In this discussion I have spent most of my time talking

about motives not to appeal to. What ones should you make use of then? The one you select in any particular chore-learning situation depends, of course, on your estimate of a relevant, significant feeling in your child, an appeal to which will effectively motivate him to perform the chore. You have seen that when Tim's mother wanted to motivate him to learn to come in when called, she selected his desire to go on playing. This was effective because Tim wanted to keep on playing and because his mother thought continuation of play was suitable. (It would not have been effective to appeal to Tim's desire to play unless he had wanted to go on playing now; and, of course, his mother could not have made use of this desire unless she was willing to have him continue to play.) Thus, selection of an effective motive is a complicated question, in which you have to take into account time, place, and circumstance, as well as your child's motivation. If you want to look ahead to an account of other motives which, in general, are likely to motivate a child to learn to perform chores, see the opening discussion of Chapter 8, Guidance in Business Activities, pp. 210–11.

5. It is essential to take your child's whole life into account in planning his guidance. Sometimes, after you have made such an over-all appraisal you will find that you can concentrate pretty much on the immediate situation that needs attention (Julie's restlessness at sleep time); at the other extreme there will be cases (for instance, the thumb-sucking 2-year-old) in which it is necessary to concentrate on the total context rather than on the behavior that is causing the trouble.

Over and over again I have focussed on how important the motive to which you appeal is in guiding your child if you wish to have him acquire attitudes which will lead him to want to behave in ways that foster his long-range development and at the same time take account of other people's needs.

In all of the discussion of learning, I have taken for granted one extremely important point—that is, what it is the grownups want the child to learn. I cannot go any further in talking about guidance without having you think about this. What do you want your child to learn?

3

What Do You Want Your Child to Learn?

WHAT DO YOU WANT your child to learn? You are the only one who can answer this question. You may not want to bother with it, but all the same, whether or not you take time to think through your answer, you will be determining what he learns in everything you do and do not do. Hence, it is worthwhile seriously considering your answer to this question. You may have ideas quite different from mine about what children should learn. But however much we differ in our aims for guidance, of equal use to us both will be the methods of guidance I have been discussing. These methods are the means for carrying out aims, whatever they are.

I am going to tell you what my aims are, not in an effort to get you to agree with me, but to give you a starting point for thinking about your own aims for your child. I emphasize this, because, in talking about your child, it may sound as if I am trying to persuade you to accept my goals for him. It is true that, since I think these are important goals, I hope you will come to agree with me. But of much more importance than any such agreement is your reaching your own decision as to what you want. To reach a sound decision, you must take into account your child, yourself, your husband or wife, the rest of the family, the kind of life you lead, and the kind of world you think your child is going to have to live in. Quite a large order.

As you think over what you want your child to learn, it is reasonable to distinguish between long-range aims and aims for immediate learning situations. For example, you probably want your child to spend his money wisely when he grows up, and to earn it, too—these are long-range aims. And right now, let us say, you want him to learn to close the door after he comes in the house—an immediate aim.

Let us consider long-range aims first.

Long-range aims

DEVELOPMENT OF POTENTIALITIES

I hope your child will develop his potentialities sufficiently to take his place productively and confidently in the world of his adulthood. And when I say "develop his potentialities," I mean the whole complex of interrelated aspects of personality—intellectual, physical, social, emotional, and all the rest.

ADAPTABILITY

I expect you will agree with me that your child ought to be able to adjust to the kind of world that exists when he grows up. What will it be like? Of only one thing can you be sure: it is likely to be very different from what you know today. Clearly, your child will have to be adaptable to get on in the world of *his* adulthood. Does this make you feel that there is little sense in trying to guide him, because you do not know what conditions he will have to meet? I think that is all the more reason for parents to use their wits to the best of their ability in child guidance. If now, in childhood, children are learning to choose their behavior according to its consequences, they are getting preparation for adaptation to whatever situations they may find themselves in later on.

SECURITY

And, of course, children need more than an ability to adapt. They need an inner sense of security. It is stylish to talk about security nowadays; everyone is in favor of it. But it is important to distinguish between two kinds of security.

Dependent and interdependent security contrasted. Dependent security is the kind of security which a little baby or small child has when he is lovingly and wisely looked after, when his needs are tended to as they occur, and when he is suffused with a sense of well-being. This kind of security is fine in babyhood, but as a person gets older, such dependence would place him in a vulnerable position. For his own sake, an individual needs to progress toward *interdependent* security. (There is today no such thing as independent security.) This will enable him to care for his needs in part through his own efforts, instead of being utterly dependent upon other people.

Interdependent security. In the long run, what kinds of attitudes are likely to be involved in an interdependently secure attitude? A variety of interests in things and in people is important. Indeed, to talk about having a variety of interests is simply another way of talking about the development of an individual's many potentialities, of which I spoke a moment ago. Moreover, a variety of interests makes for security; an individual with very limited interests is in a vulnerable position, for if anything interferes with these few, all-absorbing interests he has little to fall back on. Hence a variety of interests, and the varied skills to which they are likely to lead, promotes self-confidence and the probability of contacts with other people.

To be interdependently secure, an individual needs to have a sense of his own worth and adequacy; he also needs to accept his inabilities, when these cannot be remedied. He needs inner resources—not only breadth but depth of interest—which enable him to derive satisfaction from activities pursued on his own.

He also needs satisfying relationships with other people. To this end, a general attitude of consideration and of give-and-take is likely to be helpful, and is therefore desirable. It is to be hoped that the people he is fond of are fond of him in return.

Further, there will be many requirements and tasks in his life, often uninteresting, but necessary to keep daily living going efficiently—making repairs, writing letters, tending to the manifold jobs that keep a household or a business going. Toward these he needs an attitude of acceptance and responsibility, combined with enough skill to accomplish them promptly with reasonable efficiency. This will relieve him from the nagging and burdensome effects of putting off such matters, including the justifiable complaints of other people inconvenienced by his procrastination.

There are other attitudes of mind essential to interdependent security in a democracy which are likely to be helpful to your child when he is fully grown and living in a world about which we know so little now. Among these are a habit of trying to think for himself and of trying to solve the inevitable problems which arise when efforts to do something are not immediately successful. Another extremely important attitude is a willingness to accept the consequences of his behavior. How different this is from attempts to escape such consequences and find excuses for himself.

Then there is the matter of making decisions. It is so easy, instead of learning to face up to decisions, to have an attitude of postponing or agonizing over even the most trivial matters, with resultant uncertainties and unpleasantness.

Lastly, an individual needs the ability both to express and to control his feelings adequately.

These, then, are some of the long-range aims which I think are important for your child. You may not agree with them all. Or, even if you do, they must sound pretty vague and, if your child is only 2, or 3, or 4, probably very remote. But actually, everything that you do now bears on these long-range aims. They need not be vague because the quite specific things you do right now will tend to make these aims concrete.

Promoting long-range aims through everyday experiences

For instance, if you plan things well, even as your little child is enjoying himself in play, he can be learning attitudes (such as self-reliance and adaptability) which will stand him in good stead all the days of his life. In the next few pages I shall show you how this can happen.

SOME IMMEDIATE AIMS FOR YOUR CHILD'S PLAY AND WAYS OF ACHIEVING THEM

Learning to take the initiative in finding something interesting and constructive to do. If you agree with what I said about long-range aims, you should encourage your child to take the initiative in finding something interesting and constructive to do. The key words here are, of course, *initiative, interesting,* and *constructive.* Taking them in order, I hope that he learns to choose things to do, on his own, without reliance on grownup suggestion; further, that what he does is interesting to him, that is, that it brings him satisfaction; and lastly, that it is constructive. I know of a 4-year-old who, all in one day, backed the family car out of the garage, put a kitten in the toilet, and emptied the vacuum-cleaner bag over his mother as she sat taking a bath. Quite a display of initiative, but hardly constructive!

To be constructive, an activity must not be harmful either to persons or property, and must give your child a chance to be using his skills and developing his potentialities. This he can do only if he has suitable play materials and equipment, what we might call "constructive" play materials. What are they?

Constructive play materials. Most "constructive" play materials offer various possibilities for use. Snow, for example, can be shaped, rolled, thrown, built up, slid in, not to mention tasted, if it is clean enough or no one is there to say no. Blocks can be lined up by a 2½-year-old, or built into elaborate structures by a 4-year-old. These materials lend themselves to alteration and manipulation according to the skills of the user. The diversity of activity which they offer helps a child develop sustained interest and persistence, as he shifts his attention, not necessarily from one play material to another in order to get variety, but from one aspect of a particular play material to another. Contrast with these "constructive" materials the limited possibilities of a mechanical duck; once it is wound up, the duck does the rest while the child stands by. My conclusion is not that all wind-up toys should be banned, but that play materials be heavily weighted on the side of "constructive" playthings which encourage varied, interesting activity by the child himself.

Sufficient variety in play materials. Your child also needs considerable variety in the kinds of things available for his play—sufficient variety so that as his attention shifts (it is bound to because of his very nature), he continues to be exposed to materials which help him develop skills and interests of many different kinds rather than a few limited ones. To mention a few of these, I hope that his play surroundings promote his physical coordination involving large-muscle activity as well as finer motor control; that they also foster his ability to solve problems; further, that he has opportunities to enjoy working with color, and shape, and form, and texture in different kinds of materials (with due regard for ease of supervision). I hope that there is provision for housekeeping play, so that he can act out his ideas about family life when he wants; that he has a chance to develop his imagination in the use of the materials provided, as well as through the kind of experiences that books geared to his developmental level can give him; in addition, that he has the opportunity to enjoy music and to take part in musical activities. These are just a few of the many aspects of his development which I hope are being fostered.

Varied interests and skills: their contribution to interdependent security. Why should you be concerned about variety in play possibilities if your child is content without it? You can anticipate my answer from what I have said already about long-range aims. I want your child to develop a variety of interests and skills. A variety of available play activities is likely to help him be resourceful in finding occupation right now. He will probably not be in the position of a 2-year-old I know who was content, day after day and month after month, to spend all of her outdoor time swinging. For your child, I care about the development of interests and skills both for what they mean to his own enjoyment and for their usefulness in promoting contacts with other people. I care about them, too, because they have a direct bearing upon his sense of competence. How will a variety in skills and interests involving not only things but people increase your child's sense of his own adequacy?

First, varied interests and skills are likely to make him more interesting to other people, and so increase his range of contacts and friendships with other children and with grownups, too. To put this another way, varied interests and skills are likely to promote his belonging to a number of social groups. (By definition, it takes just two people to make a "social group.")

Many social groups have at their core—as their reason for being —a particular skill. Here is an obvious example: suppose that your 10-year-old daughter (though I am adding a few years to your pre-school child's age, the principle is the same) and a group of friends have formed a cooking club and that you, in your enthusiasm for this interest, have bought all the children aprons. On the strength of this, your child is elected president. Now if this were a purely honorary position, no harm would be done, but let us suppose that the president has a lot of responsibility in planning the food to be prepared, in arranging where meetings will be held, and so forth. Your daughter is simply not good at this. She knows less about cooking than most of the girls and tends to forget her responsibilities. Since the president should be one of the most capable cooks in the club, your child's false status places her in an insecure position. And let me advance the converse: if a person's status in a group reflects his skill in the activity which is the core of the group's existence, he is in a secure position (unless he disagrees with the status given him by the other group members).

It is obvious that there are advantages in belonging to a number of groups in order to develop a general sense of competence. If her cooking club were your hypothetical daughter's only activity, what an insecure position she would have in her dealings with other people. Enough of this example. Here is another, also involving a 10-year-old girl. Let us say that she belongs to a cooking club, too, and is inexperienced and poor at it; but at least her status in the group reflects her skill in the kitchen. This girl belongs, in addition, to a number of other groups. She sings in a glee club, and because she has a true, pleasant voice, the other children count on her as a mainstay in the singing. She is also on the volleyball team, where, unfortunately, she sometimes tends to get excited and play wildly, to the annoyance of other members of her team. At home, however, because she reads well, she enjoys taking turns at out-loud family reading. Neighborhood children and their parents like to have her come to play, because she is almost always full of good ideas about something interesting to do.

My point is that it is helpful to an individual to be a member of a number of groups. Not only does this give him varied interests, but it contributes to his sense of adequacy through sufficient competence in some of these groups to give him a sense of worth. Belonging to a number of groups helps him, too, to accept realistically his status in the groups in which he is rather inept. I have already said that both of these attitudes are important for interdependent security: a feeling of adequacy derived from reasonable competence in activities of some variety and a feeling of acceptance of one's inabilities when these can hardly be remedied.

A sense of his own worth helps an individual in his relationships with other people, too. As Anna Wolf says so well in The Parents' Manual, "Love for one's fellow man, if it is really to become free from admixtures of its opposite, depends to a very large extent on a fundamental esteem for oneself and faith in one's dignity and power."

To get back to your 3- or 4-year-old (2-year-olds are being left out for the moment), belonging to a number of social groups will be equally helpful to him. I hope that your child has enough diversity in contacts with other children so that he learns how to get on in a variety of social situations, occasionally being one of the children most advanced in ideas and skills, occasionally being one of the least advanced, often having a chance to play with children who are at just about his own stage of development, for only with them is there a chance to develop real give-and-take in attitude and behavior. This involves, among other things, your child's learning to stand up for his own rights and to respect other people's as he moves through the years of preschool age.

Through his status, then, in various play groups (as well as, of course, in the other groups to which he belongs) he will be getting a sense of his own competence. If you think this notion of status is farfetched for children of this age, watch any group of 3- or 4-year-olds who play together regularly. You are likely to see some one child who often seems to be favored by the others, sought after, heeded when he puts forward ideas. Or there may be several children of this type who seem to have pretty much of a give-and-take relationship with one another. Other children may be hangers-on, who are merely tolerated, and still others may be excluded. As I have said, it is important that your child's status in play with other children has some variety if he is to learn social versatility. It is important, too, to his sense of adequacy not to be consistently in a position of low status. Therefore, if he tends to be the underdog in a particular group, I hope that this experience is balanced, to some extent at least, by his having a more favored position in some other play group. If, on the other hand, he is a resourceful child with a lot of appeal to his companions, who tends to dominate his playmates, I hope that his role is sometimes reversed, as he, in turn, is dominated by some other able, resourceful, but pleasant child.

I have excluded the 2-year-old from my remarks about group play since if he is close to 24 months of age and, therefore, does not interact with other children in his play as he will later on, it might seem odd to talk of his "belonging" to play groups. But he, too, should have opportunities to play alongside other children, both because this is pleasant for him and because it helps to pave the way for group play when he is ready. And long before his third birthday, the remarks I have made about the 3- and 4-year-olds will begin to apply to him, too.

THE IMPORTANCE OF PARENT-CHILD FEELINGS TO
DEVELOPMENT OF YOUR CHILD'S SENSE OF ADEQUACY

If you agree with me that a sense of personal adequacy and self-worth are fundamental long-range aims, then not only your child's relationships with other children but his relationships with grownups are very important. I hope your child has a sense of security in your love and in your ability to make him behave reasonably if he needs direction. I hope that you are able to accept him for what he is, without trying to turn him into something he is not, even as you try to further development of his potentialities. This may be hard if the father involved is a dedicated athlete with a dreamy little son, or if the mother who wanted a feminine companion has a vigorous tomboy daughter who cannot wait to go outdoors to play ball with the boys.

Remember how conditioning operates. Tone of voice and facial expression can easily give the lie to what you say if your words do not reflect your feelings. It is very difficult for your child to develop a sense of adequacy if he feels that he is under a perpetual cloud of parental disapproval.

But what can you do if you really disapprove not just of some aspect of your child's behavior or appearance, but, more fundamentally, of what he seems to be like in general—of the kind of person he seems to be? You can acquaint yourself with what it is reasonable to expect in a child of his developmental level, which may be helpful if you are expecting too much of him. You can try to search out the source of your attitude if you find yourself unusually emotional about some particular aspect of your child's behavior (pp. 70–71). Fortunately, a persisting attitude of thoroughgoing disapproval of a child by his parent is rare, but some parents seem to go through such extensive phases of seeing the dark side of their child's nature that their attitude is close to the sort of wholesale disapproval I have been discussing.

At the other end of the scale, in contrast to a general attitude of disapproval, is one of such blind admiration that parents feel a child can do no wrong. This extreme is no kindness. It is likely to give him an unrealistic picture of his own status in relation to other people. Far from contributing in the long run to his sense of adequacy, such blanket approval can make it hard for him to learn to get on happily with other people.

This blind admiration and approval of a child is quite different from an attitude of real acceptance by his parents—quite different from a love which can be counted on and is not conditional on good behavior, but which neither blinds them to the child's need for guidance nor prevents them from using discrimination in appreciating what is genuine achievement on his part.

THE INFLUENCE OF COMPETITION ON A SENSE
OF ADEQUACY

The way competition is handled in the groups which make up your child's life also has a marked influence on his sense of adequacy. When he is of preschool age, I hope that his performance is measured against his own efforts, not other people's, for there is enough pressure in the lives of children of this age without adding to it by adult-sponsored competition. "Let's see if you can keep busy dressing and be ready to open the door for the milkman the way you did yesterday" has quite another effect on your child than "Let's see if you can beat Sam getting dressed" or "Why can't you do a quick job of dressing like your brother Sam?" If children of preschool age spontaneously introduce competition into play or jobs, this is different. They are not likely to agree to it unless they enjoy it and, if they do compete, are likely to feel free to stop when they want to.

The influence of competition on your child is so important as he gets older that I would like to look ahead briefly to its place in his school-age years.

By and large, for children of all ages, I hope that emphasis is on the enjoyment of an activity and on its performance in terms of a child's best efforts rather than on winning, for focussing on winning can take away the pleasure in the activity itself for all but the few at the top.

However, for a child who has a low opinion of his own adequacy,

I would make an exception to the general rule of competition only with equals. Sometimes such a child needs help in finding an area in which he can excel and, therefore, feel successful and gain status in our competitive-minded culture—which is going to keep its competitive nature however much parents try to reserve competition for evenly matched participants. I know of a teacher who in order to help a boy who was incompetent, insecure, and poor in athletics organized a competition to see who could ride a bicycle the slowest. In this contest, the insecure boy won, hands down, and for a number of weeks was copied and admired as other boys tried to equal his performance. As the winner, now a grown man, looks back on this experience, he recognizes how wise that teacher was.

When school-age children are evenly matched, competition can spur them on to greater effort and add zest to life, without the unfortunate effect of spoiling an activity for all but the ablest. This kind of competition, it strikes me, is too little used in academic learning. I know a third-grade teacher who added great interest to learning the multiplication tables by dividing her class into two teams, "The Triceratops" and "The Stegosaurus." The children were studying dinosaurs, so battles involving prehistoric monsters appealed to them. The teams were matched in arithmetical ability as evenly as possible. The winning side of each daily "battle" entered its victory on a wall chart. Children became so interested that they studied their tables at home with real zeal in preparation for the next day's contest.

Turning from academic learning to athletics, I hope that at the high school level, interschool competition is not reserved for the first-string athletes but that each school has a number of teams of varying ability, all of which have a chance to play with teams of comparable skill from other schools.

FRIENDSHIPS WITH GROWNUPS OUTSIDE
THE FAMILY

Returning now to your preschool child, I have been asking you to think about how you can help him develop a sense of his own worth. I have mentioned relationships with other children (which led me to talk of competition) and with you, his parents. But I hope, too, that your child has a chance for friendships with grownups outside the family, and so finds that there are other adults besides his parents whose company he enjoys and who enjoy him.

SOME IMMEDIATE AIMS FOR YOUR CHILD'S
BUSINESS ACTIVITIES

Let us turn from thinking about your child's play and his relationships with other people to the business side of his life. For him, these are the activities designed to take care of his physical needs, such as eating, sleeping, going to the toilet, as well as activities necessary in conformance to certain customs, such as wearing clothes and tidying up his belongings. Toward these activities, I hope that he is developing attitudes of acceptance and responsibility, attitudes which will serve him not only now, but when he is grown up, and, in addition, that he is acquiring the skill to look after his needs and to meet requirements efficiently. Such attitudes and skills have an enormous effect on the flavor of home life. Efficient, responsible performance of tasks can free you and your child for more interesting, creative use of time, and eliminate a major source of unpleasantness and irritation.

AIMS FOR DEVELOPMENT IN BOTH BUSINESS
AND PLAY ACTIVITIES

Though it is convenient for purposes of discussion to divide up your child's life into play and business activities, much important learning goes on in both situations.

Learning to think for oneself. The way your child is guided in all his activities—in work and play—will affect his ability to think for himself. Take even such a humdrum matter as forgetting to flush the toilet. Suppose instead of just telling him to do it you say, "You forgot something." This encourages him to figure out what he has overlooked, instead of your doing his thinking for him. Or suppose he is working a puzzle and asks, "Where does this go?" as he holds up a piece. If you think that the piece he has in his hand is particularly difficult, tell him, "That is a hard one." Then, putting another in front of him which you think will be one of the easiest pieces to identify you might say, "Where do you suppose this goes?" If it is still too hard, you give him further help: "Where do you suppose that long narrow part fits? Can you see any space like that?" If he is successful this time, you add, "If you find the easiest pieces first, it will help to find the harder ones later." This way you are helping him learn to solve a problem, not solving it for him and not depriving him, besides, of the fun of feeling that *he* has done it.

Learning to make decisions. Suppose your 4-year-old is wandering around aimlessly; you are going to be busy for a while and it would be nice if he were busy, too. Instead of saying, "Why don't you make a tea party for your stuffed animals?" you leave the decision up to him by making more than one suggestion: "Come on, let's look around and see what there is to do. There are your tea dishes, if you want to have a party for your animals, or you can use your drawing paper and your crayons, and there are paste and colored paper if you'd like to use those. What are you going to do?"

Learning to take the consequences of one's behavior. This is another important attitude which, once learned, will be invaluable to your child all the rest of his life. It is one of the mainstays of interdependent security. In the example below, Mrs. A is helping Sandra learn about consequences:

> *Sandra is using paste. She puts a glob in her mouth. Mrs. A explains, "You need to keep it out of your mouth. If you don't manage, then away it goes, and you find something else to do."*
>
> *When another glob is consumed, the consequence follows. Paste is put away.*
>
> *A short time later, Sandra wants to use paste again. The reply is, "Yes, if you manage to keep it out of your mouth." And this time she does.*

Learning to express and to control feelings adequately. An important aspect of interdependent security is the ability to express and to control feelings adequately. On the expression side, I often think of a 4-year-old boy who combined very high aims for his own achievement with a habit of holding in his feelings. In carpentry work, for example, he wanted every nail straight and every piece firm, yet his lack of skill made this impossible. He would keep on with determination in the face of frustration until finally he would go all to pieces. He needed to learn to express his feelings as he went along. This boy was helped by having a grownup talk with him as he worked. "It does make people cross, doesn't it, when nails bend," he would hear, and at the same time a suggestion would be made as to how he could hammer to help prevent nail bending. At last he learned to say, "Darn it, that nail's bending," instead of holding his frustration in until he exploded.

None of us who have dealings with young children need examples to remind us of the emotional outbursts they have and which, in the long run, they need to learn to control.

Acquiring a sound foundation for some of the complicated aspects of life. While we are on the subject of your child's feelings, I hope that in these years from 2 to 5 he is living through experiences which are helping him develop a foundation of feeling and understanding about many of the complicated aspects of life—a foundation on which he can build further as he grows in understanding and maturity (and not have to reject because he finds it does not fit the facts as he comes to know them), about such complex matters as sexuality, religion, honesty, a sense of responsibility for using his talents to the best of his ability, to name only a few.

Developing one's intellectual potential. Everything I have been discussing—from variety of constructive play materials to learning to make decisions or expressing and controlling feelings—has a bearing on intellectual development. And conversely intellectual development has a bearing on these.

In focussing on what is conducive to full development of your child's intellectual potential, the last thing I have in mind is an overearnest attitude on the part of parents, forever looking for a chance to educate their child, like the mother who always greeted her husband after his weekly walk with their 2-year-old with the somber question, "What did you see today that was worthwhile?"

What I do have in mind is the sort of unforced stimulation that is likely to occur in the natural course of events for a child who has the kind of surroundings I have already described and who has also sufficient freedom in the use of these varied, constructive play materials. As he interacts with his physical environment, he will be gaining many concepts of how things work and of what the world is like. Much development, of course, could never take place in a social vacuum, but will also occur in the natural course of events for such a child—language development, for instance. There is increasing evidence that since language is important to the formation of many concepts, it is a necessary condition for other kinds of intellectual growth. Your child will benefit by being exposed to the kind of language experience that most grownups adopt naturally with a baby and a small child—not baby talk, not talking down, but speaking the key words slowly, clearly, and distinctly: "Yes, that is a great big truck, Johnny." "The swing goes high." "There's Daddy, way over there." "More? More dinner, Johnny?"

From his earliest days on, as a child explores his surroundings (first with his eyes and mouth, then with his hands before he walks, and finally with all the inquisitive faculties of an into-everything toddler and an active preschooler), let him hear judicious comment about the world around him. What a wealth of intellectual stimulation and of intellectual heritage is then coming his way. "That's an interesting picture you painted. A red shape in the center, and white spaces all around." Or, in song form,

> Five little chickadees, no room for more,
> One flew away, and then there were four. . . .

Numbers, colors, spatial and temporal relations, relative sizes, cause and effect—all these concepts and many more are learned by a young child in a stimulating social (and physical) environment, almost without the parents' being aware of what is happening. As a matter of fact, until psychologists became involved in studying the tragic effects of cultural deprivation, it was hard even for them to realize how much a beneficent environment for tiny babies and growing children promotes their intellectual development. But a word of caution. I have found that interested parents tend to over-stimulate rather than understimulate their child. Therefore quell the impulse to fill your child with information, to jump the gun on school learning, to talk so much when he is playing on his own that he loses interest in his activity. Later I shall have more to say about interacting with your child in a variety of situations.

Things to take into account when setting aims for your child's behavior

So far I have talked about the sort of long-range aims that I would have for your child (aims that I hope you will decide to adopt) and about the sort of day-to-day activities and immediate aims that will help bring these about. Now, whether you are thinking about long-range or immediate aims, there are a lot of things you need to take into account.

KEEP IN MIND WHAT YOUR CHILD IS LIKE

In setting an aim for your child's present behavior, keep in mind his developmental stage (that is, what children are like at his stage of development), as well as what he is like as a person distinct from all other people. You must do this in order to be reasonable in your expectations and to gear them to his abilities to meet them.

TAKE INTO ACCOUNT THE KIND OF PERSON YOU ARE

You need to take yourself into account, too, since you are the one who decides what is reasonable to expect your child to do. If you happen to be an exacting person, which means you probably have high standards for yourself as well as other people, bear this in mind. You may need to give particular attention to the matter of your child's readiness (in terms of maturity) to meet your expectations, in order to avoid aiming too high for him. To expect too much of a child is always frustrating for everyone concerned. It reminds me of a pair of parents who had excellent long-range aims for guidance; they wanted their child to be considerate in playing with other children and to look after her needs efficiently (to name just two of their aims). The trouble was that they expected behavior far beyond her capacity at 2. She was supposed to defer to other 2-year-old guests and let them take away playthings she was using when they came to her house to visit. And she was made to feel that she had lapsed badly when she failed to get to the toilet in time. This little child wanted to please her parents, but too much was expected of her. She could not rise to their ideas of consideration; she did not stay dry. Her "failures" worried her (she bit her nails down to the quick) and made them all unhappy.

If, on the other hand, you expect too little of your child, the chances are he is not learning what he needs in order to adjust well to other children and to meet what will be required of him by people outside his home. Then you should take this tendency of yours into account as you plan for him.

As you think over immediate aims for guidance, if some aspect of behavior seems important to you out of all proportion to its seeming importance to other parents, try to figure out why. I know a parent who exploded with irritation whenever his 3-year-old daughter used what he called "bad grammar." Actually her speech was typical for a child at her developmental level. "I was tooken to the doctor yesterday," for example, was par for her age group. Why did this father feel so unreasonably emotional about these grammatical lapses? One reason may have been that he simply did not know what to expect of a child of his daughter's age. But there was more to it than that. My guess is that he had come a long way, socially and professionally, from the status of his childhood home and that he looked on his daughter's incorrect speech as a step backwards into the lower status which he wanted to leave behind.

I know another father whose child had a habit of bending her arms sharply at the elbow and gesticulating with her hands, with mouth slightly open, when she was watching someone else in (what seemed to her) a rather precarious or exciting position— another child swinging very high, for instance. This father remarked at nursery school, in a severe tone, "Don't let her do that. She has an aunt who acts that way. She is not to make those motions." Why did he feel this way—so strongly unsympathetic toward behavior which his child seemed to use as a tensional outlet when she stood by passively? Probably his feelings were related to his attitude toward the aunt he mentioned; he seemed to be afraid that the aunt's "queer" behavior was recurring in his child.

All of us need to try to understand our attitudes if particular behavior on the part of children seems to carry an unreasonably strong emotional charge for us. It may be that such behavior is related to our own childhood experiences. If we can become more aware of how our attitude came into being, we may be able to gain perspective.

PARENTS SHOULD TALK OVER AIMS TOGETHER
AND AGREE ON PLANS FOR ACTUAL GUIDANCE

You have to take into account, too, the kind of person you are married to, and his or her feelings and attitudes. It is important for your children that both of you be active in planning guidance and putting it into effect. At least some of the time, the two of you are going to have different ideas of what your children should learn and how you should guide them. When you do disagree, it will be helpful to your children's learning if you talk over your differences and reach a compromise at the level of actual guidance (out of children's hearing, of course). This is often not easy—neither are a lot of other important things. But guidance is ineffectual if parents operate at cross-purposes in dealing with their children.

MAKE UP YOUR MIND WHAT YOU WANT YOUR
CHILD TO LEARN

Be honest with yourself. You need to be very honest with yourselves, both of you, in figuring out what you really feel about your child's learning. Sometimes parents go through the motions of thinking they want to change their child's behavior when they really do not want to at all.

For instance, a pair of parents came in for consultation because their 4-year-old was getting into all sorts of mischief. Putting grass in car gas tanks, slipping glass into mailboxes, building a fire in a neighbor's garage were only a few of his milder activities. They thought they were worried, but actually they were not. As they talked of their son, I could see that they really did not want to do anything about this kind of behavior. They were amused by it and proud of him because they thought he was enterprising. Then there was the mother who sought advice because her 2-year-old often climbed into his parents' bed at 2 A.M. What should she do? It turned out that she did not want to do anything. She preferred to let him keep on with this behavior, though she had not been aware of her real wishes when she came in for consultation.

I emphasize again the importance of reserving attempts at guidance for occasions when you really want to modify your child's behavior and when, in addition, you have worked out a plan for learning which seems feasible and sound, both for him and for you. Otherwise, you are teaching your child to ignore you, probably with irritation and annoyance on his part thrown in. You are building up an attitude in him which will make it much harder to guide him in some other situation.

DECIDE ON IMMEDIATE AIMS FOR
DAILY ACTIVITIES

Think in detail of your child's day from the time he wakes up in the morning until he goes to sleep at night. How do you want him to act, what do you hope that he feels as the day moves forward? He is in bed in the morning; he is awake. What do you want him to do? Stay there until you come to his room? Get up, go to the toilet, and return to bed? Or dress when he wakes, with or without your help? And then what about breakfast? What would you like him to eat? Suppose he and a small sister both pounce on a plaything. What do you want your children to learn about how to deal with this kind of conflict? Perhaps your reaction to these questions is to say, "I play the whole day by ear." If this is how you feel, I differ with you. Since your child is going to be learning in any case, why not at least try to have this learning move in directions which will benefit him and the rest of the family, too? Now, of course, you cannot anticipate everything that is going to occur. But you can meet situations with a point of view—even as you take necessary action—a point of view in which you ask yourself what your child is likely to learn from what is happening and how this fits in with your other aims for learning. This approach may lead you to plan to deal differently with similar situations when they come along in the future.

SUMMARY

In this chapter we have been concerned with what you want your child to learn. Until you reach a decision on both long-range and concrete, immediate aims, you obviously cannot make any effective plans for guidance in moment-to-moment, everyday living. I have described what seem to me to be desirable aims, chiefly in order to get you to think through what your own aims are.

In the remainder of the book, I shall be assuming (in what I say about specific techniques of guidance) the aims that I have discussed here. Where you differ with me, you will simply have to devise learning situations to bring about your own aims instead of mine.

You have two ways of influencing your child: first, through the surroundings you arrange for him; and second, through the ways you deal with him directly, in actions and in words. In the next chapter we will turn our attention to the first of these: arranging your child's surroundings.

4

Arranging Your Child's Surroundings

IN THE YEARS from 2 to 5, when your child is having to learn so much, he can easily get the idea that someone is telling him what to do all the time. This may make him feel bossed constantly, or it may lead him to expect that everything he does will be talked about. The first is liable to make him irritable and resentful, even defiant; the second, to make him demand continual attention instead of getting a good deal of his pleasure out of what he is doing. If he actually is being told constantly what to do, and heeds what he hears, he has little chance to develop initiative for finding something constructive to do. For this reason and also because of what a child can learn from constructive play, he should have a great deal of freedom in play to use his own ideas.

You may remember that in talking about learning by consequences I advised trying to plan your child's play surroundings so that when he was active in them, he would be likely to be learning what you want him to learn, and to be gaining satisfaction from his activity. Carrying out such a plan is our present job. But your child is not the only one who needs home arranged to fill his needs and give him satisfaction. What about the rest of the family?

74

What home should be for each
person in the family

One of the best ways to go about planning home for everybody is to try to think through what each person in the family would like it to be. There will be many cases in which what one person wants is just what another does not; plenty of compromises will have to be made. But the starting point is sound—to think over everybody's needs and likes. The next point is to see how much of what is desired can be realized.

What are the preferences of family members? How, for instance, is the living room to be used? Is it to be a playroom? If you are willing, does your husband or wife agree? Is it all right for toys to be strewn around, or do you want the living room to be a place where a grownup can sit down and read the paper in relative tranquillity? And what about the kitchen? As long as no cooking is going on, do you not mind having all the pots and pans spread over the floor? And what about other children in the family? Do they object if a child of preschool age has access to their belongings?

Now, if everybody in your family is content to have a 2- to 5-year-old free as a breeze in every part of the house, you have less arranging to do than most people, certainly less than I would have. But you will still need to curb your child in other people's homes, because most people will not want everything inside four walls turned into boisterous play space.

ARRANGE THE SURROUNDINGS TO RECONCILE
VARIOUS NEEDS AND DESIRES

In making the necessary compromises, the aim is to be fair to everyone, including yourself. I shall now describe a home in which other members of the family feel the need of limiting the child's activity in many areas. The task is, then, to reconcile the desire of the older members of the household for limitations on the child's play with the child's need for activity and the importance for him of freedom to play as he would like. Let us suppose that the living room is to be kept free of scattered playthings, that most of the kitchen equipment is out-of-bounds, as are most of the things in Father's desk, that Father's and Mother's bedroom is not a sports arena, that an older child's belongings are to be left undisturbed when he is not at home to look after them (and when he is home, too, unless he has agreed to their use by the smaller child), and that the baby's room is not to be visited when he is asleep. How can one arrange the surroundings to foster these compromises? Here are some measures which can be taken:

In the living room, when a child is a toddler and a 2-year-old, keep a box of playthings which he spies on entrance and can use on the spot in the presence of the rest of the family—just a few objects, which are varied from time to time to hold his interest. There should not be enough of them to create a confused mess in the box or to be scattered all over the place. When he goes out of the room, the things go back in the box. In the kitchen, one drawer, easy to get at and in which he is free to explore, can be devoted to kitchen equipment he may use. The items in this drawer should also be varied from time to time to interest him. If Father's desk is fascinating, and located in a commonly used part of the house, perhaps a bottom drawer could be similarly equipped. Now, this attempt to plan surroundings will not be successful if the desk drawer, for instance, contains only objects which the child has long since tired of; hence the stress on need for change of contents. What about Brother's and Sister's rooms? Older children need a place to put belongings where they will be safe from prying preschool hands. You must see that this place is respected, if necessary by using fastenings on doors. This is far more likely to promote generosity and harmony than is insisting that what one child regards as private property must be used (and possibly ruined) by another member of the family. As far as the baby goes, a lock on his door will keep the small child out if he does not heed instructions. But I hope the runabout child has plenty of chances to be near the baby when sleep will not be disturbed.

ENVIRONMENTAL ARRANGEMENTS MUST BE
SUPPLEMENTED WITH DIRECT GUIDANCE

Always do as much as you can through environmental arrangements to reconcile the needs and desires of everyone in the family,
but environmental planning alone is never enough. You will often
have to step in, with the consequences you devise, to help your
child learn what you want him to. And how active he is! Every
one of his actions has a consequence, and it is your job to see that
these consequences foster the learning you desire. You have to help
your child learn how to carry on the activities of his choosing in
such a way that other people can manage to exist reasonably comfortably alongside of him. You have to help him learn what may
be done where.

If he brings his paints into the living room, have him remove them
then and there. (Remember the importance of consistent, relevant,
significant consequences.) If, still in the toddler stage, he gets into
the "wrong" drawers and kitchen cupboards, wedge them with paper
so he cannot open them. If you are busy cooking and he gets too
close to the stove, set up a marker in the kitchen, perhaps a couple
of chairs. "They mean, stay on the other side because I'm using the
stove," you might say. If he does not heed you, then the kitchen is
not the place for him on this occasion. If shouting and boisterous
running are ruled out for indoors, you need to help him learn this:
"Back you go and walk. You're in the house now," or "Out you go
and have a good shout there."

BALANCE IN ACTIVITIES THROUGHOUT THE DAY

You may think that what I am saying here about restricting a
young child's activity for the sake of other members of the family
contradicts what I said in the last chapter about his need for a
variety of interesting activities. But there is no conflict. Your child
does not need access to all of the activities all of the time. If you
feel that the dining-room light fixture should not double as a
trapeze but that your child should have a chance to swing and

climb, then arrange the surroundings accordingly. In short, it is in your child's life as a whole that he needs the variety of activity I have talked about; and, each day, he needs a balance in activities to fit the kind of creature he is. In his preschool years he thrives on physical activity (and he is much easier to live with when he has enough of it). Therefore, you should try to have him spend the major part of his day in a place where he can carry it on safely and happily, without constant warnings or a lot of comment and instruction from you, but with adequate supervision. This is quite different from having him turn the whole house into a gymnasium. On the other hand, if your family is content with a gymnasium-home, that is your business, and you will have little arranging to do and few compromises to make.

Safety measures

There can be no compromises about your child's safety. Surroundings have to be vigilantly baby- and child-proof, so far as possible, to try to prevent the serious, even fatal, accidents which the 2- to 5-year-old's inquisitiveness can so readily produce.

Though this is not an exhaustive list, here are some of the measures to be taken:

Upper-story windows need to be guarded to prevent falls. Secure screens which cannot be opened from the inside serve this purpose well.

Stairs need protecting gates for babies and very young children.

Electric outlets should be guarded from curious hands. When feasible, place heavy furniture in front of these outlets. As a matter of standard practice, all metal objects small enough to go into such outlets should be kept away from children (pins, bobby pins, paper clips, bits of wire, and so forth).

Electric cords and equipment must be kept in safe condition. You cannot assume that new electric equipment is free from shock hazard.

Such devices as electric coffee makers with cords hanging down are so dangerous for babies and small children that there should be no possibility of children of this age having access to them.

Pots and pans must be placed on stoves without handles projecting over the stove edge.

Young children should not be in the vicinity of dangerously hot food or cooking equipment.

Open fires, heaters, and furnace outlets hot enough to burn need secure barriers to prevent children from coming too close.

The hot-water supply should not be dangerously hot.

Sharp objects must be kept out of children's reach—knives, scissors, needles, pins, razor blades, of course. But also, playthings need rigorous inspection, for sometimes they have exceedingly sharp edges which may become increasingly hazardous if the metal gets bent out of shape.

Matches must be inaccessible.

Substances which are harmful if swallowed must be inaccessible. These include: medicines (aspirin, sedatives, etc.), tobacco, many disinfectants, many cleaning materials (cleaning fluids, lye, toilet cleaners, ammonia, stove cleaners, many furniture polishes), shoe polish, gasoline, kerosene, ink, oil of wintergreen, paint, pest and weed poisons.

Paint containing lead must not be used on any objects that a child might suck or chew.

Playthings and equipment should have rounded rather than sharp edges and corners.

Plastic bags should be inaccessible.

Ropes should be used only under sufficient supervision to ensure prevention of accidental choking.

Car doors should have a child-proof lock that cannot be opened without adult help.

Swimming pools must be inaccessible to children.

Discarded refrigerators must have the doors removed.

As your child moves from 2 to 5, you will, of course, be helping him learn caution, based on an awareness of hazards, which will eventually, as he grows still older, come to replace your vigilance. But you should not expect that your child's good judgment can be counted on in these preschool years to keep his curiosity in check. In short, the first job in arranging your child's surroundings is to try to prevent serious harm.

A *place designed expressly for your child*

Now, let us consider an area in the house designed expressly for your young child. He needs such a place, even if you are living in cramped quarters. If you are lucky enough to have a separate room for each child in the family, you have gone a long way toward promoting harmony in relationships. If rooms have to be shared, then mark off space, even with makeshift equipment, so that each child feels he has a place for his belongings. Here I shall optimistically assume that your 2-, or 3-, or 4-year-old has a room to himself, and make suggestions for furnishing it to promote his development.

He needs low shelves for his play materials so that he can easily see what is there, remove it, and put it back. Why not a toy chest? Because, though neat from the outside, it encourages chaos, breakage, and frustration, as anyone who wants a particular object discovers as he rummages around to find it in the inevitable jumble within. Besides, having play materials in view suggests things for your child to do. Shelves need not be costly; secondhand shelves, unpainted furniture (mail order or otherwise) or shelves made from stout wooden boxes and sturdy boards (well sanded and finished) will be equally satisfactory for your young child. These latter should be fastened together securely so as not to invite dismantling, since what you want to cultivate is a shelved supply of playthings, not a dump yard for them.

A child-sized table and chair are extremely useful all through the preschool years. Get a table with rounded corners, large enough so that at least two children have space to sit without having elbows and playthings in each other's way. A table top about 2 by 4 feet serves this purpose well. A cover of oilcloth or some durable plastic material, tacked firmly in place with the tacks out of sight on the underside, will be helpful. (You will need to keep a close eye on the tacks, obviously, to make sure they do not work loose. Tack the cover when your young child is not around, so that you do not call attention to tack pulling as an interesting activity.) Formica is a splendid table surface, but costly. If you have twin tables for children in different rooms, you will find them useful placed together sometimes for such affairs as birthday parties, with borrowed child-sized chairs; or long after the two tables are outgrown as a place to sit and play, they may come in handy as supports for a sheet of plywood to house an electric train, to mention just one idea. Here again, if you are willing to do some work yourself, you can often find an unpainted kitchen table which is suitable if you cut the legs off to make it low enough. It is worth compromising on table height so that the table can be used during all the preschool years; having the table top about 21 inches from the ground and using it with a chair whose seat is 14 inches off the ground works pretty well. Ideally, of course, it is good to have your child's feet resting easily on the floor. When his legs dangle, he is likely to wiggle around. But if he has a sturdy chair (well balanced, with no sharp corners and designed to encourage good posture), with a rung for his feet, he can be reasonably comfortable for a number of years with this arrangement. School supply houses offer chairs which meet these requirements.

Outdoors, a fenced-in play area is a wonderful help, especially in your child's toddler and 2-year-old days. And if you happen to have a tree which he can enjoy climbing when he is 3 or 4, you are lucky. This, of course, like most interesting occupations, involves some hazards. If the tree is tall, you will have to have an understanding with him about how high he may go.

Play materials

PROVIDE CONSTRUCTIVE PLAY MATERIALS
OF SUFFICIENT VARIETY

Now what about actual things to play with? I am not going to make exhaustive suggestions. I shall just remind you of what I have already said about constructive play materials, give some examples, and suggest where you may read more on the subject. Bearing in mind necessary safety precautions, keep an open mind as to what interesting, constructive play material is. An object does not have to be designed as a plaything to be a good one, though a great many of the so-called "educational playthings" are both enjoyable and stimulating.

Remember, too, that your child needs a sufficient range of things to do to develop varied interests and skills instead of quite limited ones.

The cost of playthings. In calculating cost, always bear in mind the length of time your child is likely to use particular play materials. Since most constructive playthings will be useful throughout the preschool years, initial cost should be judged accordingly. Of course, if you have the luxury of an unlimited budget, you will not have to worry; but by making some of your child's toys, you can not only save money, but also have fun. What is good for children is good for parents—devising constructive playthings means being creative and imaginative at the parent level in thinking of play materials which will help your child learn to be creative and imaginative. But a word of warning. It is not fair to feel put out with your child if something you have provided does not "take." Of course it is disappointing, but try to figure out why your creation is unsuccessful. Perhaps it is not suited to his level of development, and will be later on. Perhaps, in having preferences, he is becoming more of a person in his own right. Think up something else that may meet with better luck in interesting him.

SAFETY, DURABILITY, AND COMPLEXITY OF
PLAY MATERIALS

The first concern in choosing playthings for your child is safety. Objects he plays with should have rounded corners and edges. If there is any chance he will put them in his mouth, they must not be finished with paint containing lead; nor should they be made of brittle plastic, which can break off and be swallowed.

By and large, it is worth providing strong, durable play materials rather than easily broken ones, which encourage frustration, destruction, and an attitude of "if it breaks, get a new one." You need, of course, to gauge the difficulty of play materials to your child's abilities, mental and physical, so that he can have the fun of solving problems without being completely frustrated by complexities he is not yet ready to cope with.

WHAT TO LOOK FOR IN PLAY MATERIALS

Choose play materials which will encourage activity and which will promote physical coordination of both large and small muscles; constructive, even creative, use of materials; problem solving; imaginative play; play with other children as a child is ready for it, rooted in "something to do"; and, of course, satisfaction and real enjoyment.

Bear in mind the kind of imaginative play which is apt to be fostered by a plaything. There are, for instance, no military toys among the playthings I propose for your child because I am not in favor of suggesting "war" as a play activity to preschool children, or of encouraging them in war play by the addition of glamorous models (from their point of view) of military equipment. Nevertheless I do not advocate flat prohibitions of war play, since a wholesale veto may whet their appetites. Tactful discouragement is probably more effective. If a group of parents whose children play together agree to discourage war play, they can accomplish a great deal by a unified front in their disapproval of the purchase of war toys. In any case, if your child is to receive a war toy, I would see to it that the toy is an economy model rather than some splendid object that will become the center of attention among his playmates.

War toys apart, do not let yourself become infatuated with many of the intricate, glamorous toys that capture a child's attention in a toy store—beautifully strong trucks and realistically designed road-working machinery, for example. If you can afford one (or more) of these, choose a versatile model; your child may derive a great deal of lasting pleasure from it. But do not feel that his life is blighted forever if it is too expensive. Concentrate on a variety of constructive materials that you can afford. And, to cheer you up if you can only yearn for the heavy-duty equipment, remember that a child may lose interest in his own efforts because he is surrounded with play equipment too finished and elaborate in itself.

These same remarks hold for costly housekeeping equipment. If you can afford such equipment, get the kinds that offer variety in use. A sturdy doll bed into which your child himself can climb is an example of this. Tables and chairs which accommodate both children and dolls are another example. But remember, if these are beyond your budget, how much fun your child can get from so quickly made a plaything as a cardboard carton converted with a few crayon strokes into a "stove."

I shall be extremely specific in the suggestions made, for it is much easier for you to alter precise details than to wrestle with the task of translating vague suggestions into actual play arrangements.

The baby before he walks. First, here are a few thoughts for the baby, before he has reached his walking days. Everything must be able to be mouthed, chewed on (therefore, not of a size on which he can choke), and fallen onto without serious injury. There should be no long strings in which he can become entangled.

> *When he is tiny (before he can hold objects, but can fixate them with his eyes), a large brightly colored object, perhaps a mobile, fastened near him during waking intervals so that he can see it readily.*
>
> *When he is old enough to notice, a chance to lie watching shifting leaf shadows on a wall, in sufficiently soft light.*
>
> *When he can hold objects, a rattle, a squeak toy, a small block, given him whenever his diapers are being changed.*
>
> *When he reaches the playpen stage, a few playthings at a time (three or four), washable animals and dolls (some of which squeak), rattles, teething rings, things to mouth.*
>
> *As he is able to manipulate objects more and more, still give him a few things at a time, with interesting substitutions made as needed (not so often, however, that he expects new arrivals every few minutes). A double boiler, a pan and spoon, two different-sized measuring cups nested together, two colored cubes which can go into the cups, old-fashioned clothespins set round the edge of a firm, nonbreakable plastic can, a simple pegboard, a simple color cone (he will take these last three items apart and mouth and chew on them for many months before he thinks of putting them together).*
>
> *When he likes to reach through the bars of his playpen, one or two of his objects of the moment placed outside the bars within reach.*

A book with large, clear, brightly colored pictures of familiar objects on sturdy pages.

Floating water toys for his bath.

The toddler and the 2-year-old. Many of the above objects still hold his interest. Because a child of this age is so geared to large-muscle activity, outdoor occupations and playthings (some of which can be brought inside) will be mentioned first.

Push-and-pull toys. For example, a toy lawn mower, a toy baby carriage, a lightweight, well-balanced wagon, a cardboard carton with a rope attached like a sled rope (but not so long as to be dangerous).

A chance to walk outdoors from the time he is able, to investigate objects he sees and to pick them up (for example, leaves, feathers, moss, stones, little sticks, pine cones); a pail or other container to put them in if he wants.

A chance to pick a few flowers, put them in a nonbreakable container, and have them in his room, either out of reach or where spilled water will not matter.

A chance to look at the moon and stars.

A chance to watch the traffic go by.

A pile of loose sand or a sandbox. Sand should be kept damp enough to hold its shape readily. So-called plasterer's sand (which can be purchased from a cement-mix company) is much more satisfactory than some types of sand bagged for children's use that do not hold their shape well even when quite damp.

A child needs something to sit on in the damp sand and should be taught to use it so that he stays dry in cool weather.

If there are cats around, sand should be covered when not in use. Eight by four feet is a good size for a sandbox if you look ahead to the time when two children may be using it. Very helpful instructions for making a sandbox or other play equipment can be found in a Children's Bureau publication called Home Play and Play Equipment, which does not mention, however, that old bricks make an excellent floor for a sandbox. You will need to adapt the directions for making a sandbox if you wish to build one of the size I suggest.

An earth-digging place (not adjacent to the sand if you hope to keep sand and earth separate).

A garden trowel or sugar scoop and cans to use in sand or earth; in due course, a muffin tin, a dump truck, or a steam roller for added interest.

Water, in warm weather
—in cans, in the sand;

—in an old-fashioned washtub (under close supervision), to sail a boat in (though sailing indoors in the bathtub is easier);

—in the earth hole; your child wearing next to nothing, something old and expendable;

—in a tin cup, to use with 1½-inch or 2-inch paint brush to "paint" outdoors in hot weather;

—in a wading pool.

Strong wooden boxes and planks to use with the boxes. At least two boxes and two planks for one child, double this for two, are recommended; planks, 6 feet long, a foot wide, and three-quarters of an inch thick are a good size, with all sharp edges and corners rounded (a wood rasp helps), sanded smooth, and finished so as to resist weathering and consequent splintering. Using these in toddler and 2-year-old days will require close supervision, like almost everything else a little child does. Later in the preschool years a child who has learned what is involved in making secure arrangements can use them with more casual supervision.

The boxes and planks can be arranged in many ways. For example, boxes can be sat in; an inverted box with one end of a plank rested on it, the other on the ground, makes an inclined plane; two inverted boxes with a plank between them are a walking board. As a child reaches 3 and 4, the boxes may be "autos," "train engines," "airplanes," "earth satellites," whatever strikes his lively fancy; they can be played with all during the preschool years, and even later, if they last.

A place to climb, which may be supplied by an arrangement of the boxes and planks described above or, even better, by equipment especially designed for climbing.

Fit-together toys of various sorts. For example, color cones (disks of varying sizes which slip over a central pole and which your child can arrange according to size when he gets the idea on his own), pegboards (with the holes encircled in color, to provide opportunity to match peg color to corresponding hole when he gets hold of this idea in his spontaneous play), interlocking trains without wheels.

Nested toys (purchased ready-made, or, if you prefer, made at home with cans of varying sizes painted different colors, or out of a cut-off milk carton with a smaller-sized cutoff cream carton nested inside) to be used under supervision in case there is too much chewing and swallowing.

A disappearing-objects can. If you like to make things, get hold of a shortening container without any sharp places on it, with a fit-in cover which your child can remove and, preferably, with a pail-like handle. Then cut an opening in the cover to form a slot large enough to admit poker chips or milk-bottle tops (not to be eaten). Pound all the edges of your slot down firmly, making sure there are no sharp edges or any possibility of your handiwork loosening up to form sharp edges later. Or, if you are content with a disappearing-objects can with a brief life, make a slot in the top of a cardboard oatmeal cylinder.

A pounding board.

Play materials requiring a screwing motion can be handled by a number of children of this age. Some toy companies manufacture large wooden screws and bolts.

Stuffed animals (with nonremovable eyes); washable baby dolls; an unbreakable toy baby bottle, particularly if there is a real baby in the family.

Housekeeping equipment: a toy mop, unbreakable doll dishes (these are fun in the sand, too), a few blankets or other covers for dolls and animals, a carton made up as a doll bed, doll furniture. If you buy or make a doll bed, it will add greatly to interest and varied possibilities for use if it is sturdy enough for your child to get into and curl up in, as mentioned earlier.

"Table" blocks. Little blocks, brightly colored, about 1½ inches or 2 inches square, sixteen or so in a durable open box into which they exactly fit.

Cars and trucks. Little ones your child can hold in his hand; one truck large enough to load with his table blocks, or to hold a doll or a toy animal.

Floor blocks. (See comment in the suggestions for 3- and 4-year-olds.)

Dress-up clothes. Colored scarves (pieces of cloth) and hats give a lot of pleasure and are easily put on and off; a durable cast-off hat from some family member is often just as much fun as a costume hat bought for the purpose; an old purse is a valuable object.

PAPER, CRAYONS, PASTE, PAINTS, CLAY, PLASTICENE:

Large paper, about 18 by 24 inches, to suit a young child's broad arm motions. The cheapest paper is unprinted "newsprint," obtainable from many newspaper companies and also from school supply firms, often cut to the size you request.

Crayons. Large ones, suited to a child's motor coordination at this stage (to be used under supervision).

If you want to go through the preparations and supervision involved, pasting, painting (easel and finger), clay, and plasticene activities are fine for 2-year-olds. (Supplies are described in the 3- and 4-year-old section.) If you give your child a chance to paste, you should cut, ahead of time, vividly colored construction paper into two or three simple shapes (circle, square, triangle, for example), at least 2 inches in one dimension and have these shapes available to use with a large newsprint base sheet.

Books. Available for your child to look at by himself (unless he tears or eats them) and for you to read out loud to him. See pp. 101–9.

Music. See pp. 109–11.

Tumbling, scrambling, and playing "chase" with a gentle, older person can produce peals of joy.

SOME PLAY MATERIALS ARE EQUALLY SUITABLE FOR VARIOUS AGES

Because many constructive play materials offer varied possibilities for use according to developing abilities, they hold interest through the preschool years.

It should be noted, however, that some playthings which offer little diversity for use are constructive, nonetheless, and highly desirable at suitable levels of development; puzzles, for instance, of a particular complexity may be of absorbing interest at a particular age, too hard or too easy at other ages. This is also true of certain kinds of pegboards and form boards.

ROTATE YOUR CHILD'S PLAYTHINGS

It must be made clear that even though many constructive materials remain suitable throughout the preschool years, a child will lose interest in his play surroundings if they are unchanged. In most families, this does not mean that a child needs more playthings, but that, once he has a sufficient supply, his toys will be more likely to remain attractive to him if you have only part of this supply in sight at any one time.

From babyhood on up, your child's interest will receive an encouraging thrust forward if you rotate his playthings. Begin to do this, as already suggested, in his playpen days by having a few objects at a time available for him, of a sort likely to hold his interest during one particular playpen interval. Of course, if he is there for an unusually long time, he may need some substitutions, but do not make changes so frequently that he expects something new to arrive every few minutes. You want him to feel content to explore what he has, not always to be demanding something more.

In his toddler days, as soon as he has enough playthings to make it practicable, sort them into two groups, roughly matched in the variety of activity which they offer. If he is very plentifully supplied, you will need more groupings. Then have one group available for use at a time. Now, of course, if he is attached to particular objects, keep those available all the time, but find out which the preferred objects are by putting a whole group away and producing any objects he specifically asks for. You will have to do this sorting when he is not around, and when fetching things out he has asked for, keep the others out of his sight, for if he sees them he is going to want the whole supply.

As he gets on toward 4, he can probably assist in arranging the groupings, unless he is the kind of child who is made unhappy by helping because he feels that each object he looks at is indispensable right now. If the system of producing objects from the stored supply when he requests them gets out of hand by his asking for everything to be out at once (presuming always that his current supply offers sufficient variety in things to do), then you can institute a system of having each object produced on request replaced in the stored group by one from the current supply on hand.

How often should you rotate your child's toys? This depends upon his memory and his attention span. When he is in the neighborhood of 18 months, every three or four days works pretty well. As he gets older, you need to lengthen the time between shifts to keep things fresh and interesting when they appear.

Rotation of playthings may sound like a lot of work, but you can get it down to a system that takes only a few minutes. Keep a carton to hold each group of playthings, with a list of the contents attached, which you worked out earlier in order to offer sufficient variety in activity in each of your groupings.

As your child outgrows playthings, do not be in a hurry to dispose of them. Even when he is of school age, some will prove welcome additions to a supply to be used when he is sick in bed, both because when he is feeling under par he may enjoy simple things to do and because the playthings will have novelty if long stored away. Furthermore, when he has passed his preschool days and no longer plays with toys suitable for small children, you will find that a select supply of preschool playthings which can be produced at a moment's notice is a great boon to adult and small visitors alike, not to mention you, the host.

If you live in a one-climate region, you will need to give more thought to getting diversity into outdoor occupation than if you live where change of season does a lot of this for you. One of the advantages to having some simple outdoor equipment which can be moved around is that it lends itself to your child's making changes in play setup. Even so, sometimes you can be the one to change it around to make outdoor life more interesting.

ADDING NEW PLAYTHINGS—SPREAD YOUR
ADDITIONS THROUGH THE YEAR

Your child will be helped to keep interested in his surroundings if your gifts of play materials are spread throughout the year instead of coming in a deluge on his birthday and at Christmastime (which can be overwhelmingly bewildering to a very little child and can devalue the enjoyment of the various play materials for a 3- or 4-year-old).

You can do a lot to build up fresh interest in old materials by adding accessories from time to time: another doll blanket; a toy cooking pot; a cardboard carton, with burners drawn on, to serve as a stove; a flour sifter to use in the sand; new shapes of soft wood for carpentry and a new supply of nails; a book; colored newsprint instead of the usual white; a pair of blunt scissors when your child is ready for them; a watering can; and so forth. It is also useful to keep on hand a small stock of new playthings so that you can easily produce one at strategic moments. Remember, I am not suggesting that you spend more on toys than you otherwise would, but that you spread out the distribution. One more word about distribution. Do not overdo novelty by giving your child something new all the time. Too frequent additions to his play supplies can produce in him a sham appearance of taking initiative for finding interesting activity, when he is really just responding to novelty. This is quite different from encouraging his resourcefulness through the well-timed arrival of new materials.

ARRANGEMENT OF AVAILABLE PLAYTHINGS

On your child's low shelves, have materials stored close to each other which are fun to use at the same time. For example, when he is responsible enough to have these kept available, see that his paper and his cutting, drawing, pasting supplies are conveniently located beside each other. By the time he is 3½ or 4, a cutlery box with partitions in it to hold various supplies to use with paper can be very welcome if he enjoys paper work.

Have space for block accessories on or beside the block shelves. And always remember, your child is likely to use together what he finds near at hand. (This reminds me of a mother who despaired when her 3-year-old sawed the top of the piano. Yet when asked, "Where was the saw?" she replied, "On the piano bench." If saws are left on piano benches, sooner or later you can expect trouble.)

Small-sized shallow cartons which fit well on shelves are very useful to house play materials which your child likes grouped together.

SCRAP MATERIALS

Keep a supply of cardboard cartons in many sizes. Save cans, wrapping paper, strings, rubber bands, empty thread spools, empty typewriter-ribbon reels, film spools, food containers, boxes of all kinds.

THE 3- AND 4-YEAR-OLD (WITH ALL THE PRECEDING COMMENTS IN MIND)

Before he is 3, your child may be ready for many of the activities mentioned here. And 3- and 4-year-olds will enjoy many of the items listed for the younger ages, particularly with accessories added to give their wider abilities and interests scope in play.

> *Instead of just collecting nature objects, the 3- or 4-year-old may want to display them or use them as constructive materials. Leaf*

necklaces, leaves mounted on paper, stones made into stone sculpture (a cement which works well with stones is sometimes obtainable in tubes from hardware and building-material companies), these are examples of elaboration of earlier activities.

He may enjoy making flower arrangements.

Interest in sand or earth play will be increased by occasional availability of toy farm equipment, people, and animals. (Your child can learn to wash these off in a pan of water and set them out to dry before bringing them back in the house.)

If there is space for digging in the earth, get a T-handled trench shovel from a government surplus store. It is about 2 feet long, and an excellent digging tool.

Space permitting, let your child have a garden, which he plants with seeds likely to grow speedily and well in your locality. Let him use regular garden tools in addition to his T-handled trench shovel (under supervision, with instructions for safe use) rather than the flimsy miniature sets, which break easily.

Outdoors, he will welcome more wooden boxes and planks. If you wish to buy large hollow blocks, these are a fine outdoor play material.

Two sturdy sawhorses, to be used with boxes and planks, add a great deal of interest to life.

Large pieces of cloth (old sheets are fine) available in the dress-up box will sometimes be welcome to drape over the sawhorses.

A sturdy, well-balanced tricycle is an investment likely to give your child a great deal of pleasure throughout his preschool years.

A small wagon, sufficiently well-balanced to hold a passenger safely and which can be attached behind the tricycle, will add versatility to the tricycle's use.

If your child has ready access to swings in a nursery school or park, and unless you have generous outdoor space, the chances are that home play space can be better utilized for something else. If you have a swing, be sure to equip it with a soft seat rather than an old-fashioned board seat, which can cause serious injury.

A tree house. It need not be elaborate, but one or more sturdy platforms large enough to hold the number of children who are going to use it at one time can offer plenty of occupation.

Carpentry tools and materials (to be used under supervision). A regular-sized, well-balanced hammer, nails with big heads, soft wood in varied shapes, to start with. A small, well-made saw, and a vise to hold wood in place. If you get a workbench, select a height with long-term use in mind; provide your preschool child with a strong wooden box of the right height to stand on now.

A carpentry construction box. Add new materials to a carpentry construction box from time to time to keep it interesting: spools with nails long enough to hold them down, film reels, rubber bands, colored wires (provided the hazard of electric outlets is sufficiently controlled), bottle caps, and any other useful materials that turn up.

It is fun to paint finished carpentry constructions. To provide a paint which rubs off less easily than that used for making pictures, dissolve powdered paint (pp. 94–95) in commercial liquid starch, just as it comes from the bottle.

When your child is getting on toward 5, supply him with a coping saw and cardboard cartons to cut as he likes. The liquid-starch paint described above works well on cartons.

A pulley, with a length of twine (not so long a piece as to be dangerous), which he can use to hoist objects up and down.

Floor blocks. A good set of floor blocks and shelves to store them properly are one of the best investments you can make for your child. Get them before your child is 3 (but wait to produce them, and then only a part of the set, until he is over 2½). It is worth getting what educational-playthings manufacturers call the "large kindergarten set." Buy from a manufacturer who permits you to buy additional units by the piece for your set at a later date—new shapes to whet interest or an increase in old ones in short supply.

Store your child's blocks on low open shelves, with identical units piled in the same location and help him put them back where they belong when he is finished.

MATERIALS FOR COLORING, PASTING, CUTTING, SEWING, PAINTING:

Some children take little interest in drawing, cutting, pasting, and painting until close to kindergarten age and then turn into dynamos, creating in paper at a great rate. A number of children, on the other hand, enjoy this activity well before 3. Being with other children who like making paper constructions has a lot to do with stimulating a child's interest in this area. If your child is not interested, do not overencourage him to carry it on. But expose him, every once in a while, to a chance to use these materials.

A word about protecting your child's clothes and the house when using paint and other such materials. Make a smock from a man's old, long-tailed shirt by shortening the sleeves. Have your child wear it backwards, buttoned up the back, with the end of the cutoff shirt sleeves tucked well under his own sleeves. When weather permits, roll sleeves up above the elbows.

When paint or clay is used indoors, waterproof floor protection (oilcloth, for example) is desirable. If cost is of little concern, a linoleum remnant is excellent, for it is easily wiped clean. Several layers of newspaper offer a fair amount of protection, but are rather a nuisance to put in place.

Paper in large sheets. (See comments about unprinted newsprint in the toddler and 2-year-old section, p. 87.) For painting, about 18 by 24 inches; for drawing, about 12 by 18 inches (easily cut down from the larger sheet). Newsprint is often available in several colors (at a slightly higher cost), which may add interest to paper work.

Construction paper in a variety of bright colors. Instead of providing your child with simple shapes already cut for him to paste, as was suggested for 2-year-olds, let him do his own cutting.

Colored paper of all sorts, salvaged from wrapping paper, an out-of-date wallpaper catalogue, advertisements, and the like, to be used in making montages, with other materials. This can be enjoyed long after preschool days.

All sorts of other materials which can be cut and/or pasted: ribbons, macaroni and other pasta in various shapes, dry cereal, pine needles, bits of egg shell, just about anything that is not harmful and can be stuck on paper. Paste made quite thick and colored with powdered paint is fun with these.

Paste. Powdered wallpaper paste, which you mix with water to the desired consistency, is a good inexpensive paste to use in quantity. (Make sure it is not harmful if swallowed; some wallpaper paste contains an insecticide.) Put just enough in a container at a time to almost cover the bristles of your child's paste brush when he dips it in. A stiff, flat brush about half an inch wide with a handle 3 or 4 inches long is easier for him to manipulate than a regular paste spreader. (Both of these usually can be purchased at a paint store which deals in wallpaper. School supply firms also sell paste brushes and paste.)

Scissors. Blunt-ended, 4 or 4½ inches long.

Crayons. Keep your child supplied with a respectable set, not a lot of old stubs. If he seems uninterested, remove them altogether and keep them stored for a while.

Blunt-ended tapestry needle and wool or cotton yarn, to be used to sew paper, coarsely woven cloth, or for stringing paper constructions, leaves, cranberries. Tie a half knot to hold the yarn on the needle. Provide a specific storage place for the needle and keep charge of it yourself.

Paint. In bright primary colors and black. Powdered (nonpoisonous) water-soluble paint bought from a school supply house or many paint stores is much cheaper than ready-mixed poster paint. Mix it so that it is a good strong color. To be used with a long-handled paint brush, with a brush about one-half or three-quarters of an inch wide.

An easel (of a size to hold unprinted newsprint, 18 by 24 inches, with a trough for containers of paint) encourages painting, but is not indispensable.

Finger paint. This can give a lot of pleasure, but you need to prepare well for it, including having a container of water and a cloth right at hand for your child to clean and dry his hands and arms when he is through. His reversed-shirt smock will protect his clothes; be sure to have his sleeves above the elbows when finger-painting.

When your child first begins, let him work directly on oilcloth fastened firmly on a table top. When he wants to save his products, use butcher paper, about 18 by 24 inches. It needs to be wet, and spread out smoothly on a horizontal, waterproof surface. You will need to spoon out the finger paint.

Here is a simple recipe for finger paint:

Mix 1½ cups Linit starch in 1½ cups cold water. Add slowly, while stirring constantly, 4 cups boiling water. Place over low heat, stir constantly until cooked clear in color. Remove from stove. Mix in 1½ cups Ivory or Lux flakes. Pour into containers (jars work well). Stir into each container powdered paint to desired shade. Cool. Finger paint will keep longer if stored in a covered jar in the refrigerator. A preservative such as glycerine can be added, but is expensive.

"Gooshy" clay. It is easier to buy it ready to use than in powder form, and should be kept damp. Store it in a sturdy plastic bag, preferably set in a covered container. Prepare child and floor as for painting activity.

Let your child have a good-sized lump of clay at a time (as big as a grapefruit) rather than little dabs.

Unpainted dried clay products can be reclaimed for use by tying them in a cloth, pounding to break them up, and soaking the bag in water. Then after draining, with the bag still tied up, knead the clay smooth and let it dry out in the bag to the right consistency.

Clay is a fine material for small children, from toddlers to 5-year-olds, to manipulate and pound. As long as your child's enjoyment is mainly in manipulation rather than in the end result, do not encourage him to save his clay products, but put them back in the supply of damp clay at the end of a session. By the time a child is about 4, he is likely, on his own, to want sometimes to save his clay products. After they have dried, they can be painted, though, unhappily, dry clay breaks easily.

Plasticene. This involves no such preparation as for clay, merely a greaseproof surface. You may need to work plasticene in your hands to warm it to a pliable consistency. Store it in pieces about the size of an orange, not in little bits. When purchasing, get as much as a pound at a time, not the miniature sets with very small amounts of plasticene.

Dress-up clothes. Castoffs can give great pleasure. Old hats, old shoes, old handbags, shirts and blouses, cutoff trousers, colored squares of cloth, scarves of some "floaty" material, even old pajamas. Scarves and cloths in which a child has draped or wound himself can be held in place by blanket clips, which he can fasten himself.

I know two children for whom an old slipcover from a sofa proved inexhaustibly fertile play material. It served as all manner of wrap-around costumes, as a "tent" draped over sawhorses, as a "sail" attached to a pole, as a tree-house "roof," and even, finally, in third grade, as an admired dragon costume.

Have the supply of dress-up clothes available for your child to use when the spirit moves him.

Table toys of various kinds. Table block sets which through the use of pegs inserted into holes make it possible to build structures that are hitched together and may be put on wheels.

Table block sets which snap together.

Tinker toys. Get a length of round elastic, of the slim size used to hold women's hats in place. Put this in the tinker-toy box to give added interest to constructions after your child has explored the usual possibilities.

Puzzles, hard enough to involve problem solving, but not beyond your child's capacity.

A magnet.

A magnifying glass.

A blackboard, mounted on the wall. Get one with a trough to hold chalk and eraser.

A bulletin board for your child to display paper work encourages creativity, though any wood surface to which cellophane tape can be attached will serve well. (Cellophane tape damages walls if left in place any length of time.)

A chance to help in the kitchen. What is work for you may be play for your child. There are endless kitchen jobs he will enjoy if you do not have too high a standard of performance. (I am not suggesting, note, that his doing them will save you time.) Scrubbing carrots or potatoes, shelling peas, washing nonbreakable dishes, helping mix cookies are four possibilities.

Growing bulbs indoors has great appeal for some children.

HOLIDAY ACTIVITIES AT YOUR CHILD'S LEVEL
OF ABILITY

Christmas decorations. Supplies: construction paper in Christmas colors, blunt-ended scissors, paste, yarn and a tapestry needle for stringing. When he is 4, he can use household glue in a plastic container provided with a spout to spread on his creations, which can then be sprinkled with glitter for added interest. (In using glitter, have him carry on his work in a large, shallow box. You can then easily dump the spilled glitter back into the main supply.)

Preparation of materials: holiday decoration time is one occasion for providing stencils or patterns, which you have designed to suit your child's cutting skill. As a steady diet, however, they keep him from using his ideas and abilities in drawing and may make him dissatisfied with his own efforts. Make your stencils or patterns out of cardboard and keep them simple enough not to tax his patience in the cutting if he wants to make decorations in quantity. (Bells can be designed very simply; stars require more cutting skill.)

When your child is skilled enough with scissors, trace the Christmas shapes ahead of time onto different-colored pieces of construction paper, so that they are ready for him to cut out. Later on, he may be able to trace around them himself.

Cut strips from colored construction paper for him to use to paste cutout decorations to, one at either end if he wants, as an easily hung decoration on the Christmas tree.

When he is around 4, show him how to make strips into chains. (Strips about 1 inch wide and almost 8 inches long, which allow a generous overlap of an inch, work well. If you make the strips too short, he will have trouble working with them.)

Christmas cards. Last year's Christmas cards, scissors, paste, crayons, colored construction paper marked into rectangles for your child to cut and use as a base to mount the Christmas-card cuttings of his choice can give a 4-year-old a pleasant time making his own cards.

Christmas presents. There is so much emphasis on gifts for children at Christmas, that thought of their giving presents may be overlooked.

From the time your child is 3, encourage him to make presents for other members of the family from materials he uses in constructive activity.

Perhaps one of his paintings, which he chooses for this purpose, could be rolled and tied with ribbon, possibly with a calendar pasted on it.

Boxes of various sizes (useful, for instance, in bureau drawers) can be decorated or covered with decorative paper.

Empty spools, put into such a box, provided with a long-tipped string (wound at the end with cellophane tape) make an acceptable gift for another preschool child.

Carpentry constructions are often welcome to another child. (You may have to suggest a few changes to make them safe and sturdy.)

Another gift for a child is a picture book, made from magazine pictures pasted into a scrapbook.

And, of course, your child can go along shopping when presents are bought for other members of the family.

Out-loud reading on Christmas Eve. A 3- or 4-year-old can understand that Christmas is the celebration of the birthday of Jesus (though he probably is confused as to who Jesus may be, like the child who told his dinner companions at nursery school, "Jesus goes to my Sunday school"). The Nativity is a story which tends to hold great interest for children. I happen to be in favor of reading the King James version of the Bible, so that a child can hear the music of the language even though he may understand the words very little. (Such a selection, however, is an outstanding exception to what I am going to recommend for your child's literary fare—books geared in language and in content to his level of development.) Follow the reading with a familiar hymn or carol which your child can join in singing.

In any case, some pleasant family activity, which comes to be traditional on Christmas Eve, in addition to hanging up stockings can mean a great deal to children.

Valentines. If you get a kit, choose one suited to your child's motor skills. However, he may well have more fun with raw materials which you provide: cardboard heart patterns of different sizes, red construction paper, plus other colored paper for further decoration, paper doilies of an appropriate size, paste, and, if desired, crayons. If your child wants envelopes for this type of valentine, buy them first and cut your patterns to fit.

Apply to valentine-making the suggestions given on using patterns for Christmas decorations.

Easter eggs. Let your child help dissolve Easter egg dye and dye the eggs, deciding what colors he wants to make them. This, of course, takes close supervision.

May Day baskets. If your child has access to flowers which he may pick, help him make a little paper basket with a handle. Design a very simple one so that he can make more by himself if he wants from supplies which you have traced. Let him fill the basket with flowers and surprise a friendly neighbor by leaving it at the door.

SUPPLIES TO BRIGHTEN BLEAK OCCASIONS FOR
2-, 3-, AND 4-YEAR-OLDS

Rainy days. Some parents have a "rainy day supply," with objects in it not available at other times.

When your child is 2, or 3, or 4, large cartons, big enough to get into, can provide a lot of occupation on a rainy day if reserved for this time.

Save a supply of empty cans and other food containers that your child can use to play "grocery store" on a rainy day if he wants to. When he becomes old enough to notice letters of the alphabet, make a practice of opening cans from the bottom so that he can set out what appear to be intact cans, with the labels right side up.

Illness. Here are a few suggestions for a "sick box" of toys, in addition to the outgrown playthings I mentioned earlier:

> Small (about 1 inch square) blocks painted so that they make various designs according to the way they are placed together are appealing to most children from preschool days well into school days, if reserved for infrequent use. These are expensive, but remember that their cost is likely to be spread over a number of years.

Pipe cleaners.

A magnet.

A set (purchased ready-made) consisting of pieces of felt of various sizes and shapes and a base board on which the felt pieces stay in place temporarily as located by the child.

Construction sets like tinker toys, but perhaps in colored plastic.

A "magic slate."

A slate made of the kind of shiny composition material which can be wiped clean with a cloth after being drawn on with soap-base (rather than wax-base) crayons.

Old magazines.

A kaleidoscope.

A comb with tissue paper on it to sing through (or a kazoo, if you can find one).

An unbreakable mirror, particularly if your child can catch a beam of sunlight and flash it around the room.

Old Christmas cards to look at.

When the sitter takes over. (I have in mind here a rather short occasion, when you go out for dinner, for example, while your child is still up.) Need for special planning depends upon many things, of course, including the kind of person the sitter is and the way your child feels about your going out. If your child enjoys the sitter's company and the sitter is good at keeping life interesting during waking hours, there is no need for any special plans. It is often helpful, however, to have some suggestions up your sleeve as to pleasant ways to pass the time: perhaps to be read to out of a favorite book, to take a walk, or to listen to records.

If your child happens to be going through a phase of being upset when you leave, it sometimes works wonders to provide a small present, well wrapped so that he cannot guess what it is, with the stipulation that it cannot be opened until you have actually left. This has been known to turn sad apprehension into an eager "When are you going to go?" Your child should not get the notion that he will receive a present every time parents step out, but this system, judiciously handled, can be a real help to him if he is not deeply disturbed at the prospect of your absence.

This completes my suggestions for constructive play materials and activities, with the exception of comments about books and music for your child. For further suggestions as well as discussion of constructive play materials, I recommend *The Complete Book of Children's Play* by Ruth E. Hartley and Robert M. Goldenson.

Books, music, television

BOOKS BEFORE 5

I may as well tell you at once that I am highly in favor of doing everything you can to interest your child in books. Television offers stiff competition in its appeal to growing children. Therefore encourage your child's enjoyment and interest in books right from babyhood. Start before your child is a year old with a book that consists of pictures of objects your baby often sees, in the hope that it will have significance and attraction for him. I know a baby who had such a book with a simple, clear, colorful drawing of a spotted dog. He used to crawl around the open book as it lay on the floor until he was looking at the picture right side up. Then he would settle back and say "Duh" (one of his first words) triumphantly. There was a Dalmatian in his family.

From babyhood through the preschool years children are busy finding out what the world is like. They are immensely interested in it. They do not need to have it dressed up into something it is not; indeed, they will become confused if make-believe enters in before they can recognize it for what it is.

Some people believe that children's imagination is better nourished on make-believe in the preschool years. Just the reverse is true, I contend. What fosters imaginativeness at this age is a book that conveys through words and manner of presentation the feeling of an experience. When, for example, a toddler hears in *The Animals of Farmer Jones* that the animals are hungry and need to be fed, his imagination is being called on to make a link between himself and them. To tell him, however, that the moon is made of green cheese, or that people can jump into a fiery furnace and emerge unharmed, or that tiny fairy creatures live in a mushroom patch will not foster his imaginativeness. These are just as reasonable to him as most of the statements of fact he hears. Why should he not take them at face value?

Many months before children are 2, they will enjoy looking at pictures and hearing "stories" (in extremely simple language, concocted by the storyteller)—stories of children like themselves, of familiar animals, of such common objects as cars and trucks. The children in the stories should behave in childlike ways; the animals, the cars, trucks, and other objects in the story should act and be as they really are; "things" should not be animated to have feelings and faces. Until a little child knows that animals do not talk, the animals in his stories should make only their animal noises. Just think how fascinating it is to find out that each kind of animal makes a special kind of noise. Animal conversation and animated things should wait until later, when a child recognizes this pretending for what it is. It is ideal if a little child is given a chance to see in real life what he finds in his books.

Here are a few examples of the kind of book I have in mind for the toddler not yet 2; all of them can be found on the book list for 2-, 3-, and 4-year-olds (pp. 106–9), since they are also appropriate for some of these ages: *Time for Bed*, *The Animals of Farmer Jones*, *The Little Family*, *Papa Small*, *Busy Timmy*, and *Guess Who Lives Here*. (The last two are included in *A Treasury of Little Golden Books*.)

A well-illustrated, well-chosen selection of Mother Goose is enjoyable in toddlerhood. I happen to like particularly *The Tall Book of Mother Goose*, illustrated by Feodor Rojankovsky, with the exception of "What are little girls made of?" and "What are little boys made of?"—a difficulty that can be surmounted by gluing two pages firmly together and so deleting them from the collection.

During all the preschool years, you need to look over ahead of time any stories or poems which your child is going to hear to make sure that you approve what they offer and that he is ready for them. If a story is fine except for a few details, it is easy to make it suitable for him. If, for example, a story says that "the wicked nail pierced poor Donkey Donkey's ear," remove the "wicked." Children need to realize that running into things does not involve malice on the part of the objects bumped into; why suggest the opposite in a story? Or, if a story for a 2-year-old, suitable in other respects, tells him that a pilot "feeds" his airplane gas, change the verb to fit the fact that the airplane is not alive Or, if a poem states that "the big, big wheels of thunder roll," I simply would not read it to a preschool child. It is better to wait until he wonders what causes thunder, and then tell him in a way consistent with the facts.

You may well think me fussy about children's books. So I am. This is because I think it important to gear your child's literary fare to his level of development and to your aims for his experience with books. Among mine are enjoyment, encouragement of curiosity, of wonder, and of imaginativeness at the same time that your child is finding out something about what other living creatures are like, about the nature of things, about how events take place in the world of nature and in the world devised by man.

As your toddler gains in knowledge of the world, he will be ready for stories in which animals talk. At first, the animals should be realistic in the sense that their talk is in character with the kind of animals they are, and so continues to inform him, rather than mislead him, about the nature of such animals. As your child's knowledge widens during the next two years, he will be ready for more fanciful tales, but they should always be sufficiently rooted in his own experience for him to recognize fancy for what it is. And he will continue as a 4-year-old, of course, to be interested in stories based in the real world, depicting what real people, real animals, and real things are like. Fairy tales belong to kindergarten days and beyond.

Keep on the lookout for stories and poems (and illustrations, too) which combine the realism and familiarity needed by your child at this age with something more—with the ability to capture the essence of an experience of real interest to him. This takes artistry. You cannot expect to find it in all of his literary fare, but watch for it. In stories, it is often a joint product of illustration and text.

I realize, of course, that the appeal of literature is personal. Furthermore, you and I are adults, guessing at what has appeal for a child, and, at the same time, setting up some standards which we want his books to meet because of our interest in and aims for his development. Here are some examples of literature for children which for me have the additional dimension I am talking about. For under 2-year-olds, *The Animals of Farmer Jones,* for the reason already mentioned that a little child may feel a kinship with the hungry animals as the story asks, "But where is Farmer Jones?" And also, to some extent, *Guess Who Lives Here,* bringing with it the notion of other people in other houses who are quite a lot like the small "reader" and his family. Or, some of the Mother Goose rhymes, together with their illustrations by Rojankovsky, in *The Tall Book of Mother Goose* ("Little Boy Blue," for example, or "Cold and Raw the North Winds Blow"). For 3-year-olds, *The Noisy Book,* with its tale of the little dog Muffin with a bandage over his eyes, and all the things he could nonetheless hear (though I feel the illustrations do not come up to the level of the text). Or, for 4-year-olds, whether or not they are city children, *Little Boy Brown,* who regularly lived in a hotel in a big city but spent one day in the country. Or the poem "My Cat," by Dorothy Baruch, in *Sung Under the Silver Umbrella.* Or *The Color Kittens.* You may feel at first sight that *The Color Kittens* contradicts suggestions I have made about suitable literature for children of preschool age, since the kittens are all dressed up in clothes and they are mixing paint. But a 4-year-old will not be misled by kittens who act like this. He is likely to respond to the happy combination of imaginative text (by Margaret Wise Brown) and equally imaginative illustrations (by the Provensens). Together, these tell of the colors mixed and the kittens' dream (which is effectively dreamlike), and portray the very essence of kitten behavior when the Color Kittens wake from their dream and pounce about. Do not demand this imaginative quality in all your child's books; much that is rather pedestrian and run-of-the-mill will nevertheless give him pleasure.

Well-selected collections of poems or stories make a special contribution to your child's literary fare. Two collections of poems I like for children of preschool age are *Sung Under the Silver Umbrella,* by the Association for Childhood Education International, and *Very Young Verses,* by B. P. Geismer and A. B. Suter. The first of these has drawings by Dorothy P. Lothrop interspersed throughout the book (not one to every page), and the pictures do not refer to adjacent poems. This takes some explaining to a child who points to a picture and says, "Read me this one." Despite the repeated explanations probably necessary before your child grasps the fact that pictures and poems do not go hand in hand, I very much like both the imaginative black-and-white drawings in the first book, its selection of poems, and the fact that the poems themselves are not illustrated, for I favor having the words of poems speak for themselves. Poems are, after all, created out of words to evoke feelings and images. Let them do it. Illustrations for poems often hamper imagination rather than enhance it. This is true of *Very Young Verses*, but the collection of poems is so good for preschoolers that it merits recommendation.

Collections of stories often make available well-loved stories which are no longer in print as individual books. Collections also frequently contain some stories which rely almost entirely on words alone, without illustrations, to produce the story's effect. Such stories develop your child's imagination in the way good poetry does: they stimulate him to create his own imagery instead of just following the play-by-play account furnished by illustrations. This comment is not a criticism of generously illustrated books. The point I wish to make is that both stories with and stories without illustrations are highly desirable in order to foster your child's interest in literature.

One more word about stories for preschool years. They do not need to come between the covers of a book. Most young children greatly enjoy stories which parents make up about everyday doings, including true stories of babyhood. Stories of his own babyhood can help a young child who has a baby in the family to realize that he, too, went through this stage.

In this section, Books Before 5, I have been concentrating mainly on the *content* of children's literature. When I am writing of how you act with your child, rather than of his surroundings, I shall have more to say about looking at books with him and about occasions for storytelling (p. 180, pp. 190–92). Enjoying literature with your child is a shared experience which can go on bringing you close together all through the school years.

EXAMPLES OF BOOKS FOR 2-, 3-, AND 4-YEAR-OLDS

The examples below are not an all-inclusive book list; they merely illustrate the kinds of books I recommend. I have included a few books which, at this writing, are not in print, and have indicated when this is so. Some of these may still be found in bookstores. Not infrequently, of course, children's books are reprinted. In any case, regular trips to a well-stocked children's library are likely to enhance your child's interest in books.

Individual stories and a few information books. The number in parentheses after the title indicates the age for which a book is particularly suited. But take this rough indication with a grain of salt, for many stories continue to hold interest as a child grows older.

BENDICK, JEANNE. *All Around You* (4). McGraw-Hill.

BERTAIL, INEZ. *Time for Bed* (2, 3). Doubleday.

BRENNER, BARBARA. *The Five Pennies* (4). Knopf.

BROWN, MARGARET WISE. *The Color Kittens* (4). Golden Press.

BROWN, MARGARET WISE. *Goodnight Moon* (2, 3). Harper.

BROWN, MARGARET WISE. *The Noisy Book* (3). Harper. This is one of a number of "Noisy Books" by this author, the rest of which are better suited to 4-year-olds.

BURTON, VIRGINIA LEE. *Mike Mulligan and His Steam Shovel* (4). Houghton Mifflin.

BURTON, VIRGINIA LEE. *The Little House* (4). Houghton Mifflin.

CARTER, KATHARINE. *The True Book of Oceans* (4). Childrens Press.

CRAIG, M. JEAN. *The Dragon in the Clock Box* (4). Norton.

DONALDSON, LOIS. *Karl's Wooden Horse* (3, 4). Whitman. Not in print.

DUVOISIN, ROGER. *Donkey-Donkey* (3, 4). Grosset & Dunlap. Not in print.

FLACK, MARJORIE. *Angus and the Cat* (2, 3). Doubleday. Also, *Angus and the Ducks* and *Angus Lost* for these same ages.

FLACK, MARJORIE. *Ask Mr. Bear* (2, 3). Macmillan.

FLACK, MARJORIE. *Tim Tadpole and the Great Bullfrog* (3, 4). Doubleday.

FLACK, MARJORIE, AND WIESE, KURT. *The Story about Ping* (3, 4). Viking.

FREEMAN, MAE AND IRA. *You Will Go to the Moon* (4). Random.

FRISKEY, MARGARET. *The True Book of Birds We Know* (3, 4). Childrens Press.

GALE, LEAH. *The Animals of Farmer Jones* (2). Golden Press.

GAY, ROMNEY. *Cinder* (2, 3). Grosset & Dunlap. Not in print. Also for ages 2 and 3 *Cinder's Secret* and *A Joke on Cinder*, both out of print.

HARRIS, ISOBEL. *Little Boy Brown* (4). Lippincott.

HUNTINGTON, HARRIET E. *Let's Go Outdoors* (4). Doubleday. The magnified photographs should be used in combination with a child's firsthand experiences with the creature described.

KEATS, EZRA JACK. *The Snowy Day* (2, 3, 4). Viking. An effective combination of text and pictures show the pleasures of snow for Peter, a little Negro boy.

KOHN, BERNICE. *Everything Has a Shape* (4). Prentice-Hall.

KOHN, BERNICE. *Everything Has a Size* (4). Prentice-Hall.

LEAF, MUNRO. *The Story of Ferdinand* (4). Viking.

LENSKI, LOIS. *The Little Auto* (2, 3.) Walck. Also for 2- and 3-year-olds, *The Little Family*, *The Little Farm*, and *Papa Small*.

LENSKI, LOIS. *The Little Fire Engine* (3, 4). Walck. There are several other Lenski books with titles similar to this, such as *The Little Airplane* and *The Little Train*. Examine them to see whether the information provided is sufficiently up-to-date so as not to be misleading. *The Little Train*, for example, is a steam engine. If trains mean diesels to your child, this may not tell him what he wants to know about trains. *Cowboy Small* and *Policeman Small* are also well-known Lenski books. Suit the complexity of the details you read aloud to your child's interest and understanding.

LENSKI, LOIS. *On a Summer Day* (3, 4). Walck. Your child may get some ideas about play activities from this book, particularly if you help by making available appropriate play materials.

LINDMAN, MAJ. *Snipp, Snapp, Snurr and the Red Shoes* (4). Whitman.

MC GOVERN, ANN. *Zoo, Where Are You?* (4). Harper.

MITCHELL, LUCY SPRAGUE. *The Taxi That Hurried* (3, 4). Golden Press.

PAASCHE, CAROL. *Count With Me* (4). Golden Press.

PHLEGER, FREDERICK. *Ann Can Fly* (4). Random.

POTTER, MARIAN. *The Little Red Caboose* (3, 4). Golden Press.

PROVENSEN, ALICE AND MARTIN. *Karen's Opposites* (4). Golden Press.

SCARRY, RICHARD. *Richard Scarry's Best Word Book Ever* (3, 4, and far beyond). Golden Press. The pictures interest preschoolers. Older children will enjoy reading the book well into their school years.

TRESSELT, ALVIN. *The Rabbit Story* (3, 4). Lothrop.

TRESSELT, ALVIN. *Rain Drop Splash* (4). Lothrop.

WILDSMITH, BRIAN. *Brian Wildsmith's A.B.C.* (3, 4). Watts. This is notable for the reproductions of Brian Wildsmith's paintings which accompany the letters. Though I suspect their appeal may be greater for adults than for children, I highly approve of exposing children to them.

Collections. You need, of course, to choose carefully from the poems and stories in collections to find those suited to your child. Occasions when a child is confined to bed and bored with trying to amuse himself are often opportune times for reading poetry or stories with few illustrations.

POEMS AND VERSE

Association for Childhood Education International. *Sung Under the Silver Umbrella.* Macmillan.

Geismer, B. P., and Suter, A. B. *Very Young Verses.* Houghton Mifflin. Not in print. See the earlier discussion of this book and *Sung Under the Silver Umbrella* (pp. 103–4).

Rojankovsky, Feodor. *The Tall Book of Mother Goose.* Harper. I have already commented about this collection (p. 102). It is pleasant to sing the nursery rhymes for which you know tunes.

STORIES

A Treasury of Little Golden Books, selected and edited by Ellen Lewis Buell. Golden Press.
An excellent collection of forty-eight stories, originally published individually as Little Golden Books, illustrated with pictures selected from the originals. Many of these stories would otherwise be out of print. Some, however are available as individual books; others may be reprinted. I strongly recommend in the case of favorite stories that, whenever possible, you duplicate stories in the collection with individual Little Golden Books so that your child may peruse all of the illustrations originally devised.

Association for Childhood Education International. *Told Under the Blue Umbrella.* Macmillan.
This collection contains a number of stories which create their effect chiefly through words, without the assistance of illustrations. (For further comment about the value of your child's exposure to this kind of story, see p. 105.) Among my favorites for 3-year-olds are "Little Sheep One, Two, Three," by Marjorie Allen Anderson, and "A City Street," by Lucy Sprague Mitchell; for 4-year-olds, "William and Jane," by Dorothy Aldis. Attractive black and white illustrations are interspersed

throughout the book. You yourself may be interested in the article entitled "The Experience Story," by Eloise Ramsey, at the end of the book.

Bayley, Verna Hills. *Martin and Judy in Their Two Little Houses.* Beacon.

This is the first volume of a recommended series of three. It is designed to describe for 3- and 4-year-olds experiences which may serve as background for religious faith later on, whatever the religion in which parents wish to bring up a child; it is also intended for use by parents who do not subscribe to "any historical faith at all." It succeeds well in its aim, I think, and is interesting to children of 3 and 4.

Child Study Association of America. *Read-to-Me Storybook.* Crowell.

This is also one of a series, the others being *Read Me Another Story, Read Me More Stories,* and *Read to Me Again.* These books are attractively illustrated in black-and-white, but also give your child an opportunity to visualize happenings without the aid of illustrations. This is a highly successful series in terms of its appeal to children of preschool age.

MUSIC FROM 2 TO 5

I think that the nicest kind of music for a baby, a toddler, and a young 2-year-old is his parents' singing, even if they do not have particularly good voices. What I have said about the content of stories and poems for children applies equally well to the songs a young child hears and eventually learns. He is indeed lucky if his mother and father like to sing spontaneously. There is no need for them to confine themselves to songs written for children, though one hopes their repertoire includes a number of such songs. Some of the songs should be very simple so that he can come close to them in his own spontaneous singing. Take such a song as "Swinging" (in *Singing Time,* by Satis N. Coleman and Alice G. Thorn), with its very pleasant, simple tune:

Swinging,   Swinging,   now we go up   now we go down,
Swinging,   Swinging,   Betsy goes up   Betsy goes down.

If a little 2-year-old is swinging, sing this to him, substituting his name in the song.

Or, take the following song (source unknown):

The thunder makes noise,
And dark grows the sky,
Where faster and faster
The storm clouds race by.
Soon down will come dashing
The warm summer rain.
And dusty brown meadows
Grow green once again.

I know a child a little under 2 who was apprehensive about many noises, but who seemed to feel relaxed about thunder, as this was sung to him by one of his parents whenever a storm was in the offing.

Or, here are two homemade songs (by a father who had a very pleasant singing voice but was not adept at carrying a tune) which gave a lot of pleasure to his children.

WHAT KIND OF NOISE

What kind of noise does a train make?
Choo choo choo choo, all the day long.
What kind of noise does a cow make?
Moo-oo, moo-oo, all the day long.
What kind of noise does a clock make?
Tick, tick, tick, tick, all the day long.
What kind of noise does Johnny make?
It all depends on the time of day.
When he gets up, he says, "Good morning."
When he goes to bed, he says, "Good night."
When he sneezes, he says, "God bless you."
When he goes outdoors, he says, "Walk around, walk around."
When he's hungry, he says, "Like more, like more."
It all depends on the time of day.

THE TRAIN SONG

Daddy and Mommy and Johnny
Went to a train one day.
They said to themselves, said they,
Let's go to a train,
Let's go to a train,
Let's go to a train, today.
The gates went down,
The train came in,

The people got off and got on.
The train started up
And went down the tracks,
Puffing and blowing
And making big noise.
The gates went up
And we went home
And that is the end of this song
Do you see,
The end—the end of this song.

In short, I hope that songs about what your child does, some-times sung when he is carrying on the activity described, are a part of his life, and that they continue to be a part of it during all his preschool years, along with nursery rhymes, folk songs, songs about different animals, about cars, trucks, ships, airplanes, and other familiar objects, about cowboys, about people in other countries, about interesting happenings that come with changes in season—songs, indeed, which reflect his interest in the world around him and in the wider world he comes to know secondhand. In addition to the song book by Coleman and Thorn already mentioned, I highly recommend Fletcher and Denison's *The New High Road of Song for Nursery Schools and Kindergartens.* MacCarteney's *Songs for the Nursery School* is also good.

In addition to songs, I hope your child has a lot of other music in his life, music presented to him in many different ways: listening to records, exploring sounds, moving to music (preferably outdoors, which offers more space and consequent freedom than he can have inside). If you want to read more on the subject, I suggest Emma Dickson Sheehy's *There's Music in Children*, where you will find both discussion and quite specific suggestions. *The Complete Book of Children's Play*, by Hartley and Goldenson, contains in its appendix suggestions for recordings and song books.

TELEVISION

You can probably guess how I feel about long hours spent in front of a television set from everything I have said about constructive play materials, and my hopes that your child will learn to take the initiative for finding something interesting and constructive to do. As a matter of fact, I feel so strongly about the detrimental effects of television on preschool children that it is hard for me to be open-minded. I object to television first because of the activities a child is missing as he sits passively watching; second, because television has such compelling fascination for children that it tends to absorb more and more of their time. I view with genuine horror the fact that the first word some babies speak nowadays is the name of a product which they have heard advertised on television.

My third objection to television involves the content of what a child sees, not simply what he is missing by sitting there. Too many parents let their children view scenes which they would never approve in real life. It now seems to be established that witnessing aggression leads an individual to act aggressively himself when in a similar situation. It is a fact that children who have been watching aggressive cartoons act more aggressively in their play afterwards than do children who have been watching more peaceful cartoons. I invite you to look at everything your child watches on television for a week, and then decide how much of it you think contributes positively to his development. One last word: of course I am aware that there are genuinely worthwhile programs on television; but I believe that by and large what is served up for children's entertainment sadly needs improvement.

SUMMARY

This chapter, concerned with arranging your child's surroundings to promote enjoyable, constructive activity, has been a long one. Keep watching for ways to set your child's surroundings to work for you, even more than you do at present, to help bring about your aims for his learning. And remember two points with which you began this chapter: (1) well-arranged surroundings can do a lot to free your child from constant warnings and allow him to act the way his spirit tells him to without getting into trouble; but (2) even the most astutely arranged environment can go only so far in guiding your child. What you do and say as he is active in his surroundings is of crucial importance. Our next concern, then, will be direct guidance, the techniques you use in guiding your child.

5

Techniques of Guidance

SO FAR I have been emphasizing how you can arrange your child's surroundings in order to take into account his needs and desires as well as those of everyone else in the family. Now I am going to talk about your activity in these surroundings—that is, about guidance of your child by your words and actions.

Preparing yourself for direct guidance of your child

Keep in mind everything said so far: what children of your child's developmental level are like in general and what he is like in particular; your knowledge of how people learn; your speculations about your child's motives and behavior. Make up your mind, being quite honest with yourself, about what you want your child to learn, both from a long-range and an immediate point of view. Set his surroundings to work for you as far as possible so that the consequences of his behavior when he is active in these surroundings foster the learning you hope for.

APPRAISE YOURSELF AND YOUR HOME

Before you step into action, take a good look at yourself, too, at your home, and at the rest of the family. Try to size up what kind of people and what kind of place are involved in your home. If you happen to be a person with a hasty temper or a rather exacting, severe attitude, who expects a lot from people, what you need to bear in mind in guiding your child is likely to be something quite different from what is needed if you have endless patience and gentleness or such an easygoing attitude that your child lacks the security of a pattern for his life, suited to his needs, and lacks, too, an understanding of what you expect of him. It is hard for anyone to appraise himself. Obviously, the more realistically you get a line on yourself and other members of the family, the better use you can make of my suggestions for guidance.

FROM TIME TO TIME APPRAISE YOUR CHILD'S WHOLE LIFE

This is so important that I shall put down more or less in outline form the kind of questions you need to ask.

Does your child show ability to take the initiative for finding something constructive to do?

> Is he fairly resourceful, or does he spend a lot of time at loose ends?
> If he does take initiative in finding activity, is it constructive?

Does he have varied interests?

> What, specifically, does he do, and what, particularly enjoy?
> If his interests are pretty limited, why is this the case?

Does he have varied skills?

> What does he do competently? What does he have trouble with?
> To ask this another way, what are his skills in various aspects of development: gross motor coordination, fine motor coordination, language, and so forth?

What kinds of relationships does he have with others?

In the family, where are satisfactions and dissatisfactions in relationships?

Outside the family, does he have a chance for different kinds of relationships, including give-and-take with peers?

What about his feelings, his emotional expression and control?

What situations are frustrating, worrisome, frightening?

How does he cope with problems?

Does he express feelings adequately, hold in too much, or lose control too readily?

How does he feel about making decisions and abiding by the consequences of his actions?

Taken as a whole, how does he feel about himself as a person; how do all his experiences tally up for him in terms of satisfactions and dissatisfactions?

There are many reasons why it is important to make a periodic appraisal. One, already mentioned, is that in applying learning by consequences, you sometimes have to deal with the whole situation rather than the specific behavior about which you are concerned. Also, such an appraisal may call your attention to deficiencies—dissatisfactions—which can be remedied. I remember a little girl who seemed to feel timid a good deal of the time. An over-all appraisal suggested that she was particularly apprehensive about climbing and other gross motor activity, and further (because of the way she looked at books), that she might not see well. This proved to be the case. As soon as she was fitted with glasses, her confidence and interest in large-muscle activity increased enormously. And I remember a little boy with very limited interests; he spent most of his time in a sandbox. The remedy here was to give him more chances to play with children on his own level of development, without being surrounded by boisterous children zooming around on bicycles or moving at a fast pace in general. The sandbox must have seemed a sanctuary to this little boy, who was small for his age and geared to play at a slow rate.

Thus an appraisal is not just an imaginative exercise. It is to help you to see your child in perspective, to plan desirable changes, and to figure out consequences for his behavior which are likely to bring him satisfaction and to motivate him to behave in desirable ways. Then you can go into action in translating your conclusions from the appraisal into actual experiences for him.

Feelings are basic. A lot of effort, energy, and emotion are involved in raising children. Feelings are basic to guidance. I shall not keep talking about their fundamental importance, but I shall always be bearing it in mind, and ask you to do the same.

Perspective about the whole job of being a parent will promote the kind of feelings that make it easier for you to guide your children effectively. How do you gain this kind of perspective? Precisely by going through the kind of thinking I have been recommending: by looking, for example, at your own child's behavior against a backdrop of knowledge of what children of his age are like in general; by making appraisals of everyone in the family.

Try for a relaxed attitude toward life in general and your child in particular. If you can manage it, an attitude of relaxation, both toward life in general and your child in particular, is very helpful. He needs to be loved. But he needs to be loved and guided in a relaxed sort of way. One aid to feeling relaxed is having the kind of perspective that I just mentioned. Another is knowing how to guide him effectively. Such knowledge is likely to reduce your feelings of tension and concern. Then your sense of relaxation will be picked up by your child, help him feel secure, and so further the effectiveness of your guidance.

Now, perhaps you respond, "This is a pretty picture, but not realistic. Granted, if concern and worry about how to guide a child are creating tension, then effective guidance can reduce that tension. But there are so many angles to life which create tension and interfere with a relaxed attitude." I agree; feelings are not made to order, nor is life made smooth for the benefit of children. Yet you can do a lot to reduce tension. I have great confidence in what people can accomplish if they think it worthwhile, and reducing tension is.

Take the matter of having to hurry through the day. This can put everybody in the family on edge. Part of the remedy for this may be being more realistic about the length of time required to do various things. Or suppose getting the family fed and on its way in the morning is a scramble. Getting up half an hour earlier may make the difference between a relaxed and a harassed start.

Perhaps tension is being produced by overfatigue. Then can you hire outside help for especially tiring jobs, even as a temporary measure? Or perhaps you should revise your views downward as to how much must be done to keep the household running smoothly.

Whatever is done to promote relaxation in life and reduce tension is going to have its effects directly or indirectly on everybody in the family.

Recognize behavior-on-the-way. Keep alert, as you live with your child, to behavior-on-the-way—behavior which should be encouraged or discouraged, as the case may be, because of its probable outcome in the long run. Here is an example of such behavior-on-the-way, undesirable in itself, but nonetheless a step in the right direction:

> Ronnie, just 3, usually lets go and cries when other children try to take something from him. He is playing outside and has just picked up a large block, at some distance from a block building he is making. Margaret, almost 3½, a forceful little girl who often gets her own way, walks toward him, with a determined look. Ronnie lets out a scream and Margaret stops advancing toward him.

Now there were a lot of different ways to guide Ronnie. One of the watching grownups remarked, "He's got to learn not to scream like that." The staff member who knew Ronnie best felt different:

> She goes close to him and asks, "Ronnie, do you want to keep on building with blocks?" He nods. "Then hold on tight to that one." To Margaret, "Ronnie got here first. If you want to build with blocks, I'll help you see where to get them."

This staff member thought that Ronnie screamed because he was afraid that Margaret would take away his block. Of course, his scream was undesirable in the long run, but at this stage it was a step in the right direction, an attempt by Ronnie to stand up for his rights. To say "There's no need to scream like that" would not have fitted the facts, for probably the scream actually stopped Margaret's would-be grab for the block. Ronnie was encouraged to keep holding onto what he was using, because that was the first step in standing up for himself. Later on, when he was ready for it, he would be encouraged to tell children in a firm way, "I got this first."

Here is another example, this time where the grownups did not look ahead to the kind of habit that was likely to develop from their child's behavior:

> From the time Gretchen was given a little rocking chair, when she was close to 2, she used to rock herself to sleep in it at night. Her parents were delighted with her pleasure in the chair. Once she was asleep, they would put her to bed. All went well for several months, but then she began to take an increasingly long time to fall asleep. When they came for consultation, they were in a quandary. She was rocking as late as ten o'clock almost every night. She was clearly worn out. But they were afraid that any attempts to get her to change her habitual rocking would result in such marked upsetness that they dreaded trying to do anything about it.

Hindsight is always easier than foresight, but I believe Gretchen's parents could have predicted that they would be in difficulties if their little 2-year-old was permitted to rock herself to sleep. If, when the chair first appeared, it proved so inviting that it led to rocking instead of staying in bed, that was the time, if necessary, to remove it from the room.

Before you start guidance be sure you have a reasonably workable plan and that you really want to carry it through. If your child is acting in a way which you would like to change, your first step is to figure out what seems an effective plan of guidance. If you cannot, then let the matter go. Why? Because, ineffective guidance is detrimental in many ways, as I have said more than once. If you do not get results, you are likely to keep repeating yourself, to feel irritated and frustrated. Your child will probably feel nagged, resentful, even hostile, or defiant, and be inclined to believe you do not mean what you say, and thus encouraged to be inattentive the next time you tell him something. I think such ineffective guidance may be partly responsible for the self-centeredness and selfishness of school children which, as I mentioned in the Introduction, many parents report. If attempts at guidance take on nagging overtones, it is small wonder if children's uninterested attitudes toward grownup instruction carry over into school.

Even if you figure out a plan of guidance which you think will be effective, take time to decide whether you really want to go through with it. It is far better to do nothing than to start guidance and abandon it. I do not mean that you should never change a plan of guidance once it is under way, if you feel that you have made a real mistake. I am saying, though, that as a general principle, once you have said something you should stick to it. You need to try to anticipate the consequences for everyone, including yourself, of trying to shape your child's behavior. Unless you are sure that guidance is worth it, leave matters where they stand.

Keep requirements to a minimum. As I have already stressed, a young child is learning so many things that it is easy to make him feel bossed all the time. It is also easy to make him dependent upon being told what to do, instead of encouraging him to use his own ideas. Think over carefully what you expect of him; then really require it. But keep your requirements to a minimum. For if you tell your child to do things for which there is no very good reason, you are likely to be inconsistent in two ways. First, you may change your mind after telling him what to do, because there was not much point to it in the first place. Second, what you require one day, or one minute, you may not require the next. Under these circumstances, your child will not learn to act as you want him to act. In contrast, minimum requirements will help him pay attention because you are not after him all the time. And your efforts to keep requirements to a minimum during all his growing years will give your child less to rebel about at adolescence when he is trying to assert his independence and to find his place as a young adult.

Have a consistent pattern for your child's life: what he does and how he does it. As a reaction against the overemphasis upon habit training which was popular in the twenties and thirties, many parents swung too far in the opposite direction. Overdoing permissiveness, they forgot that a child derives security from a pattern of life designed to meet his individual needs, and from parents who work out what it is reasonable to expect of their children, parents who make up their minds what they do expect, and who are able to help their children learn to meet these expectations.

Consistency in the pattern for your child's day, in what he does, how and when he does it, should not be confused with inflexibility. Of course, the pattern will need to change as he changes or as circumstances demand. But do not undervalue the importance of a pattern geared to his individual needs, of regular hours for mealtimes and midmorning and midafternoon snacks, of regular times for afternoon sleep and bed at night, of a pattern for play which includes plenty of opportunity for strenuous outdoor activities as well as quieter ones. Remember that this kind of pattern helps your child have an accepting attitude toward the day's events and allows his body to regularize itself so that he will generally feel hungry at mealtimes and sleepy at bedtime; it also gives his system a chance to regularize bowel movements if he tends toward regularity.

A pattern to his day can give him events to look forward to that you can utilize in his guidance. Suppose it works well in your house to have some pleasant family activity just before your child's bedtime, reading a story perhaps, or singing songs, or looking at the stars. This will put him in a relaxed mood, give you a cozy time together, and provide a pleasant bedtime atmosphere. Now suppose that when he is 4 and quite able to get ready for bed with dispatch, he takes to dawdling. You will find it useful to tell him, "Too bad. You took so long getting ready for bed that there is no time for a story. I'll remind you tomorrow night to keep busy so there will be time if you want one."

Work out ways to minimize need for instructions. However much you have tried to plan your child's play environment so that he can be free in it (and so that the consequences to his activity bring him satisfaction and promote desired learning), there will still be occasions on which you will need to give instructions. You can minimize these by working out procedures that fit your child and your home setting.

Suppose, for example, he likes to take toys outdoors to use in earth play, but in bringing them back inside scatters dirt around. Have him learn to leave them just outside the door, or, if he is old enough, provide him with a pan of water and a brush so that he can clean his toys. Or suppose he enjoys water play in the kitchen sink, but tends, naturally enough, to get wet. Keep a little plastic apron handy which he learns to put on first. Or suppose he likes to climb a particular tree, but the tree invites too high climbing to be safe. Then have an understanding with him as to how high he may climb and mark the tree accordingly. Of course, you will have to see to it that your child follows the procedures you work out. Remember the purpose of the procedures: they are designed to minimize need for instructions, but remember, too, they are requirements. This means you have to see that he either adheres to them or promptly experiences an unsatisfactory consequence.

SUMMARY: PREPARING YOURSELF FOR DIRECT GUIDANCE OF YOUR CHILD

Up to this point in this chapter, I have been describing how you get ready to use techniques of guidance: by making use of everything you have considered so far in this book; by appraising yourself and your home; appraising your child's whole life from time to time; bearing in mind how important parents' feelings are to guidance; and by cultivating certain attitudes. It is important to try for a relaxed attitude toward life in general and your child in particular; to recognize behavior-on-the-way; to be sure, before you start guidance, that you have a reasonably workable plan and that you really want to carry it through; to keep requirements to a minimum; to have a consistent pattern for your child's life—what he does and how he does it; to work out ways to minimize instructions.

A *record of children at "family" play*

It will be helpful, in thinking about your words and actions in guiding your child, to take a look at the spontaneous "family" play of some children in nursery school—play which reflects how these children think parents act. They have built a house of large blocks and parked a tricycle nearby. The characters involved are Rob, the father (4½); Nan, the mother; Tad, the child (both two months younger than Rob); Catherine, the child of a neighboring family (a year younger than her brother Tad). Mother and Father are inside the block house. Tad is outside:

TAD: *I want to ride the bike.*

NAN (*to Rob*): *Daddy, can he ride the bike?*

ROB: No.

NAN (*running over to Tad*): Honey, he says, "No." (*Tad looks quite genuinely put out. He and Nan go back to the "house" together.*)

NAN: *Honey, do you want a nut?*

TAD: *Yes.*

NAN (*taking him some pebbles*): *Here are two, honey.* (*Then to Rob*) *Have you some sugar?*

ROB: *Yes, I have some sugar and honey.*

TAD (*calling*): *I want a cookie.* (*Nan takes him a pebble. Then she starts to sweep the house.*)

NAN (*to Tad*): *Now you lie down. It's your naptime.*

TAD: *But you're not lying down.*

NAN: *We don't take naps, honey. Now lie down.*

CATHERINE (*who has come running over to the block house*): *Daddy says that you can come to tea.* (*Nan starts out at once with Catherine, but then returns.*)

ROB (*to Nan*): *I'll take care of the baby.* (*Nan nods, then runs after Catherine, but comes right back just as Rob starts to talk.*)

ROB (*to Tad*): *Do you want some honey?*

NAN: *What are you giving him?*

ROB: *Honey.*

NAN: *Give him some tomorrow. (Then she turns to Tad.) Take off your shoes, honey.*

ROB *(to Nan): We're lions, aren't we?*

NAN: *No. (A pause.) Ding-a-ling.*

ROB: *I'll answer the door.*

Did you notice the guidance techniques used by these "parents"? First, Mother passed the buck to Father when Tad wanted to ride a bike and Father's "No" was automatic. Notice, too, that grownups are privileged characters ("We don't take naps, honey. Now lie down"). Note also, Mother knew her own mind. Though Catherine's invitation to tea was apparently directed to the whole family, Mother accepted it so quickly that no one else had a chance to come along and Father was left holding the bag. And "Give him some tomorrow" is a postponement technique which many parents use without much more reason than this mother. Mother Nan and Father Rob would have done well to do a little more thinking about family life and child guidance.

Guidance techniques for children of any age

The techniques which follow are effective with children of all ages, though the illustrations are of 2- to 5-year-olds. Though some of these techniques may sound superficial, each serves a purpose. For instance, some reduce tension, some create a relaxed atmosphere, some get your child to heed what you say the first time you say it. After these guidance techniques for children of all ages, I shall describe techniques suited to particular developmental levels. Remember throughout that I am not talking here about your companionship with your child, I am speaking simply of those occasions when you have to get him to do what needs doing.

SLOW DOWN; RELAX

When your child was a baby, you probably used the way you did things for him to promote the feelings you wanted him to have—

feelings of security and well-being. For instance, if you went to do something for him, you moved slowly, and held him in a relaxed sort of way. As your child has grown older, you may have forgotten how much he picks up attitudes and atmosphere from the way you act. Make use of the fact that he does this. You will need to stand off and take a good look at yourself. Watch yourself, for instance, when you are bustling your child into his coat, helping him tidy up his room, or putting him to bed as dinner guests are due to ring the doorbell.

Try slowing down in your motions, in the way you talk to your child. Relax physically when you do things for him. You will get just as much done. At the same time, be realistic about the amount of time it takes to do things comfortably. Remember, I am not just trying to get you to put on an unhurried act when you are really taut and your mind is racing. I am hoping that you will come to feel unhurried from the inside out. Hurry is often just a habit.

WAIT TO TELL YOUR CHILD WHAT TO DO UNTIL IT IS REALLY NECESSARY

One reason for waiting to tell your child what to do until it is really necessary is to give him a chance to think for himself. Another is that he may stop the activity himself without being told. Suppose he has your car keys in his hand, having just welcomed you home, and that they touch the highly polished surface of a table as they dangle down. A remark about what he is doing may spring to your lips. But the dangling of the keys may well be over before you ever finish your remark. It was an accidental happening or, at most, a fleeting interest. By holding back your remark, you save your child from one piece of instruction for that day. Furthermore, not saying it may serve to avoid calling his attention to the very activity you would like to discourage.

GAIN YOUR CHILD'S ATTENTION BEFORE SPEAKING TO HIM

How do you gain your child's attention before speaking to him? By letting out a bellow? No, that would create just the kind of atmosphere we are trying to avoid. Make a habit of going up close to him before you start to talk when this is practicable, and it is most of the time. With a little child it helps to start off by saying his name, or if he is absorbed in what he is doing, it may help to gain his attention physically—by touching him on the shoulder, for instance. (However, if he does not like the gesture, drop it at once.) In a word, see that you have his attention before you say anything more. If your child is going through a particularly inattentive phase, get down to his level physically, squatting beside him before you say anything. Even when your child has reached school years, it can save a lot of frustration and annoyance if you keep on making sure you have his attention before you tell him something. Many a school-ager has been heard to say, "You never told me to get dressed," or ". . . rake the leaves" or ". . . come to dinner," or whatever. Save your breath until you are sure he is attending.

TALK QUIETLY

You may say that this is impractical—that your child will not hear you. He will. You just need to get close enough so that he can.

SOUND DEFINITE

I do not mean by this that you should bark out what you have to say like a drill sergeant. You can be definite and pleasant at the same time. A friendly, definite attitude helps your child know that you mean what you say. I was once involved with some small children who spoke only French. Although I had worked hard to get my French ready, my uncertainty about how to say things carried through into my tone of voice, and the children reacted accordingly. But when I managed to keep my words moving along confidently, they responded by acting as if they thought I meant what I said.

TELL YOUR CHILD WHAT TO DO INSTEAD OF WHAT NOT TO DO—THAT IS, SAY THINGS POSITIVELY

Suppose your 2-year-old is out in the garden and starts to pull up a plant stake. There is a world of difference between "No, no" and

"That's there on purpose. If you'd like to use a stick, there's one over there." (Of course, part of the difference is that you are suggesting a satisfactory substitute.) For a toddler, when he reaches for a lamp, there is a real difference between "No, no" and "That stays there." "Watch what you're doing," as your child absent-mindedly starts to spill water from a glass is a better approach than "Don't spill." Saying things positively helps your child learn because you are emphasizing what to do. Also, if he constantly hears "No" he is likely to rebel and to feel that he needs to assert himself by handing the "No" right back to you.

SAY THINGS JUST ONCE

Suppose you say to your child, "Lucy, time for dinner." You thought you had gained her attention, but she just gazes out the window. Or suppose she responds by asking "What?" Quell your natural impulse to repeat what you said. If you do repeat things frequently, you are teaching your child that there is no need to pay attention on the first go-round. Therefore, see that your first remark takes effect. One technique is to ask, "What did I say?" The chances are your child can tell you. If he cannot, tell him again, now that you really have his attention. Do not ask him a second time to repeat what you have said; this would just be tedious and probably make him feel resentful. If your child has developed a habit of inattention, it pays sometimes to preface what you say with "Listen, so you'll understand." But do not run this into the ground or it will lose its meaning.

This technique of "What did I say?" is more suited to older preschoolers than to the average just-2-year-old. It is often sound, when you have said something to your 2-year-old, to follow up with action. Suppose when you say to him, "We're going downstairs now," he runs off along the hall. Do not say it again. If you start down, he may follow right along, too. When you do this, go down in a forthright way, not pausing to look back to see if he is coming. Or go up to him and, with a relaxed hand, take his, or even pick him up and say, "I'll help you get started," as you put him in his going-downstairs position at the head of the stairs. This is the same principle, adapted to a younger level.

If you see to it that whatever you do or say counts the first time, you will eliminate a great deal of irritation now and in the future. Nagging spells trouble for everyone.

HAVE ONE PERSON AT A TIME TELL YOUR CHILD WHAT TO DO

Sometimes two or even more people pitch in at a time to tell a child what to do. Let the person who starts a situation carry it through. This not only helps your child attend the first time he is told something; it also helps to keep his inattention from leading to exciting consequences. If he were feeling contrary, it might add zest to life to get everybody talking to him at once.

DO ONE THING AT A TIME

There is another thing to bear in mind in order to have what you do or say effective the first time. Wait to talk or act until what you do will get results. Now suppose your 4-year-old is playing outdoors with several other children. Suddenly you hear excited shrieks, and look out. They are dancing up and down, laughing and shrieking, "Oh, look at that funny old man," as a forlorn cripple slowly makes his way down the street. You go outdoors, but excitement is so high that you cannot cope with all the children at once. Then deal with one at a time. You probably begin with your own child, unless one of the others is clearly the ringleader. You go right up to him, perhaps take hold of him to get his attention, and say, "Come here, I want to tell you something," as you take him away from the others. Then you give him an explanation, perhaps something to this effect: "The man does walk in a different way from most people. That's because he must have been badly hurt sometime. It's not the thing to do at all to talk about him out loud or make fun of him. You find something else to do." You can effectively deal with each of the children singly. If you try to deal with all of them at once, you will probably just add to the general hullabaloo.

WHEN YOU HAVE TO CHANGE WHAT YOUR
CHILD IS DOING, SUGGEST HOW HE MAY DO
WHAT HE WANTS IN AN ACCEPTABLE WAY

Your child starts to climb on the fence. You want to discourage this, for it may lead to scaling the fence, so you have provided a bench for climbing; there is also a suitable tree in the yard. "If you want to climb, climb in a climbing place" is both an instruction to stop what he is doing and a suggestion of how he can still do what he wants, at least to some extent. So are "If you want to throw gravel, do it over by the fence where there aren't people around," "If you want to use sand, keep it away from other people's faces," "That stays there. If you want to use a stick, there's one over there" (when your 2-year-old, a while back, began to pull out a stake in the garden), and "If you want to shout, you need to go outdoors."

Use this technique whenever you can, but of course some things you simply cannot allow. These have to be handled another way, and you will find that your child is more likely to be impressed with flat prohibitions if they are used sparingly.

SPEAK IN SUCH A WAY THAT YOUR CHILD CAN
UNDERSTAND WHEN YOU EXPECT HIM TO DO SOMETHING
AND WHEN IT IS A MATTER OF CHOICE

Take a look at the phrase "Do you want" in "Do you want to go outdoors now, Johnny?" If you are really asking whether or not Johnny would like to go out, well and good. If, however, what you mean is "Johnny, you are going out now," then you are setting yourself a bear trap. For if Johnny says no, you will either have to change your tactics—or your mind.

Here is another example. Suppose you sit down to take off your shoes and realize you forgot to get your slippers. If you do not feel that your child *ought* to get them for you and want to let him choose whether to or not, then this is worth emphasizing. You can do so by saying, "Johnny, you don't need to, but would you like to bring me my slippers from the closet?" Incidentally, it is not fair, if you put something to him this way, to feel put out if he chooses not to do it. If he does help you, thanks are in order, for he is doing you a favor.

PHRASE REQUIREMENTS IMPERSONALLY

"Mommy thinks it's time for bed" has quite another connotation than "Time for bed." In the first phrase, Mother sounds like a creature of whim. Or take "I guess you'd better put on your rubbers." If you really want your child to be in on a decision about wearing rubbers, then make it clear: "Let's take (or you take) a good look to see if you need your rubbers." However, if this is to be your decision, state it in terms of facts. "It's wet, so you need your rubbers."

SHOW BY THE WAY YOU TALK WHAT IS YOUR CHILD'S RESPONSIBILITY

The time has come to tidy up your small child's room. "Johnny, help Mother pick things up" suggests that picking up is Mother's job. In contrast, "Things go away now. I'll help you tidy up" carries the opposite meaning, even though with a little 2-year-old Mother does most of the work: the job is Johnny's responsibility.

Or consider "Let's put our coat on now." This kind of "we" is very natural; it grows out of babyhood when many things a baby did were a matter of "we." But a 2-year-old has outgrown it. (I am always reminded of a nurse I once had in a hospital who used to say cheerily, "Now let's take our temperature." "Whose temperature is it, anyway?" I wanted to snarl.) When you say, "Now let's put on our coat," you are losing a chance to have your child begin to get the idea that it is his job.

Of course, sometimes "we" is appropriate, as in "What story shall we read?" "What song shall we sing?" "Where shall we take a walk?" But not "our coat," please.

SAVE THANKS FOR SITUATIONS THAT DESERVE IT

Whenever a child does someone a favor, thanks are in order, but in his business activities—getting dressed, tidying up, going to the toilet, eating, and so forth—it is not sound to thank him for performing efficiently. Thanks for jobs which *ought* to be done imply that your child is doing you a favor to perform them, just the reverse of the attitude you want him to develop toward these jobs.

LET YOUR CHILD KNOW WHEN HE HAS
ACHIEVED SOMETHING

Approval, in distinction from thanks for efficient performance, is something else again. Parents are often much more ready to tell a child when he does something wrong than to comment about achievements. Showing approval for achievements has greater importance. Suppose your child rather frequently knocks over his glass of milk because he is inattentive. Then for several days his milk glass stands unspilled. Tell him something to this effect: "You certainly know how to be careful of your milk these days, don't you? You look at what you're doing." Save approval for occasions when your child has achieved something. Otherwise, it will lose its meaning.

PHRASE APPROVAL IN TERMS OF BEHAVIOR

Phrase approval in terms of *what* your child does. "You certainly know how to be careful of your milk these days, don't you? You look at what you are doing" is an example. It highlights the behavior concerned and conveys something quite different from "You're a good boy." It is also not likely to give him the idea that you love him only when he is being "good." (I talked earlier of the importance of how you phrase approval [pp. 46–49] and of the importance of your child's not feeling that your love is conditional upon good behavior [pp. 44–45].)

RESERVE DISAPPROVAL FOR BEHAVIOR THAT MERITS IT

Perhaps you remember the plea made earlier to take into account your child's motives and behavior when appraising his conduct (pp. 47–48). Reserve disapproval for behavior which merits it.

PHRASE DISAPPROVAL IN TERMS OF BEHAVIOR

Suppose your 4-year-old (I have seen one do it) on a sudden and astounding impulse whacks a visiting lady as she leans over to pick up her gloves. "That's no way to act," with appropriate consequences if you feel they are needed, carries quite a different implication from "Tommy, you bad boy." It is important for your child to feel not that *he* is bad, but that what he has *done* is at fault. If he becomes convinced that he is bad, he may think that there is no use trying to do any better; furthermore, feeling that he is bad is likely to make him unsure of your affection.

Similarly, being told he is slow, lazy, selfish, inattentive, clumsy, noisy, or rude is likely to confirm him in the belief that he *is* this kind of person, and it is certainly not apt to motivate him to try to be different.

KEEP DISAPPROVAL TIED TO THE BEHAVIOR WHICH DESERVES IT

It is all too easy to carry disapproval from one situation in your child's life to another. If it spreads like a cloud to each new situation, you are complicating his learning and inviting misbehavior. To be sure, he may take special care for a while not to offend you. But tension begets tension; annoyance on the part of one person stirs up responsive feelings in others.

Now, you may feel I am asking too much of you here, to confine your annoyance to a particular situation in your child's life. You may even quote my own words back at me. "Feelings are not made to order, nor is life made smooth for the benefit of children."

I stand by this; I am not asking you to be superhuman. If you restrain your feelings too much, they will come popping out in some other guidance situation. Nonetheless, a sense of proportion in your annoyance, if you can manage it, will help your child's learning. Granted, he needs to know that when people become cross and irritated they stay that way for a while. But he will have plenty of chance to learn that, without your plunging him into a prolonged atmosphere of disapproval.

What about you, though? What can you do with the annoyance you feel? Of course, you and I, like most adults, are going to be childishly put out sometimes, out of proportion to the cause which triggers off our reactions; and sometimes we are going to be thoroughly infused with feelings of annoyance. But we can try to do for ourselves what we aim at doing for our children: we can try to discover the real cause of our feelings and then express these feelings in ways that do not hurt other people.

"KEEP BUSY," NOT "HURRY UP"

When you want your child to do something with dispatch, you probably tell him to hurry. I have been emphasizing the value of trying to take the pressure out of life. "Hurry up" puts it back in. "Keep busy," on the other hand, tells him what you want, but without stressing speed. So do "It's already time for dinner, so you need to keep busy getting washed" and "You're taking too long. You need to finish up."

SHOW THE REASONS FOR GRANTING REQUESTS

"Mommy, can I go over to Janie's house?" "Yes, there's time before dinner" is an example of showing the reason for granting a request. Or suppose your child has been wanting to get into a wagon which is already filled, with no room for more. When one of its passengers leaves and your child asks, "Can I get in?" "Yes, there's room" shows him why he may and gives him a basis for figuring things out for himself. But notice, you are not going into lengthy explanations.

WHEN YOU GIVE YOUR CHILD ATTENTION, GIVE
YOUR FULL ATTENTION; WHEN YOU WANT TIME TO
YOURSELF, MAKE THIS CLEAR AND STICK TO IT

You are about to sit down to write a letter which takes some thought.
Your child enters the room with a new book, points to an unfamiliar object and asks, "What's that?" Unless you are in a
desperate hurry, here is a time when some wholehearted attention
from you will be pleasant and interesting for him. It does not even
have to be for long, but give him your full attention while you are
giving any. Then, when you have to write your letter, tell him so.

Halfhearted attention ("That's lovely, dear" as your child waves
something at you while you study a shopping list) will not satisfy
him. Nor will absent-minded comments while you are trying to get
something done.

You must, of course, give your child in his life as a whole the
full measure of attention he needs. But being together will mean
more to both of you if your child learns to respect your time when
it is necessary. And it is good for him if it is necessary some of the
time.

KEEP FROM TALKING ABOUT YOUR CHILD
WHERE HE CAN HEAR YOU IF YOUR
WORDS ARE NOT MEANT FOR HIM

This is more than a suggestion for guidance; it is an injunction.
Parents who are otherwise understanding have been known to talk
about their child in front of him as if he would obligingly turn stone
deaf during these conversations. If you are saying something about
your child that is fine for him to hear, then bring him into the conversation: "Susie did something very interesting with her blocks
today. Susie, would you like to show them to Aunt Jane?" But if
you want to say, "She's been fussy all day and screams at the slightest
delay in what she wants," or "She didn't eat any dinner," or "She
hit the baby with her ironing board," or "She pays no attention to
a word I say," then wait until your child cannot hear you. If you

are in the habit of talking about your child in front of him, you may find it hard to change, but once you have learned, you will find it quite possible to let people know what you want them to without having him hear you.

If it is your friends who do the talking, just politely ignore the remark and turn the conversation to something else. Be relaxed about it. Remember, what you do and the attitude you have matters much more to your child than a chance remark on a friend's part. I recall admiring a pair of parents in this predicament. Their 2-year-old had not yet begun to talk and they were naturally concerned about it. As they stood with him on their front porch, a neighbor walked by and called out, "Has Lou begun to talk yet?" They waved in a friendly way, apparently relaxed, and did not answer at all. Later on, when they had a chance, they passed on the word to keep from talking about Lou in front of him.

GUIDE YOUR CHILD SO THAT HE LEARNS TO THINK FOR HIMSELF AND TO SOLVE PROBLEMS

I have saved for the last this matter of guiding your child to think for himself and to learn to solve problems, partly because it involves so many of the points already made, partly because it calls for a fuller discussion than any of the other points.

Guiding him to think for himself in business activities. Let him alone to see if he remembers what to do. I have already given two reasons for waiting to tell your child to do something until you see that it is really necessary: to avoid needless instructions and to avoid calling his attention to an undesirable action which may hold only a fleeting interest for him.

Another and extremely important reason is to give him a chance to think for himself. Take such a humdrum affair, for a grown-up, as learning to hang up a coat. When 2½-year-old Hal gets out of his coat with your help, wait to see what happens next. If he remembers to hang it up, good. Your watching-and-waiting has spared him an unnecessary instruction. But what if he walks off, leaving it on the floor? Then

Act in such a way that you get him to figure out what needs doing. It would be easy to say, "Hal, hang up your coat." It is just as easy, though, and much more helpful in the long run if you say, "Hal, you forgot something." This is a lead, but not a solution. If, even now, he does not get the point, you can still leave something up to him by asking "What about your coat?" or "Where does it go?" Or, for that matter, you can just point to it. In itself, dealing with the coat seems inconsequential, but this is just one of many similar events in a little child's day. If you think of these as learning situations, you can guide your child to think for himself and to take the responsibility for necessary tasks. Then some fine day your child will remark with obvious pride, "You know what? I can manage to remember to put away my bicycle myself," or "I can settle down when it's time to go to sleep," or "I closed the door so the dog won't run out." When that day comes you will find how much it reflects about his development, and about your guidance—and how much time there is left for more important things.

Gear requirements to your child's ability to meet them. Hal had a problem on his hands when, after he walked off, you told him, "You forgot something"; he had something to figure out because you had decided on a standard for his behavior. Make sure that you gear what you expect to your child's abilities to meet the standards you set. It is unreasonable, for example, to expect him to eat his dinner neatly when he is just learning how to handle his silverware. Corrections at this time will bring no appreciable improvement in manners, and they may interfere with eating. And remember that success in accomplishing anything depends upon much more than ability, if "ability" means the skill necessary to perform what is involved. Achievement depends, too, upon motivation and persistence. A father I know forgot about this when he expected his 3-year-old to lace up his high shoes all by himself every morning. It only put the little boy in a bad humor because it took him so long. Hence, when I say, "Gear requirements to your child's ability," I mean not only physical ability, but ability to focus on tasks long enough to get them done.

Be consistent in what you expect. And if you really want your child to learn to meet a standard, you simply must be consistent in what you expect of him. Otherwise, he will not learn. Remember what I said about consistent consequences in learning by consequences (pp. 29–32). It will help your child learn if you arrange satisfactory (to him, that is) consequences of any behavior you want him to learn, and unsatisfactory consequences of behavior that you do not want him to learn or that you want him to unlearn. Further, these consequences (satisfactory or unsatisfactory, as the case may be) should *always* happen *at once*.

Let us suppose in the example of Hal and the coat that he wants to go play. If he hangs up his coat right away, he is free to go—a satisfactory consequence for desirable behavior. When he forgets, and starts off without doing it, you let him know that the coat has to be hung up before he is ready for play—an unsatisfactory consequence. If these consequences *always* happen *at once*, he will learn to hang it up. But if half the time you see that he meets this requirement and the other half you do not, he is not going to learn to hang it up consistently. Perhaps you do not really want him to. It may be easier to hang it up for him. Fine, if that is the way you want it. But then do not clutter up his life and yours with inconsistent instructions about coats. We are back to thinking about the importance of minimum requirements.

To sum up what has been said about guiding your child to think for himself in business activities: first, let him alone to see if he remembers what to do; then, if he needs reminding, act in such a way as to get him to figure out what needs doing; gear your requirements to his ability to meet them; finally, be consistent in what you expect of him.

Guiding your child to think for himself in play. When you suggest something to do, always make at least two suggestions and let him choose between them. Suppose your child is at loose ends. Rather than mentioning just one possibility for play, suggest at least two: "What would you like to do? There's your watering can. I'll fill it up if you want to sprinkle the sand, or here's a brush and cup if you want to paint with water, or there's a sheet you may use with your planks and boxes if you'd like. What are you going to do?" This is an important technique for encouraging your child to make decisions and to learn to take the initiative for finding something to do.

Let him alone to make an attempt to tackle a problem. Many times in his play, problem situations will come up for him. Use these to help him learn to think for himself. As a general rule, let him alone to tackle a problem by his own efforts, just as you let him alone in business activities to remember (or forget, as the case may be), before giving a reminder. If you leap in as soon as he comes up against a problem in his play, he does not have a chance to think for himself.

Suppose your child is working a puzzle, trying to put a piece in the wrong place. Why step in? Who is working the puzzle, anyway? Let him alone so that you will not rob him of the wonderful satisfaction which comes from solving a problem by oneself. I know a little boy named Henry, just 3 years and 3 months old, who was working on a puzzle. It was hard for him; he worked away for a long time trying to fit pieces into the wrong places before trying them somewhere else. But he did not become frustrated; he did not get tired. Finally he was done. I will never forget the satisfaction with which he exclaimed, not to the world at large, but almost to himself, "I did it! I did it! I did it! I did it! I did it! . . . I did it!" sixteen times in a row. I counted them.

This general principle "Let your child alone to make an attempt to tackle a problem" should not, of course, be carried too far. If you let him alone in situations too difficult for him to handle, he may not bother to try to solve problems, or he may develop a habit of becoming upset over them. If a situation is too difficult or too dangerous, it may be unwise to let him find out what he is up against. Otherwise, however, the general principle is sound.

Help your child figure out how to solve problems when help is needed. Here is an example of a child getting the help needed to solve a problem, instead of having the problem solved for her:

> *Three-year-old Belinda has climbed up onto a tall box. Now she wants to get down. She holds out her arms to a grownup, asking, "Help me down." Instead of lifting her at once, the grownup asks, "How could you get down?" Belinda just looks at her. Then, "If you turn around and go down backwards, I think you can manage." Belinda does, sliding onto her stomach, dangling her feet down*

against the vertical side of the box. Thus she reaches the ground. The grownup stands close by, but does not have to help.

If Belinda had not understood, the adult would have helped her get into the right position. Of course, if Belinda had been really frightened, the grownup would have lifted her down; what Belinda probably would have learned from this was to ask for help after climbing up. As it was, she went through the motions of helping herself—at least a first step toward learning to get down on her own.

Of course, when your child is tackling a problem, do not let him alone so long that he finally explodes with frustration. Help him before he reaches that point.

Here is an example of a child faced with a problem which he does not have the skill to solve:

Sammy, almost 4, combines high aims for his activity with rather poor motor coordination. He also gets upset easily in the face of frustration. He is trying to cut around a crayon drawing he has made, but his cutting skill is clearly not up to his aims. His face reddens; he is close to one of his frequent emotional upsets.

This is not an easy situation for guidance. Suppose Mrs. A says, "That's too hard, Sammy. You'd better find something else to do," and Sammy follows her suggestion. What he will probably learn from this is that there is no use trying to cut crayon drawings. In this event, though the frustrating situation has ended, so has opportunity for Sammy to practice the very motor skills which need improvement. Or suppose she says, "That *is* hard, Sammy. Let me do it for you." Obviously what Sammy will learn from this is to get grownups to do things for him when he has trouble. And he will not be beginning to harmonize his aims with his abilities to accomplish them. What Mrs. A actually does is this:

She says, "That drawing is too hard to cut, Sammy, because the wiggly lines are very hard to follow with your scissors. If you'd like to cut, how about trying an easier one?" Quickly, she draws a simple shape, quite within his capabilities, and hands it to him. Sammy does choose to cut it out. Even this is not easy, but he is clearly pleased with the product and pastes it on a piece of colored paper.

In this case, when Sammy was faced with an obstacle which he could not overcome, Mrs. A decreased its difficulty; she suggested a substitute he could cope with, as much like what he was trying to do originally as she could make it.

Another example of this same technique would be the substitution of an easier puzzle for one which is too difficult.

You will notice the way Mrs. A talked to Sammy in offering him a substitute activity. She left it up to him whether or not to take the suggestion: "If you'd like to cut, how about trying an easier one?" She was not dictating to him. This was play, not business, and Mrs. A respected Sammy's freedom to choose his activity. Similarly, in suggesting an easier puzzle for one beyond a child's abilities, she would say, as she produced the easier substitute, "That *is* too hard. If you'd like to work a puzzle, here is one that is not so hard." But before saying this, she would have watched the child to make sure that it really was too difficult. And even so, whether she would just let him lose interest and abandon the puzzle on his own, or whether she would make the suggestion indicated, would depend upon what she thought was best for that child in those circumstances. For instance, if a child were going through a phase of antagonism to grownup suggestion, she might let him alone for a while to struggle in vain and become upset; then her comfort and suggestion might be welcome, whereas if offered earlier it would merely be an annoyance.

SUMMARY: GUIDANCE TECHNIQUES FOR CHILDREN OF ANY AGE

I have suggested so many techniques for guiding your child that you may feel surrounded by a positive forest of techniques. One by one, perhaps they make sense, but in the aggregate they seem rather bewildering; there are so many of them! Yet actually, they are only common sense, the putting into practice of points of view already discussed in this book. Also, the order in which techniques have been considered was not just higgledy-piggledy. They involve the *manner* in which you do things (for example, Slow Down, Relax; Gain Your Child's Attention Before Speaking to Him; Talk Quietly; Sound Definite); the *timing* of what you do (for example, Say Things Just Once, or Let Your Child Alone to See If He Remembers What To Do); what you say (Tell Your Child What to Do . . . Say Things Positively; "Keep Busy," Not "Hurry Up," for example). It may help you to translate them into your own patterns of thought and action to sort them out in this way. As you use these techniques, you will find that what are listed as separate points are, in actuality, related ways of thinking and acting that follow one another in logical sequence when you are dealing with your child. I shall list them again, in the order in which I discussed them:

Slow down; relax

Wait to tell your child what to do until it is really necessary

Gain your child's attention before speaking to him

Talk quietly

Sound definite

Tell your child what to do instead of what not to do—that is, say things positively

Say things just once

Have one person at a time tell your child what to do

Do one thing at a time

When you have to change what your child is doing, suggest how he may do what he wants in an acceptable way

Speak in such a way that your child can understand when you expect him to do something and when it is a matter of choice

Phrase requirements impersonally

Show by the way you talk what is your child's responsibility

Save thanks for situations which deserve it

Let your child know when he has achieved something

Phrase approval in terms of behavior

Reserve disapproval for behavior that merits it

Phrase disapproval in terms of behavior

Keep disapproval tied to the behavior which deserves it

"Keep busy," not "hurry up"

Show the reasons for granting requests

When you give your child attention, give your full attention; when you want time to yourself, make this clear and stick to it

Keep from talking about your child where he can hear you if your words are not meant for him

Guide your child so that he learns to think for himself and to solve problems

>Guiding him to think for himself in business activities

>>Let him alone to see if he remembers what to do

>>Act in such a way that you get him to figure out what needs doing

>>Gear requirements to your child's ability to meet them

>>Be consistent in what you expect

>Guiding your child to think for himself in play

>>When you suggest something to do, always make at least two suggestions and let him choose between them

>>Let him alone to make an attempt to tackle a problem

>>Help your child figure out how to solve problems when help is needed

If you think these techniques make sense, why don't you try them? But do not expect magic. In the first place, if you have been doing things differently, it will not be easy to learn new habits. Your first step in learning will probably be to think of the new way of doing things just after habitually acting in the old way. That is all right. That is how people learn. Keep on thinking about the new techniques; eventually you will learn to apply them before you act. Do not try to learn all these techniques at once. Deal with a few at a time until you incorporate them into your daily life, then work on some more. But after all of them have become habitual ways of thinking and acting, you still cannot suspend thinking about how to guide your child. He is too important and changes too frequently to lend himself to a rubber-stamp set of techniques. This brings me to my next point, that in addition to these techniques, which are suitable for all ages, you will need other techniques that are appropriate at particular stages of development.

6

Supplementary Guidance Techniques for Particular Stages of Development

THE GUIDANCE TECHNIQUES I am now going to describe do not stand by themselves. They must go hand in hand with those discussed in the last chapter. These are simply supplementary techniques to use as your child is ready for them. I do not mean to imply, as I move from one age to another, that you are to discard techniques effective at younger age levels as your child matures, unless I specifically say so. But as he grows older, you will, of course, adapt to his level of maturity the techniques which retain their usefulness. Take the matter of talking sparingly, for example, especially when it is time for business. For an easily distractible 2-year-old, this means paring your conversation down to a bare minimum when you want him to get a job done. By the time your child is 4, he may be learning to combine business with conversation. As always, you need to tailor what you do to his needs.

But remember, too, that a child's progress toward maturity is uneven, whether reckoned during the course of one day or over longer periods. The fact that a child has reached a particular age, say 4, is no reason why he should always act like a 4-year-old. When he does not, his parents may be cross or disappointed, or think that it reflects on his intelligence. It does not. Being told that he is acting like a baby will probably only accentuate his feelings, even though he may try to hide them if he is made to feel ashamed. When your child does revert to behavior more characteristic of younger stages, you need, of course, to try to seek the causes and to remedy them if you can. As we all know, there are many circumstances which may contribute to immature behavior—fatigue, illness, emotional upset, desire for attention, to name a few of the most common ones. As always, even as you are trying to figure out your child's motivation, you will be having to deal with him, and so to decide what seem the best techniques to use. In short, this is another reminder that the techniques suggested for so-called "stages of development" may well be effective at different ages.

Some of the techniques mentioned here for particular stages of development have already been suggested as useful for children in general. I repeat them because of their particular applicability to the developmental level under discussion.

Supplementary guidance techniques for 2-year-olds

SUIT YOUR TECHNIQUES TO WHAT YOUR 2-YEAR-OLD IS LIKE

The 2-year-old is still very much of a baby in quite a lot of ways. Sometimes it is easy to forget this, to think of him as a kind of inefficient, clumsy 4-year-old in the making, who needs to come up to standard. Sometimes, on the other hand, parents keep on thinking of their 2-year-old as a baby to such an extent that they do not give him a chance to begin growing up. Usually, however, parents' attitudes toward him have changed a great deal since babyhood. One mother's remark I mentioned in the Introduction illustrates this: "For a long time, when a baby or a toddler does something we don't like, we think it's our fault. But the time comes when we think it's his fault." Most parents feel this pretty often by the time their child is 2.

You need to be careful not to put too much pressure on a 2-year-old. But you also need to help him learn to get on in a world where other people have rights and where there are approved ways of doing things. Do not stimulate him too much at this time in his life when he is already being greatly stimulated by what goes on around him, when he is developing at a colossal rate. I stress this because a lot of interested parents tend to bombard small children with too many stimuli. Listen to what sometimes happens to a 2-year-old on a walk. "Oh, look at the bird. There, way up in the tree. See? See it? Look, there it is. Oh, now it's flown away. See the big dog. There's a truck. What a big one it is! I hear something. What do you suppose it is? See that flower, over there? There's a feather if you'd like it." And so on. If you are on an outing with your child at this age, let him sometimes be the first one to see something, even though he misses out on something else in the process. If he is happily busy picking up stones, what if a big truck does go by? There are other big trucks in the world. He will see them again. Now, of course, there is such a thing as not stimulating a child enough. Perhaps you have a placid child who keeps on so contentedly with what he is doing that he misses out on much that would give him pleasure and needed stimulation. Then, by all means, go ahead and tell him about the truck that you see coming. This is just another reminder that, as you apply what I say here, you must take into account the particular person your child is.

You may remember that one of the techniques advised for helping any child think for himself in play is that when you suggest something to do you should always make at least two suggestions and let him choose between them. In using this technique with your 2-year-old, he will probably profit from being presented with no more than two play possibilities to choose between at a time. If neither has appeal, then suggest another pair. Facing a small child with too many possibilities for decisions can be confusing—and an overrich diet of decisions-to-be-made can contribute to feelings of insecurity.

In guiding your 2-year-old, you particularly need to bear in mind the hither-thither pattern of his behavior. Remember, for instance, when you walk to the corner that every stick and stone and fluttering leaf may beckon to him. Does this mean that you always let him spend endless time meandering around when you are in a hurry? Of course not. But it does mean you should give him a chance in his daily life to do the meandering and investigating that his spirit tells him to, when you are not in a hurry and where you will not have to keep telling him what to do. On the other hand, if you really need to get to the corner in a hurry and have to take him along, you will probably carry him. But if you have time on the way back, let him go at his own pace.

You can help him not to be distracted when you have a set plan for him by clearing the decks of distractions, as far as this is practicable and convenient. When, for instance, you want him to sit on the toilet for a few moments, do not leave the new book, which is much too large to be held, lying on the floor in the bathroom; keep it out of sight. This is just an example, of course, of arranging his surroundings to encourage behavior you would like.

In describing the typical 2-year-old, I said earlier, "He wants what he wants when he wants it." When he has to postpone doing or getting something he wants and lets out a wail of disappointment or anger, remember that from his point of view he is not just postponing it for a moment. He is being deprived of what he wants in the here and now—the time he lives in. Between 2 and 3 he will learn that sometimes the way to get what he wants is to do something else first, but he needs consistent, understanding guidance if he is to accomplish this with a minimum of frustration.

And because his time is in the here and now, think twice before you tell him not to do something because something else is going to happen in just a moment. Suppose a 2-year-old brings a book into a room where a grownup is occupied, disappears, and returns with another. Then off he starts again. If he is about to go on a family expedition, it may seem sensible to remark, "Johnny, you'd better leave your books in your room because we're all going outdoors pretty soon." But "soon" for you is a long time for Johnny. He probably has plenty of time to fetch his books; it will take only a moment to help him put them back when you are actually ready to go.

In guiding a 2-year-old, remember the so-called "negativistic" stage which may come along between 2 and 3. Why does it come? A large part of the answer lies in the strong drive for independence which children in our culture tend to have at this time. Of course, it is not operating constantly. Sometimes they are glad to be dependent, but many children are dealt with in such a way that they may feel they have to fight for independence. Think of the barrage of noes which many a 2-year-old comes up against. Think of the way many grownups react to the 2-year-old's hither-thither pattern of attention. Grownups usually want to accomplish something by moving ahead in a straight line and having their child come right along with them. Yet left to his own devices the 2-year-old charts a zigzag course—as he attends first to one thing, then another. If this irritates the grownups in his life, he may respond by feeling negative. Then there is the matter of hurrying. If you are always after a 2-year-old to hurry up, you can easily make him balk in protest, because he is just not geared to hurry. Conversely, if you cater too much to what a 2-year-old wants instead of what he needs, you can turn him into a tyrant whose demands are, in part, an expression of contrary feelings. In short, remember that the best way to start off thinking about guidance techniques is to try to imagine what it feels like to be the child concerned.

WHENEVER POSSIBLE HAVE AN ATTITUDE OF "YES, IF YOU'D LIKE"—AND LET HIM KNOW YOU HAVE IT

Suppose your 2-year-old is going down a walk and points to a deep drift of snow. "Da?" ("There?") he asks. You know it will probably be hard for him to walk in the drift. You may be inclined to say, "It's too hard to walk there. No, stay on the sidewalk." Instead, let him try it. Perhaps you say, "Yes, if you'd like," or "All right. But it's hard to walk because the snow is deep." He tries, falls down, but wants to keep on. Then let him. But if he becomes increasingly frustrated because he cannot cope with the deep snow, then he is faced with the kind of insurmountable obstacle I talked of in the last chapter (pp. 138–39). You may need to end his struggle by lifting him out of the snow and saying, "That's just too hard. I'll help you find some snow that's not so deep" (if that is possible). Otherwise, it will just have to end with "That's too hard. The sidewalk's a better place to be."

I have seen a 2-year-old who had been showing signs of negativism reflect the laissez-faire attitude which his parents were creating with their yes-if-you'd-likes and all-rights by chanting happily to himself as he walked along, apropos of no immediate remark, "All right, all right, all right, all right, all right." It was music to the ears of grownups who had been hearing "No."

TALK SIMPLY, SLOWLY, AND DISTINCTLY

There are several reasons for this. A flood of conversation flows over a 2-year-old like a river; he simply will not heed you if you talk too much. At least, this is often the result. Sometimes he reacts by becoming an overstimulated little chatterbox, who is so busy talking that he does nothing else. Another reason is that it helps him in his language development to hear distinct, slow speech made up of key words and simple phrases which he can incorporate into his own speech.

It is no coincidence, in my opinion, that most of the children I have known who were slow in language development were exposed frequently to a grownup whose characteristic speech consisted of a positive torrent of rapid sentences, flowing together with scarcely a pause for breath, often indistinctly pronounced, with little emphasis on key words. At nursery school, in talking to children who are behind in language development, our staff members make a practice of using the kind of brief, slow, distinct speech I have been advising, gearing its complexity to gains in the child's speech. The language skill of children who have been dealt with in this way has shown decided improvement during the nursery-school year.

TALK SPARINGLY, ESPECIALLY WHEN IT IS TIME FOR BUSINESS

This does not mean that you should never have a nice conversational time with your 2-year-old. But he usually cannot talk and do something else at the same time. When he is having a chance to investigate something on his own, when he is playing interestedly in his own way, or when you want him to carry out an activity, keep your conversation sparse.

Here is a record of a grownup who did just the opposite of this. She is helping a 21-month-old child pick up his room, or rather, "he is helping her," from the way she describes it. He is having a happy time, but the atmosphere which she creates is one of playing together, not getting a job done. Also, the way she talks is likely to give Johnny the impression that he is doing her a favor to tidy up. But the main drawback to her technique is that once his room is tidied up, he tends to keep on with the conversational flow and spends all his time talking to Mrs. Chat; he has lost interest in outdoor play.

In this record, the phrases the grownup uses are simple, but how many of them there are! As it starts, she has just arrived in his room and has pointed to things on the floor.

MRS. CHAT: *Pick them up. Wouldn't that be a good idea?* (*She starts putting things away.*)

JOHNNY: *Man. Yady* (*Lady*). (*People he has seen recently.*)

MRS. CHAT: *Uh-huh.*

JOHNNY: *Man. Yady.*

MRS. CHAT: *How about giving me a hand here? Help Chatty here. Give some help to Chatty.*

JOHNNY: *Man. Yady. Man. Yady.*

MRS. CHAT (*sings*): *Ha ha ha.*

JOHNNY: *Coa?* (*Coat?*) *Mitt?* (*Mittens?*) (*He is thinking about what comes next.*)

MRS. CHAT: *Uh-huh.*

(*Johnny picks up a block.*)

MRS. CHAT: *Thank you.*

(*He picks up another.*)

MRS. CHAT: *That's fine.*

(*He picks up another.*)

MRS. CHAT: *Thank you. Get those over there for Chatty.*

(*He gets one.*)

MRS. CHAT: *Thank you.*

(*He gets another.*)

MRS. CHAT: *Thank you.*

JOHNNY: Em more (Some more).

MRS. CHAT: *That's it. Get some more. (She keeps working away busily.)*

(Johnny stumbles momentarily.)

MRS. CHAT: *Up-si-daisy.*

JOHNNY: More, more, more, more.

MRS. CHAT (laughingly): *All right.*

JOHNNY: *Joke.*

MRS. CHAT: *Get a block for Chatty.*

JOHNNY: Hi.

MRS. CHAT: *Hi, Johnny Smith.*

JOHNNY: Hi.

MRS. CHAT: *Hello.*

JOHNNY: Da all *(That's all).*

MRS. CHAT: *Oh no, there's some more.*

JOHNNY: Em more. *(He pauses.)* Man. Yady. Man. *(He laughs.)* Hi. More. More. More.

MRS. CHAT: Uh-huh.

JOHNNY: Hi.

MRS. CHAT: *Hello.*

MRS. CHAT (as Johnny starts to walk into a shelf): *Watch out.*

JOHNNY: Yady.

MRS. CHAT: *That's right.*

JOHNNY: Yady. Man. Em more.

MRS. CHAT: *Now then, going to change Johnny's pants. (Actually, she is going to put him into dry diapers. Since a child can help in this only by lying still, this is an appropriate time for conversation and songs.)*

JOHNNY: Pants. Change pants.

MRS. CHAT: *Hey.*

(Johnny laughs.)

MRS. CHAT: *Hey.*

(Johnny laughs again.)

JOHNNY: Sam. Sam. Sam. *(Sam is a gardener who comes to work twice a week.)*

MRS. CHAT: *He won't be here today. We're having fun, aren't we? Oh, we're having fun, you and I.* (*She picks him up and raises him, then lowers him a little.*) *Up-down.* (*She lowers him a little more.*) *Down.*

JOHNNY: *Sam.*

MRS. CHAT: *Whee.* (*She raises him up high again for a moment, then lays him down on his back on a bureau and starts changing him.*) *Up-down. How are you? Are you fine? Hello. Ha ha ha.* (*Sings.*) *Ha ha ha. Hee hee hee. Johnny Smith, how I love thee.*

JOHNNY: *Ha ha ha.*

(*Mrs. Chat sings the song again, then laughs.*)

JOHNNY: *Ha ha.*

MRS. CHAT: *Ha ha ha. You and me.* (*She laughs.*)

(*Johnny laughs.*)

(*She gives a make-believe laugh.*)

MRS. CHAT: *Peekaboo.*

(*Johnny laughs, then laughs again.*)

MRS. CHAT: *Here we are. Peekaboo.* (*Conversation missed.*) *See you. Peek. There he is. There he is. Peekaboo. Way up. Way down. Up. Down.* (*She has finished changing his diapers and has just lifted him down to the floor.*)

JOHNNY: *Peek. Peek. Sam. Sam. Johnny. Johnny Smith. Johnny. Ha ha ha. Man. Yady. Man. Yady. Car. Car.*

MRS. CHAT: *Peekboo. Peekboo.*

JOHNNY: *Peek.*

MRS. CHAT: *Peekboo.*

JOHNNY: *Come.*

MRS. CHAT: *Just a moment.*

JOHNNY: *Da? (That?) Da? Da?*

MRS. CHAT: *Uh-huh.*

MRS. CHAT: *Now shall we come: Peekboo. Peekboo. Peekboo.*

JOHNNY: *Peek. Peek.* (*He starts down the hall.*)

MRS. CHAT: *No, we don't have to go in Chatty's room today. Let's go down this way.*

JOHNNY: *Tick-tick.*

MRS. CHAT: *We don't have to go down into Chatty's room today. Chatty has her tick-tick.*

(*They both start downstairs.*)

MRS. CHAT: *Let's not play on the stairs. That is right. Just come downstairs.*

JOHNNY: *Ha ha ha. Peekboo.*

MRS. CHAT: *Wait till you're downstairs.*

MRS. CHAT: *Now, peekaboo. Where's your boots?* (*He starts to pick up some others.*)

MRS. CHAT: *No, those are Mommy's boots. What would Mommy do when she needed her boots?*

JOHNNY: *Mommy.*

MRS. CHAT: *Not Mommy's boots, Johnny's boots.*

(*He gets his.*)

MRS. CHAT: *That's a good fellow.*

JOHNNY: *Ay boy (Attaboy). Mitt?*

MRS. CHAT: *Yes, Chatty has your mittens and your coat and your hat.*

JOHNNY: *Coa.*

(*They carry them away to put them on.*)

Johnny's mother, concerned over his lack of interest in outdoor play, decided to be the one to help him tidy up his room and put his outdoor clothes on before he went outside under Mrs. Chat's supervision. Since his mother was acquainted with the point of view I have been describing, she used techniques which would encourage Johnny to feel that tidying up his room was his job and that he should get the job done with dispatch. Here is a record taken while she was helping Johnny, just five weeks after the earlier record with Mrs. Chat. When she came into the room, Johnny was standing at a table, looking at a book.

JOHNNY: *Da. Da (There. There).* (*He puts his finger on objects in the picture.*) *Out?* (*Meaning, is he going outdoors now.*)

MRS. SMITH: *I'm going to help you put things away.*

(*Johnny still looks at the book.*)

MRS. SMITH (pointing to a new arrangement of shapes slipped onto a pole not previously used for this purpose): That's an interesting thing to have made. We'll put it up for a decoration.

JOHNNY (looking at it, then at a page torn out of a book lying on the floor): Too bad. Too bad.

MRS. SMITH: It is too bad it got torn. (She hands him a box in which are kept one of the four kinds of blocks that are spread about on the floor. He begins collecting that particular kind at once, putting them in the box. Mrs. Smith also puts things away. Johnny has picked up all the blocks of this type in sight. He leans way over and reaches under the bureau.)

JOHNNY: Reach.

MRS. SMITH: There, you got all of those. Now what?

(Johnny just stands and looks out the window.)

MRS. SMITH: I'll help you get started over here. (She picks him up, puts him down by another group of blocks and places their box by them.)

JOHNNY: Box.

MRS. SMITH: I'll help you get started. (She puts a few blocks in the box.)

(The first thing Johnny picks up is a car which belongs on the shelf.)

JOHNNY: Da? (That?)

MRS. SMITH: Well, where does it go?

(Johnny takes it over to the shelf, pleased with himself.)

JOHNNY: Ay boy (Attaboy).

MRS. SMITH: Yes, that's where it goes.

(A noisy airplane goes by outside. It just happens that this morning there is more air activity than usual, though plane traffic is often heavy.)

JOHNNY: Plane? Plane?

MRS. SMITH: Yes, it is a plane.

(Johnny returns to the blocks, picks up a transparent one with an animal fastened inside it.)

JOHNNY: Da? Da?

MRS. SMITH: Well, what is that? Do you know?

JOHNNY: Da? Da?

MRS. SMITH: *That's an elephant. (He puts it in the appropriate box.) How about those over there? (Johnny puts some more blocks in their box. Another plane is heard in the distance, its sound fading out. Johnny runs to the window. There is nothing to see. Mrs. Smith picks him up and puts him down beside the remaining toys.) Can you see anything else? (Johnny finds a small truck and puts it on the shelf. Everything now seems to be put away. But under the shelves he spies a "sailor-boy peg boat" which is sometimes kept on a high shelf.)*

JOHNNY: *Peg boat up? Peg boat up? (He picks it up and carries it toward the high shelf.)*

MRS. SMITH: *You can have it up there if you'd like.*

JOHNNY *(handing it to her)*: *Peg boat. Peg boat. (Another plane goes by, closer this time.)*

JOHNNY: *Plane. Plane. Walk around. Walk around.*

MRS. SMITH: *Walk around after dry pants.*

JOHNNY: *Toidy? (Toilet?)*

MRS. SMITH: *Do you need the toidy?*

JOHNNY: *Change pants. (Then, in a speaking voice) Baa baa black sheep.*

MRS. SMITH: *Would you like to sing that song? (She sings it all the way through, as she picks him up, then lays him down and starts changing him.)*

(Johnny says something indistinguishable.)

MRS. SMITH: *What do you mean?*

(Johnny repeats it.)

MRS. SMITH: *I don't know what you mean.*

JOHNNY *(as a noise is heard)*: *Train?*

MRS. SMITH: *I think that's another airplane.*

JOHNNY: *Airplane. (He gurgles, a pleased sound.) See it?*

MRS. SMITH: *You can't see it from the window (meaning it does not come into view there). You can see planes when you go out, can't you?*

(The noise grows louder.)

JOHNNY: *Big plane?*

MRS. SMITH: *Sounds like a big one.*

JOHNNY: *Big plane?* (*He marks in his hand.*) *Mark it with J.*

MRS. SMITH: *Mark it with J and toss it in the oven for Johnny today.*

JOHNNY: *Plane come?*

MRS. SMITH: *I don't know.*

JOHNNY: *Plane go?* (*Sings the first line of "Baa baa black sheep." Mrs. Smith sings along with him, and then finishes the song herself.*)

(*His diapers are now changed.*)

MRS. SMITH: *All right. Downstairs now.*

JOHNNY: *Walk around now?* (*He starts toward the stairs at once.*) *Daddy car? Daddy car? Daddy car?*

MRS. SMITH: *No, Daddy's working now.*

JOHNNY: *Daddy. Mitts now? Mitts?*

MRS. SMITH: *Yes.*

(*Johnny reaches the stairs and goes down at once. He reaches the bottom.*)

JOHNNY: *Mommy working now?*

MRS. SMITH: *Mommy's going to work again.*

JOHNNY: *Boots? Boots?*

MRS. SMITH: *Yes, sir, uh-huh.* (*Johnny collects them. She collects his other clothes.*)

MRS. SMITH: *That's everything.*

JOHNNY: *Boots? Mitts now?*

MRS. SMITH: *They're all here.*

JOHNNY: *Chatty?*

MRS. SMITH: *Yes, Chatty's going to help you put them on.*

Notice that in her desire to cut down conversation, Mrs. Smith several times effectively substituted actions for words. When she handed Johnny a box for blocks without saying anything, he started putting them away at once. Twice, as he stood at the window after hearing airplanes, she picked him up and placed him beside things to be put away, saying the first time, "I'll help you get started over here," saying the second, "Can you see anything else?" Here again,

Johnny got on with his business pretty well, even though he was distracted by the sounds of airplanes.

He even seemed interested in doing a thorough job, for he reached under the bureau for blocks after he had put away all those of a particular kind in sight. And when he put a car on the shelf, he was pleased with himself: "Ay boy," he said.

You probably noted that, except for Mrs. Smith's remark about Johnny's interesting and unusual (for him) construction when she first arrived, it was Johnny who initiated all conversation and singing in this business event of the day.

Note, too, that when it was time to go downstairs, Johnny went at once without playing en route.

Mrs. Smith reported that this kind of tidying-up procedure over a period of a month's time showed definite results in Johnny's finding things he was interested in doing outdoors, instead of constant chatter with the grownup.

TALK CONFIDENTLY

As you talk to your 2-year-old simply and slowly, sound relaxed. But, at the same time, sound as if you take it as a matter of course that he will do what you say. If you say, "We're going outdoors. Coat goes on now" as though it were a question, he is likely to react to the implied uncertainty, perhaps by dashing into the living room and starting to look at a magazine.

ASSUME THROUGH YOUR ACTIONS THAT HE
WILL DO WHAT YOU SAY, EVEN THOUGH
HE MAKES AN INITIAL PROTEST

Suppose after you announce, "We're going outdoors. Coat goes on now," your child says "No" and stands in the hall. Instead of launching into an "Oh yes. Why we always go outside now," I suggest that you reach for his coat, or, better still, if it is where he can reach it, ask, "Where's your coat?" Treat his "No" as if it were a yes. Just go forward confidently with what you have planned.

FOLLOW UP WHAT YOU SAY WITH ACTION
IF YOUR CHILD DOES NOT RESPOND

I do not mean anything forceful by this. As a matter of fact, unless you are casual and relaxed you will lend drama to his refusal or failure to respond—drama which is likely to motivate him not to do what you tell him. Suppose you have just said, as your child reaches the top of the stairs, "Wash hands for dinner now." (Of course, if he is at the stage where the mere mention of dinner makes him want it at once, then you will not mention it until he is all ready for it.) Instead of following directions, he starts into his room. Take his hand in yours, yours being a friendly, relaxed hand. In this connection, remember how short his arms are. Reach far enough down whenever you take your child's hand so that he is not being held with one arm high up in the air. Or suppose he has just washed and stands with dripping hands. "What next?" perhaps you say. If he does not respond, turn him toward his towel. Now, note, you are not pushing him about. You are giving him an initial steer in the right direction in order to cut down on your talk. If he does not like this steering —if, for instance, he shrugs when you do it—then either use gestures which do not involve touching him (for example, giving his towel a pat to call his attention to it), or fall back upon asking him what you said, as you would with an older child (p. 126). Getting him to take that first step gives him a chance to be thinking of washing as *his* business; it also gives him a chance to express some of his independence. But you will probably need to help him, once he takes the first step, if you want him to have really dry hands.

SUMMARY: SUPPLEMENTARY TECHNIQUES FOR 2-YEAR-OLDS

Here, by way of summary, are the main points discussed in this section:

Suit your techniques to what your 2-year-old is like

Whenever possible have an attitude of "yes, if you'd like"—and let him know you have it

Talk simply, slowly, and distinctly

Talk sparingly, especially when it is time for business

Talk confidently

Assume through your actions that he will do what you say, even though he makes an initial protest

Follow up what you say with action if your child does not respond

I hope this discussion of supplementary techniques to be used in guiding a 2-year-old has conveyed the basic idea that what you are trying to do is to make life interesting and satisfying for him; to bring about a relaxed atmosphere in a setting planned to meet his needs, where life has a consistent pattern adapted to these needs. He is developing important attitudes; the way you act and talk is extremely influential in their formation. This is no time for a "Life is real, life is earnest" approach to your child. Nevertheless, you need to say what you mean—in a way understandable to a 2-year-old —and mean what you say. You need to keep your patience, a large supply of it, and your sense of humor.

Supplementary techniques for the child who is feeling negativistic

SOME BASIC CONSIDERATIONS

I have already discussed some of the possible reasons for the "negativistic" phase which many children in our culture go through sometime between the second and third birthday, characteristically near 2½ (pp. 145–46). Sometimes it comes later, when a child is 3 or 4, or even later than that. If the guidance principles and techniques already described are used, they can go a long way toward preventing the development of a ripsnorting negativistic phase. But however skillful and understanding your guidance, you will have at least some refusals and protests to deal with, and if you have not been taking any preventive measures, you may already have a full-fledged case of negativism on your hands. Therefore, it seems worthwhile to put together here some techniques for dealing with negativism. A number of them repeat what has been said earlier. Obviously, guidance which is useful in keeping negativistic feelings at a minimum is also likely to be helpful in dealing with these feelings once they have occurred.

Try to find out why your child feels the way he does; take his whole life into account. Though you may be getting tired of this refrain, I keep repeating it because it is the first step in effective guidance. Once again, try to think yourself into your child's shoes to get a picture of the satisfactions and dissatisfactions he is experiencing in being the person he is in your family. When a child feels at odds with the world, you included, he is often having a pretty thin time of it. Effective guidance may thus lie mainly in trying to stress more satisfactions in his life so as to sweeten his whole outlook. You need, of course, if your child is feeling negativistic, to focus particularly on all the probable causes for his contrary behavior, too.

Try to figure out the factors that contribute to your child's feelings of refusal and protest. Is he feeling well? (It is always wise to explore the possibility of physical causation. If you think your child is under par, consult your doctor.) Is he getting adequate sleep and rest? If his balkiness seems associated with a particular time of day —late morning or late afternoon, for example—this may be a clue that he is tired or hungry. Does he have plenty of opportunity to express his developing independence? Is he hearing instructions and prohibitions all the time? Is he feeling a need for more attention and making a bid for it through negativistic behavior? Is he bored? Does he get satisfaction from the drama of refusal? Is he being frequently interrupted or thwarted in what he wants to do by another child, or by an adult, even though well intentioned? Is he being teased? These are just a few of the questions to ask in trying to think through the factors contributing to his contrary feelings.

How you deal with your child depends upon his motivation. As always, how you deal with your child depends upon what you take to be his motivation. Therefore, select from the techniques I am going to describe those which seem most relevant.

I have arranged my suggestions under three headings in order of increasing negativism: Techniques for a Child Who Is Showing Signs of Negativism; Techniques Useful When Your Child Has

Formed a Habit of Protest in a Particular Situation; Techniques to Use When Your Child Is in the Process of Protesting.

TECHNIQUES FOR A CHILD WHO IS SHOWING
SIGNS OF NEGATIVISM

A number of the guidance techniques which follow are designed to create a permissive atmosphere and to give your child a chance to express his feelings and his growing independence. He needs to be encouraged to express his feelings in ways which do not take the form of a protest at requirements.

Reduce requirements to an absolute minimum. Even though you believe that your child's life already involves only minimum requirements, look at them again carefully if he is feeling negativistic. For this is a period in his life when it is particularly important that requirements are minimal. I do not mean that you should discard the fundamental pattern of his life, but see whether it is adapted to his present needs.

Suppose you have been keeping to a bedtime of six-thirty. Your child has taken to protesting loudly and crying for an hour before going to sleep. Perhaps he needs less sleep, and, therefore, should stay up longer. Of course, this is just one of many possibilities. On the other hand, suppose he has not had any particular bedtime; he has stayed up until he dropped in his tracks. Setting a time adjusted to his needs is a *necessary* requirement, which will make life easier for both of you.

Or suppose you have kept your child restricted to the grass in front of your house, although there is a vacant lot which lies beyond. This is probably an outgrowth of the days when he was unsteady in his walking. He wants to go into the vacant lot. Then how about letting him?

Be consistent. This is tremendously important for a child who is feeling negativistic. A consistent pattern for various events in the day is a great help, for then he knows what to expect and can learn the "ground rules" around home. If a young child's life is too changeable, that alone may make him feel resistant.

See that he has plenty of interesting things to do, including activities which help him let out his feelings. It is hard to overestimate the importance to a little child of the materials with which he plays. Remember that a 2- to 3-year-old needs lots of opportunity for gross motor play—things to lug around outdoors, a place to climb. Three- and 4-year-olds need plenty of chances for active play, too, and gain a great deal from companions of the same age. Mud is wonderful for a negativistic child to play with; so is clay, the wet, gooshy kind that he can slap and pound and squeeze.

Unless there is a real need for redirection, let your child play in his own way. This is important for any child, but especially for one who is feeling negativistic.

Make sure he is getting a full measure of your attention and companionship. Since your child may take to refusal and protest in order to get attention, it is important to make it unnecessary for him to resort to negativism to gain needed attention. Does he have opportunities to have fun with each of you, each of his parents? And do you sometimes really give him your full attention? Looking at books together, or singing him songs (the fact that you are doing it is what matters, not whether you happen to have a good singing voice), is a pleasant way for a child to have your attention; so are walks, and chances for some (not too) rough-and-tumble play, hopefully with Father.

Be on the lookout for other ways to have good times together. See, too, that you give your child merited praise for achievements.

Show in the way you talk that your attitude is one of minimum requirements. I have already stressed the importance of showing in the way you talk to 2-year-olds that your attitude is one of minimum requirements. This is as useful in trying to decrease contrary feelings as it is in trying to minimize their development. Remember that if your child asks to do something, it is a good idea to answer in terms of "All right" or "If you'd like" or "Yes, if you want to," for such replies create a permissive atmosphere and let your child know that a lot of things are up to him.

If you suggest something to him, be sure to make clear that it is optional. "You don't need to, but if you'd like, would you open the door for the milkman?"

If you change a procedure to which he is already accustomed, make it clear that it is provisional till you see how it works. For instance, if you change the requirement that your child stay on the grass in the front of your house, say something to this effect: "You have been staying just on the grass in front of the house, but let's see how it works if you play in the deeper grass beyond, if you'd like to." Then if the change does not work, going back to the old procedure will be consistent with what you have said.

Have one person at a time tell him what to do. I repeat this because of its importance in guiding a negativistic child.

Avoid rushing him. This is another technique already described for children in general which is also important in guiding a child who is feeling negativistic. But remember, even your 2-year-old needs to learn to do necessary jobs with dispatch. How to bring this about will be discussed in the section on specific business activities (pp. 255–61).

Time interruptions tactfully. This does not mean to pussyfoot around until you think your child is looking agreeable before telling him to do something. It does mean to take a good look at what he is doing before you interrupt him. Suppose you have come to take him to the toilet; he is almost through fitting some blocks into a little wagon. Then wait until all the blocks are in place.

Give him a chance to do things for himself until he feels a need for help. Sometimes a child will take to protesting when you come near him because he thinks you are going to swoop down and do something for him that he wants to do himself. To him it seems not that you are helping him, but that you are keeping him from doing what he wants. Therefore, let him try, even though you are convinced he will not succeed. You might say, as your child tries to buckle a sandal, "Barbara, tell me if you'd like some help." There is more to it than this, of course, since sometimes it is reasonable and necessary in the long run for a child to be willing to accept help, and he needs to learn this. This sort of drive for independence is likely to arise in business matters such as dressing, which still hold interest and are hard to do. Guidance designed to give your child a chance to help himself, but at the same time to get him to accept *necessary* help, will be discussed later (p. 257).

Give your child an opportunity to say "No" about pleasant things. This is a useful technique in dealing with a child who is in the habit of refusing. Here is an example:

Danny, singing with a group of children, is asked, "Danny, would you like to be a galloping pony?" (which we know he enjoys). Danny may automatically answer "No." Sometimes one can see a child discover that he has cut off his nose to spite his face. If he changes to a yes before another child has been offered the chance, he may have his turn; but if he is too slow, then he hears, "Teddy is going to be a pony now because you said no." There is no icy sweetness, nor any "Now see what you've done" in this explanation. Such an attitude would complicate a child's motivation; it might make him feel more negativistic. He will find out that "No" is sometimes not such a good idea, without your preaching about it.

Create the atmosphere that you take it for granted he will do what you tell him. Since you are deeply involved in how your child acts and feels, it is easy to be irritated when your child is balky. But if you counter his negativism with irritation, you are going to make him feel even more negativistic, although you may succeed in getting him to stop a particular kind of behavior at a particular time. I am not suggesting that you bottle up your feelings until you finally explode, probably over some trifle. If you feel a lot of irritation, express it, but leave your child out of the picture when you do so. How? You may smile at my next suggestion, for it will sound childish. Get away from your child where he cannot hear you; then, say what you feel. More than this, if you feel like giving him a thorough shaking or a sound spanking, do just this—not to him but to a pillow. You may reply, "How about just giving my child a good paddling? That *will* relieve my feelings, and probably make him more reasonable, too." You can guess my reaction to this from everything I have said earlier about relevant, consistent consequences. I agree that it would serve to vent your irritation, but in the long run it would not help your child.

The knowledge that your child is going through a phase common to children in our culture should help give you perspective about his refusals. If you become thoroughly interested in trying to see the world through his eyes, this, too, will help minimize your irritation. The less ruffled your feelings, the easier will it be for you to act as if you take it for granted that your child will do what you tell him.

So much for feelings on your part that would interfere with sound guidance. Now for techniques to create the atmosphere that you take it for granted your child will do what you tell him. They are applications of guidance already recommended for 2-year-olds in general.

Talk confidently. Even though your child is exasperatingly contrary, always have your voice sound as if you expect him to do what you say. Speak with confidence, definitely, firmly; keep your voice pleasant.

Assume through your actions that he will do what you say, even though he makes an initial protest. If he says "No," do not take it at face value. Carry on as if he has said "Yes." If he persists in refusal, what you do then is important not merely in terms of this particular situation, but in terms of how it affects the feelings that cause his negativistic behavior. Guidance when your child is in the process of refusing is discussed in the second section below.

SUMMARY: TECHNIQUES FOR A CHILD WHO IS SHOWING
SIGNS OF NEGATIVISM

Reduce requirements to an absolute minimum

Be consistent

See that he has plenty of interesting things to do, including activities which help him let out his feelings

Make sure he is getting a full measure of your attention and companionship

Show in the way you talk that your attitude is one of minimum requirements

Have one person at a time tell him what to do

Avoid rushing him

Time interruptions tactfully

Give him a chance to do things for himself until he feels a need for help

Give your child an opportunity to say "No" about pleasant things

Create the atmosphere that you take it for granted he will do what you tell him

TECHNIQUES USEFUL WHEN YOUR CHILD HAS
FORMED A HABIT OF PROTEST TO A
PARTICULAR SITUATION

Once again, the first thing to do is to take a good look at the situation to see whether it should be revised in the light of your child's present needs. Assuming this is not the case, but that he has formed a habit of protesting at a really necessary requirement, then the following techniques are often useful:

Get the activity under way tactfully. Here is an example. Your 2-year-old, who is about to have supper, is playing in the living room. It is time he washed his hands, which you have decided is a minimum requirement. But lately when you have said, "Johnny, come wash your hands now," he has sailed into a screaming, crying protest. So instead of mentioning washing, pick him up in a relaxed way and say, "I'm going to give you a ride."

By the time your child is about 3, other techniques are better for dealing with this habitual kind of protest. By then, because he is not as distractible as is a 2-year-old, he knows what you are about. To get an activity under way by distracting him from what is happening would amount to evasion when he is this old. He is capable of understanding that he has a deliberate choice in regard to how he acts; at this age he needs to find out that it is to his advantage to choose to do what is required of him. How to go about helping him learn this is discussed later in this chapter (p. 169, pp. 174–75).

Give your child a forewarning of the coming event about which he has protested. You cannot use this technique with most young 2-year-olds, for, typically, a young 2-year-old's time is so much in the here and now that either he does not really take in your announcement of a coming event or he thinks you are telling him to do it now. But by the time he is getting on toward 2½, he is probably ready for this technique. So give him a forewarning of a coming event—for example, "In just a little while I'm going to tell you it's time to get washed," perhaps adding, "so if you want to finish loading that truck, you need to do it now." This gives him a chance to come to a stopping place in his activity. Give only one forewarning. Follow it up with "Now it is time to . . ."

The length of time advisable between the forewarning and "Now it's time" depends upon your child's maturity and the complexity of his activity. A minute or two is enough for a 2-year-old. Considerably more time may be desirable for a 4-year-old busy with an elaborate block construction.

Suggest something positive for him to do in terminating an activity. This is another technique suited to a young 2-year-old. He is outdoors, clutching to his chest a piece of moss well supplied with a muddy foundation. It is time to go inside. "Johnny, where are you going to put your moss so you can have it when you come out again?" is a useful procedure. He will then get in the habit of finding a parking place for loved objects that are not to be transported indoors, instead of having a tantrum at separation from them.

Get him to listen to your explanation. An alternative to getting things tactfully under way with a younger child, this technique is useful at all preschool ages if a child has a habit of protesting. You judge from his past behavior that he will make a row when you tell him it is time to get washed. Then give your explanation to him before the row starts. Pick him up or get down on his level as you tell him, "Listen, so that you'll understand." It is very helpful in giving such an explanation to

Start by acknowledging that you know what he wants. Suppose he is in the living room looking at a book. If he is still small enough for you to do so easily, pick him up, complete with book, before you tell him, "Listen, so that you'll understand." Then, instead of beginning to talk about what he does not want to do, talk about what he wants. "You do want to keep on looking at the book, don't you? All right, that's just what you may do when you are through washing."

If he has a habit of refusal in a particular situation, change the situation. This is particularly useful when it appears that your child does not have any fundamentally deep negativistic feelings, but rather has developed a habit of protest which is cued by a particular situation. Suppose he leaves his milk untouched, although you are convinced he does not really dislike it. Then it may help to give it to him, without comment, in a new glass, say a bright red one. Or suppose when you spread his snowsuit out on the floor in the front hall, he has taken to letting out a bellow and running away. Putting it on in a different setting sometimes does the trick.

Talk over with him the situation he objects to, not when it is in the offing but some other time when he is feeling agreeable. This is emphatically not a technique for 2-year-olds. It would just amount to a lot of undesirable grownup chatter. But usually by the time a child is 3 it will be helpful. I am assuming, as I have all along, that what he objects to is something really necessary for him to do, that you are keeping requirements to a minimum. Let us suppose he protests when it is time to get dressed in the morning, but that he needs to dress promptly because you have other things you must do. Then, sometime when he is feeling agreeable, talk it over with him. Here is one tack you might take: "You know, it really is silly, fussing in the morning about getting dressed. You're very grownup about a lot of things. How about seeing if you can't manage without any fussing at all? What do you think will help, anyway?" Perhaps he will come up with an idea. Arousing *his* interest in remedying the situation is an enormous step forward. If he does not have a suggestion, you make one—perhaps "I'll spread out your clothes on your bed in the order you put them on," or "How about your bringing your clothes into our room to dress, if you can really keep busy in there?"

SUMMARY: TECHNIQUES USEFUL WHEN YOUR CHILD HAS FORMED A HABIT OF PROTEST TO A PARTICULAR SITUATION

Get the activity under way tactfully

Give your child a forewarning of the coming event about which he has protested

Suggest something positive for him to do in terminating an activity

Get him to listen to your explanation

Start by acknowledging that you know what he wants

If he has a habit of refusal in a particular situation, change the situation

Talk over with him the situation he objects to, not when it is in the offing but some other time when he is feeling agreeable

Lastly, here are

TECHNIQUES TO USE WHEN YOUR CHILD IS
IN THE PROCESS OF PROTESTING

Remember the importance of relevant, satisfactory consequences for desirable behavior and (for undesirable behavior) relevant, unsatisfactory consequences designed to motivate your child to behave in a desirable way. You are well aware, I know, that what you do in guiding your child depends upon your understanding of his motivation—your estimate of the feelings which prompt his behavior. Often the feelings which make him behave negativistically are unsatisfied needs. If he is making a bid for attention, for example, see that his protests are not a means of accomplishing it. Be on the lookout for ways to satisfy this need by giving attention for desirable behavior. He may be finding life rather dull and needs some added interests.

Meet the refusal in a relaxed way. I have already suggested the value of treating an initial "No" as if it were a yes. The protest may just evaporate. This technique is particularly useful before a child is nearing 3. When he is getting on toward 3, but is still full of re- fusals, meeting his protest in a relaxed way on a verbal level is often a good idea. Here is an example:

> Harry, 2 years and 10 months old, who is sitting at a table working on a puzzle, has just been told it is time to put his puzzle away and go outdoors. "No, I won't," he replies, and keeps sitting there. "All right," says Mrs. A in a relaxed way. She pulls his chair, with him in it, away from the table so that he cannot keep on using the puzzle, and says nothing for a moment. Then, "Wait as long as you like till you are ready." Within a quarter of a minute Harry puts the puzzle on the shelf and goes outdoors.

Have a good long pause between your agreeable "All right" and what you say next. Often a child will look taken aback at the "All right." He may have been hoping to create a stir.

Assist your child to carry out what you have told him. Suppose you have treated your young 2-year-old's "No" as if it were a yes, but he stands by his protest. Perhaps he is refusing to climb down from a teetering table. Then just lift him down, but in a relaxed way, not with sudden, tense movements which may convey irritation or lend drama and excitement to his refusal. Or suppose he is refusing to go upstairs. Then say, "I'll help you get started," and carry him over to the stairs. If he still just stands there, carry him up. Now it may be that halfway up he will protest, "Johnny walk up." That is fine. Use his desire to be independent to accomplish what you want. "All right, if you'd like, walk up yourself." But if he does not walk up with dispatch this time, pick him up again and carry him all the way, still relaxed. He has had his chance at independence in stair climbing. Do not give him another one on this trip up. (Incidentally, a good way to carry an already protesting child, who may want to kick, is to hold him like a sack of meal, with one of your arms around his middle as you rest him above your hip, his head projecting in front of you, his feet out behind.)

This kind of assistance may lead to the following technique, if your child likes to be independent: "Can you do (whatever it is) by yourself, or do you need some help?"

Show him the consequences of his behavior and let him choose what to do. You must be sure to wait to use this technique until your child is developmentally ready for it. I have just shown how assisting your child to carry out what you have told him may lead to his making a choice between doing something by himself or being helped to do it. In such cases you need to put before him relevant, significant consequences to choose between. All the considerations discussed in connection with finding such consequences to guide your child have bearing here.

I illustrated this technique a moment ago in the guidance of Harry. After the grownup's relaxed, "All right. Wait as long as you like till you are ready," he was free to choose to wait all morning if he wanted to. But he chose to do right away what had been requested. This was a sound technique with Harry because he was developmentally ready for it. A younger 2-year-old, even most 2½-year-olds, would not have been. A little 2-year-old might have a sad or mad time, because he thought you just were not letting him go outdoors. A negativistic 2½-year-old would be likely to hang on like grim death to the "wrong" choice.

Here are a few techniques that are useful when your child is actually yelling, crying, or expressing his protest in some other vigorous way:

Ignore his noisy protest when you can. Just let him yell or cry without doing anything about it when he first starts. This is particularly important when a child who has not yet shown signs of feeling negativistic first begins to protest. If you ignore his behavior, he will find out that protest is ineffective as a way of getting what he wants. If his protest makes you angry, it is a good idea to walk out of the room till you cool off. Otherwise, just carry on with whatever activity was in order.

When you cannot ignore it, refer to it as "noise." Though this may seem a very picayunish point, it really takes away some of the dignity of protest. Deglamorize protest whenever you can. "That's too much noise because little Pam is still asleep," you say as you move your yelling child to a less strategic spot for rousing the household.

When it is all right to "make noise," say so. Suppose some of the time it is highly undesirable if your child makes a lot of noise, so you have had to tell him to be quiet when he begins a noisy protest. But now suppose he starts yelling or crying at a time when it does no harm. Then say to him, "It's all right to make noise now because (for example) no one is asleep." There are two reasons for doing this: first, the obvious one, of minimum requirements; second, the fact that you may thereby remove his motive for yelling. Since he is feeling negativistic, he may well be making noise because he thinks he should not do so. When he knows it is all right, he may stop. You need to be relaxed about this and really mean "It's all right to make noise."

Shift his attention to something else. Be agreeable and friendly as you do this, but do not try to entertain your child out of his negativism by being especially jocular and amusing. To give him the feeling that you are standing on your head to get him to stop a protest makes his refusal worthwhile. A technique that sometimes works with a young 2-year-old who is making a protesting noise is to say, after you have let it run on for a moment or two, "That's one kind of noise. What's another kind? What kind of a noise does a pussy make?" He may be delighted to respond to this and other questions along these lines.

Or, with a 2- or 3- or 4-year-old who is protesting against a reasonable, customary requirement, introduce an interesting topic of conversation.

If crying or upset yelling still persist, then you will have to deal with them as you would with any other prolonged emotional outburst stemming from annoyance or anger (pp. 271–74).

SUMMARY: TECHNIQUES TO USE WHEN YOUR CHILD IS IN THE
PROCESS OF PROTESTING

Meet the refusal in a relaxed way

Assist your child to carry out what you have told him

*Show him the consequences of his behavior and let him choose
what to do*

Ignore his noisy protest when you can

When you cannot ignore it, refer to it as "noise"

When it is all right to "make noise," say so

Shift his attention to something else

Supplementary techniques for 3- and 4-year-olds

Remember to take your 3- or 4-year-old's whole life into account in
planning his guidance. This is still another reminder that guidance
should never be thought of exclusively in terms of techniques. Techniques are merely the on-the-surface reflection of fundamental considerations about your child which are basic to planning effective
guidance. Remember, too, how important it is to think yourself
into your child's shoes periodically, to appraise the satisfactions and
dissatisfactions he is experiencing in being the person he is in your
family.

TECHNIQUES FOR YOUR 3- OR 4-YEAR-OLD
ADAPTED FROM THOSE RECOMMENDED AT 2

As you will see, some of the techniques suggested for your 2-
year-old are just as useful when your child is 3 and 4. Others need
to be modified to suit his increased maturity.

*Whenever possible have an attitude of "Yes, if you'd like"—and let
him know you have it.* This is as good a way at 3 and 4 as it was at 2
to get across to your child your attitude of minimum requirements.

Remember that at these older ages, as well as at 2, your child is likely to feel the weight of prohibitions and instructions.

Suit the complexity of your speech to your child's language development; speak distinctly. If your child is slow in his language development, he will profit from hearing the simple, slow, distinct speech that is so advantageous at 2. In any case, suit the complexity of your speech to his language development and to his understanding, and remember that speech simple enough for him to incorporate will help him learn; so will hearing words pronounced distinctly, now and in the years ahead.

Talk sparingly, especially when it is time for business. This is still good advice. Your 3- or 4-year-old can easily become irritable and heedless of your remarks if you deluge him with directions. Also, if you fire conversation at him when it is time for business, he is likely to be sidetracked from performing the job.

Talk confidently. A 3- or 4-year-old is every bit as quick to pick up hesitation and indecision from tone of voice and manner as is a 2-year-old. Mean what you say and sound as if you mean it.

Assume through your actions that he will do what you say, even though he makes an initial protest. This is a good technique as long as it works effectively right away. However, if your child keeps on doing what he wants, contrary to instructions, you need to be ready to follow through right away with other techniques suited to your 3- and 4-year-old.

Follow up what you say with action if your child does not respond. In using this technique with a 3- and 4-year-old, sometimes you can apply it just as you did at 2, but see that you gradually replace it, as your child moves from 3 to 4, with other techniques designed to get him to think for himself. For 2-year-olds, my examples were: relaxedly taking hold of your child's hand and leading him where you told him to go (if he has started in the wrong direction); and getting him to think of the next step in washing by turning him toward his towel or giving it a pat. If your 3- or 4-year-old really does not know the next step in performing a job, this is still a useful technique. But if he has had consistent guidance, he should know by now what is involved in the business side of his life. Furthermore, he is not nearly as distractible as is a 2-year-old; he can pay attention if he wants to. Therefore, if you overdo this technique at 3 and 4, you will be doing your child's thinking for him. Instead, get him to think of what needs doing and to choose to do what is required.

However, the technique of substituting action for words can be very useful whenever your child is going through a period of seeming not to hear a word you say. But first, take a look to see whether his heedlessness may not be a protective device because you are talking too much—in the form of directions, advice, or even just conversation. In order to get him to attend to necessary directions, it sometimes pays to point to what needs doing, instead of talking. By cutting way down on speech in this and in other ways, you can often get your child to heed what you say. Then you can gradually go back to relying once again on spoken instructions.

So much for the adaptation of 2-year-old techniques to the greater maturity of your 3- or 4-year-old. Now I shall show how your child's strides in development are related to the way you deal with his refusals to do what is required.

DEALING WITH REFUSALS WHEN YOUR CHILD
IS 3 OR 4

If your 3- or 4-year-old is full of refusals, look in the sections on negativism for guidance suggestions. But in any case, even though no rash of refusals comes along at 3 or 4, from time to time your child is going to object to what you tell him and refuse to do what you say. Console yourself; otherwise, he might grow up to be a doormat. Like the 2-year-old, he needs to find that refusals do not bring him what he wants—avoidance of what should be done. But he needs more than this. He needs to learn to make a deliberate choice to do what is required.

Help your 3- or 4-year-old learn to make a deliberate choice to be willing to do what is required. When at 2, or 2½, your child refused to do what you told him, your techniques consisted chiefly in seeing that it got done promptly anyway. Treating his "No" as if it were yes is an example. Another is the "Can you manage by yourself or shall I help you?" choice that I recommended putting to a child at these earlier ages. If he is given such a choice, whichever alternative he takes leads to prompt compliance with what was required in the first place.

Quite different techniques should be used with an older child. Remember Harry's refusal to put his puzzle away and go outdoors, and Mrs. A's response (p. 168)? Her "All right. Wait as long as you like till you're ready" is a special application of showing your child the consequences of his behavior and letting him choose what to do. Here is another example with Harry, who is refusing in much the same way and being dealt with in an identical manner:

> Harry, sitting at a table fitting pegs into a board, throws one on the floor. When he is directed to pick it up, he refuses with a "No, I won't." Mrs. A's reply, "All right. Wait as long as you like till you are ready," produces a continuation of I-won'ts, but even in the process of saying them, he picks it up.

The alternatives offered to Harry are quite different from those open to a child when he has to choose between either accomplishing promptly by himself what is requested or doing it with grownup help. When you give your child the option of waiting, you must mean it. You have to be genuinely willing to wait yourself, since prompt compliance does not necessarily follow this technique.

Now there are many times in a household when such a procedure simply will not work because there is not time. In such circumstances, if your 3- or 4-year-old refuses to do as directed, you will have to carry through with the younger age-level techniques. But arrange family life so that an "All right. Wait as long as you like till you're ready" can sometimes be used with your 3- or 4-year-old. Such a technique is essential to his finding out that there are disadvantages to refusal and that the way to get what he wants is to be willing to perform necessary activities. If instead you keep on carrying through with what needs doing as you would have when he was younger, he may derive a good deal of undesirable satisfaction from this, particularly if his drive for independence is considerably lower than that of the hypothetical 2-year-old I have talked about.

Your child's readiness for the particular set of consequences involved in the "All right, wait as long as you like till you're ready" technique shows how much he has developed since typical 2- and 2½-year-old days. Remember, a typical 3-year-old is quite a reasonable person. As suggested earlier in the description of 3-year-olds in general, this is partly because he generally understands that one activity needs to come before another and is even a means of attaining the other. You can reason with a 3-year-old. You can put choices to him without having him try to take both alternatives at once or seize on the "wrong" one (as he might well do at 2½), or without having him misunderstand what is going on altogether (as he might at 2), in thinking you were just keeping him from doing what he wanted.

The technique I have been talking about here is one way of helping your child take an important step toward interdependent security, which will contribute to his well-being all his life: making decisions geared to his level of development and taking the consequences for them.

The Harry whom you have twice seen refusing to do as directed was developmentally ready for the "All right, wait . . ." technique. That it and the other measures taken with Harry were successful in guiding him is shown by the records we kept. He was a little boy full of refusals, both at home and in his early days at school. During his first eight weeks of school (when he was present 29½ days), there were twenty-three occasions on which Harry received consequences designed to get him to change his behavior. During the next eight weeks (when he was present 32 days), there were only two such episodes. As a result of using the kinds of techniques I have described, including four instances of "Wait as long as you like till you are ready," Harry chose to conform to minimum requirements. It is fair to say, on the basis of his behavior, that he found school highly enjoyable.   •

FIGURING OUT YOUR CHILD'S BEHAVIOR—
RECORDS HELP

You can see from the example of Harry how useful records are in figuring out a child's motives and in appraising the effectiveness of the guidance used. If you can find the time, keep records of your child's behavior and of how you guide him. You may want to limit your records to one particular kind of behavior about which you are especially concerned. Quite apart from serving as a record of how your child acted and what you did, I think that the mere act of putting things down on paper will ensure that you will think more carefully about what you are doing than you otherwise might. It is also likely to give you objectivity in viewing your child's behavior, and make you feel less emotionally involved.

A COMMENT ABOUT CHOOSING CONSEQUENCES
FOR YOUR 3- AND 4-YEAR-OLD'S BEHAVIOR:
SIGNIFICANT ALTERNATIVE CONSEQUENCES

Almost three-fifths of the situations requiring disciplinary consequences for Harry involved infringement of other children's rights. The adult-designed consequence which he most frequently experienced for this behavior was removal from the group. Removal was effective in getting Harry to choose to respect other children's rights, because he enjoyed playing with these other children. But lest either you or I slip into the false assumption that appeals to a child's desire to remain with other children are always effective with 3- and 4-year-olds, let me tell you of the experience of a friend of mine who directed a nursery school in an underprivileged neighborhood. Since the children who attended that school came from crowded homes, they loved to play by themselves and would deliberately misbehave in school to have a chance to play alone. Removal from the group was, therefore, completely ineffectual as a means of motivating them to play happily together with due regard for each other's rights, or to perform business activities with dispatch.

Remember, when you put alternative consequences to your

child they must be ones which he can understand, which have significance for him, and which will really happen. I know of one parent who offered the following alternatives to her child when he wanted to go outdoors on a cold day without his coat: "If you go out without your coat, you'll catch cold. If you put it on, you won't." He chose to go out without the coat—and he did not catch cold. This is no matter for a 3- or 4-year-old to be making a choice about. The fact that this child did not catch cold does not prove that going coatless in cold weather is sound procedure. If a child who is developmentally ready to choose between alternatives refuses to put on his coat, the choices open to him should be of quite a different order. If his mother does not care whether he goes out or not, but thinks he wants to go, then the choice might be between going out with his coat on or staying indoors with it off. On the other hand, if she wants the child to go out, then the choice might be (providing he likes to be independent) between getting into his coat himself or being put into it. In other words, as always, the alternatives must have significance to the child concerned.

SUMMARY: SUPPLEMENTARY TECHNIQUES FOR 3- AND 4-YEAR-OLDS
Here, before concluding this chapter with suggestions which apply only to 4-year-olds, I summarize the supplementary techniques described above for 3- and 4-year-olds.

Techniques for your 3- or 4-year-old adapted from those recommended at 2
> *Whenever possible have an attitude of "Yes, if you'd like"—and let him know you have it*
>
> *Suit the complexity of your speech to your child's language development; speak distinctly*
>
> *Talk sparingly, especially when it is time for business*
>
> *Talk confidently*
>
> *Assume through your actions that he will do what you say, even though he makes an initial protest*
>
> *Follow up what you say with action if your child does not respond*

Dealing with refusals when your child is 3 or 4

> Help your 3- or 4-year-old learn to make a deliberate choice to
> be willing to do what is required

Figuring out your child's behavior—records help

A comment about choosing consequences for your 3- or 4-year-old's
behavior: significant alternative consequences

Further suggestions for 4-year-olds

The suggestions which follow reflect certain aspects of your 4-year-old's development which set him apart from a 3-year-old.

HELPING YOUR 4-YEAR-OLD ENJOY SOCIABILITY
WITHOUT LETTING IT GET OUT OF HAND

One of a 4-year-old's outstanding characteristics is his sociability. I have already talked about how much he needs the companionship of children at his own stage of development. But he also needs help keeping sociability under control so that it does not turn into oversociability, which can result in both overexcited, nonconstructive play and inefficient performance in business activities.

Here are a few examples of what I mean by oversociability:

> Four-year-old Peter pours sand all over Scott, laughs excitedly, rolls in the sand.

> Peter runs around with three other 4-year-olds, screaming loudly. (They had been told, not long before, "If you'd like to play together, then find something you'd all like to do," with various suggestions for activities which could occupy four children.)

> As several children are singing "Happy Birthday," Peter shrieks and laughs, whereupon some of the other children who have been singing join in his shrieks.

Now perhaps your reaction is, "Oh, let them have a good time. Of course they're boisterous, but they're having fun. Leave them alone." My answer is that overexcited, oversociable, nonconstructive play tends to breed more of the same and so to replace constructive activity. Of course one wants children to enjoy themselves, but enjoyment does not depend on overexcitement. Accordingly, here are a few suggestions which will be useful in helping your 4-year-old keep his sociability under control, whether in play or in business activities. Additional suggestions will be given later in the sections on play with other children (pp. 199–201) and on particular business activities (p. 225, p. 258).

Sociability at 4 needs to be based in an interest in some thing. Emphasis on a permissive atmosphere for children often has the unintended effect of leaving 4-year-olds to alternate between boredom and oversociability. Children of this age tend to become oversociable so readily because, although they are very sociably inclined, they are not yet skilled in their sociability. To be able to be sociable without having their sociability run away with them, their interest must either be based in some *thing* or else harnessed to some interesting activity which is more than mere socializing. If they are bored with what their play surroundings offer, they will readily turn to the kind of overexcited, nonconstructive play illustrated by the examples of Peter.

Remember as you try to keep your 4-year-old's environment stimulating to him that his horizons are expanding; this is one of the reasons for going on excursions to places of special interest—a farm, a kennel, a dairy, a shipyard, or an airport, for example. Often your child will pick up new ideas to bring home to his play. Still another way of adding interest to your 4-year-old's play is by thoughtful variation from time to time of the play materials available to him, as suggested in the section on arranging your child's play surroundings (pp. 88–91).

Sociability also easily disrupts the daily business activities of 4-year-olds; the tasks involved seldom hold enough interest in themselves to keep sociability from taking over if the opportunity is offered. For this reason, you need to devise techniques which help your 4-year-old want to get through his business activities with dispatch and which reduce opportunities for oversociability at these times.

Use transitional activities to relax the tempo of your child's life and to reduce keyed-up sociability. Sometimes you will find that children have reached a pitch of overexcited, nonconstructive play (most liable to happen when several children as old as 4 are playing together, but not unlikely even when your child has only one playmate). Suppose you decide it would be a good idea for the children to go to the toilet and then have a drink of fruit juice. If you let two or more children crowd into a bathroom, your facilities would not be equal to keeping the children busy—not unless your bathroom has two or more toilets in it! You would just be inviting oversociability. Instead, see that they come in one at a time, and set the change of atmosphere as they do so. Suppose a child starts to rush pell-mell toward the bathroom. Stop him. Put out an arm if necessary as you say, "You're in the house now so you need to walk." If you wish, have the juice all ready so that each child is given it individually right after he is finished with the bathroom. If you have time and are feeling inclined, this would be a good moment for a story, when you have just used toilet and juice activities to relax the tempo of play and reduce keyed-up sociability.

Choose combinations of children to do things together with both enjoyment and a tendency to oversociability in mind. Suppose four children are playing in your yard and you are going to ask two of them to come with you to help carry a midafternoon snack outdoors. Choose a combination which is likely to produce a relaxed, businesslike attitude toward the job at hand.

It is a good idea, as you watch children playing together, to notice which ones your child seems particularly to enjoy—and to play well with, too. This includes playing together without dissolving all the time into sheer undiluted sociability. Then you can help foster friendships for your child which are both pleasant for him and likely to promote constructive, interested play.

GUIDING YOUR 4-YEAR-OLD'S TENDENCIES TO
ASSERTIVENESS, SELF-PRIDE, AND BELITTLING
OTHER PEOPLE'S EFFORTS

In addition to oversociability, as you will remember, assertiveness, self-pride, and belittling other people are also typical 4-year-old tendencies. You really do not need to feel that your child is becoming a permanent critic of the human race when he greets other children's efforts with "That's no good." Nor need you feel he is a hopeless egotist if he remarks, as a child I know did to a companion block builder, "Let me do it. I'm so clever with the blocks," or if he frequently calls attention to his accomplishments. These are all typical 4-year-old feelings. One of the best ways of dealing with them is by the kind of play situations you arrange for your child. If 4-year-olds who are about equally assertive and skillful play together, you can let the assertiveness bounce back and forth, for then it is not hurting anyone, yet is having a chance for expression.

BALANCE RESPONSIBILITIES WITH THE
SATISFACTIONS OF BEING MORE
GROWNUP

Because you expect a 4-year-old to be more responsible than younger children, make sure that you balance the responsibilities you think he should assume with satisfactions in being a more grownup person. He needs to find that being 4 years old is an enjoyable state, not just one in which he is expected to accomplish tasks that younger children cannot manage and to exercise better judgment generally. In other words, it is important for him, as it is for all ages, that you keep his whole life in mind and make sure that he derives plenty of satisfactions from being the person he is at the same time that he is called upon to make decisions suited to his level of maturity and to meet standards of behavior which will help him progress toward interdependent security.

SUMMARY: FURTHER SUGGESTIONS FOR 4-YEAR-OLDS

In this section I have discussed the following points:

Helping your 4-year-old enjoy sociability without letting it get out of hand

> *Sociability at 4 needs to be based in an interest in some thing*

> *Use transitional activities to relax the tempo of your child's life and to reduce keyed-up sociability*

> *Choose combinations of children to do things together with both enjoyment and a tendency to oversociability in mind*

Guiding your 4-year-old's tendencies to assertiveness, self-pride, and belittling other people's efforts

Balance responsibilities with the satisfactions of being more grownup

Turnabout is fair play: children using these techniques

Now, by way of concluding this chapter, let us look briefly at the techniques which a group of 4-year-olds in a nursery school used both on each other and on the grownups who were guiding them.

Jennifer (age 4¾, in her third year at nursery school) is piloting her little brother Clark (age 2¾) through his first days at school. She is eating dinner with him. He does not like meat and is having a hard time eating liver. He is grimacing and not swallowing it.

Jennifer: "If you take a bit of the milk, Clark, that makes it juicier. I tried it before." (Note the tone of this. It is not a command. It leaves the whole matter up to Clark, but indicates a way to make things easier.)

Jennifer to Nancy (age 3¾), who is riding a bike and bumps into Clark, also riding: "Don't bump into Clark, Nancy." (Jennifer could improve on her choice of words here.) "He's still very little."
Nancy: "But I want to go fast."
Jennifer: "Then you can go around him on the gravel the way I do." (Here she describes an acceptable way for Nancy to do what she wants.)

Jennifer and Clark are painting at separate easels. Jennifer says, "Clark, you can cover your name if you'd like" (by "cover," she means cover with paint). "Just do it gently the way I do and it won't get all covered up." (Here again, note the way in which this is said. Incidentally, the content of the suggestion in distinction from the form is entirely Jennifer's, for although the children's names are put sometimes on their paintings-in-the-process, staff members say nothing about leaving names showing.)

Jane (age 4½, in her second year of nursery school) is standing with a group of 4-year-olds who are watching Julie (age 4¾) climbing high in a tree. The others are clustered around the bottom.
Jane: "Be careful of Julie, she's way up high."

Jane is sitting in the Senior playroom. Marguerite (age 4) walks over to the table where she is sitting.

Jane: "Bring a chair over if you want."

Nancy (who has had a year and a half of nursery school before the present year) has found a sow bug. Other children crowd around her so closely that they interfere with one another's view. Nancy points at them, saying, "You go . . ." (meaning, apparently, back up). "It's too crowded." They enlarge their circle, whereupon she shows the bug to each of them individually.

The use of a wagon has been withdrawn from Ben (age 4¼, in his second year of nursery school) because he and another 4-year-old knocked down Marguerite and then ran the wagon into an easel. They have been occupied with something else, but now run up to Mrs. A.

Ben: "We want a wagon. We think we can keep from running into things."

Jennifer chooses to sing a particular song. Miss B, who wonders whether she wants piano accompaniment, asks, "Shall I play it?"

Jennifer: "You can if you want."

So you see your child will use on you the techniques you use on him—still another reason for you to choose techniques wisely!

7

Guidance in Play

IF YOU AGREE WITH ME, you want your child to learn to take the initiative in finding interesting, constructive activity. You hope he will gain varied interests and skills, so that he is developing his potentialities in many ways. You want him to be getting from his play experience an over-all sense of his own competence and worth as a person. You want him to have satisfying play contacts with other children his own age, to be learning to get on well with others, learning consideration for their rights and learning to stand up for his own rights, too.

I have discussed in considerable detail how to arrange your child's play surroundings so that, in so far as possible, when he is active in them these aims will be realized (pp. 74–112). Of course, as I have said, these surroundings cannot do the whole job, however adroitly you plan them; but the better you make your environmental arrangement, the less will you need to step in directly to give instructions or take part in your child's play.

Your part in your child's play

Now perhaps as you read that last remark, with its emphasis on minimizing need for your taking part in his play, your reaction is

that you *want* to join in his play. Where is a place for that in my
scheme of things? Let me work up to my answer by talking first of
ways to encourage your child's interest and satisfaction in using his
own ideas in constructive play, without your joining in. After that I
shall discuss playing with your child.

IF YOUR CHILD IS PLAYING CONSTRUCTIVELY
AND CONTENTEDLY, LET HIM ALONE

If your child is playing constructively and contentedly, let him
alone to enjoy what he is doing in his own way. After all, you want
him to use his ideas, not rely on yours, don't you? As a general
policy, then, show your interest in his play by how you react to it
rather than by taking part in it yourself.

WAYS TO SHOW YOUR INTEREST WHICH
ENCOURAGE HIS RESOURCEFULNESS

He can gain a great deal from the interest you take in what he does.
Watch his efforts. Be ready to recognize development in the way he
uses materials and ideas.

*Comment about achievement in play; use constructions for decora-
tions.* Suppose, when he is just 2, that for the first time he has piled
some of the disks from a color cone with some square blocks to make
a little tower. Perhaps you say, as you point to each part of it at
tidying-up time: "My, that is interesting. You have a red circle and
a square, and a green circle and a square. How about having it on
the shelf for a decoration instead of taking it apart to put away?"
Or suppose your 3-year-old has painted a picture. In the main, up
until now, he has tended to cover the whole page with paint. This
time, however, he has made shapes and left spaces around them.
Then say something on the order of: "That's an interesting picture,
with the solid blue shape in the center and the other colors in spots
around the outside. Would you like it put up for a decoration?"

*Keep from implying that your child's products should represent real
objects.* "What is it?" is a question which readily springs to grownup

lips, but why suggest to your child that the materials which he puts together ought to represent something readily nameable? Lots of efforts of children of preschool age are simply an experimental, manipulative trying-out of colors and shapes and textures. If you would like to encourage your child to talk about what he has done, but without implying that his efforts ought to represent "something," such a question as "Would you like to tell me about it?" conveys quite a different meaning from "What is it?" But do not overdo this, either. Have a very receptive ear for his spontaneous comments, but do not prod for them if they are not forthcoming.

Talk in terms of what your child has done in play, not in terms of what he is. You will notice, too, in the examples above that in commenting about what your child did, you did not remark, "Aren't you clever." You talked about what he did as meriting comment.

Now these remarks about expressing your interest in your child's activities do not imply that every time he raises a hand to play with something you go into raptures over what he does. As always, reserve your comments for activities which deserve them— but recognize constructiveness on his part.

When you suggest something for your child to do, make at least two suggestions. This point has already been made in connection with encouraging your child to think for himself in play activities, and qualified in its application to 2-year-olds (p. 144). Although you try to arrange your child's surroundings so that he takes the initiative for finding interesting activity, sometimes he will be at loose ends and will profit by suggestions. Even so, leave a choice up to him by making at least two suggestions: "There are lots of things to do outdoors. Would you like to take your farm animals and farm machinery to the sandbox and have more water there? Or would you rather load leaves into your wagon, or spade up the earth for your new garden?"

When your child is old enough, provide a place to store partially finished products which can be completed later. Be ready, when your child has matured enough to want to carry over an activity from one day to the next, to help him carry on such sustained activity. Suppose, at 3½ or 4, he has to stop before he finishes a collage (bits of various kinds of objects pasted on a sheet of paper). You might produce a special box and say, "How about putting that in here and setting it on top of your shelf? Then if you want to work on it later, it will be handy." See that such partially finished products are stored in a conspicuous place. He may get in the habit of peering into his box to see if he wants to resume some activity started at an earlier time.

When your child is old enough, let constructions remain in place rather than helping tidy them up at the end of a play session. Another way to help your child keep interest in an activity sustained (and also to save him from the frustration of having to dismantle a creation he has put together with prolonged, loving care) is by letting block constructions stay up overnight, or for several days, rather than having them tidied up with your help at the end of a play session. Wait to do this until there is a real reason for it. Most 2½- to 3½-year-olds will be quite content to have blocks go away on their shelves at the end of daily play. In fact, at this age a block structure would just be in the way if left in position. But by the time your child builds elaborate constructions, he will often want to play for several days with what he has made, or keep it up to admire. Let him. Try, however, to figure out whether what he really wants is to keep the blocks in position for their own sake, or just to avoid tidying up.

Willingly help your child tidy up after play which involves a lot of work in the tidying-up process. It is important, if you want to foster your child's interest in block building, to keep tidying up from being too large a task; otherwise he may choose not to use blocks. This would be a pity since blocks are a satisfying activity which invites creative and imaginative use with many kinds of accessories. Be willing, therefore, to help him tidy up, but do not do the job for your child. A useful formula is, "I'll be glad to help, but you need to keep busy, too." (This implies a logical consequence if it turns out you are doing a solo job. That would be, "I'm stopping tidying up now because you aren't doing any of the work. When you're ready to keep busy, I'll help again.")

Be ready to suggest additional activity for particularly creative efforts. Suppose your child's usual carpentry constructions consist of a piece of wood with two or three rickety nails in it. Then, one day, he goes beyond this and is pleased with the result. You might say: "You have two pieces there, don't you?—nailed firmly together. If you'd like to paint them, I'll mix some powdered paint into starch [p. 93]. What color would you like?"

Or, after an interesting clay product has dried, your child may enjoy painting it.

HELPING YOUR CHILD COPE WITH PROBLEMS IN USING PLAY MATERIALS

I have in mind here not the problems which involve other children and their rights to play materials, but problems in using the materials themselves—solving puzzles, for example, or putting movable outdoor play equipment together. Recall the discussion of letting your child alone to tackle a problem and helping your child figure out how to solve problems when help is needed, including the remarks about gauging the difficulty of the problem facing your child not in terms of skill alone but also in terms of his feelings. But don't forget that your child can get a lot of pleasure and satisfaction out of learning to solve problems in play. Remember 3-year-old Henry's triumphant I-did-its, sixteen times in a row, after he had managed to put a hard puzzle together (pp. 136–39).

This concludes my suggestions for encouraging your child's resourcefulness and interest in constructive play without taking part in it yourself. Now let us deal with the question I raised at the start of this chapter. Suppose you *want* to take part in your child's play. Where is a place for that in my scheme of things?

PLAYING WITH YOUR CHILD

You can probably guess that I think you should play *with* your child in a way that does not discourage him in the long run from finding enjoyment in seeking and carrying on his own activity. It will help him to play contentedly on his own if he knows in advance when play with you is going to happen. Work out enough of a pattern to his day so that he knows when to expect you to play with him. Perhaps the middle of the morning, just after juice, is a good time for him to count on play with Mother. Father's arrival home, if it comes at a likely hour for a play session (not when a small child is overhungry or needs to go to bed) and if Father is willing and enjoys it, is an excellent time for a child to count on play with Father— a boisterous romp for a 2-year-old, for example. You and your child can have a lot of fun doing many things together—a walk, stories, moving around to music, singing (some of it simple enough so that he can join in), a chance to help cook, a chance to help in the garden, sufficiently gentle roughhouse.

What about your using your child's constructive play materials? Here your superior skill and grownup resourcefulness call for discretion. It would be easy for you to make something so handsome and finished that he loses all interest in using such materials himself because your products so far outshine his crude efforts. With such constructive materials, then, which are going to reflect the skill of the user in the finished product, you should keep to just about his level of performance.

Suppose your 2-year-old is wandering around at loose ends outdoors. You think he would enjoy some sand activity, once he got started. Over you go to the sand, saying "I wonder if this is damp enough." This gambit is enough to get him started, but you would like to join in and play with him. This is not the time for a magnificent castle, far beyond his capacities, complete with moats and steps and tunnels and towers. No—instead, you might say, "This will keep its shape in a big mound," as you pile up the sand and pat it down. Or maybe you fill a muffin tin, and then dump it out. You are using constructive material at your 2-year-old's level of development.

The test of your success in whetting your child's interest in carrying on an activity in his own way is: When you step out of your active part in his play, does he want to keep on?

Here is another example. Suppose on a rainy day your 4-year-old is at a loss for something to do. You fetch some new plasticene, sit down at a table with him, remarking, "This needs to be softened up," as you work it with your hands. Then, once it is soft enough, perhaps you form it into shapes, but not such elaborate ones that he cannot approach your products.

Now consider a different situation. Suppose your 4-year-old comes up to you and says, "Draw me a Christmas tree." If you oblige, with a beautiful, finished picture, he may be discouraged from trying to draw for himself. Therefore, instead of making one, say, "I'll help you find a picture of one; maybe that will help to draw it." Or you might say, "Here are some old Christmas cards. They might give you an idea of how to draw one, or perhaps you'd rather find one to cut out." If your child decides to cut out a picture from a Christmas card, he is no longer being encouraged to draw. But the point is that he attains what he wants through his own efforts, and does it in such a way that he is likely to find further activity and enjoyment in the process.

This point of view about the way you play with your child does not mean that you never make a drawing for him at your own level of skill. But you need to turn skilled drawing for him into a special occasion which is distinguishable in his mind from his own play efforts. You might have a special drawing book, that you use when it is storytime—that is, at a time of day when he expects to do something with you. Perhaps he asks for different kinds of pictures and you make them as you go along. I have seen drawings in such a book, made by a father and carried on as a play activity with his child at play-together times. These did not diminish the child's interest in his own drawing efforts during his playtime on his own.

ENCOURAGING YOUR CHILD'S ENJOYMENT OF BOOKS

Perhaps you remember from my discussion of Books Before 5 that I am highly in favor of your doing everything you can to interest your child in books. You already know the importance I attach to choosing interesting, suitable books for your child and, further, to selecting (or adapting when desirable) what you actually read out loud from the printed text (pp. 101–5). I hope that your child will enjoy books by himself as well as in the company of other people.

Make access to interesting books easy and cultivate care in their use. Before your child can walk, put a book with clear, colored illustrations of familiar things and living creatures where he can look at it; if he shows some interest, turn the pages for him. By the time he is a toddler, keep a few books at a time available on his low toy shelves, where he has ready access to them. Once in a while show him how to turn the pages by the corner (in order to minimize tearing) and mend any tears promptly without blame, though a little regret may be in order: "Too bad it is torn. I'll mend it so it won't tear any more." Needless to say, the books readily available at this age should not be family heirlooms or costly treasures, for rough handling is bound to occur sometimes if your child looks at books on his own.

As he grows older, widen his ready access to books. By the time he is 3½ or 4, he will probably be responsible enough to have all of his own books and other books of special interest to him located in one area on bookshelves where he can easily find them and look them over. But even so, display in some prominent place a few books particularly likely to be appealing at the moment; change this display often enough to keep it fresh. Encourage careful use of good books by fostering reasonably clean hands, and keep up your system of prompt repair of torn pages.

Enjoying books with your child. Suppose you have followed my advice and your crawling baby has responded with interest to one or more of the pictures in the book you have chosen with his experience in mind. Give him a chance to look, to really examine the picture before him. Then, if you have time and it is fun, make a very simple comment—perhaps one word, perhaps a phrase—spoken slowly and distinctly. "Cat." A pause. "Cat like Ginger" (the family cat). Another pause. Then, if your audience is still with you, "Cat goes meow." (And if you enjoy this sort of thing, make that "meow" as Ginger-like as you can.) If your baby likes it, you have helped him start his enjoyment of books, an activity which can give him pleasure all his life.

As he grows older, continue to adapt the complexity of your comments about picture books to his language skill and understanding. Make a point of speaking slowly and distinctly in order to foster the development of language.

Once he is ready, in terms of understanding and attention span, it is fine to read him the text of books. It is often pleasant at the end of a story, particularly the first few times a book is read, to go back over the pictures with comments, or to comment about them en route, so long as interruptions do not spoil the story's effect.

Occasions when your child is confined to bed are often opportune times for reading him stories and poems with few illustrations, as I suggested earlier.

Daily experience with books. I hope your child's experience each day includes not only the regular access to books which I have suggested, but also a time he can count on for enjoying books with grownups— Father or Mother. It is ideal if this comes at the same time every day—at bedtime or naptime, for example, or just before dinner or supper—in any case, after he has had a chance for active play, since quiet occupation then will have special appeal. Choose a congenial time for all concerned. It is hard to overestimate how much such daily experience can contribute to your child's pleasure now or how much it can widen his horizon and foster his intellectual development.

Settling conflicts over play materials

Now let us turn to the matter of settling conflicts over play materials. If you have more than one child, or if your child has companions in play (as I hope he does), conflicts over play materials are going to arise again and again. The way such questions are settled can have a lot to do with how children in the same family feel about each other and with how your child gets on with all children. What you do in the way of guidance depends on a number of different considerations, and I shall arrange my recommendations so as to bring these out.

PLAYPEN RIGHTS

Let us suppose you have two children, close in age. When one of them starts his playpen days, the other is in the stage of wanting to play with whatever he sets his eyes on.

Since a baby old enough to be holding a rattle or some colored blocks is likely to be equally content with a substitute, it makes sense, if an older preschooler wants what the baby is using, to suggest he find something for the baby to use which he will like as well. "It has to be shaped so he can't hurt himself," you might tell your 2-year-old as you help him find a substitute. Then, let him offer it through the bars. If the baby drops what he is using and takes it, your older child has won the other toy by fair means, with no harm done to anybody, at a time in his life when it does him good to feel he can gain what he wants in this way. As the baby grows old enough to want to keep on with whatever he is using, then you will employ a different technique. By then, however, your older child will himself be in a different stage of development and more used to having a younger child in the family.

PRIVATE POSSESSIONS

Children need a right to their own belongings. A child's own possessions are not to be confused, though, with play materials which are not private property, but rather meant to be used by two or more children. Let us say your hypothetical children are now 2 and 4. If your 4-year-old's belongings are not unduly disturbed, he is more likely to feel cordial toward the younger member of the family. He needs to have a means of protecting his property from a wandering baby, who can be destructive. It is a sound procedure, therefore, to provide him with a place to which the younger child does not have ready access—the top of a bureau which the little one cannot reach, for example, and where things can be kept out of sight, or even a storage place with a fastening which the smaller child cannot undo. Explain to the older child that it is fine to reserve his possessions for his own use, provided he keeps them out of the baby's way. But if he leaves them around in places where the younger child plays, then the baby is entitled to use them.

Children must learn to respect the property rights of other people. Part of this learning depends on having their own rights respected. For this reason, if one of your children wants to use the private possession of another, leave the decision up to the owner; do not try to enforce sharing. Your children are much more apt to work out a system of "If you'll let me use . . . , then you can use . . ." if you are not trying to mastermind everything. Sometimes, of course, the prospective lender and borrower will need advice because some objects (balloons, for example) are so fragile that being on loan is equivalent to being destroyed or lost forever. And sometimes a child will profit by being reminded, "Teddy let you use his xylophone, remember? If you let him use your watering can now, he'll probably feel like letting you use something of his again."

JOINT PLAY MATERIALS AND EQUIPMENT

It is reasonable and beneficial for children close in age if much of their play material is joint property. But make clear to them what is jointly and what is privately owned. About the best way of doing this is to let each child in the family have his own shelves for private possessions, and have another source of supply (a "toy closet," say) for joint materials. As a child feels willing to let another child (or other children) use a private possession of his at any time, he may agree to store it in the joint-supply place.

"Sharing" and "taking turns." When children are disputing over something that is a joint possession, many grownups think it reasonable to have them share use of the object, or else take turns, with the grownup dictating the turns. Though these techniques are useful in special circumstances, you will find they have serious disadvantages if you try to use them as your principal techniques for dealing with disputes.

As far as sharing goes, at preschool ages this is often sharing in name only. If peace reigns, it is likely to mean monopolization by one of the sharers and acquiescence by the other. Of course, if two children of preschool age spontaneously want to share a piece of play material, well and good. It is often wise to say, though, "That's fine, if you can manage it. But if it doesn't work, then David, you're the one to find something else since Roger got the blocks first."

And as regards taking turns: there are two disadvantages to this technique. First, children are forever dependent upon the grownup to apply it for them. Second, it promotes constant references to the grownup in play: "It's my turn now. Tommy's had it longer than I did," and so forth. In very special circumstances, however, grownup-dictated turns are sound. When some new activity has great appeal, then taking turns is the fairest way of letting each child take part in what he is yearning to try out, without having to wait a long time because the novelty of the material keeps holding the user's interest.

In general, however, a much sounder principle to follow in regard to joint property is to

Let the right to use something depend on who got it first. The advantage here is that, unlike the system of sharing or taking turns, the children can apply this principle themselves. They can understand, "Sally got it first. I'll help you see when she is through so that you can get it." Or, "If you want to keep on using it, hold onto it. If you leave it, someone else is likely to get it."

The idea of "right." So far, I have been talking about how to get disputes settled with a minimum of quarreling. But you want more than efficiency; you also want your child to learn the idea of right, or equity. Therefore, I shall suggest some techniques for helping him learn both how to respect the rights of others and how to stand up for his own. In describing these techniques, I shall assume that a child has a "right" to a joint plaything if he got it first. Of course, if you have a different idea of what his rights are, you will have to adjust these techniques accordingly, but the principles I am illustrating will still hold.

1. Let us suppose one child is using a wagon. Another grabs it away. The first child wanders off. So far, the consequences of behavior for each of these children promote exactly the opposite of the learning desired. Probably you need to step in. But do not assume that the original user would like to keep on with what he was doing.

Find out. Otherwise, if you rescue whatever was taken and return it to the child concerned, only to discover he does not want it, you have interfered unnecessarily. So ask, "George, did you want to keep on using the wagon?" Suppose he says, "Yes." Then what you do depends upon his developmental level. If he is a little 2-year-old, perhaps you pick him up, carry him over to the wagon, set him down by it as you hold it in place, put one of his hands on the wagon, and hold it there, saying, "If you'd like to keep using it, you hold on"; then redirect the other child. However, if George is older, perhaps you take his hand to give him reassurance as you go over to the wagon. And you might add "Tell Nelly you got it first" to your original suggestion, "If you'd like to keep using it, you hold on." In each case, you are helping the child who lost the wagon learn how to cope with the problem created when someone else takes something away from him. And you are seeing to it that the consequences for each of the children, grabber and grabbee, promote the learning you hope for.

2. Now suppose two children are struggling over some plaything and you know who got it first. If it looks as if the rightful user is going to hold his own, do nothing. But be ready to lend a helping hand to settle the matter with dispatch and to keep rising tempers or sorrow from dominating the scene: "That's right, George. Hold on tight. You got it first"; or—if he is developmentally ready for it—"Tell Paul you got it first"; or perhaps, "Tell him in a big voice so he can really hear you," if George happens to be speaking in a whining or fearful voice. Then to Paul: "Paul, George did get it first. I'll help you see when he is through"; or "If you'd like something with wheels, I'll help you find it."

3. But often when two children are struggling over something, you do not know what has gone on. What are you to do now? Rather than allocate the disputed plaything arbitrarily, it is better to say, "I just don't know who got it first, so the trike had better go away now and we'll bring it out later." Or, if both of the children are getting on toward 3 or are older, it would be sound to see if they could settle this matter themselves. You might say, "I don't know who got it first. If you can settle who is going to use it now, fine. Otherwise it will just have to be put away for a while." Suppose

the children manage to agree who is to be the present user. Watch their play carefully from now on so that you will be in a position to know what has happened if similar conflicts arise. It is not good for either of the children involved if the same child always surrenders in order to keep the peace.

4. Now, suppose once more that children are in conflict, not about who has a right to a plaything, but about who prevails in a joint enterprise, say the way a block building should be made. If one of them hits the other, what you do depends, as always, on what you want them to learn. If you want them to learn to talk to each other instead of hitting, then ask the hitter, "What do you want to tell so-and-so?" Let us say he answers, "I want an opening here for the truck to go through." You reply, "Then tell him; he can hear." You may need to add in this case, "Of course, when you're using blocks together, you both have ideas about how they should go. If you want the building to be just the way you want it, then you'd better not build with someone else."

If your children are to learn to settle disputes with words instead of blows, see to it that, by and large, reasonable requests by one child to another are respected. Otherwise your children will learn that words are ineffective and so will resort to hitting.

Let us say Jenny is pulling a wagon. Roger comes up and starts to push it, at greater speed than Jenny wants. She protests, "Stop. I want to pull by myself." If Roger does not respond, then you need to see that the protest is effective. "You heard what Jenny said, Roger. She wants to pull by herself. Maybe if you ask her she'll let you ride in the wagon."

Play with other children

HELPING CHILDREN TO BE WILLING TO
PLAY TOGETHER

Note this last remark. "Maybe if you ask her, she'll let you ride in the wagon." It is fair to leave the answer up to Jenny, because she got the wagon first. If you think Roger should have a ride in a wagon, then give him one when the wagon is free. In the meantime, if Jenny wants to use the wagon by herself, help Roger find something else interesting to do. And, incidentally, though you should not make sour remarks to Jenny if she chooses to use the wagon alone, it would be appropriate if she does give Roger a ride to tell her it is nice of her to do so.

It will be clear to you that I think children should not be dictated to about playing together—it should never be mandatory. But one child sometimes needs help in being accepted by others. Let us suppose, now, that several 4-year-olds are active in the same location, two of them playing house, a third on the fringe, wanting to be included. Unless the would-be joiner is a child for whom a pattern of rejection has developed, the chances are that the three will play together harmoniously once they get started. It may help to suggest, "Maybe if you knock on the door [a pretend "door" made of large blocks] they'll let you in." Perhaps you add, "There's a mother and a baby in the house. Who else might live there?" Notice that your suggestion proposes a definite action. If this kind of definite suggestion for a part in play tends to result in acceptance, encourage children to use this technique on their own instead of the wistful "Can I play with you?" which more often than not results in flat rejection.

An enormous help for children, certainly by the time they are 3, is having opportunities to play with other children their own age in situations where the number involved is not so small that playing together on the part of two children means the exclusion of a remaining child from all group play. This is one reason, of course, why a good nursery school has so much to offer a child. For when a number of children are present, if two children choose to be clubby and to exclude a third (without overstepping their rights to equipment), grownups can help the excluded child find other companionship. This is much harder at home, but the principle of help is the same: try to see that the child excluded by one group of children has a pleasant time with someone else. Inviting a child to your house to play who is likely to prove congenial may help a lot if exclusion by other children is going on.

If your child tends to be left out pretty generally, you need, of course, to figure out why—and to do it objectively. You will need to appraise your child's whole life to figure out the satisfactions and dissatisfactions he is experiencing, in addition to concentrating on probable reasons for his exclusion. If your child attends a nursery school, have a talk with the teacher. She may be able to make suggestions for improving the situation. Perhaps she will suggest that your child bring to school some plaything he does not love so dearly that he minds having other children use it, and one which is likely to have appeal for other children. Perhaps she will have suggestions about children to invite home for play—one at a time—who she thinks may prove congenial. Perhaps cooperative transportation by two parents will encourage companionship at school between the children involved.

Make the play opportunities at your home interesting, so that a visiting child enjoys himself. But do not expect your child to defer to the visitor at a grownup level of sociability. Let the first-come, first-served policy I have already described be in effect with visitors. If your child has possessions he wants to keep for his own use, help him think what they are and store them out of sight before the visitor comes. It is also a good idea to set the length of visits on the short rather than the long side.

One more word of caution about visitors: just because you are eager for the visiting child to enjoy himself, do not feel hesitant to step in to instruct the children when it is necessary. This is much better than letting play get out of hand with ensuing overexcitement, even chaos, and finally a necessity for drastic action on your part.

OVERSOCIABILITY AND NONCONSTRUCTIVE
ACTIVITY

How do you guide children if they become oversocial or nonconstructive, or both? Exactly as you guide them in any other situation where you want to modify their behavior—through the consequences to the behavior in question. Suppose your child and a visitor are playing in a sandbox. They start scooping up trowelfuls of sand and flinging it over each other's backs, with shrieks of laughter. Sand in eyes is no joke; besides, this nonconstructive, overexcited play is likely to lead to more of the same. Take your child by the hand and lead him out of the sandbox. Perhaps you ask, "What do you think I'm going to say?"—and he knows the answer. Or you tell him, "You know all about how to use sand. Keep from throwing it." And, to the visitor, "That's the way it works at our house. The sand is not for throwing." At this point you will have to size up, rapidly, various ways of directing the play into more constructive channels. It is probably a good idea to sit down with both children and talk over some play possibilities. If they want to keep on using sand, it might add interest to bring out some accessories—small cars or animals, for example. Or, if sand is not appealing, you might produce two bottles of soap-bubble liquid and their bubble makers, which you have tucked away for just such an occasion.

But maybe your attempts at redirection do not work: the not-so-good companions, who chose to go back to the sand, are soon throwing it again. Or bubble fluid is being smeared on faces. In either case, that activity should end. Where do you go from there in your guidance? If overexcited, nonconstructive play keeps turning up when a particular pair of children play together, you may well conclude that the combination does not work. You will have to find other congenial companionship for your child. But in the meantime, the visiting child is still on your premises. As long as he is there, you need to control the situation. The best way out may be to take the children on a walk, perhaps to see a new house under construction. Or you might try to produce a marked change in play by using a technique already described: have the children come inside, wash up, have a glass of fruit juice, and listen to a story (to fill in the time until your visitor goes home). As a last resort, you might even have to separate the children: "You two keep needing so much reminding that it just doesn't work to have you play together. Now, each of you sit down, you over there, Johnny, and you over here, Paul. Each of you think what you'd like to do separately." Offer suggestions if necessary.

Incidentally, if you operate, as many parents do, on the visiting system that host parent and visitor parent each transport the child visitor in one direction, it is often sound for the host parent to choose the trip taking the visitor home. Then the length of the visit can easily be gauged to its success for both children. Remember to keep the visits short enough so that play is terminated while both children are still having a good time. You want to have your child visitor leave your house in the frame of mind to come back soon for more play.

To sum up your guidance efforts relating to oversociable, non-constructive play: first, try to prevent it by having play surroundings interesting enough to direct children's energies into constructive activity. Be ready with suggestions likely to have appeal. But if a pair of children cannot be helped to "think of something really interesting to do," then you may have to promote grownup-sponsored activity which does not lend itself to overexcitement; as a last resort, you may have to separate the children.

If a child tends to become overexcited easily when he plays with others, this may be because he does not have enough chances for group play. The main remedy in the long run is, of course, plenty of opportunities to play with other children under wise supervision.

DUPLICATE PLAY MATERIALS

If your children are close enough in age to use the same play materials, or if your child frequently plays with friends his own age, provide a sufficient supply of constructive materials (housed in separate containers) so that two children can be occupied with the same activity without being thwarted by running out of materials. Remember, when one child would like to use exactly what another child has chosen, he is not being ornery. His interest has been aroused by the other child's play—he is made that way.

Table blocks are an example of the kind of play materials advantageously stored in duplicate containers. If the right proportion of different shapes is not available, a child is likely to get a construction partially made and then run out of the block shapes he needs. Crayons are another example. These should be available in individual sets so that a child does not have to wait until someone else is through with the color of his choice.

The extent to which you find it helpful to have duplicate supplies of materials will depend upon how often one child wants to use exactly what another child has. If this happens frequently, as is probable if your children are close in age, then it tends to make life pleasanter to have a good deal of duplicate material available. But remember, you certainly do not need to duplicate everything.

CONSOLIDATE DUPLICATE MATERIALS WHEN YOU NO LONGER NEED TWO SOURCES OF SUPPLY

As your younger or youngest child advances in age in his preschool years, you are likely to find less and less need for duplicate storage. You will find, if your children's playthings consist of the kind of constructive materials I have discussed, that a double-sized source of supply is still advantageous. For this gives an older preschooler or school-age child scope to use his abilities for the more elaborate constructions he is now capable of making.

HELPING TO PARCEL OUT ONE ADEQUATE SUPPLY OF PLAY MATERIAL BETWEEN TWO OR MORE CHILDREN

There are lots of materials—plasticene, for instance—which do not need to be put in duplicate containers. But have enough available, so that all the children who play together can use it at the same time without running short. Even so, disputes may develop, for when another child starts to help himself, the first child may object. Then you step in, with an "Oh yes, there's enough for more than one person. Here's a piece for Sally that is not being used." Suppose the first user still protests, "I need that one." Then you reach in for another piece, with "Then you're not using this one." There are just so many pieces a child can actually be using at once. If, on some occasion, he really wants to make a supercolossal plasticene construction (which happens seldom with the preschoolers I know), then you may need to make special arrangements for him to use the whole supply.

Here is a different case. Suppose you have two sets of trains, and one of your children has them all hitched together. Another one wants a train, too. Since there actually is a double supply, it makes sense to divide the trains up. Make clear to the original user what you are doing and give him his choice throughout the division: "There are two trains here and Sally wants to use one too, so I'll help divide it up. There's an engine and there's an engine; which one would you like?" and so forth, till the trains are separated.

PREVENTING AND DEALING WITH ONE CHILD'S
DISTURBING OR SPOILING ANOTHER
CHILD'S CONSTRUCTIONS

Children sometimes need grownup help to protect them in their play from interruption, disturbance, or the spoiling of constructions by another child.

In a family, it is often the older child who needs a sanctuary where a younger one will not spoil what he is doing. He is more likely to feel kindly toward a younger brother or sister if he knows he is free to play by himself when he wants to. If necessary, have hooks on his door which he can request you to fasten. But suppose, for instance, that children are playing in the same area, and each is building individually with blocks. Then try to avoid trouble by seeing that the constructions start far enough apart so that each structure has room to grow without encroaching on the other. See, too, that the building sites are so located that both children have easy access to the block supply.

When children sit down at a table, make sure that each has room for what he is using, to avoid difficulties arising through crowding.

Now, suppose one child starts to use what another child is using. If the children are pretty much on a par developmentally, it may work well to ask the original user, "David, is it all right if Roger uses the tinker toy with you?" If the answer is "Yes," collaboration is in order. If it is "No," Roger may need redirection to find something else to do. If the children are of quite unequal developmental levels and if previous experience has indicated that only difficulty can come from such attempts at combined use, it will probably be sound to redirect the would-be sharer at the outset.

Now sometimes, of course, one child will deliberately spoil what another child is doing. If one knocks down another's block building, say firmly, "If you want to take something down, you need to build it up first." If you can, catch this sort of thing before it happens. You might take firm hold of a 2-year-old's arm as he prepares to knock down another child's construction, give him an explanation, and direct him to where he can find play materials.

By and large, if one child spoils another's plaything, the grownup should try to help the destroyer repair the damage. By the time a child has an allowance, it is reasonable to expect him to contribute from it if there are costs involved in a repair job, but be careful how you handle this kind of situation. Do not blame him for his feelings if he has felt hostile toward another child, but help him realize that he should not damage other people's possessions and that it is to his own advantage to respect others' rights. (In the long run, one hopes, too, that he will be prompted to be kind to other people through genuine consideration for them.) I shall have more to say about guiding your child's aggressive feelings when I am focussing particularly on emotional development (pp. 267–74).

Some further examples of guiding your child's play by the way you phrase instructions

The phrasing in every case is designed to help your child learn desirable play procedures and to suggest the consequence which will follow if he does not heed the instruction. I have grouped the examples under headings which indicate the underlying reason for the guidance shown.

DANGER RULES AND HEALTH PRECAUTIONS

"If you'd like to climb, climb in a climbing place."

"If you want to use the plasticene, you need to keep it out of your mouth." (Needless to say, if your child is still in the stage of putting lots of things in his mouth, he is not yet ready for plasticene.)

"You need to sit if you're riding in the wagon. If you want to stand, stand on the ground."

"If you'd like to use the earth, keep from throwing it" (presuming this to be necessary because more than one child is using earth for play).

"If you'd like to use water, you need to ask me. Grownups turn on the faucet."

"Take a look. Is it steady?" (to a child building with large outdoor blocks, precariously arranged so that they are likely to tumble down on him; if he gives a contrary-to-fact "Yes," have him look at the source of trouble). "How could you make it steady?"

To a 3- or 4-year-old in the kitchen: "It's nice to have you in here when I'm cooking, but you need to stay on the other side of that chair so you won't be too close to the stove."

To a child starting to sit in damp sand in cold weather: "If you'd like to sit, sit on the wood. The sand's too damp to sit in."

CONSERVATION OF PROPERTY AND MATERIAL

"Apron first" (to a 2-year-old wanting to paint).

"Brush stays in the jar" (as the child starts to walk around with it).

"If you'd like to pound, use your pounding board," or ". . . use your hammer and wood."

In regard to floor blocks: "Keep them from crashing when you take them down," or "Crashing knocks the corners off and then they don't stay up well." (If you decide that building blocks without crashing is a minimum requirement, the consequence to a second crash must, of course, be significant to the child. To let the consequence be gradual ruination of the blocks merely means that avoiding crashing is not a minimum requirement.)

To a child who is pasting quantities of expensive colored paper, one piece on top of another, apparently simply for the pleasure of mass pasting: "If you'd like to paste lots of paper together like that I'll make some white pieces [or some newspaper pieces] and you paste as many as you like. Colored paper costs a lot."

To a child cutting colored paper into tiny pieces, apparently for the sheer pleasure of cutting: "If you'd like to cut lots of paper, I'll make some white [or newspaper] pieces and you cut as many as you'd like."

FAMILY COMFORT

As a child brings a drum or whistle into the living room: "If you'd like to use a noisemaker, you need to do it in your part of the house."

"If you'd like to shout, do it outdoors."

To a child talking in a very loud voice: "You don't need to talk so loud. I'm right next to you." (Or, in conversing with the child who is talking very loudly, talk very quietly yourself.)

"Back you go and close the door. You left it open."

MANNERS

To a child spitting outdoors: "If you'd like to spit, spit in the toilet."

SUMMARY

You may not agree, of course, with the minimum requirements assumed in these examples—for instance, you may not object to your child's spitting outdoors. But whatever the particular play procedures and minimum requirements you decide on, you can use the methods of guidance I have advocated and illustrated. That is, see to it that the consequences of his behavior are relevant to the situation, significant to your child, and sufficiently consistent to motivate him in the long run to do what you desire him to do. And, of course, always use techniques suited to his developmental level. With a 2-year-old, you are involved most of the time in putting him through the right motions; with a 4-year-old, in getting him to choose to do what is required, once he has learned what is expected. Thus, when your 2-year-old starts to climb over the fence which separates his play yard from a busy street, you lift him down with "If you'd like to climb, climb in a climbing place," as you carry him to an appropriate spot. On the other hand, if your 4-year-old scales the fence, the consequence might be to be brought into the house—all the way in before you say anything, in order to make your remarks more effective. Then, presuming he likes to play outside you might say, "Do you know why you're inside?" If he needs an explanation, he receives it, along with the statement that if he wants to play outdoors, he needs to manage to stay inside the fence; he must always ask before he goes outside. This kind of treatment follows from what has been said about guidance at different developmental levels.

Remember, you help both yourself and your child when you use effective methods of getting him to meet requirements; both of you are saved from the irritable effects of inefficient nagging.

Effective guidance is necessary to help your child learn the ground rules which will enable him to have a maximum of freedom within a framework of reasonable consideration for other people and for property. Effective guidance is necessary to help him learn to get on in his play setting with a minimum of directions from you.

Bear in mind, as you try to keep play requirements to a minimum, that you are guiding a changing child in a changing family, that the needs and desires of children and parents do not remain constant. You have to stay alert to necessary revisions in what is expected of everyone at home and keep in tune with changing conditions.

Perhaps your reaction to my advice about guiding children's play is: "It sounds like a good plan of guidance, but how in the world can I have time to know what is going on and to give the kind of guidance you are talking about?" My answer is that it is just one of the facts of life that young children make great demands on your time. You need to cudgel your wits to work out ways to give your family—grownups and children—the time and companionship they need with you, without exhausting yourself in the process. Because children of preschool age do need so much supervision, this is a time in your life to sort out what is essential for family living from what can be dispensed with. And do not forget, years roll along quickly. Soon your children will be in school. Then, if you are the woman in the family, you will have more time to write poems, to cultivate outside interests, perhaps even to take a job if that especially appeals to you. In the meantime, make the most of these preschool years in your children's lives.

Here are the points I have dealt with in this chapter:

Your part in your child's play

> If your child is playing constructively and contentedly, let him alone

Ways to show your interest which encourage his resourcefulness

> Comment about achievement in play: use constructive products for decorations
>
> Keep from implying that your child's products should represent real objects
>
> Talk in terms of what your child has done in play, not in terms of what he is
>
> When you suggest something for your child to do, make at least two suggestions
>
> When your child is old enough, provide a place to store partially finished products which can be completed later
>
> When your child is old enough, let constructions remain in place rather than helping tidy them up at the end of a play session
>
> Willingly help your child tidy up after play which involves a lot of work in the tidying-up process
>
> Be ready to suggest additional activity for particularly creative efforts

Helping your child cope with problems in using play materials

Playing with your child

Encouraging your child's enjoyment of books

> Make access to interesting books easy and cultivate care in their use
>
> Enjoying books with your child
>
> Daily experience with books

Settling conflicts over play materials

> Playpen rights
>
> Private possessions
>
> Joint play materials and equipment
>
>> "Sharing" and "taking turns"

Let the right to use something depend on who got it first

The idea of "right"

Play with other children

Helping children to be willing to play together

Oversociability and nonconstructive activity

Duplicate play materials

Consolidate duplicate materials when you no longer need two sources of supply

Helping to parcel out one adequate supply of play materials between two or more children

Preventing and dealing with one child's disturbing or spoiling another child's constructions

Some further examples of guiding your child's play by the way you phrase instructions

Danger rules and health precautions

Conservation of property and material

Family comfort

Manners

8

Guidance in Business Activities

IN CHAPTER 3, What Do You Want Your Child to Learn? I mentioned possible aims for your child's learning in business activities: learning an attitude of acceptance toward the things that need doing, and taking responsibility for getting them done; acquiring sufficient skill to accomplish business activities efficiently, with dispatch.

Motivating your child to perform business activities

Your job, of course, is to motivate your child to perform these business activities as you want him to. How are you going to do this?

Some business activities are related to physiological needs, as I have already suggested. You want your child to feel hungry at mealtimes, sleepy when it is time for bed, a need to urinate or to have a bowel movement when he goes to the toilet. To this end, arrange a pattern to his day suited to his needs. But as I remarked before, sometimes your child's physiological need is not enough to motivate him to perform a particular business activity. He is hungry, but he dislikes the meat you want him to eat. His eyes are heavy with sleep, but he wants to stay up. He is clutching himself and needs to urinate, but he does not want to bother to go to the toilet. If the physiological need involved is not sufficient to motivate him to carry on what you consider to be a necessary business activity, how are you going to motivate him? And what about business activities that are quite unrelated to physiological needs?

Here you are faced with the same kind of problem which occurs in any learning which you have in mind for your child. So you must find in your child a motive to appeal to which is both really relevant to the situation and significant to him. Now, in general, in addition to physiological needs, there are three motives to which to appeal for performance of business activities by your child. These are:

1. *A desire to play* (for example, "As soon as you've finished dressing, you'll be ready to go outdoors to play").

2. *A desire to be independent* (for example, "If you can manage by yourself to get washed for dinner, fine, but if you take too long I'm going to help you so that you'll be ready on time").

3. *A desire to remain with other people* (for example, at the dinner table, "You're talking so much, you're forgetting what you're doing. If it is too hard to keep from talking so much, I'll move your dinner plate so you can finish by yourself and be through in time to have more, if you want it").

Let us go on now to talk of specific business activities.

Eating

I hope that in all of your child's babyhood, taking in food was something he did because he felt like it, and that when he had had enough he stopped; in other words, that he did not have more food shoved at him than he wanted. I hope that new foods were judiciously introduced while he was still young enough not to be overly opinionated. If he had the kind of guidance in eating during his first year which Dr. Benjamin Spock describes in detail in his *Baby and Child Care*, by his first birthday he was eating "a pretty grownup diet." I hope, too, that when he showed an interest in feeding himself, you let him have a spoon, and that you gradually gave him more chance and more need to use it. If so, eating is probably something he now enjoys and manages by himself without your feeding him; in all likelihood he accepts a variety of foods.

But, alas, sometimes the cards are stacked against parents. Perhaps, for example, your child showed an allergic reaction to a lot of foods in babyhood, so your doctor had to keep him on a limited diet. Now, at 2, he can have more variety, but he is so set in his ways that he does not want to try new foods. Or perhaps your child has been ill a lot, and you could not resist trying to put more food into him than he wanted. Or you still feed him, because, as you say, "He does so much better than when he feeds himself." In any case, let us say he is 2 and start our advice from there.

YOUR CHILD'S HEALTH

I am assuming throughout this book that your child is under a doctor's care and that right along you have received his advice about your child's eating. If your child seems to lack interest in food, he should have a medical checkup to see whether there is any physical basis for his uninterest.

PLAN YOUR CHILD'S DAY TO PROMOTE HUNGER
AT MEALTIMES

The pattern to your child's day should promote hunger at mealtimes. Let us assume he is healthy. Does he have opportunity for plenty of active play? Is he getting adequate sleep and rest? Are his meals spaced so that he has a chance to become hungry for each one without going so long between meals that he is too empty? In other words, do meals come about five hours apart? Do midmorning and midafternoon snacks tide him over to the next meal, without taking away his appetite? Fruit juice (plus a cracker or two if your child has a large appetite) fills this bill well. As you can see, I am all in favor of regular hours for meals, keyed to your child's individual needs. Regular meal hours help him feel hungry at mealtimes and foster regularization of other physiological needs, such as afternoon and night sleep and bowel movements.

The kind of activity which occurs just before mealtime may affect your child's appetite, too. It is a good idea, if he seems keyed up by boisterous or exciting activity carried on right until time to eat, to have him engage in some pleasant, quiet activity for long enough to unwind a little before mealtime, perhaps some occupation in the kitchen, perhaps a story, perhaps listening to records.

ARRANGE SURROUNDINGS TO FOSTER YOUR
CHILD'S EATING HABITS

Since a preschool child's attention is easily diverted, arrange the setting for his meals so that he is not exposed to distractions, which make it hard for him to get on with the business of eating.

Advantages of eating apart from the family. When he is 2, being at the family table is likely to prove too distracting. Your child will profit by having his meals apart from the rest of the family (probably ahead of time); then his enjoyment of sociability will not have to compete with his attention to food. The extent to which this is advisable for a 3- and 4-year-old depends on a lot of things, including parents' convenience and the extent to which a child of this age is distracted from eating by sitting with the rest of the family.

Often mothers say, " I want Janie to have dinner with us, for otherwise she just doesn't see her father, he gets home so late. But she's tired by that time, almost too tired to eat." Here is a clear case where an earlier supper for Janie will make life easier for everyone. Then she can enjoy her father's company when he comes home all the better for having her own supper out of the way.

Equipment scaled to his size. A comfortable chair, suited to your child's size, set at a table of a convenient height for self-feeding, is important. A dish with rather steep sides helps him get his food onto his utensil; a large soup plate does nicely. (Even better, when he is just learning to feed himself, is the kind of child's dish with compartments—which not only provides the steep sides that help him get food on his utensil, but makes it possible to give him a variety of foods without having them get all mixed up together.)

Your child needs utensils easy to handle. When he is 2, a

straight-handled baby spoon does very well. Have only one spoon at his place; a second utensil is just something to play with. When he is 3½ or so, a regular-sized teaspoon and a salad fork are convenient equipment.

A straight-sided glass with a rather heavy bottom (so it does not readily tip over) and holding about four ounces of milk is easy for your child to handle. You will see in a minute a second reason for my preference for a small glass.

Arrange the setting so that spilling will not matter much. It is important to arrange the setting for eating so that spilling will not matter much. A preschool child is going to spill sometimes, knock over his milk, drop food. Being prepared for spilling will help you not to overreact. A washable floor covering under his table is essential; also a table surface which will not be spoiled by spills. While your child is still under 2½ or so, plastic bibs are a boon. It is handy to tuck the end of the bib under his dish, to form a kind of hammock into which spilled food drops. If you do this, you are gambling that your child will not give a vigorous tug to his bib, knocking his dish on the floor. But I have seen this system work month after month without such a mishap.

Make it easy to add additional servings to the small ones given at the start of a meal. If you want your child to feel that eating is something he wants to do, it is a good idea to serve him *less* than you think he is going to want. Arrange things so that it will be easy for you to give him additional small servings as he wants them.

One way to do this is to have a tray with the serving dishes on it near your child. Covered refrigerator dishes which can be heated work well for this. If your child is eating previously cooked food, be sure not to rob it of vitamins by overheating.

Serve food that needs cutting in bite-sized portions. In order to help your child manage his food, serve whatever needs cutting in bite-sized portions. Of course, he can manage foods he finger-feeds (like apple slices) by biting off pieces.

Serve attractive combinations of food. This may sound unnecessary, but I think the color and texture of food make a real difference. For instance, a menu of baked fish, mashed potatoes, apple sauce, and custard is improved by substituting a colorful, raw, crunchy vegetable—carrot sticks, say—for the pale apple sauce, and colorful fruit or jello for the custard.

HOW YOU ACT IN GUIDING YOUR
CHILD'S EATING

So far, I have been concerned with arranging the pattern of your child's life and his surroundings so as to make him likely to be hungry at mealtimes and to manage to feed himself with ease. This is in keeping with the basic plan of setting surroundings to work for you to foster desired learning, as far as they can.

Now let us get to the way you act in guiding your child's eating, and first take a look at

A trend in children's attitudes toward food. This is a tendency, which has been on the increase in recent years, for children to be uninterested in eating and to have very limited food likes. What has caused it?

I think it may well be an unforeseen by-product of a permissive attitude plus concern about children's eating. In addition, this tendency may result from parents' misinterpretation of the sound advice that they should be relaxed about their children's eating—and not give children the idea that eating is something grownups are forcing them to do. This is good advice. More than that, it is indispensable to a child's enjoyment of food. But do not go to the extreme of a completely hands-off policy in regard to eating, whereby children eat as much as they like of a favorite food and leave a less-liked food alone. For it is important to help your child learn to accept and enjoy a variety of foods at the same time that you are fostering in him the attitude that eating is his responsibility—and this means that it is really up to him whether or not he eats.

I am quite aware that the advice I am going to give about guiding your child's eating may surprise you, because you have probably been told to take it easy at mealtimes, that since your child is well-nourished you may relax and leave him alone. But you will see that what I am going to advise is only another application of the kind of guidance I have been talking about all along. It is designed to motivate him to want to eat a variety of foods. It is extremely important not to make your child feel that eating is something you are eager for him to do—that you are happy when he eats well and displeased when he does not. These feelings only complicate his learning and interfere with sound eating attitudes. Urging your child to eat takes away his appetite. So does having him sit down to a plate too laden with food. It discourages him before he starts. What you want to do is to create an atmosphere in which your child is the one who is asking you for more. And remember, he is the best person in the world to know how much he feels like eating. Let him tell you. But arrange the eating situation so that he is likely to want to ask for more.

Give small servings. Give your child small servings, considerably smaller ones than he will want in order to satisfy his appetite. If he feels he has been robbed when he looks at his plate, especially if he has been a poor eater, that is fine—that is just what you want. You are already beginning to create the atmosphere you are after— that eating is something your child wants to do, that it is his responsibility. If he protests as he looks at his small serving, if he says he wants more, tell him, "You may have more if you'd like as soon as that's gone." Keep from acting eager about it.

But perhaps you believe that if you give him little servings, he will not ask for more. Maybe he won't. But if so, this only shows that you have been getting him to take more than he really wants. If he is not very hungry, all the more reason to offer small servings. The chances are his appetite has been affected because he has felt people are pushing food at him. He probably will eat less than usual for a while if you give him small servings. But in the course of time, he is likely to respond with an increased appetite, and a totally different attitude toward food. However, if my proposed procedure worries you, do not adopt it. Remember everything I have said about being sure you want to try to change some aspect of your child's behavior before starting efforts at guidance (pp. 71–72, pp. 118–19).

What do I mean by small servings? I mean a teaspoonful of foods he likes. If your child habitually wants more, then increase the initial serving, but always give considerably less than he is apt to want at a meal. If you have been using this system during baby-hood and saying to your child, "Would you like some more?" before you give him an additional serving you judge he wants, one of his first words is likely to be "More." And he will probably think of eating as something he wants to do.

Start off this program by serving only foods he likes. Start off this program by having your child's meals composed entirely of foods he likes (and ones that are appropriate to the meal in question), or, if he is indifferent to all food, at least choose foods he does not actively dislike.

After about a week, if the eating program is going well (i.e., if he is finishing what you give him and quite often asking for more), then occasionally (not more than two or three times a week) include a less favored food in a meal.

When a disliked food is on the menu, be sure that the other foods present are ones he really likes, so that he will have an in-centive to eat and ask for more. I shall have more to say in a moment about helping him overcome food dislikes.

Give him some of each food in the entire meal at each serving. A dish with partitions makes it easy to give your child some of each of the foods in that meal at each serving, without having the food run together on his plate. Until your child eats regularly with the family, include a serving of dessert along with the main course. Re-member in this connection that desserts for children should not be the rich, sweet kinds which cut off appetites. Rather, they should be raw or stewed fruits, jello, custard—important parts of his diet. If you give him a serving of dessert along with the rest of his food, you do not put a false premium on it.

By the time he is eating meals regularly with the family, it would be a nuisance to include dessert with his main course. However, even when he eats with the family, continue to see that dessert servings are proportional to what is eaten at the main course: "Two servings of dessert, if you'd like, because you've had two servings of dinner." By the time your child is getting on toward kindergarten age he is likely to be indoctrinated with the notion that dessert is the treat of the meal, even though you have done your best to avoid it. If so, make use of it. "If you want to be ready for dessert, Janie, you need to finish up. If you are all through now, then ask to be excused." But, until your child does pick up the idea that dessert is the climax of dinnertime, do not put a premium on dessert by highlighting it in your guidance of eating. Use his desire for more of the foods he especially likes to motivate him to finish what he likes less well.

Cultivating manners. The years from 2 to 5 are not ones in which to lay stress on table manners. Your child has enough to do at this age in learning more fundamental things about eating. To stress holding a utensil "properly" or chewing with his mouth closed is liable only to interfere with his eating. There are, however, certain standards of behavior worth holding to, more because they help your child attend to the business of eating than because the behavior involved is polite.

Sitting facing the table. It is reasonable to expect your child to sit facing the table at mealtimes. Try to seat him so that he can look at what interests him without having to turn around. If he does turn around, tell him, "Around this way," as you pull up his chair (if it is too far away). If he keeps turning away from the table, probably he is not hungry, and it is best to end the meal.

Getting feet comfortable. If your child is twisting his feet about, it may help to tell him to "get your feet comfortable so you won't need to wiggle." I am presuming his chair fits him, and that he does not need to go to the toilet.

The way your child asks for more. By the time he is about 3½, I would expect him to ask for additional servings in what amounts to a polite way, but I would not insist on a single magic phrase for politeness. If he blurts out, "More," suggest there are several more grownup ways of asking for more food, "May I please have some more?" or "Could I have some more?" or "May I have some more?" This paves the way for giving him the idea that it is the attitude underlying manners that counts, not a set phrase.

I shall deal with other standards of behavior shortly when talking about play during mealtimes.

After you have put your child's plate in front of him, leave him alone unless he is playing. By "leave him alone," I do not mean go out of the room; I mean do not urge him to eat. If he just sits there without playing, turning around, or twisting his feet, let him sit. If you cannot keep from looking anxious, read a book (to yourself, not to him). If he is a child who normally eats well, not eating may be a sign he is not feeling up to par. Urging him to go ahead is the last thing you should do. If he is a "poor" eater, and you are starting a program to encourage him to want to eat, it is extremely important to let him alone as long as he is not engaged in play which interferes with eating.

When eating time is almost over, tell him so. I mean just this. Wait to tell him that eating time is almost over until that is actually the case. What is a reasonable time for a meal? Twenty-five or thirty minutes is likely to be long enough for any meal in a setup just for children. (Dinner with the family would need to be somewhat longer.) When fifteen minutes have gone by and your child has not eaten, tell him that in just a little while breakfast (dinner, or supper) will be over, so if he is going to have it, he needs to keep busy. You will notice the way I phrase this. It fits in with the whole idea that eating is his affair. Tell him just once. And while you are waiting to say it, do not keep eyeing your watch like an official at a track meet. If he does not then begin to eat within a minute or two, tell him the meal is over. I emphasize again, he is to hear only once that dinner will soon be over. Repetition is nagging, and nagging certainly gives him the idea that eating is something you are anxious to have happen. A child who is not very hungry in the first place will be quick to realize he has a potent weapon in his hands by refusing to eat if his parents are worried and let him know that they are worried. This is not because he is ornery, but because he is human. If your child has sat most of a mealtime without eating and has only just started to go ahead when it is time to be through, do not prolong the meal. Be pleasant about ending it, but mean what you say: "It's too bad if you want to keep on, but dinnertime's over. If you keep busy from the start at supper, you'll have plenty of time." Incidentally, if your child is hungry during the afternoon, do not give him a bigger snack than usual, but give him his supper early. And keep from moralizing. He will get the idea without that. This brings us to

Keep from telling your child to eat or talking about his eating where he can hear you. You will come to see, as I continue discussing your child's eating, that I am advising you never to tell your child to eat, or to hurry up. Saying "It's just about time for dinner to be over, so if you want to have that, you need to keep busy and finish up" conveys something quite different from "Hurry up and eat your dinner."

And whatever you do, do not talk about his eating or the lack of it in front of him. For instance, if you are discussing the matter with your doctor, leave your child in the waiting room, with a plaything to keep him amused. Similarly, never give your child the idea that you are either pleased or displeased by the amount he eats or leaves on his plate. I know this is hard. If you have busied yourself in meal preparation, you are likely to feel irritated if people do not enjoy their food. But remember, something important is at stake; do not complicate your child's learning by letting your pleasure or displeasure become one of the consequences of his behavior at the table.

"Helping" your child put food on his spoon. When a child has finished most of a meal on his own, sometimes with a last bite or two, or with a disliked food, scraping it onto your child's spoon for him can be a help. But only scrape up food once or twice during each serving, for if you scrape up many spoonfuls, you are urging him to eat. Be sure you do not put an extra big portion on the spoon. He is liable to dislike this; it may even make him gag. You might say, as you scrape up the bite you are helping with, "Maybe this will

help you finish up." Once you have scraped up the spoonful, set it on the plate. Let your child be the one to put it in his mouth. If he does not want to, then have him be through, and put up his plate. Do not actually feed him either liked or disliked foods.

Occasionally, if a child is faced with a tiny bit of disliked food, it may help him if you scrape up a small portion of something he does like and then put the tiny bit of disliked food on the same spoonful, so that he will eat it first. But do not do this as a general rule, for it will help your child to accept a new taste if he eats a food by itself rather than in a mixture.

Servings of milk. You probably remember that I advised a small glass, holding about four ounces, for milk. If your doctor recommends more, give it when your child has a second serving.

Keep from referring to specific items of food by precise name—especially in the case of disliked foods. Though you may think I am being rather silly here, I think there is a real point in not putting neon lights around a child's food preferences by stressing their names. So when your child asks for "more" with tomatoes still on his plate, instead of saying "When you've finished your tomatoes," say, "Yes, as soon as you're through."

Have your child finish up all of one serving before he gets more. This advice, again, is not stylish at the moment, for it seems to make an issue of eating. But this system really does not make an issue of eating, and it does help your child learn to accept a variety of foods. Here is how to go about helping him.

You have given him small servings of everything. If he wants more before he is finished, say, "When you're finished, you'll be ready for more." Being finished means drinking his milk, too. Suppose he does not want to finish up? The question you need to ask yourself is: Does he feel generally indifferent toward the entire meal, or does he have a real dislike for one of the foods? If the former— if he really does not care about eating—then let the mealtime be over. Say, "If you're all through with dinner, then your plate goes up. Are you through?" If he says, "Yes," that is that. Put his plate up matter-of-factly. Irritation on your part will only hinder his learning.

Disliked foods. But suppose you decide it is not disinterest in the meal as a whole, but dislike of one food that is holding your child back.

At once reduce in amount a food which proves to be disliked. At once, without comment, take his plate away and remove all of the disliked food except a tiny bit, say an eighth of a teaspoonful. Leave the other portions as served. Do this promptly, because if you wait until he has stalled around, you are just teaching him that by dawdling over his food he can get you to remove some. Bring his plate back and set it in front of him without comment. If he asks why there is less of the disliked food, tell him it is to make it easier to finish up. If he finishes up and wants more, fine. But be sure on the second go-round to give an extremely small portion of the disliked food. Suppose on the other hand he does not want to finish up. That is all right. Be agreeable about it: "If you've finished, up goes your plate and away you go from the table."

Scale frequency of inclusion in the menu and size of serving to your child's acceptance of a food. Once you have discovered a food which your child dislikes, leave it off the menu for several weeks. When you include it again, make sure that all the other foods at the meal are ones he really enjoys, so that they will serve as an incentive to want "more." You want to make it very easy for him to accept the foods served him, so you give him only an eighth of a teaspoonful or even less of any disliked food.

Try to anticipate your child's food dislikes in this way so that you are rarely involved in reducing the size of a portion once it is on his plate. This will promote his getting used to the idea that he eats what is there, instead of coming to expect you to take away some of his food.

If another child asks, "Why does Janie have only one pea?" you can answer, "Because she is learning to eat them," and let it go at that.

Try to remedy whatever aspect of the food your child dislikes. Try to figure out what makes your child dislike a particular food: taste, temperature, consistency—one or more of these may be the answer. If taste is the problem, what I have advised so far is the way to deal with it. If, however, it seems to be the consistency which puts him off, help him out further if you can. A number of children object to peas because they seem to dislike the skin. If you think this is the case, then mash his tiny serving with a fork. (No conversation about it.) As your child comes to accept the food, gradually reduce the amount of mashing until you can discontinue it altogether. If the consistency of meat bothers him, tear apart with a fork the small serving you give him. Gradually decrease the degree of pulling apart you do as he comes to accept the food.

Keep conditioning in mind to avoid creation of food dislikes. And always remember the conditioning process. Make sure that the food you serve is neither too hot nor too cold. I have seen a child develop a dislike for string beans which lasted for months, because one serving of beans was so hot that it burnt him. Or, if your child happens, say, to be coming down with intestinal flu when he has a particular food, the feeling of nausea may become attached to it. This is not likely to occur if you have been following the advice I have been giving, because feeling sick generally leads to a lack of interest in eating which you would respond to by suggesting that he end his meal if he has had enough.

As a child comes to accept a disliked food, gradually increase the size of the serving until it approximates that of the other foods at that meal.

When your child dislikes milk. If your child heartily dislikes milk and you have been urging him to drink it, then, in keeping with my advice to serve him only foods he really likes till the eating program has been going well for a week, discontinue serving milk. If he asks for some other liquid, just say it does not go along with dinner (or breakfast, or supper). You do not want to get him accustomed to a different beverage at his meals.

Then, after the eating program has been going pretty well for a week or so, reintroduce milk. Remember, now, that your first goal is simply to get your child to have an accepting attitude toward milk, not to have him consume a specified amount. It is worth introducing something different for him to drink out of, on the chance this will help—a small red plastic glass, say. Introduce it without comment. If your child asks about it, you might say you thought it might be nice for a change. No talk of milk drinking.

If your child is really set against milk, barely cover the bottom of his glass. If his dislike is not so pronounced, scale the amount to his ease in accepting it, but keep it small. From here on, deal with his milk drinking as you would deal with any other food dislike. If he finishes all his meal except his milk and asks for more, say, "Yes, as soon as you're all finished."

Discourage conversation about disliked foods. Sometimes, especially if more than one child is eating at a table, conversation keeps going on about a disliked food. Discourage such talk, but be accepting of the fact that the child does not like the food in question. "Yes," you may say, "I know how you feel. But we all heard you the first time. There's no need to keep talking about it." Then introduce another topic of conversation, if he is not apt to be distracted from eating by your talk. If he insists on going on about his dislike, you may need to tell him that he will have his meal by himself so other people do not have to listen. Be sure you mean this before you say it. If you decide to say it, say it just once. Then, if necessary, follow up with the implied consequence.

Introducing new foods. Keep to a system of giving small portions of a new food on the first serving, small enough so that once your child has taken a taste it is likely to be all gone. Increase the portions when it is clear he likes the food. And, of course, serve the new foods along with ones he really likes.

Play at meals. In the preschool years, play at meals often interferes with eating. Therefore I recommend that you cultivate the attitude that it is fine to have a nice time at meals, but meals are not the time to play. How do you do it?

The play of a 2- or young 3-year-old is likely to be with his food or utensils. A useful technique for dealing with utensil-play is to say, "Your spoon's for eating. It goes on your plate if you're not using it." You may need to set it there. Another technique (be agreeable about it) is to take the spoon and put it down out of reach. Wait till your child notices it is gone and reaches or asks for it, then tell him why you took it away. Give it back if he wants to use it to eat with. You can do the same thing with his dinner plate.

If he is playing because he has had enough and is no longer interested in eating, then it is time to end the meal. "If you're all through, your plate goes up." As for 4-year-olds: they also play with food and utensils, but they are more likely to indulge in play with another child. If it is social play that is interfering with eating, there are various ways to control oversociability at mealtimes. Suppose silly wordplay is going on, the kind 4-year-olds often find amusing. It may be that introducing an interesting (not too fascinating) topic of conversation will do the trick. Or perhaps "That's lots of fun. I'll remind you of the words you were saying when it's playtime" will take care of the matter.

When your child is distracted by other people at mealtimes. If your child is so interested in watching and listening and talking at the family table that he forgets to eat (perhaps because he is not developmentally ready to be there yet, and you have made a mistake in including him), you may need to remove him as you tell him something to this effect: "There's so much to watch and hear that you're forgetting all about dinner. I'm moving your plate out to the kitchen to make it easier to finish up, so you'll have time to have more if you want." This is as close as I would get to speaking directly of a child's eating. It still does not fall into the category of "Hurry up and eat." But remember, if your child is distracted a good deal by family sociability, it will be much easier to have him eat ahead of time, and so be able to take part in sociability when the rest of the family eats. Whether this is advisable will depend in part, of course, on how convenient it is for you.

FLUCTUATIONS IN APPETITE

You need to remember all along that your child's appetite is going to fluctuate. Do not think that what he eats when he is most hungry is par, and that anything else is less than he should take. Be sure to let him be the one to set the total amount he eats.

When your child is sick, you will have to watch yourself like a hawk to see that you do not put pressure on him to eat when he does not feel like it. A feeding problem can easily begin at such a time.

It is natural, of course, to be concerned about your child. But if you leave him alone to let his appetite catch up when he is over his illness, the chances are he will make up for lost time.

THE EXAMPLE SET BY THE PEOPLE YOUR CHILD EATS WITH

It is hard to overestimate the influence on your child's eating of the attitudes toward food of the people he eats with. If other people are forever talking about what they do not like (or even what they do like) or picking at their food, you can hardly expect your child to learn to accept what is put before him. Now grownups should have some privileges. I do not hold that you have to eat everything your child does. But I do think it will be a big help to his eating if you can bring yourself to use the same system you demand of him. Take a tiny serving of a disliked food, instead of passing it up altogether. You may surprise yourself and learn not only to accept it, but to like it.

SUMMARY: EATING

Here are the points covered in this section:

Your child's health

Plan your child's day to promote hunger at mealtimes

Arrange surroundings to foster your child's eating habits

Advantages of eating apart from the family

Equipment scaled to his size

Arrange the setting so that spilling will not matter much

Make it easy to add additional servings to the small ones given at the start of a meal

Serve food which needs cutting in bite-sized portions

Serve attractive combinations of food

How you act in guiding your child's eating

A trend in children's attitudes toward food which has been on the increase in recent years

Give small servings

Start off this program by serving only foods he likes

Give him some of each food in the entire meal at each serving

Cultivating manners

> Sitting facing the table

> Getting feet comfortable

> The way your child asks for more

After you have put your child's plate in front of him, leave him alone unless he is playing

When eating time is almost over, tell him so

Keep from telling your child to eat or talking about his eating where he can hear you

"Helping" your child put food on his spoon

Servings of milk

Keep from referring to specific items of food by precise name—especially in the case of disliked foods

Have your child finish up all of one serving before he gets more disliked foods

> At once reduce in amount a food which proves to be disliked

> Scale frequency of inclusion in the menu and size of serving to your child's acceptance of a food

> Try to remedy whatever aspect of the food your child dislikes

> Keep conditioning in mind to avoid creation of food dislikes

> When your child dislikes milk

> Discourage conversation about disliked foods

Introducing new foods

Play at meals

When your child is distracted by other people at mealtimes

Fluctuations in appetite

The example set by the people your child eats with

If you follow these suggestions, you are likely to feel the satisfaction which we did in our nursery school when a 4-year-old eyed her dinner plate and announced to the world at large, "I've learned to like liver." Talking this way was her idea.

Sleep

AIMS FOR YOUR CHILD'S SLEEP

It is not too much to hope that your child has an attitude of real acceptance toward going to bed, at naptime and at night; that, once put to bed, he chooses to settle down, relax, and let sleep take over. But he is going to need some help to feel this way during his preschool years, more help at some times than at others. What can you do to promote this kind of attitude and behavior about bedtime?

YOUR ATTITUDE TOWARD SLEEP IN GENERAL AND TOWARD YOUR CHILD'S SLEEP IN PARTICULAR

If your child is growing up in a home where he hears talk of people's difficulties in getting to sleep, of waking at dawn, and so forth, it is likely to interfere with fostering the attitudes toward sleep just described. Keep him away from talk about other people's sleeping problems.

And never use going to bed as a punishment or as a place to park your child. Bed is a place for sleep—hopefully, an inviting, friendly place, for a small child who is sufficiently tired out by the day's activities.

How much sleep does your child need? This may be a question which worries you. If so, talk it over with your doctor, out of your child's hearing. Be sure you do not have an exaggerated idea of how much sleep your child needs. If you do, you are apt to make him dislike going to bed by putting him there before he needs to go.

A PATTERN TO YOUR CHILD'S DAY TO HELP HIM FEEL SLEEPY AT BEDTIMES

Work out a pattern to his day which helps your child feel sleepy when it is time for bed. Regular hours for sleep, keyed to your child's individual needs, help him both accept bedtimes and feel sleepy when they come.

During the day your child needs plenty of vigorous activity, preferably in the open air. Before bedtime he will profit by quiet activities, quiet physically and psychologically, to help him feel relaxed instead of keyed up. Blood-and-thunder television is not likely to help.

NIGHT SLEEP

Pleasant, quiet activities before bedtime at night. What sort of pleasant, quiet activity can be carried on in your home before your child's bedtime depends, of course, on what else is happening then. If he has had his supper earlier than the rest of the family and goes to bed before they eat, perhaps he can have a regular date to be read to by one of his parents. Or he can listen to records. Records have a great advantage over television: you know what they hold in store. A quiet, enjoyable activity before bedtime can both put your child in a pleasant frame of mind and remind him that bedtime is on the way.

When bedtime comes, remember to phrase requirements impersonally: "Time for bed." Carry him if he is still small enough, or lead him by the hand. You want to keep the tone of life pleasant and cozy.

Arrange surroundings to encourage your child's sleeping. I hope that from the time your child is big enough to be in a playpen, you have encouraged him to acquire the attitude that bed is the place for sleep. When he was a baby, you let him know the playpen meant play by giving him playthings to use there. You let him know, too, that bed was a place for sleep by the way you settled him down and by the absence of toys, except for the special ones he snuggled down with.

Suppose your child is sick in bed; you will probably need to help him learn to mark off playtime from sleeptime. If he is old enough to have playthings in bed, you can help him realize that the time has come to settle down for day or night sleep by putting away the toys he has been using. If he is not too ill to put things away with your help, have him do so. A shift in bed position, if you can manage it easily, is also a good idea for the playtime of a sick child. Move his bed near the window, for instance, so that he can see out. Then when sleeptime comes, return it to its usual place.

Every day, well or ill, it helps to have your child's room reasonably tidied up before it is time for bed—at least I think it helps. If you agree, see that this activity gets worked into the day's events regularly, well before bedtime. The end of the last play session in your child's room is a good time for this. Suppose the sequence of events is: helping him tidy his room, bath, supper, quiet play in another part of the house. A tidy room is more tranquil than a cluttered one, and your child is less likely to be lured out of bed by playthings if they are not lying around practically under his nose.

When bedtime comes, have your child go through his pre-bedtime chores. He probably wants to take something to bed. This is fine, but limit the toys that go into bed at sleeptime to soft ones, and a reasonable number of those, to prevent him from raising the ante in pre-bedtime arrangements. Go-to-bed toys should not encourage such active manipulation that they tend to keep your child awake. It is a good idea to foster a little diversity in what he takes to bed—not always his teddy bear, sometimes his woolly lamb. This will keep him from becoming so attached to one object that it is a catastrophe to lose it. If he is still in the chewing stage, be sure he is provided with his "chew thing," as a child I know calls it. Or if he is using pacifiers, have one in bed, or several if he tends to lose them in the night and call out.

The manner in which your child actually gets into bed is worth some thought. Avoid lowering the side of the crib when your child is nearby, so that he never sees it moved or in a changed position. As long as he is small enough, lift him in and out of bed. When he is bigger and it is easier for you to have him climb in by himself, set the stage to encourage him to stay put by always placing something for him to climb on, say a sturdy chair, next to his crib and then moving it out of reach as soon as the climb is completed. Of course, he may well take to climbing in and out despite this climbing chair. If he does, there is no longer a point in the myth of the climbing aid. I have known children brought up on the climbing-chair arrangement, though, who once in bed tended to stay put. I have also known children, encouraged to climb into their cribs without aid, who made a habit of climbing out and prancing around as soon as they had mastered the climb in. I even know one whose favorite midnight occupation well before he was 3 was to climb out of his crib, go downstairs, and run the vacuum cleaner.

As long as your child's crib is comfortably roomy for him and as long as he tends to stay in it, there are great advantages to keeping on using a crib rather than shifting to a bed without sides. A regular bed encourages roaming. Save the shift from crib to bed until your child is ready for the kind of guidance which involves showing him the consequence of his behavior and letting him choose what to do (p. 169, pp. 174–77).

Incidentally, the term "bed," throughout the discussion of sleep, does not imply that your child has graduated from a crib.

If the presence of some particular object in the room proves so inviting that it leads your child to get out of bed, step in right away before a habit is formed. If this had been done with Gretchen, the little girl I told you about earlier, her parents would have been spared the problem of how to deal with a fixed habit a year and a half later—rocking each night for as much as two hours before finally falling asleep in her chair (p. 118).

Always clear the decks of any distraction, then, that make it hard for your child to stay in bed. He may still climb out, of course, but he is less likely to.

A young child enjoys a certain amount of ritual at bedtime. Do not, however, let it become too time consuming. Let us say, first toilet and teeth are taken care of; then your child has a small drink of water; next he gets into his crib; his lamb goes with him, too; you sing one good-night song, and then—that's that. Good night, and out you go.

You are used to the idea, I trust, that the rest of the household does not have to tiptoe around because a child has gone to bed. Neither, though, should loud, enticing noises broadcast the fact that he is missing life, stowed away as he is in his room.

Now, before discussing various bedtime problems, let us talk of settling down for day sleep.

DAY SLEEP

It is worth cultivating a pattern for your child in which day sleep comes right after his midday meal. He has had a full morning's activity. His hunger is satisfied. Sleep now will give him the latter part of the afternoon in which to be active, so that he has a chance to become sleepy again for bedtime at night at a fairly early hour. If he goes to bed as soon as he is through his midday meal, he does not have to be interrupted in a play activity.

The midday meal itself is a sufficiently quiet activity to be a good prelude to sleep. Just as at nighttime, have his room reasonably tidy, the light subdued, and go-to-bed procedure an accustomed ritual, hopefully briefer than at night. Tuck him in, say "Good night," and leave him.

TROUBLES AT BEDTIME AND DURING THE NIGHT

Protest at bedtime. Suppose that instead of the pretty little picture I have painted, you no sooner close the door than he starts yelling bloody murder. What then?

Bedtime evasions. As always, the first question is: What motives are prompting this behavior? Suppose your child usually settles down happily. Then one night he sets up a howl once his door is closed. Go back at once to see what the trouble is, but do not be dramatic. If you rush in as if to rescue him from a sinking ship, you are likely to be encouraging him to howl in the future.

Ask him what he would like to say. His reply may give you some clues. Suppose he has thought of some loved object left outdoors. Help him by rescuing it, but the next night be sure that rescue work occurs before bedtime. Suppose, however, he says he wants to kiss you again, or that he wants his elephant in his crib, or that he is hungry. This suggests he has nothing more on his mind than a desire for more sociability and playtime. One can sympathize with the feelings of a small child who wants to postpone the end of the day, but it is a kindness to him to help him accept bedtime without protest and sorrow. Be firm but cheerful. Lingering over your farewell is going to make him feel it pays to keep on with evasions. Tell him he can give you an extra big hug in the morning—"Good night." Or, point out that he chose Lamb tonight; Elephant can have a turn in bed tomorrow. Or, if he says he is hungry, say that he can eat an extra big breakfast tomorrow. This is good night. And off you go.

Now, of course, there is such a thing as real anxiety at the prospect of being separated from you. Dealing with this is a different proposition.

Real anxiety at bedtime. Children may develop intense anxiety which interferes with sleep, particularly around the age of 2. One cause may be any sudden change in the life a child knows. Perhaps, for example, you went away on a trip, leaving your child behind, or perhaps your family has moved and uprooted him from familiar surroundings. In any case, he has reacted by being deeply disturbed for fear you are going to leave him. Such feelings are likely to be at a high pitch at bedtime. Your child is not angry at the prospect of your going out of his room. He is deeply frightened, even panicky. The best thing to do, once you are convinced that he is really anxious, is to settle down comfortably and stay put until he is sound asleep. It will help if you look sleepy, too, if you relax physically, close your eyes, breathe slowly and deeply, and keep quiet. Do not keep peeking at him. This will just give him something to stay awake for.

I realize, of course, that what I advise here is just the opposite of the prompt, firm, cheerful withdrawal recommended a moment ago. You are now dealing with an entirely different kind of emotion. Your child needs reassurance; he needs it badly. Once he has overcome his anxiety, you will probably be left with a problem of protest, even violent protest, when you start to go out of his room at night. And then you will have to cope with that. So, to the best of your ability, do not magnify in your mind the kind of common bedtime evasions which most children try their hand at—do not attribute these to deep anxiety. A 2-year-old will give you many indications if he is deeply fearful of the possibility of separation from you.

Readjustment to being left at bedtime, once anxiety has been overcome. When your child has overcome his anxiety, and has also become thoroughly used to your being in his room at go-to-sleep times, then you have the job of helping him readjust to going to sleep without your company. Wait until you are sure his anxiety has gone—for if you start your program of readjustment and have to discontinue it, you will only be teaching him that protest pays off. Once his anxiety is over, though, it is better for both of you—and for the rest of the family, too—to get yourself disentangled from his bedtime.

To accomplish this you are going to have to go back to your original prompt, firm, cheerful departure, not by easy stages but, once you start, absolutely consistently. He will probably cry, hard and loud. He is angry. Leave him alone and do not go back. It is a good idea every night to jot down the time you leave his room and the time he finally stops making noise. This record will help you to see that progress is being made.

This readjustment period is a poor time for you to go out for the evening. You need to be on deck until the fireworks are all over so he will not become anxious over your whereabouts.

What are you going to do if your child keeps climbing out of his bed and coming out of his room? Take him back, promptly, and put him in bed. If he persists, arrange his surroundings so that he will not come out.

Now, I am fully aware of the psychological disadvantages of fastening a child's door. But sometimes it is the least of other evils. In this case, install a fastening on his door, out of his reach on the outside, which keeps the door from moving (for if it moves even a little, this is likely to make your child more angry). If you have to install a door fastening to keep him in his room at bedtime, try to arrange matters so that it is useful to your child on other occasions. For instance, if there is another child in the family who often disturbs him when he wants to be by himself, you can encourage him to request the fastening of his door when he wants to be alone. At bedtime, tell him that he needs to be in bed and that if he keeps coming out of his room, the door will have to be fastened. Once said, do it if he comes out again. If he protests as the fastening goes on, go back in at once (rather than delaying) and say, "If you can manage to stay in by yourself, fine. You won't need the door fastened to help you." If he chooses this, he has to do his part. Coming outside the room then means the fastener goes on to stay for the rest of the evening. Be sure to have it unfastened before he wakes in the morning.

This period of readjustment when your no-longer-frightened child is trying through anger to make you stay with him is hard for you. But do not despair. Once he is convinced you mean what you say when you tell him good night, you may be surprised how quickly he learns to settle down without protest.

Mild bedtime fears. Your child may go through a stage in which, while he does not feel deep anxiety over separation from you at bedtime, he has fears of a milder sort and is reluctant to see you go. Reassure him without resorting to staying in his room. If he takes to clinging to you, with a long, loving farewell, transfer your good-night hugs to another room, before he actually gets in bed. It may help him to have the other parent put him in his bed, the one to whom he has not been clinging. In any case, be cheerful and matter-of-fact.

In such circumstances, time your departure to avoid going out for the evening just at bedtime. Have a thoroughly reliable sitter whom your child knows and likes arrive well before bedtime. And follow the suggestions given in other sections for helping your child feel comfortable with a sitter and easy about your departure (p. 100, p. 340).

In all of these examples of protest at bedtime (bedtime evasions; real anxiety at bedtime; readjustment to being left alone at bedtime, once anxiety has been overcome; and mild bedtime fears), it is your child's feelings at bedtime that have been interfering with his settling down comfortably for the night. Your job all along has been to try to figure out precisely what his feelings are and to modify them so that he will feel secure. As far as possible, see to it that his experiences throughout the day reassure him. Suppose you decide he is afraid of getting wet at night. You may have put too much stress on staying dry. Then stop doing it and assure him it is all right if he does get wet. If, instead, it is jealousy of another child in the family that is keeping him awake at bedtime, you will have to help him feel comfortable and secure despite having a brother or sister. Your job, in short, is to help him cope with his feelings and to guide them so that they do not interfere with his peace of mind and disrupt his sleep. You will find various specific suggestions for helping your child cope with jealousy in the next two chapters (p. 296, pp. 321–23).

Troubles and wakefulness during the night. When your child, who normally sleeps through the night, wakes and cries or calls out, go to him promptly and try to find out what the trouble is. There are many possibilities. He may, for example, feel sick, or have a pain, or have had a bad dream, or feel fearful about something.

As a general policy it is sound to comfort and assist him without taking him out of bed. You are less likely to wake him up thoroughly. Even more important, you minimize the chances of making it worth his while to wake up just in order to have your company. If you walk around with him or take him into your room, certainly if you take him into bed with you, you are only inviting him to keep on with nighttime disturbances in order to be with you.

What you do to make him comfortable depends, of course, on what you decide is the matter. If you think he is sick and running a fever, taking his temperature may be in order. If this in itself is an emotional ordeal, however, then by all means try to avoid it during the night unless it is strongly indicated for reasons of health. If it is an earache, naturally you follow your doctor's directions to ease the pain. If it is a bad dream, a pat and "You're all right" may be all he needs.

If, on the other hand, your child wakes in the night with intense anxiety, you will simply be faced with the necessity of using the kind of guidance advised for severe anxiety at bedtime: put on something warm, if necessary, and stay with him until he is asleep. Again, I urge you, do not take him into bed with you. You will pay too dear a price for this—the formation of a habit of getting into bed with you during the night.

Though you may think I am hardhearted, I would keep from livening up nighttime by various ministrations. You need your sleep, too. Though sometimes he might be more comfortable if you gave him a drink of water, other things matter more: development of a habit of going back to sleep if he wakens during the night, giving you a chance to have the sleep you need.

In the case of severe nightmares, which may leave your child immersed in his dream, your job is different. You need to rouse him enough to feel reassured. Suppose he has just awakened from a nightmare. His eyes are open—wide, frightened eyes—but you doubt if he even knows you are there. Talk to him to rouse him. This is one time to take him out of bed, to hold him in your lap if you think it will help to reassure him and wake him from his dream. But keep him in his room. When he quiets down, put him back to bed. Stay with him while he needs comfort for his fear.

If he has frequent nightmares, a large part of your guidance should occur in the daytime. During the day, try to get across to him the notion that everyone has bad dreams; there is just one good thing about them—when a person wakes up, he knows it's just a dream. Try to figure out what may have contributed to nightmares; worries of some sort, scary stories, movies, or television, physical discomfort, even just being covered too warmly may produce bad dreams. Eliminate causes if you can, but do not be surprised if you discover no clues at all and have to resort merely to comforting your child when nightmares occur.

PROMOTING QUIET IN THE MORNING

What do you want your child to do when he wakes in the morning? A lot depends on how old he is. If you want him to play quietly in bed till you come to get him up, then place something in his crib after he goes to sleep which will give him occupation in the morning. Three or four interesting books may appeal to him, or a manipulative toy. But I would not expect him to stay in bed after waking in the morning for more than half or three-quarters of an hour, at the outside. He probably wants to be up and doing, and he has a right to be if it is a fairly civilized hour. You know already that I am in favor of encouraging the myth that he needs to have you place a chair beside his crib in order to climb out. You should not make him wait too long if you want him to keep on with this practice. If you do not care whether he climbs out of bed by himself, and you hope to snatch a few more winks, you can have his bathrobe and slippers right beside his crib. Tell him the night before to put them on before starting to play. But do not be surprised if this system results in his starting the day at 2 A.M.

HOW TO DEAL WITH NAPTIME PROBLEMS

Motivate your child to settle down instead of playing. Unless your child is emotionally upset, the chances are that when he is close to 24 months of age he falls asleep readily when he is put down right after his midday meal. As he gets closer to 3, he becomes more and more able to keep himself awake. You will then need to motivate him to settle down for afternoon sleep. What can you do in addition to your consistent day-by-day practice of having afternoon sleep come right after the midday meal—and in addition to the procedures already suggested for creating a situation conducive to his going to sleep? How can you motivate him to lie still enough so that if he needs to sleep he will choose to stay quiet enough to do so?

One procedure, already referred to, is to remove objects from his room which might entice him out of bed for play. I know one 3-year-old who had to have all his playthings removed from his room for a week (of course, he could use them when it was playtime). At the end of that time, he felt he could manage to leave them alone at naptime if they remained in his room; and he did.

Another procedure is to leave him alone in his room though you know he is playing until about ten minutes before it is time to get up. (I should say here that if your child has not gone to sleep after a rest of an hour's duration, he should be allowed to get up.) Then about fifty minutes after he has been put down, go into his room and tell him, as you tuck him in, "If you had settled down and had a real rest it would be time to get up now. But since you didn't, you need to finish up your rest before it is time to get up. Get in a comfortable position." Then go out of the room, but stay close by. Once he has lain still for two or three minutes, let him get up. Make it easy for him to comply with your requirement that he lie still. It is actually better that he not go to sleep now, it is so late. Sleep which starts now can interfere with going to sleep at a reasonable hour after supper.

You will note that I did not suggest telling your child that he did not sleep. The suggested talk was all in terms of settling down. It is important not to stress sleep itself; your child has the upper hand here. He can keep himself awake if he wants to. On the other hand, if he conscientiously tries too hard to go to sleep, he may keep himself awake trying. Emphasizing settling down so that he has a "real rest" highlights the behavior which is likely to lead to sleep, but without stressing sleep itself.

You will notice, too, that I did not recommend your popping in at the start of your child's rest to tell him to settle down. The reason is that he would probably find this a satisfactory consequence. He enjoys your company. It is nice that he does, but if you go into his room whenever you hear him moving around, you will make it worth his while to be restless in order to get you to come in.

When he omits his usual daytime sleep, compensate with an earlier bedtime. Tell him that since he did not happen to have a sleep today, it is time for bed early. It is sound to make this earlier bedtime significant to him by the absence of some event he enjoys in the usual pre-bedtime activities. "No time for a story tonight," for instance, "because it is bedtime now." If he feels sad, be sympathetic and comfort him. This is not a punishment. You are simply trying to make him want to settle down at naptime. The next afternoon when you put him down, remind him, if he is old enough to think this far ahead, that if he happens to have a sleep he will not need to go to bed early after supper.

End afternoon sleep in time to avoid interference with bedtime at night. With your doctor's approval, see that your child wakes from his afternoon sleep before it has lasted so long that it appreciably puts off going to sleep at a reasonable hour at night. By the time he is 2½ or 3, the chances are that if he sleeps much longer than an hour and a half or two hours, his day sleep will substitute for night sleep. Suppose you put him in bed about quarter of one, after his midday meal, and he usually falls asleep within about 20 minutes. Suppose that when he sleeps past three in the afternoon he tends to stay awake in bed at night a good deal longer than usual. In this case, get him up at three o'clock. If it makes your child cross to be wakened, when you go into his room put up the shades and rattle around doing something. As he rouses, you might mention something pleasant that will take place when he is up. I do not mean a gilt-edged special occasion. Maybe it is just a kind of fruit juice he especially likes which he is going to have in a few minutes; maybe it is a walk to see the new puppies next door.

Let your child get up from afternoon sleep as soon as he wakes. It is only fair to your child, and conducive to his feeling that bed is a place for sleep, to let him get up from afternoon sleep when he wakes, unless, of course, he happens to be roused from sleep by some occurrence well before an hour is up. Then you may need to tell him it is not time to get up yet; but let him up pretty soon if he does not fall asleep again.

When sleep drops out, encourage rest with quiet activity. Children vary a lot in the age at which sleep in the afternoon drops out. It is important to distinguish between play which interferes with needed daytime sleep and a lack of need for sleep. When your child's sleep begins to drop out, this takes the form, as you probably know, of skipping sleep altogether some days and continuing to sleep on others. Most children who need afternoon sleep keep on sleeping well past their fourth birthday if they are motivated to lie still enough to fall asleep at the start of their afternoon rest.

Once it is pretty clear that afternoon sleep has become a rarity, let your child have some play materials during a rest after his midday meal, rather than trying to motivate him to lie still. Consult him about it. Tell him that he needs to have a quiet time after dinner (lunch). Does he think it will work to play quietly if he is up in his room, or would it be easier if he lies in bed? In any event it is not reasonable to extend afternoon rest beyond an hour.

SUMMARY: SLEEP

Here are the points covered in this section on sleep:

Aims for your child's sleep

Your attitude toward sleep in general and toward your child's sleep in particular

A pattern to your child's day to help him feel sleepy at bedtime

Night sleep

Pleasant, quiet activities before bedtime at night

Arrange surroundings to foster your child's sleeping habits

Day sleep

Troubles at bedtime and during the night

Protest at bedtime

Bedtime evasions

Real anxiety at bedtime

Readjustment to being left at bedtime, once anxiety has been overcome

Mild bedtime fears

Troubles and wakefulness during the night

Promoting quiet in the morning

How to deal with naptime problems

Motivate your child to settle down instead of playing

End afternoon sleep in time to avoid interference with bedtime at night

Let your child get up from afternoon sleep as soon as he wakes

When sleep drops out, encourage rest with quiet activities

Elimination

AN HISTORICAL PERSPECTIVE ON GUIDANCE OF ELIMINATION

During the thirties, along with an emphasis upon habit training, which was prevalent at that time, the desirability of early toilet training was stressed. Wobbly little infants five or six weeks old were placed on chamber pots, often after insertion of a suppository to induce movement of the bowels. It was common for babies less than a year old to be subjected to bladder training. Later, the pendulum of child-rearing practices swung in the other direction, away from the early habit-training approach. Permissiveness was the watchword in the forties. This was due in part to the influence of Freudian concepts with their emphasis upon the importance to infants and small children of instinctual interests and pleasures (among them eliminative functioning, particularly of the bowels), in part to other influences which led to a needs-centered approach to child rearing. Some people, in their concern to avoid the early toilet training which now came to be regarded as detrimental to a child's well-being, went so far in the other direction that they failed to take advantage of children's readiness to use a toilet. Certainly, if one has to choose between a hammer-and-tongs program of rigid toilet training and a program in which a child is left entirely to his own devices, I would choose the latter. But the choice does not have to lie between these two extremes. I am in favor of watching for signs of readiness and of encouraging children to function at the toilet when these signs occur.

WHO TAKES THE RESPONSIBILITY FOR THINKING OF GOING TO THE TOILET?

As I have just said, some people feel it is best to leave entirely up to a young child when he goes to the toilet. However, I think it makes more sense for a grownup to take the major responsibility when a child is 2, 3, and just 4—to tell him it is time to have a try, at certain times of day which fit his pattern of elimination. A preschool child, absorbed in play, can easily forget about going when he needs to. It is sound to encourage him to get used to an interruption of his play activities long enough to tend to his toilet needs with reasonable frequency. In the year before kindergarten, gradually let him be the one to toilet himself as he feels the need, by waiting to see when he will think of it and noting how urgent his need seems to be when he actually gets to the toilet. If he is putting it off too long, tell him, "You're getting big enough to take yourself to the toilet when you need to go." If he still puts it off too long, go back to telling him when it is time.

ATTITUDES TOWARD YOUR CHILD'S ELIMINATION— YOURS AND HIS

Perhaps you have been waiting patiently for your child to show signs of readiness for toilet training. Now you are beginning to wonder how long to keep waiting, for he seems content to go on forever functioning in his pants or diapers.

Or perhaps you have been impatient, convinced that your child was deliberately having a bowel movement in his pants or getting wet. Your feeling may be based on the fact that he told you right after functioning; you felt he could have told you ahead of time. But actually, announcement after functioning is a stage which comes before learning to express a need in advance. Or perhaps you have campaigned so intensively for training that you have put your child's back up by making him feel you are ordering him around about this toilet business. Particularly if he is in the neighborhood of 2, with characteristic feelings of independence, some of this strong drive for independence may lead him to resist efforts to make him function at the toilet.

Or it may be that he is frightened at the prospect of elimination. Perhaps functioning has hurt him, or the flushing of the toilet has made him afraid. Or, still another possibility, he may be worried that he will get wet; he keeps saying he needs to go to the toilet, though all he can do is squeeze out a few little drops of urine.

Whatever the case, think over your child's experiences to date with bowel and bladder functioning, including your attitudes toward his elimination, for they form the background for any plan of guidance at this time.

MAKE SURE NO PHYSICAL CONDITIONS ARE CONTRIBUTING TO DIFFICULTIES IN FUNCTIONING

I presume, as always, that your child is under a doctor's care and that you have been in touch with the doctor all along about your child's elimination and about your plans for guidance. If bowel movements or urination seem painful for your child, consult his doctor, of course, to find out if there are any physical causes.

I take it for granted that, with your doctor's advice, you regulate your child's diet and liquid intake so that the consistency of his bowel movements is not uncomfortably hard.

CHOOSE A SOUND TIME PSYCHOLOGICALLY TO START A GUIDANCE PROGRAM

Assuming, then, that painful functioning or other conditions requiring medical advice are ruled out, you need to decide when will be a good time to start a program of encouraging your child to use the toilet.

Allow a lapse of time after unsuccessful attempts at training. If unsuccessful attempts at guidance have made your child resistant or frightened, discontinue your attempts. For how long? Perhaps several weeks, perhaps several months, or even longer. In any case, long enough for him to feel at ease about bowel and bladder functioning. It is better to err on the side of waiting longer than necessary if your child is recovering from too strenuous a training program or from some fear related to functioning than to underestimate the length of time needed to help him feel relaxed about the whole toilet process. Another reason for allowing a generous time interval after unsuccessful attempts at toilet training is that once you start again, I hope you carry through consistently, as with any other kind of guidance.

Let your child see other people use the toilet. During the time when attempts at toilet training are discontinued (or before attempts are ever made in the first place, for that matter) I hope your child has a chance to see other people use the toilet as an incidental, natural event in the day.

Choose a time when life is going smoothly. When you do start a guidance program for bowel and/or bladder control, choose a time when life is going along pretty smoothly—not, for instance, when your child is just recovering from an illness, or when there has been unusual change in his life.

Keep a record of your child's elimination. Keep a record of your child's elimination for a week before starting your guidance. What does it tell you about his patterns of elimination? I shall show how this information can be useful as I discuss, in turn, bowel and then bladder functioning.

SIMULTANEOUS BOWEL AND BLADDER TRAINING OR ONE AT A TIME?

With most children, learning to have an evacuation at the toilet comes before learning to use it habitually to urinate. Whether you deal with one kind of training before the other or with both at once depends upon your child's pattern of elimination. If your attitude is genuinely casual and friendly and you are not in a hurry for results but appreciative of achievement, it works to encourage your child to use the toilet for both bowel and bladder functions, provided he is ready for the latter learning. However, if for some reason one kind of functioning at the toilet is likely to be more difficult for him to learn than the other, begin on the one which is likely to be easier.

ARRANGE YOUR CHILD'S SURROUNDINGS TO ENCOURAGE USING THE TOILET

Clothing. Make it easy for your child to manage his clothes himself. Fortunately, nowadays, children's clothes tend to be made with ease of handling in mind—underpants with elastic tops, zippers instead of buttons.

Your child's toilet seat. There are great advantages to the kind of child's toilet seat which can be used either with a pot underneath or set up on the grownup toilet, for then, if you are going to be away from readily available toilets, you can have your equipment right along with you.

I know a mother who had to take several transcontinental trips while her children were still in their preschool years. She devised a toilet setup to be kept in an accessible place in the car. It consisted of a child's toilet seat, a sturdy waterproof wastebasket, and waterproof garbage bags. She said that having it on hand contributed enormously to everyone's peace of mind.

Make access to the toilet easy. Whether your child uses his toilet seat over a pot or over a toilet, make it easy for him to use: in the case of seat-plus-pot, by having it set up in a place where he can get to it readily (always the same place, so he knows where to find it); in the case of seat-plus-toilet, by having a sturdy stool or set of steps near the toilet so that he can learn to climb to his seat by himself.

IF YOUR CHILD IS OVERCONCERNED ABOUT TOILET LAPSES, REASSURE HIM

If your child is really anxious about getting wet or having a movement in his pants, he needs reassurance. Tell him that you will be glad to help him get to the toilet, but that if he does not get there in time, you will fix him up comfortably and he can have a try to see if he needs to do some more. You might add, "By-and-by you will find it easy to get to the toilet like everyone else, so there is no need to worry about it."

First I shall discuss guidance in regard to bowel movements, then in regard to urination.

BOWEL MOVEMENTS

A record kept for a week helps answer the following kinds of questions: When do your child's bowel movements occur? Just any time, or with some regularity? Does he assume a particular posture or facial expression when he has a movement? If he is completely irregular and shows no signs of need, then forget about trying to have him arrive at the toilet before he functions. But in contrast to this, suppose he has a pretty definite pattern, say within ten minutes after breakfast. Or perhaps he does give some signs in advance, say squatting down a little. I am assuming that he has not yet begun to use a toilet. It is sound, when he is first encouraged to use his toilet seat, to place it on the floor over a pot at the time when he is likely to have an evacuation. Then there is no chance of his becoming frightened by the flushing of the toilet, or by a feeling of insecurity because of sitting up high. Remember the conditioning process when you have him use his seat. Be relaxed physically yourself. See that the toilet seat is at room temperature. Place him on his seat and sit down beside him. You are aiming to help him accept the idea of sitting on the seat. You are also hoping that he will function there. If he does, take him off the seat and let him see what he has done. If he does not, but does not object to sitting there, have him stay for five minutes. If, however, he begins to protest or be frightened on this first occasion of sitting on his toilet, help him off gently and say, "That's fine, you had a sit on a toilet just like Daddy and Mommy." If he has a movement in his pants right after leaving the toilet, clean him up without rebuke.

If, after several days, he seems comfortable about sitting on the toilet but nothing happens while he is there, then discontinue placing him on it at this time of day. Or, if he has been irregular in functioning, follow the course of guidance about to be described. Keep your record of when he functions. When he has a bowel movement in his pants, clean him up, of course, right away, and then put him gently on his toilet seat for a moment, suggesting "See if you need to do any more." There are two reasons for this: to help him feel accepting toward sitting on the seat, and to help him realize that having a movement involves sitting on the toilet. If by any chance just not wanting to bother to sit there is part of his motivation, he may now feel that he might as well climb on before he has a movement as afterwards, since he finds that he gets on in any case. By no means leave him there any length of time, just a few seconds at first, a little longer when he is used to the procedure. If he does happen to have more evacuation there, let him know he has achieved something. "That's the way. That's a comfortable

way to have your 'evac.' Now you are all ready to go back to play."
If he uses a special word for his bowel movement, you use it, too.

Perhaps you will say at this point that if what is desired is to
build up an association between having an evacuation and sitting on
a toilet, it will not do any good to put him there *after* he has functioned. My answer is simply that this system has worked effectively
with many children.

To move to another point, you have to help your child realize
when he has had a bowel movement. If you keep your 2-year-old in
diapers at the time of day he is likely to have it, he may well not be
aware when it happens. Therefore put him in training pants.

Whatever you do, do not blame him, or shame him, or appear
disgusted when he performs in his pants. Keep the whole affair
friendly and casual.

Once your child accepts sitting on his toilet seat, there are advantages to shifting it to a position over the regular toilet. Sitting
over a pot in which he has had an evacuation may invite him to
play with his movement. You must remember, if he does so, that
he does not have attitudes toward excretory products that a grownup
has. If you leave him too long over his pot and he plays with his
evacuation, he is not to blame; if you feel you must blame someone,
blame yourself. Clean him up cheerfully, and see to it that in the
future this kind of play does not happen by fixing him up promptly.
Also see that your child has a chance to enjoy play with such materials as mud and soft clay.

Help your child to feel easy about sitting over a regular toilet
on his own little seat by the way you deal with flushing. After he is
wiped, be unhurried about flushing. The first few times he sits over
a toilet, wait to flush it until he has left the bathroom. However,
he may actually enjoy the process of flushing. Let him try it, and
help him if needed. I know a mother who always asked, "Can you
flush your toilet," for she wanted to underline the notion that his
eliminative products were his business. Not a bad idea.

Incidentally, reserve toilet flushing for occasions when the toilet
needs it. If your child starts to reach to flush the toilet when he has
not performed, tell him it doesn't need flushing because he did not

do anything. If he enjoys flushing, this sometimes gives him an incentive to function when he needs to, particularly in regard to urination.

URINATION

Everything said about elimination in general applies, of course, to urination as well as to bowel evacuation.

Readiness for urination training. Your child's bladder needs to be mature enough to make urination training advisable. Children of the same age vary greatly in their readiness to start it. What does your record, kept for a week, reveal? To what extent does urination follow a pattern? How frequently does your child urinate? Some 2-year-olds are still getting wet every half-hour or so; clearly they are not ready to start urination training. What is the longest time your child ever goes between urinations? Being dry from time to time for as long as two hours at a stretch is a good indication that your child's bladder is mature enough for you to begin encouraging him to use the toilet when he is likely to need to urinate. Remember also, small children need a chance to find out what purpose toilets serve by seeing other people use them.

Right now your aim is not to have your child stay dry all day long; it is twofold: to help him have an accepting attitude toward using the toilet, and to help him learn to urinate there. Sometimes accomplishment only comes in two steps, in this order.

How often do you take him to the toilet when you start your training program? At the start, take your child to the toilet only after he has been dry for two hours. You are gradually working up to the same system you use in bowel training, but if you begin this system at once, the chances are you would be taking him to the toilet too many times during the day and he would probably become resistant.

Keep a record of your child's urination. Continue to keep a daily record of the exact times when your child urinates during the training period.

Training pants, not diapers. Now that you have begun to encourage your child to urinate in a toilet, put him into training pants in the daytime instead of diapers. If you keep him in diapers, he may well be unaware when he urinates. Becoming aware is a necessary part of learning to get to the toilet before it happens. When he first begins to comment, he will probably tell you afterwards, not before. Eventually he will be able to tell you that he needs to empty his bladder before it happens.

"It's time to have a try at the toilet." There is a good reason for using this particular phrase when you take your child to the toilet after two hours of dryness. The "It's time to" part of the phrase shows that going to the toilet is an impersonal business requirement, not a whim. This is in keeping with what has already been said about business activities. The second part, "have a try at the toilet," reflects the fact that your child holds all the aces when it comes to actually functioning at the toilet. The psychoanalytical point of view has stressed that children have a possessive attitude toward their excretory products, bowel movements particularly. Whether you think of your child's elimination in a psychoanalytical framework or not, there is no doubt that toilet training often coincides with a child's strivings for independence. If you are dictatorial in telling him he has to perform at the toilet, you may make him feel he has to fight for his independence, and here is an area where he can fight successfully.

Keep your child at the toilet only long enough to have time to urinate if he needs to.

What if he gets wet as soon as he leaves the toilet? Put him in dry pants without criticism—and without any unspoken disapproval, either.

A pattern for toileting to fit your child's needs, plus toileting when he gets wet. Now let us suppose that quite often your child is dry for two hours and often he urinates when taken to the toilet. Your records also show that he tends to get wet about 10:30 A.M. Then anticipate his need by taking him just before this time. By the time he is urinating in the toilet pretty regularly when he is taken after two hours of dryness, the chances are his bladder is now mature enough so that you will not be taking him to the toilet too many times if you shift to "Have a try at the toilet" whenever he is wet. Change wet pants right away to help him prefer the feeling of being dry. Perhaps you wonder what is the point of taking him to the toilet *after* he is wet. The reasoning is the same as in the case of a bowel movement. When your child finds that after he gets wet he has a try at the toilet, he may feel that he might as well go there before he is wet. Furthermore, a child at this stage often has not emptied his bladder; he may need to urinate some more.

Always be ready to change the pattern of toileting according to changed needs. Be alert to keep your pattern of toileting up-to-date in terms of your child's needs. Drop unnecessary trips to the bathroom, but maintain a framework of reasonable times for a try in regard to urination; certainly before breakfast, before lunch if your child has not gone during the morning, before and after nap, before bath, before bed.

"Do you need to go to the toilet?" This question is a useful technique when your child is in a transitional stage of almost being ready to drop one of the toileting times when you usually take him. Note the phrasing. Do not say, "Do you want to go to the toilet?" which conveys something quite different. "Do you need to go . . . ?" emphasizes that you are asking your child to decide whether he needs "a try" or not. If he answers "No," abide by it. Do not ask, "Do you need to go to the toilet?" if what you really mean is that he should go.

Standing to urinate. Since a boy has to sit to urinate when he is a little fellow because of his short stature, he will probably become accustomed to a sitting position. Though there is no hurry about his standing to urinate, encourage him to do so when he is tall enough. Let him see other males function in this way, and then, sometime when he is about to urinate, say, "How about going to the toilet this way, the way Daddy does," as you guide him into position. If he is upset, do not make an issue of it. You will note that your suggestion is phrased to leave room for its withdrawal if he objects. Avoid proposing this kind of change just when a child is feeling generally negativistic. But continue to accustom him to the fact that men and boys urinate standing by letting him see this happen, and encourage him again to do so himself when he is likely to be more receptive to the idea.

Be prepared to have a little girl take it into her head to try to urinate standing, too. Once her intent is unmistakable, by her stance or by a remark, you tell her, "You sit down to go to the toilet because you're a little girl." Hopefully, she will respond to this remark before she starts to urinate. But it is not catastrophic if the explanation comes too late. Let her help clean up the floor, but without censure; stay friendly and relaxed. In connection with sitting to urinate, you may want to mention several females of whom your little girl is fond. "You sit down to go to the toilet like me and Aunt Jane, because you're a little girl and we're women." Your explanation may lead to some questions about anatomical differences; in any case you may want to add something to this effect: "Girls and women are shaped differently from boys and men. Boys stand at the toilet because they have a penis. Girls are made differently so they go sitting down." (See p. 305 for some of the reasoning behind this phrasing; for further discussion of guidance of sexuality, see pp. 302–10).

Techniques for guidance at the toilet. Here are a few more techniques useful for cultivating in your child desirable attitudes toward toileting and skills in performance:

"Can you pull down your pants?" Encourage your child to make the first motion. When he is first starting to learn to use the toilet: "You take hold of them [the pants] and I'll help you pull." If necessary, place his hands at either side of his pants, or if his hands are in place, put yours over his and "help him pull" by getting the pants down yourself. Gradually, of course, encourage him to manage this all by himself.

If he is just learning to use the toilet seat, lift him on gently, in an assured way. If he can climb up with help (and he is not in a hurry), help no more than he needs. Let him manage to climb on himself if he can do it pretty easily.

If he starts to get off as soon as you have put him on, say, "You need to sit there long enough to go if you need to." But if he is just becoming accustomed to the seat, use the procedure already described of accepting his token-sit as fulfilling the toilet requirement.

If he does not urinate promptly, tell him, "Off you get if you don't need to do anything."

Or, if he has already urinated, but still sits there: "If you're all finished, off you get."

Suppose he gets off and just stands there. You say, "Now what?" If he does not respond, add, "You need to pull up your pants." (Again, encourage him to be the one to make the first motion, but help as necessary.) As he does help himself: "That's the way."

As he manages to do more and more of the job of getting his pants up and down, recognize his achievement: "You can manage your pants almost all by yourself."

After giving him a chance to remember to flush the toilet, and finding he does not, say, "You forgot something," or tap the flusher, if necessary.

If he starts to flush the toilet although he has not functioned there: "You don't need to flush it because you didn't do anything." If he tries to keep on, put your hand on the flusher.

Staying dry at night. Most children learn to stay dry at night all by themselves when their bladders are sufficiently mature, but the age at which this happens varies a great deal.

Sometimes parents like to help night dryness along or to promote later sleep in the morning by taking a child to the toilet before they go to bed. If you want to do this, if your child goes back to sleep readily, and if he is not upset by being taken to the toilet, go ahead.

If, by the time a child is over 4, he is still getting wet at night regularly, it is sound to encourage him to stay dry. I have known children of this age who were kept in diapers and rubber pants. I suspect that they had no incentive to stay dry. It was rather cozy being wet and warm inside the various layers. If this seems to be the case, remove the diapers. Then your child's bed needs to be checked during the night. When it is wet, help him have a try at the toilet and get into dry sleepers; change his bed.

IF YOUR CHILD SHOWS A LAPSE IN EITHER BOWEL OR BLADDER CONTROL, CONCENTRATE ON CAUSES, NOT ON AN INTENSIFIED TRAINING PROGRAM

A siege of intestinal flu may well disrupt an established pattern of using the toilet for bowel movements. Do not be surprised at this. Particularly if your child has had discomfort in having bowel movements, he may need reassurance and the application of a soothing ointment. Patiently help him get used to having his evacuation at the toilet again, as you did in the beginning of his training.

Tension and emotional upset may cause temporary lapses in your child's bladder control. Rather than intensifying a program to keep him dry, try to relax life for him as you deal with his urination in the accustomed way.

SUMMARY: ELIMINATION

In this section, I have discussed the following points:

An historical perspective on guidance of elimination

Who takes the responsibility for thinking of going to the toilet?

Attitudes toward your child's elimination—yours and his

Make sure no physical conditions are contributing to difficulties in functioning

Choose a sound time psychologically to start a guidance program

    Allow a lapse of time after unsuccessful attempts at training

    Let your child see other people use the toilet

    Choose a time when life is going smoothly

    Keep a record of your child's elimination

Simultaneous bowel and bladder training or one at a time?

Arrange your child's surroundings to encourage using the toilet
> Clothing
> Your child's toilet seat
> Make access to the toilet easy

If your child is overconcerned about toilet lapses, reassure him

Bowel movements

Urination
> Readiness for urination training
> How often do you take him to the toilet when you start your training program?
> Keep a record of your child's urination
> Training pants, not diapers
> "It's time to have a try at the toilet"
> A pattern for toileting to fit your child's needs, plus toileting when he gets wet
> Always be ready to change the pattern of toileting according to changed needs
> "Do you need to go to the toilet?"
> Standing to urinate
> Techniques for guidance at the toilet
> Staying dry at night

If your child shows a lapse in either bowel or bladder control, concentrate on causes, not on an intensified training program

Dressing, washing, baths, tidying up

DRESSING

Most 2-year-olds are interested in the process of dressing, but it is difficult for them and slow. In other words, their motivation is high but their skills are low. You may well be tempted to keep on dressing your 2-year-old, since it is easier and quicker. The trouble is, if you keep on doing the whole job yourself, your child's interest will drop off. Then it may be extremely hard, later on, to get your 3- or 4-year-old to undertake the job himself. You need to take advantage of the time when he is interested in the performance of dressing in order to help him to develop dressing skills. By the time a child is 4, or even earlier, he is often bored by the process. It is much easier to get him to do the job with dispatch if his skills have already been developed than to try to get him to learn it from the ground up.

Clothes which make it easy for your child to dress himself. Even though, by and large, children's clothes are now usually designed to make it easy for a child to dress himself, look for this in clothing when shopping—for instance, overalls which zip up the front and stretchy waterproof overshoes.

Dressing should be done with dispatch. Encourage your child to feel that dressing is his responsibility, but help him get the job done with dispatch. You want him to take over more and more of the work as his skills advance, until, when he is 4, he does the whole job himself except for tying his shoes and fastening hard-to-reach buttons.

How to give help in dressing. Let us say your child is 2. It is time to get dressed in the morning. He is on his low table where it is easy for you to help him without having to lean over too far. You spread his clothes out on one side of the table. "What goes on first?" you ask him. "Can you pick it up?" You help him into his underpants. "What's next?" He reaches for his shirt, and you help him with it. "Now what?" It is overalls, which he picks up—at your suggestion, if necessary. You help him into them, pull his zipper partway up and say, "Can you zip it the rest of the way?" Socks and shoes are hard. You help him with socks; then, as you reach for one of his shoes, hand him the other, "Can you get your toe partway in?" If he does so (just his toes slipped into his shoe; any more is too hard for him), congratulate him—"That's the way"—and help him do the rest.

You have done more than nine-tenths of the job, but you are encouraging him to feel that dressing is his responsibility, and giving him the kind of part in this business of dressing with dispatch which his skills fit him for.

Perhaps you feel you do not have time to let your child take part in dressing, but if you try, can you not arrange to find the time?

When your child wants to tackle more than he can manage. Sometimes a young child wants to tackle more than he can manage. If his idea is to rip all the buttons off something in order to get out of it, or if your time is at a premium, then it is reasonable to expect him to accept help. But arrange life so that usually you can give him time to try to help himself. Perhaps moving his clothes into your room, or into the kitchen, will make it easier for you to give him a chance at self-help. After all, his drive for independence is an attitude worth encouraging. Therefore, be able to say and mean, "Tell me if you'd like some help," as you let him struggle along. This procedure will keep him from becoming resistant because he feels that you are going to swoop in and prevent him from doing what he wants, and in the long run it will foster an accepting attitude when he does need help.

Encourage your child to do more and more of the job himself. "Let's see how much you can manage by yourself" often encourages a child to do his best. Having some activity in the offing he enjoys, which will be available to him if he is ready in good time, also helps. I do not mean that he should have to hurry, but that letting the dog out or bringing in the morning paper will be an added incentive to finishing dressing.

All along, as his skills progress, give him an increasing part in the process. For instance, when he is around 2, as you "help" him put on a sweater with buttons, fasten all the buttons but one near the bottom, easy for him to reach. Push it partway through the buttonhole and say, "See if you can get it the rest of the way." Then help as needed. Gradually give him more of the job.

Shoehorns often help in getting into shoes. One good way to parcel out the shoe job—after your child has passed the early stage of "Can you get your toe in?"—is: "You do one and I'll do the other." But do not work with such lightning speed that you make him feel discouraged about his own efforts.

When play takes the place of dressing. Many a parent has been heard to say of a 4-year-old, "He can dress himself well, but I just can't get him to do it in the morning." How are you going to motivate a child this age to dress with dispatch?

It may help to change the locale of dressing, if he likes the idea. Suggest, "Let's see if it will help you to keep busy to dress where Daddy's getting up. Bring your clothes in here." If the job does not go forward with dispatch, then back the child goes to his own room.

I know one mother whose 4- and 6-year-old boys took to horsing around in the morning instead of dressing. She handled their play this way: "You've had plenty of time to dress, but you're only half finished. Those clothes come off. Pajamas go back on. Then go back to bed." This the children did, grumbling. Their final instruction was: "Wait to dress until you are really ready to keep busy." She had to fall back on this system two or three times a week for about a month, but thereafter the children decided to save their playing until dressing was over.

UNDRESSING

Undressing is a great deal easier than dressing. However, it comes at times of day when a child feels tired, so take this into account. When you give assistance, always do so from the point of view of "helping" your child rather than taking over the whole job yourself.

It is pleasant to keep a capable 4-year-old company when he is undressing. It helps him keep his mind on the task—and does not put a premium on his being helpless so as to have your company. If he is really slow about getting ready for bed, do not nag; give him one reminder. For instance, tell him, "You are taking too long. If you aren't ready soon, there won't be time for a story tonight." And stand by your guns if he does not finish his job with dispatch.

The next night, you might remind him: "Last night you took so long getting ready for bed that there wasn't any time for a story. Tonight, if you want one, keep busy and you'll have plenty of time."

WASHING

Let me preface my remarks about washing and baths by reminding you to make sure that the household water supply never becomes dangerously hot.

The extent to which you want to encourage your 2-year-old to wash his hands himself depends upon how important you think it is to get him started learning to do things for himself.

I think it is a good idea to begin when he is 2, having one time of day when he washes his own hands, maybe before juice and cracker in the middle of the morning. If you do not want to take the time, there is nothing fatal about it. But since it is another illustration of encouraging your child to assume the responsibility for a job and to accomplish what needs doing in accordance with his skills, I shall sketch how to help a 2-year-old learn to wash.

First, have a standard of cleanliness he can meet. If your child is 2, the chances are he will be charmed at starting to wash, but will not want to stop. Let us say your 2-year-old, Janie, comes into the bathroom.

"Wash hands now, Janie."

She walks over to the washbowl, but nothing happens.

"What first?"

Still nothing happens. You touch the water faucets. "Water goes on." If the procedure is new for Janie, you probably have to turn on the faucets. Janie holds her hands under the flowing water. Nothing else happens. "What now, Janie?" No response. "Where's the soap?" You get more results this time. She picks it up and starts turning it around in her hands, round and round. This is fun, but it is not learning to wash with dispatch. You step in again. "That's enough, Janie." She keeps on. "Where does the soap go?" She points. "It needs to go up now." If necessary, you can add, "I'll help you put it up." Janie is rinsing her hands under the flowing water. The suds are all gone. "That's enough, Janie. Can you turn the water off?" She probably needs help with this. If she forgets about drying her hands, you might turn her gently toward her towel, or give it a pat.

Now, if Janie is filthy dirty, and you feel you need to get her really clean, let her go through her part of the process, then say, "I'll help you get it off your wrists," or whatever. This way, without taking her job away from her, you help her meet a standard of cleanliness that is higher than she can reasonably be expected to achieve by herself.

BATHS

There is no need to talk of baths in detail. Let your child gradually learn to bathe himself. Have him get used to the idea that the business part of his bath must be over before play; this will continue to be a useful order of events when he is old enough to bathe himself.

TIDYING UP

Tidying up has already been referred to a good many times in this book. You have seen 22-month-old Johnny tidying up his room with his mother, as he received the kind of guidance that helped him attend to the business at hand (pp. 151–55). The record may now be more meaningful to you, after this discussion of guidance in business activities.

You are the only one who can decide how tidy you want your child's playthings to be. It is important both to decide on a standard for tidiness which is not too hard to meet and then to stick to it.

As you already know, I happen to think it is sound, after a play session indoors or out, to help your child leave his playthings shipshape. Cartons to house his playthings on his open shelves facilitate an easily accomplished tidying-up job. So does providing your child with a place to store partially finished products (pp. 186–87). You may remember, too, that when your child was old enough, I suggested letting constructions remain in place rather than helping tidy them up at the end of a play session (p. 187).

There is also the matter of willingly helping your child to tidy up after any play which involves a lot of work in the tidying-up process (pp. 187–88), and the way in which blocks are stored (p. 93). These suggestions were made as means of encouraging your child to carry on constructive activity.

Actually, I think a good case can be made for a reasonable degree of tidiness, solely on the grounds that it encourages constructive activity. A child then knows where to go to choose something interesting to play with, and he also has room to use the playthings of his choice if yesterday's activities are not left all over the place.

Your child will accept tidying-up time more agreeably if it is a regular activity—coming right after play—rather than an occasional event. You have to find time to help him. The formula already mentioned in connection with blocks is useful: "I'm glad to help, but you need to keep busy, too." If a 2-year-old bogs down on his part of the job, use the techniques you saw in action with 21-month-old Johnny. Ask, "What next?" Pick him up and set him down by playthings needing to go in a box, as you say, "I'll help you get started." Be companionable, help him keep his mind on the job. On the other hand, if he is old enough for the kind of guidance that involves letting him choose the consequences of his behavior, stop helping him, pick him up, set him on a chair, and tell him, "You need to wait until you are ready to get to work." You have to save this technique for occasions when you can mean it. It works best, of course, when the next item of activity for the day is something he wants to do.

In short, tidying up is just another business activity. You decide what the standard of behavior is. You make it clear to your child and hold him to it consistently by finding a relevant, significant motive to appeal to in order to get him to choose to do what is required. Throughout the preschool years, you need to keep him company in the tidying-up process and lend a helping hand.

9

Guiding Your Child's Feelings

THROUGHOUT THIS BOOK we have been concerned with your child's feelings, for anyone who aims at motivating children to learn to want to behave in desirable ways must continually be involved with their feelings. Hence there is nothing new about the subject of this chapter. But so far, we have been concerned with making use of a child's feelings to get him to keep on with desirable behavior or to change his way of acting. Now the focus is on guiding and changing those feelings themselves.

Anger and fear

WHEN ARE PEOPLE LIKELY TO BE ANGRY OR AFRAID?

What are the circumstances in which people are likely to be angry, on the one hand, or afraid, on the other? Up to a point, the circumstances are much alike. In both cases a person is being thwarted from reaching his goal. But when there is an obstacle which slows him down or that blocks him altogether, he is likely to be angry. In fear, on the other hand, the obstacle is such that he wants to with-

262

draw, but cannot. Since the circumstances are so similar, it is often difficult for an observer to tell which emotion is being experienced, but here are some actual examples, labelled as anger or fear, as the case may be, by the adults who experienced them.

ANGER

1. "*Feeling of annoyance when the car ahead of me poked along. I was in a hurry and wanted to make the light. Thanks to that slow car, I missed it.*"

2. "*I lost a purple ball-point pen and after looking everywhere couldn't find it. I was frustrated and mad.*"

3. "*Annoyance with a friend of my husband's who dropped in at 11:30 P.M. to pay a call. He awakened the baby. I resent his feeling that we have so much time on our hands that we have open house any hour of the day or night.*"

FEAR

1. "*As I was driving along a child darted in front of my car. I jammed on the brakes—fearful that I might not be able to stop in time.*"

2. "*Slipped while walking along a slippery sidewalk—had that 'sinking' sensation in the pit of my stomach. Afraid I would fall.*"

3. "*I felt a sudden fear when I woke in the night and saw someone on the balcony outside my room.*"

You will see that in the case of each emotion experienced as anger, the individual encountered some obstacle (for instance, the slow car which made him miss the traffic light), while in each emotion experienced as fear the individual wanted to withdraw (for instance, he wanted to get away from the child who had darted in front of the car).

Clearly, then, both in situations that give rise to anger and in those that give rise to fear, an individual is facing an obstacle that thwarts him from attaining some goal. Whether he feels anger or fear in these circumstances depends on how he interprets the obstacle. If his interpretation of the obstacle is such that he would like to continue his approach and is prevented (because his actions cannot keep pace with his desires), he is likely to experience anger. If, on the other hand, his interpretation of the obstacle is such that he would like to withdraw, but is prevented (here, his action of withdrawing cannot keep pace with his wish to do so), he is likely to experience fear.

Children usually do not label their emotions conveniently, as the adults did in the examples just given. But if we bear in mind the different circumstances under which these different emotions occur, we can often interpret what a child is feeling. For instance, in the following case it is reasonable to say that the emotion was anger:

> Nineteen-month-old Johnny has been opening Christmas presents. As the next present is picked up by a grownup, he reaches for it, but is told it is for Mommy. As she rips off the paper, Johnny cries hard and continues to hold out his arms for the box.

On the other hand, it is equally reasonable to call this little girl afraid:

> A 2½-year-old is standing beside a grownup, when a strange dog darts toward them. The little girl flings herself onto the grownup and almost "shinnies" up her, then clutches the grownup around the neck as she is held.

Obviously, it is extremely important for you to know whether your child is angry or afraid in any particular situation, for your guidance will depend on which emotion he is experiencing.

ANY LEARNING SITUATION INVOLVING A PROBLEM
IS POTENTIALLY AN EMOTIONAL SITUATION

Think back to two points made in talking about learning by consequences when a problem is involved:

> An individual is motivated toward a goal.
> An obstacle prevents him from attaining it.

These are precisely the circumstances which may give rise either to anger or to fear. I have made many recommendations in this book for encouraging children to think for themselves and to learn to solve problems. Obviously, then, I am in favor of your child facing situations involving obstacles, even though they may lead to anger or to fear. But remember how potentially emotional learning situations are.

In many circumstances, continuing an approach in the face of an obstacle is an excellent attitude to maintain. Only by adopting such an attitude can people solve problems. There are various names for this attitude—persistence, determination, doggedness. Here is an example of a 3-year-old who is able to overcome the obstacles which confront him through his own efforts, without any help:

> Henry wants to climb up on a large box. He tries, but he cannot pull himself up. Running off to a different part of the playground, he grabs a block, carries it over to the large box, and sets the block down beside the box. Twice more he returns for blocks, which he adds to the one already in place. Then, using this pile as a take-off platform, he easily climbs up onto the big box.

This is just the kind of case I had in mind when I recommended that you let your child alone to make an attempt to tackle a problem. If you will now reread the section summarized below, you will see that the recommendations I made there may be thought of as guidance techniques to use when children are faced with problems which may eventually lead to feelings of anger (pp. 134–39). Here are the main points in that earlier section:

> Guide your child so that he learns to think for himself and to solve problems
>> Guiding him to think for himself in business activities
>>> Let him alone to see if he remembers what to do
>>> Act in such a way that you get him to figure out what needs doing
>>> Gear requirements to your child's ability to meet them
>>> Be consistent in what you expect
>> Guiding your child to think for himself in play
>>> When you suggest something to do, always make at least two suggestions and let him choose between them
>>> Let him alone to make an attempt to tackle a problem
>>> Help your child figure out how to solve problems when help is needed

The point of all of these techniques is to let your child alone as long as the problem he is coping with is neither beyond his ability nor so frustrating that he is on the verge of emotional upset. And if and when he needs help, give it in such a way that you are helping him to learn to help himself. This may mean offering leads: "Where do you suppose this goes?" (a puzzle piece); or, to a child asking for help in getting down from a box, "How could you get down? . . . If you turn around and go down backwards, I think you can manage." It may also mean offering leads plus physical help, as was the case when a wagon wheel stuck and the child was not strong enough to free it (pp. 32–33). Or it may mean paring down the difficulty of the obstacle which is thwarting a child—to be more precise, suggesting a similar, substitute activity when a child is unable to cope with what confronts him, as was the case with Sammy, who was trying to cut a picture beyond his cutting skill. All of this guidance is aimed at encouraging approach attitudes, and helping children gain their ends in desirable ways.

The chapters on guidance techniques both for children in general and for children in particular stages of development are also relevant when considering guidance techniques to use when children are faced with problems which may eventually lead to feelings of anger.

You will remember how much emphasis I put on the here-and-now mentality of the typical 2-year-old; from his point of view, what seems to you postponement is denial—the very sort of obstacle which leads to anger if he maintains his attitude of approach in the face of the obstacle.

AVOID UNNECESSARY THWARTING

Prevention is better than cure. Until your child is old enough to realize that one activity is a means to another (instead of an obstacle in his path which prevents him from gaining what he wants), it is sound to clear the decks, literally and figuratively, to keep obstacles out of his path when you want him to do something. So, if you remember, when it was time for your 2-year-old to sit on the toilet, I advised having the big book out of sight which was too large for him to hold. So, too, I advised telling a 2-year-old what needs doing step by step. If you say, "After you've had your juice you're going for a ride," he is likely to streak out to the car, only to have to be brought back for juice protesting, perhaps in angry tears. Instead, say: "Juice now, Teddy," and then, when it has been drunk, give him the first news of a car ride.

As long as your child is in a stage of development in which he finds any change in plans upsetting, it will make life easier for both of you if you wait to tell him about the proposed change until you are reasonably sure it is actually going to happen. As he gets older, you will find yourself weighing, for him, the pleasure of anticipation against the possibility of disappointment if plans must be cancelled. Children vary a great deal in their stoicism—their ability to accept this kind of frustration. I think they are better helped by having the degree and frequency of such disappointments geared to their ability for acceptance than by being faced with many such frustrations.

Again in connection with eliminating unnecessarily frustrating obstacles, think of the standards of behavior which you expect your child to meet (pp. 69–70) and gear your requirements to his ability to meet them (p. 135). If you are always expecting too much of him, you are causing him to live continually in a potentially emotional situation. Small wonder, then, if he goes around with a chip on his shoulder, or if, on the other hand, he reacts by adopting a timid attitude. Timidity may become a refuge, a way of trying to avoid failure in measuring up to your standards by just not entering into activities. A chronically timid child interprets his surroundings as obstacles from which he wants to withdraw.

To sum up these remarks about unnecessary thwarting, the whole guidance scheme described in this book helps children think for themselves and develop skills, and also learn how to cope with the problems which are bound to arise in their lives. In this respect, this whole book is concerned with guiding your child's feelings.

Guiding your child when he is angry

IF YOUR CHILD HAS FREQUENT OUTBURSTS OF ANGER, TAKE A LOOK AT HIS WHOLE LIFE

Suppose your child has frequent outbursts of anger. Before considering how to deal with them directly, first try to figure out what lies behind them. Appraise his whole life, to find what satisfactions and dissatisfactions it contains. (Suggestions on how to go about this were given in pp. 114–16.) You may discover potential anger-producing situations that you have overlooked. You may decide that your child is using anger outbursts as a solution to problem situations.

ANALYZE THE VARIOUS PARTS OF ANGER-
PRODUCING SITUATIONS

The next step in trying to understand your child's frequent outbursts of anger is to search out the specific reasons for thwarting within any complex anger-producing situation. You need to take account of 1) his motives, 2) the obstacles he encounters, and 3) his abilities.

Motives. The more motives an individual has, the more occasions for thwartings to occur. Contrast a child who is content to sit watching other children with a 2-year-old who tries to possess anything he sets his eyes on. The second child is much more likely to become involved in anger-producing situations than the first.

Then, too, a strongly motivated, persistent child is more likely to experience thwartings than is an easily diverted child, who readily exchanges one interest for another.

Now, suppose you have a 2-year-old who, like most 2-year-olds, is geared to a slow tempo, and suppose you are always after him to hurry. Small wonder, then, if he is irritable. In this connection I remind you that I have already considered in detail how to guide your child to learn to perform necessary tasks with dispatch, without nagging him to "hurry up" (pp. 256–61).

Bear in mind also how to guide him in his play with other children, so as to learn how to gain and keep what he wants and at the same time respect the other children's rights (pp. 192–97).

Many times, whatever your child's age, you can help him accept the inevitable (that is, accept the fact that his approach to something he wants must be thwarted) if you come up with suggestions for other interesting occupations.

Obstacles. If your child is experiencing many anger episodes, try to figure out all the obstacles which come his way, from his point of view. If he is feeling under par or fatigued, thwartings which he would otherwise take in stride may prove too much for him. Certainly, if your child seems chronically under par, he needs to see his doctor.

Or is he by any chance experiencing thwarting at the hands of thoughtless people? What about teasing? It is up to you to protect your child from situations he is not old enough to cope with. Toy snatching by an older child or by an unthinking grownup, for example, is not just harmless amusement.

Abilities. Obviously, the greater your child's abilities, the fewer obstacles he will encounter. Hence the whole scheme of guidance in this book, which concentrates on helping your child to develop his abilities, is relevant here.

FOSTER DESIRABLE BEHAVIOR BY HELPING YOUR CHILD BEFORE ANGER BECOMES A LAST RESORT

Try to arrange satisfactory consequences for desirable behavior. When your baby is in a playpen, do not wait until he is fussing to offer him new, interesting occupation. Offer him something new early enough to keep him contented during the time he is to stay in his pen. When your preschool-age child is trying to gain his ends by desirable means—for example, hanging onto a shovel and saying "I got it first," as a stronger child is wresting it away—step in to see that this desirable way of trying to stand up for his rights is effective.

GUIDING YOUR CHILD'S EXPRESSIONS OF ANGER

So far I have been emphasizing that you need to think about your child's whole life, including the particular motives and obstacles that occur in specific anger-producing situations. You need to think also about what you want your child's anger outbursts to accomplish. If you want him to learn to use them as solutions to problems, see to it that satisfying, relevant consequences follow them; see to it, in other words, that he gains his ends by his emotional outbursts.

On the other hand, if, as I hope, you want him to learn to solve problems in more effective and reasonable ways, then make sure that he does not gain his ends by these outbursts. Help him find other means to his ends. But, at the same time, remember that an anger outburst is a means of communication for a small child who cannot put his feelings into words. Your treatment of his anger episodes requires wisdom, patience, and imagination.

Helping your angry child when it is all right for him to have what he wants.

> A just-2-year-old has been pushing a wagon, a piece of home equipment intended for use by either of the two children in the family. He stops for a moment to gaze at a passing truck. His 4-year-old brother dashes up, grabs hold of the handle, and runs off with the wagon, leaving the littler boy bellowing and stamping his feet in anger.

In these circumstances, I think the smaller boy has a right to have the wagon back. He did not leave it; he merely glanced up momentarily. Granted, in order to avoid future misunderstandings, he needs to learn to keep his hands on something he is using, but for the present he needs help in regaining the wagon. But how can you retrieve the wagon without his learning that anger outbursts pay off, thereby encouraging him to use such outbursts to gain his ends?

Probably, with a child of this age, an explanation, while his older brother careens around with the wagon, will only bring greater frustration. The situation must be remedied at once; but it is still possible to encourage the littler boy to communicate his wishes in more than outraged sobs. As he pauses to draw breath, it is likely that he can be reached with the kind of words that show him he is going to get what he wants. "Do you want to keep on using the wagon?" He is likely to make some kind of noise to indicate that he does. "Come on, I'll help you get it back." Then, leading him by the hand, or carrying him over to the wagon, set him down, as you hang onto it, saying "Hold on," even placing his hands on the wagon, if necessary, while you give an explanation to the older child.

You will notice there is no direct attempt to get this little boy to stop his crying. Guidance at this level consists, then, in helping him understand he can have his wagon back, and assisting him to do so. His anger outburst stopped because the source of his frustration was removed.

Here, on the other hand, is a 4-year-old who is ready for more emotional control, and the emphasis is placed on getting him to stop his crying before anything is done to help him:

> Andy is making a block house. When he leaves his construction to get more blocks from the main source of supply, Doug goes off with a block from Andy's building. Andy lets out a roar and, with tears running down his cheeks, starts after Doug. A grownup lays a detaining hand on Andy's shoulder and asks, "What's the trouble?" His answer is incomprehensible, smothered in angry crying. She hands him a tissue, saying, "If you can tell me in words, then I can understand and maybe I can help you." Andy stops crying, points to Doug, and says, "He took my block." "Then go tell him about it," replies the grownup, and goes along with Andy to lend her authority if necessary to what he says.

Sometimes children need encouragement to let out their feelings rather than to control them. Roger was a 4-year-old who hung onto his feelings too long, and needed help in learning to express them earlier in the game. In other words, what he needed to learn was not adequate control of his anger feelings, but adequate expression.

> Roger is making a carpentry construction. He lines up his pieces of wood and starts to nail, but the nail bends. He starts with another nail; the same thing happens. Though his color is rising, he gives no other sign of frustration. But the grownup knows that Roger tends to hold onto his temper for so long that he finally goes all to pieces. So she says, "It does make people mad, doesn't it, when nails bend. Sometimes it helps to say so, to say, 'It bent. That makes me mad.' If you hit the nail with little taps like this, you can probably keep it from bending."

Helping your angry child when he cannot have what he wants. I have already discussed techniques useful when your child has formed a habit of protest to a particular situation (pp. 164–67) and techniques to use when your child is in the process of protesting (pp. 167–71). Going on from these, see to it that your child does not gain his ends by anger outbursts. Here is a 2-year-old in a grocery store:

> Michael spies some lollipops, stretches out his arm and says, "Candy," with an appealing look at his mother. "No, Michael," she answers. "Here's a magazine we bought, if you'd like to look at it," but Michael, not to be diverted, bursts into angry wails and continues to howl.

The best treatment for Michael, in my opinion, would be for his mother to go about her business good-naturedly, ignore his noise, and finally, when she is ready to leave, carry him out to the car, in a "sack-of-meal" position if he is likely to kick. Emphatically, it is not helpful, or fair to Michael, to punish him by a whack or by an impatient attitude. Learning to cope with feelings, to control and to express them adequately, is complicated enough in the preschool years without being punished for expressing them. It is sound to try to shift Michael's attention to something interesting, but not in an overanxious or standing-on-one's-head-to-amuse-him attitude.

Here is a situation which was more difficult to handle:

> Two-year-old Barton started each nursery-school morning in a flannel shirt on top of a lighter-weight T shirt. As the day grew hot, he needed to take it off, but he greeted each daily occasion for shedding his shirt with protests of "No" and attempts to fight off the teacher.

Now if he had been alarmed in this new situation at the prospect of shedding his shirt, it might have been best to let him keep it on. But he did not seem anxious; he was simply mad. Helping him learn to be willing to adjust clothing to temperature seemed reasonable. But it was not easy, as Mrs. A soon learned. She had to sit down, with Barton planted between her legs so that she could prevent with her own legs his kicking her while she peeled off the shirt. This was done for five nursery-school days in a row. Throughout these days, Mrs. A had many pleasant contacts with Barton, for he was a chatty little boy who directed most of his talk to the grownups. On the sixth day, Mrs. A remarked to him, "Barton, let's see if you can't get that shirt off today without making a lot of noise about it." Lo and behold, he did, and that was the end of shirt trouble.

Although this was more difficult to handle than was Michael's anger outburst in the grocery store, the same principle was applied. The outburst itself was not allowed to become a means for either child's gaining what he wanted. One of the things that made Barton's outburst difficult to handle was that he had to be physically restrained in order to get off the shirt, and such restraint in itself is likely to lead to anger. Nevertheless, despite this complication, he did come to accept what needed doing.

Suppose Mrs. A had become angry in the process. This would have been a further complication, for Barton was an alert little boy; in all likelihood he would have been aware of Mrs. A's annoyance. It might well have given him satisfaction to know that she was put out; this would have added fuel to his protest and kept it going longer.

As children get older, techniques used to deal with angry protests and anger outbursts should change. The guidance used with Barton was an example of *assisting him* to do what needed doing (pp. 168–69). When your child is developmentally ready for it, show him the consequences of his behavior and let him choose what to do (p. 169).

> Jenny, almost 4½, has been using a doll in the doll corner. She props her up at a table, sets a cup in front of her, then spies a child coming into the playroom holding a truck, and goes over to have a look at it. In the meantime, another child goes to the doll corner and starts using the doll. Jenny runs back, but the child clutches the doll firmly, saying "You left it," and holds Jenny at arm's length with her free hand. Jenny bursts into tears. A grownup picks her up and carries her over to the tissue vendor. "Here's a hanky," she says. "Jenny, it is too bad you left the doll, but Sally got it when you were looking at Sam's truck." They return to the doll corner. "There's another doll in that bed there, if you want it." "I don't want it," says Jenny, and starts loud crying once more. The grownup carries her to an adjoining room, and, when crying pauses for a moment, says, "That's too much noise for the playroom. You make as much noise as you like here where it won't disturb other people." She sets Jenny down and sits down herself nearby. Jenny continues to yell. After about a minute the grownup says, "I need to go back to the

playroom. You may come too if you're through with your noise, or keep on with noise as long as you like in here." Jenny does choose to come back. Later, when the desired doll becomes available, it is pointed out to her.

Try to understand your child's feelings; show him that you do.

Johnny, just 4, has had a cold for a week. This is his first day up. He has settled beside his mother to hear a story, when the doorbell rings bringing callers. Johnny runs to the door, shouting "Go away."

This is a thwarting situation for Johnny. It is also hard on Mother. She may be tempted to scold him severely. She can best help herself and Johnny, though, by welcoming the callers and then taking him out of earshot to say, "It is disappointing, isn't it, when you were just going to hear a story. I can see why you feel mad. I'll read you the story later this afternoon. But even though you are disappointed, that's no way to act when people come to see us."

Have a readily available object on which to vent anger. A pillowcase stuffed with cloth works better than a regular punching bag for venting preschool anger. If you want to, draw a face on it with crayon. When your child is angry, it is sound to suggest his hitting the punching pillow to let out his madness and to say, "Talk to it anyway you like, too, in your own room where other people can't hear you."

Guiding your child when he is fearful

Now we come to fear, which, you will remember, is an altogether different attitude from anger. In fear, instead of experiencing thwarted approach, your child is experiencing thwarted withdrawal.

IF YOUR CHILD IS OFTEN FEARFUL, TAKE HIS WHOLE LIFE INTO ACCOUNT

As in the case of frequent anger outbursts, appraise your child's whole life to estimate the satisfactions and dissatisfactions he is experiencing in being the person he is in your family. (Suggestions for accomplishing this were given in pp. 114–16.) I have known cases where such an appraisal led parents to conclude that their child was finding the reassurance which followed manifestations of fear sufficiently satisfying to encourage acting alarmed in order to be comforted. For instance, here is Mona, a little over 3, who had frequent episodes of crying and screaming when another child came near her.

> *Mona is swinging. Andy rides a bike in the vicinity of the swing, though not close to Mona. She cries. Mrs. A comes up to her and says, "What's the trouble, Mona, could you tell me?" No reply, but Mona stops crying at once and goes on swinging.*

On another occasion almost a month later:

> *Mona is pushing a doll buggy on the playground. When Dave comes near her, pulling a wagon, Mona cries and screams. Mrs. A says, "There's no need to cry, Mona. Dave is not trying to take away your buggy."*

And a week later:

> *Mona is playing in the earth hole with four other children, all of whom a grownup is watching closely. Suddenly Mona starts to cry. "What's the matter, Mona?" asks Miss B. "Tell me." "I want a pan," says Mona. Miss B reminds her where the box of equipment is. Mona's crying stops at once.*

Our appraisal of Mona's life as a whole showed that much of the time she was enjoying herself. We believed that she felt more secure than her screaming and crying suggested, and that she liked the adult attention she was getting for her apparent alarm.

Accordingly, guidance was changed: she no longer got reassurance when she screamed. Instead, other ways were found to give her grownup attention and companionship. This change in guidance met with considerable success. The frequency of her outcries was reduced by half.

TAKE ACCOUNT OF SITUATIONS FROM WHICH PEOPLE ARE LIKELY TO WANT TO WITHDRAW

It is important to bear in mind the kind of situation from which your child, or anyone else for that matter, is likely to want to withdraw. What is sudden, intense, or unfamiliar is apt to produce this kind of reaction. If efforts at withdrawal cannot keep pace with the desire to withdraw, the person involved will probably experience fear. Of course, since feelings are often mixed, fear and curiosity often go hand in hand. I once knew a Sealyham who came into a familiar room where a new painting had been set on the floor against the wall. He acted like a caricature in a cartoon, stalked toward the picture, torn between his curiosity (desire to approach) and his wariness (desire to withdraw). As he moved forward, in a crouched position, I said "Boo," which was enough to tip the scale in the direction of withdrawal and send him scuttling out of the room.

Try to anticipate any potentially fearful situations and to control your child's exposure to them. During babyhood and during the preschool years try to anticipate fearful situations which your child is not yet equipped to face. Sometimes this means preventing altogether his exposure to such situations; sometimes it involves giving him support when he is likely to experience fear. Of course, you cannot always do this; you may be caught unawares, as was the mother of the 7-month-old baby who came to be fearful of running water because an electric heater happened to be turned on at the same time (pp. 19–20). Or remember the 2-year-old who was taken to see a train stop at a station, but was startled (along with his parents) by an express train which unexpectedly roared past (p. 21).

Here is another example of fear in a 2½-year-old child whose parents were caught off guard:

> It is Halloween eve. Johnny's mother, mindful of probable calls of "trick-or-treaters," has decided to tell Johnny about masked people making a call, and to be holding him in her arms at some distance from the front door when Halloween visits begin. She has not yet talked with him about it, since it is only five o'clock, but she has figured her timing wrong. The doorbell rings. Johnny goes to the door, bursts into tears, and is so alarmed at the strange, masked visitors that he can hardly be reached with words.

In all these cases, the parents involved believed in trying to control fearsome situations to which their children were exposed.

But since they were not omniscient, their guidance had to consist in helping their children after a fear reaction had occurred.

Before leaving the subject of trying to anticipate potentially fearful situations I shall say a word about moving pictures and television. Wait until your child can recognize make-believe for what it is before you expose him to frightening episodes in these vivid forms, even though the rest of the entertainment is pleasant. Let me air another prejudice here. I am strongly opposed to accustoming children to accept violence and brutality through familiarity with it on television. Even if they seem not to be frightened by a dramatic episode in story, moving picture, or television, there are other criteria of its suitability for them (pp. 111–12).

Bear in mind the conditioning process. It is important in trying to prevent the development of fears to remember the conditioning process, for many fears seem to result from conditioning (as in the case of the 7-month-old baby who acquired a fear of running water and the 2-year-old who came to fear trains). Because so many fears originate in this way it is quite possible to describe the process of unlearning a fear in conditioning terms; and indeed that is just what I did when I was discussing conditioning (p. 24). But, especially in complex cases, it is more helpful to describe the unlearning of fears in the following terms:

THREE WAYS OF LEARNING TO COPE
ADEQUATELY WITH FEARS

There are three basic ways of learning to cope adequately with fears. I shall illustrate each with an example.

Increased familiarity. First, suppose that a woman moves to a part of the country where there are many lizards. They frighten her. How can she come to feel different? It should help her to become more familiar with the nature of lizards and to find that they are harmless. Seeing them frequently with this knowledge will accustom her to them. Increased familiarity, then, both in the sense of obtaining reassuring information and of having a particular experience a number of times, may modify a person's feelings about some originally fear-producing situation; familiarity may even change his attitude in the face of the situation from one of withdrawal to one of acceptance (or to one of approach).

Development of a particular skill. Second, suppose a person who has not learned to swim is afraid of the water. What can be done? If he learns to swim well, the chances are that he will feel comfortable in the water. This is another way, then, of learning to cope with fears. Development of a particular skill may change a desire to withdraw to a desire to approach; at the least, it may very much reduce the strength of the desire to withdraw.

Adequate means of withdrawal. Lastly, suppose a person is afraid of being struck by lightning. He can inform himself about what to do if he is caught outdoors in a thunderstorm; he can learn to locate himself away from high places where lightning is likely to strike; he can put lightning rods on his house. What he is doing is providing himself with a means of adequate withdrawal.

Now, going back to the case of the 7-month-old who became afraid of water, what his mother actually did was this: for several days she warmed the bathroom and removed the noisy heater before she brought the child into the room. Then, again for several days, she left the heater in the bathroom but did not operate it in the child's presence. The first of these procedures amounted in effect to providing the child with an adequate means of withdrawal; the second, to helping him develop increased familiarity. Thus her guidance—which proved successful—followed the method I have outlined.

Similarly, the guidance used in the case of the 2-year-old who feared trains followed this pattern. First, as the train roared by, the father picked up his little boy, and, holding him securely, moved away from the tracks. Then both Mother and Father spoke of how noisy and loud the train had been, and how much it had surprised them. They stood at a considerable distance from the tracks when the slow train arrived, which the parents had been expecting. Later, when Johnny heard train whistles in the distance and looked apprehensive, they talked about where the trains were. They let several weeks go by, then went to the station again, making sure that no fast express would go through, and watched a slow, well-behaved train from a safe distance. They even got around to making up a song for Johnny about going to see trains, which he loved to hear, and which did not immortalize the loud express. Johnny gradually learned to lose his uneasy attitude toward trains.

Of course, I am not claiming that these three methods of coping with fears, either singly or in combination, can be guaranteed to do away with fears. However, I do say that often—as in these two cases and in others that I shall be describing—they will make it much easier for an individual to face formerly fearsome situations without marked reaction.

COMMON CHILDHOOD FEARS AND HOW TO HELP
CHILDREN COPE WITH THEM

Before we take a look at some common childhood fears, remember that feelings are complex and that a child's attitude is often not simply one of thwarted withdrawal. Like the Sealyham I mentioned, he is often torn between curiosity (approach) and wariness (withdrawal). It is helpful, in trying to figure out how to guide an upset child, to sort out the extent to which you want to encourage him to approach a situation and, if so, how you propose to foster this attitude, as opposed to helping him withdraw from the situation.

Always try to figure out how he came to feel the way he does. Never belittle him for being fearful, or shame him, or make fun of him, or tell him he is too big to make a fuss. Feelings are often unreasonable. However ridiculous they may seem, it is a fact that they exist and have to be dealt with. However, do not treat his fears of unlikely eventualities in such a way that you make him feel that they are reasonable.

Now for some childhood fears and what to do about them.

Going to the doctor. It is extremely sound for the sake of your child's feelings as well as his health to see that he becomes acquainted with the doctor, probably through a regular checkup, at a time when he does not need painful treatment or shots. One of the factors involved in your choice of a doctor for your child is, no doubt, his manner in dealing with children.

Going to the dentist. The remarks about going to the doctor apply equally well to going to the dentist, with the exception that many dentists advise parents to arrange a brief visit for their 2-year-old *before* he needs to have his teeth examined, even more than one visit, if indicated. The idea is to acquaint the child with the dentist and his office so as to help him feel at ease about going there for his first checkup, which is often recommended around age 3.

Getting shots. Some children accept shots during their preschool years as a matter of course (until all of a sudden, one fine day, they may be thoroughly upset by the whole process). However, even with a stalwart child, do not overdo preparation for shots. You can make him anxious by reassurance out of proportion to what he needs. On the other hand, some advance notice is always important, something to the effect of: "You're having a shot today. It certainly is good that you know how to hold still. Then it's all over with right away."

But now suppose your child is afraid of shots. How can you help him? First, by not warning him long in advance. It is a help to most young children to hear about the shot only when on the way to the doctor's office. Be honest about it, not evasive. If your child asks, "Will it hurt?" the answer is, "Yes, a little, but you can help by holding very still and keeping your arm 'easy' " (that is, relaxed). It often helps to "have a practice," and to play a game of having the child hold still while a parent "gives a shot" with his finger. The child can be the doctor, too, and give the parent a shot. I think it is also helpful to have the child know that after the shot is over, something interesting is going to happen. This is not a bribe. But "We'll go visit the pet store after you're through at the doctor's office" gives your child something pleasant to anticipate.

As far as the actual shot goes, it is important that your child never get out of the shot by making a row, even if the doctor has to hold him still while the shot is administered.

I know several children who have been helped by being told

to see how far they could count "before the shot's all over," for then they do not concentrate their whole attention on whether the shot is going to hurt. It helps, too, if they look at something else, not at the hypodermic needle, and perhaps squeeze Mother's hand, if they would like to.

As children are old enough to understand, let them know why shots are given: shots prevent unpleasant and sometimes serious illness.

Now, with all of this advice, I am not suggesting that you step in and interfere with the doctor's procedure, but the chances are that what I am suggesting will fit in with it.

Taking medicine. Many medicines for children are "pleasantly" flavored, in the hopes of making them easily acceptable. (All the more reason to keep medicines which may be dangerous completely inaccessible to children.)

Even so, children often react to the need for taking medicine by trying to get away from it, or by fighting it off. In the long run, of course, the only sound attitude is that needed medicine is something that has to happen; the sooner taken, the sooner over.

If your 2-year-old fights off a spoonful of medicine even after your explanation, it is best just to get the matter over with. When there are two grownups around, have one man the bottle and the other deal with the child. Tell him, firmly but kindly, he does need to take the medicine; you will help him. Then, if he continues to resist, have one grownup deftly put a sheet around the child which covers his arms so that he cannot knock the spoon away, while the other grownup puts the medicine in when the child opens his mouth. This should not be a surprise procedure. It is important that the child knows he is going to take the medicine. The reason for the sheet is to minimize the physical struggle in keeping the child from knocking away the spoon. This system can turn into "Can you manage to hold still by yourself, or do you need the sheet to help you?"

If two grownups are not available, the process of restraining the child with the sheet long enough to spoon in the medicine inevitably will take longer, which is obviously disadvantageous.

Hopefully, a 3- or 4-year-old will respond to an explanation about the need for accepting medicine. But if he persists in protest, deal with him as described above.

As soon as your doctor approves, it is a good idea to get your child used to swallowing pills; let him take his vitamins, for example, in pill form. If your child can swallow pills readily, it is a great advantage to him when medicine is necessary.

Being hurt. I am not talking here about a child's fear of the possibility of falls, bumps, cuts, scrapes, and the like. I am thinking of guiding him once they have happened.

As is always the case, it is important that the consequence of the hurt, as far as the amount of grownup comfort goes, is proportional to the degree of discomfort or upsetness for the child. If you overdo sympathy, you may encourage subsequent exaggeration of injuries. But do not shortchange your child in the amount of sympathy he deserves when he is hurt, for that can make it much harder for him to accept his discomfort. So, as usual, be as wise as Solomon, or at least give some thought to the relationship between the amount of your sympathy, on the one hand, and the upsetness or discomfort of your child, on the other.

I am convinced that judicious sympathy does not encourage children to exaggerate hurts. If a 2-year-old falls down and bangs his knee hard, help him up or encourage him to get himself up ("Can you get yourself up?"). If he is not too upset, give him a job to do ("Can you pull up your overall leg, and let's see where you're hurt?"). But if you think there is a good deal of bleeding, which is likely to frighten a young child, blot his injury with a tissue before encouraging him to look.

If a child is quite unhappy about a hurt, encourage him to express his feelings before starting any remedy. As you hold him in your lap, you might say, "Cry if it helps. That *was* a hard tumble." Then, after this chance to express his feelings in crying, wipe his eyes for him or offer a box of tissues so that he can pull out a "hanky" himself.

By the time a child is getting on toward 4, if his upsetness seems disproportionate to the hurt, tell him, "Sometimes crying helps, but sometimes if you keep on and on, it makes things harder." Then hand him the tissue and start treating the hurt if it needs it, giving him as big a part in the process as possible.

Medical treatment of "hurts." What you do depends, of course, on what your doctor advises. If he recommends treatment of scrapes and cuts with disinfectant, ask him to name a good one which does not sting when applied.

In general, it is sound to have your child take as active a part in the process of treatment as possible, if he finds this interesting. If a 2-year-old has a scraped knee which needs gentle washing with a nonstinging disinfectant, you probably need to do the whole job. A 4-year-old may do it himself.

Suppose that your child protests at necessary treatment and that your efforts to get him to hold still by himself are unsuccessful. Then, providing he is old enough to make this choice, you might suggest that he sit and wait a little while, if it helps, but that he must have treatment before he goes back to play. If this is not successful within a few minutes, or if he is not developmentally ready for such a choice, you will have to use different guidance. Then say, "We're going to get it over with and I'll help you hold still if you need it." If he tries to fight you off, much the same method that Mrs. A used to get Barton out of his shirt (pp. 272–73) will minimize physical struggles. Over a period of time, as your child comes to recognize the inevitability of treatment, protest is likely to change to acceptance, especially if he has a chance to watch other children calmly accept treatment. But no preaching, just an invitation to see "how Johnny manages when he needs a cut fixed." Let the demonstration point its own moral.

Hospitalization. A little child's stay in a hospital overnight or longer is a potentially fearful situation. Many hospitals maintain rigid visiting hours, asserting that children adjust more easily when parents are absent. On the other hand, some hospitals believe emotional upset can be minimized through much greater flexibility in visiting hours for parents, even to the point of permitting a parent to stay overnight with a child.

It is a good idea to inform yourself before need arises about the possibilities in your community for a child requiring hospitalization. Then, if an emergency should suddenly arise, you will be in a position to know where you want your child to go. And if you have already informed yourself about the procedures for child patients, you will be able, on short notice, to tell your child what to expect.

If a hospital permits, I hope that a parent can be present during much of a small child's hospitalization, if necessary even at night, with a cot set up near the child, particularly in an emergency case where there has been almost no chance for preparation. This may be an enormous boon to a small child in this frightening situation, provided a parent's behavior is reassuring. But unfortunately, some parents only contribute to their child's apprehension. So rise to the occasion.

Whatever the frequency and length of your visits, when you leave, tell your child when you will return, and be there on time. Consequently, even though he is upset at your departure, he will find that he can count on you to return when you say you will.

Other things you can do to make the unfamiliar less strange are: telling the child what will happen when he is admitted; describing what a hospital bed is like; explaining how baths are given in bed and how meals are served on trays; bringing along from home one of the child's go-to-bed stuffed animals (the hospital permitting); providing an interesting book for you to read out loud to him, as well as daytime occupation if the child is up to it.

Preparing your child for an operation. If an operation can safely wait until your child has reached at least kindergarten age, so much the better. But if operations before this time are unavoidable, help your child be prepared emotionally.

Be honest with your child about what has to be done, but scale what you say, of course, to his ability to understand and to his emotional vulnerability.

I know an almost-4-year-old boy, an alert, imaginative, but apprehensive child, whose adenoids were so enlarged that there was no question about the necessity of an operation. Happily, his tonsils did not need to be removed. He had never been exposed to the idea of operations. His parents, naturally enough, thought that an account in terms of gleaming knives, with part of himself being removed, might indeed make him uneasy. However, what they told him was true as far as it went. They said something to this effect: "You know what a bother all the colds you've had have been and how much mucus you've had in your nose and throat. The doctor is going to fix you up so that the mucus won't keep bothering you."

A number of days before the operation, they told him about the anesthetic (having found out exactly how it would be administered, and ascertained the extent to which his mother could be with him in his hospital room). So, having informed themselves of the precise procedures, his parents prepared him for what was to happen so as to minimize his becoming afraid because of the unfamiliarity of the experience. They told him when he would go to the hospital and explained that his mother could stay with him till bedtime, that then she would tuck him in with his teddy and then go home. Soon after he woke in the morning, his mother would be back to keep him company. Before very long he would be given some pills to make him sleepy. When it was time, he would be given something called an anesthetic, and here they explained exactly how it would be given. After he had breathed it for a while, it would make him go to sleep. They emphasized that this was a very different kind of sleep from ordinary sleep, so that he would not be likely subsequently to couple ordinary sleep with medical treatment. When the doctor had fixed him up, they said, he would be back in his hospital room, his mother would be there, and he would stay until the doctor said he could go home.

He asked questions, of course. They replied that he might not like the smell of the anesthetic, but it wasn't chosen because of its smell but because of the way it made people have a special kind of sleep. (Since there was no need for tonsils to be removed, the parents did not need to add that when he woke up his throat would hurt.) When their son cross-examined them more closely as to what the doctor would do, they said that he took away some of the mucus that had been so troublesome by scraping it away, they thought. When he asked what the doctor scraped with, they said they didn't know exactly, they weren't doctors, but some special kind of scraper just for that. "Will it hurt?" he wanted to know. No, they answered, because he would be asleep, the sleep produced by the anesthetic. You will see that what these parents did was to give their unusually apprehensive child an explanation, true as far as it went, but which omitted mention of cutting and removal of part of himself.

On a number of occasions, these parents acted out this boy's taking of an anesthetic, and let him be the doctor, too, while one of them served as the patient. On the day of the operation, his mother said, "If you're still awake when you're having the anesthetic, how about seeing how far you can count before you're asleep?" (a procedure he used to follow when he was given a shot). His mother was told later that when he was in the operating room, he showed no fear.

By way of contrast, here is what happened to another child, who had been prepared by her parents in much the same way. But just as the anesthetic was going to be administered, she was told, "If you don't like the smell, just blow it away." The trustful little child believed this new piece of information. When she found that the anesthetic had an unpleasant smell, she did try to blow it away. Of course, it would not blow away, so she went under the anesthetic, screaming with fright because she thought something had gone wrong. I need hardly moralize about this tale. The advice to blow was based on the belief that, by taking a big breath, the child would go under the anesthetic that much sooner. But it also involved deceiving and frightening her. Always be honest with children, whatever the subject, while scaling the information you give them to their intellectual and emotional capacity.

Fear of particular loud noises. Not infrequently a child develops a strong fear of some particular loud noise, say a siren, or thunder. Since a parent has no control over their occurrence, how can he help his child?

I shall talk about prevention (that is, preparing a child for the possible occurrence of a particular intense noise, so that he will not be taken by surprise) before remedies.

This is just what was done with an almost-2-year-old I know who moved to a part of the country in which thunderstorms were frequent. Since he was particularly sensitive to noises, his parents made a point of always being with him when a storm threatened. One of them would hold him up to look out the window if there were lightning and tell him that sometimes there was a noise after lightning called thunder. "If we're lucky," they would say, "maybe we'll hear some thunder. Let's listen." Also, his parents used to sing him a song about thunder, which he loved to hear (p. 110).

If loud thunder or a shrill siren does alarm your small child, the best thing you can do is not to become panic-stricken yourself, but to be a "present help in trouble," holding him, talking with him, and reassuring him.

There is no point in pretending falsely that loud thunder is music to your ears. Go ahead and share some of your child's feeling with him. "That was a loud noise, wasn't it? Shall we put our hands over our ears?"

If your child has acquired a fear of sirens, pick him up if you hear one in the offing, perhaps go indoors, and talk about where the vehicle with the siren seems to be going. If the noise is not too intense, speculation about whether it is a fire truck or an ambulance may interest him enough to forget some of his fear. Over a period of time, you may be able to help him feel more comfortable about sirens through a knowledge of how they are helpful to people.

Fear of animals. Often, one sudden intense experience, such as the dog darting toward the 2½-year-old girl who "shinnied" up her grownup companion (p. 264), establishes a persistent fear. Or sometimes the child's fear is cued off by a grownup's behavior. Fearing animals is complicated by the fact that some creatures warrant a cautious attitude. You do not want your child to rush up to strange dogs and pat them, for some dogs bite under these circumstances. Nor if poisonous snakes exist in your neighborhood do you want your child to feel so free that he handles them. More in due course about learning reasonable caution.

For present purposes, suppose your child is afraid of dogs. As far as you know, this fear originated in a startling experience when a dog, barking loudly, suddenly ran toward him. What to do? You need to protect him from experiences which will intensify his already established withdrawal attitude. Remember in this connection how big many dogs must seem to a small child. Therefore, lift him up when dogs are in the offing, remembering how much he takes in from your attitude. Lift him in such a way that the very process is reassuring, not as if you were snatching him from the jaws of death. And carry on a campaign of familiarizing him with dogs, perhaps in stories, certainly through firsthand experiences with gentle dogs, from a safe distance, probably aloft in your arms. As your child becomes more at ease, gradually see that he gets closer and closer to gentle dogs. When he reaches the point at which he wants to pat them, show him how. Finally, get the idea across to him that running away is likely to make the dog chase him. Give him your support by holding his hand until he is completely over his fright.

This prescription may sound dictatorial. But my point is not the precise procedure; I use it merely to illustrate the principles involved: 1) provide adequate withdrawal for your child, while you are helping him change his attitude toward the animals he fears; 2) see that the experiences he lives through—stories, accurate information, real life— are reassuring as he becomes more familiar with the animal in question; and finally, when he feels sufficiently comfortable to approach the animals he formerly feared, 3) help him learn skills in his behavior toward these animals which minimize the likelihood of the animals acting in ways that may frighten him.

Learning caution. Since some creatures warrant a cautious attitude, I shall now consider the question of helping your child learn necessary caution, not just in regard to animals but also in regard to other kinds of situations.

Caution is an attitude of alertness to the possibility of the desirability of withdrawal from a situation. There are many potentially dangerous or harmful situations toward which you want your child to learn adequate caution without feeling undue fear.

The principle of guidance is much the same with all of them: first, protect your child from situations he is too young to discriminate about; then gradually—by words, by your own example, and by supervised experience on his part—instruct him what to do, as you arm him with information designed to help him feel caution rather than fear and to learn the kind of skills which provide for adequate withdrawal from hazards.

Here are four examples of helping children learn caution.

Caution toward animals. Take dogs, for instance. Although most dogs are friendly, some are vicious. So you want to teach your child to be wary of dogs before handling them. The chances are that by example and instruction you can do this without instilling fear. Get across to the child the importance of not startling or hurting dogs— not walking on an outstretched paw, for example.

Safety precautions in regard to automobile traffic. Helping your child learn caution in regard to cars and trucks is very similar to helping him learn caution toward dangerous animals. When he is little, you simply need to protect him from the hazards of road traffic. As he grows old enough for greater freedom, you work out procedures for him, such as staying on your side of the street, notifying you if he wants to cross over, and doing it under your escort. As he is ready for more advanced learning, encourage him to be the one to look both ways for traffic and to decide when it is safe to cross. Have him learn to cross the street at places designated for pedestrians. Indicate the dangers of moving traffic, but in such a way that the caution instilled is a positive help, not an intense fear which interferes with the exercise of judgment.

Learning caution in regard to physical feats attempted. As children are growing up, parents must continually be deciding how much to leave them free to have firsthand experiences and how much to curtail their activity and explain why it was cut short. Some parents step in so early that their child has little opportunity to learn the probable consequence of many of his actions; what he does learn is to turn a deaf ear to warnings.

Here is a reckless, incautious little fellow of 3 who had been continually warned by his mother what not to do. Mrs. A decided to let him find out for himself the consequences to his actions:

> *Wesley, in his early days of nursery school, climbs to the top of a platform, eyes the ground, and announces to nearby Mrs. A, "I think I'll jump off." Usual procedure is to redirect children to jump from a box lower than this, for the platform is high enough to involve some hazard. "All right," Mrs. A answers. Wesley looks rather*

surprised, peers at the ground again, then leaps off. He hits the ground, hard, and tumbles over. "That's high enough to make the bottoms of your feet sting, isn't it, Wesley?" Mrs. A remarks.

Caution in regard to matches. During all the preschool years, matches should be inaccessible. But this is not enough to instill in your child the attitude he needs to develop toward them. Somewhere in the preschool years, he is likely to be attracted by them. When this happens, it is sound to let him use matches, under close supervision, for some appropriate purpose, such as lighting a grate fire. He needs to be told the hazards of fire, too.

Fear of "bad people." As always, parents need to know what experience has led to the fear in question. Sometimes such a question as the following will provide information: "You were saying you were afraid somebody might come and get you. What made you think about that, do you know?" Then, within a framework of actual facts in regard to the likelihood of the feared event, one can reassure a child.

By the time a child is old enough not to be under almost constant supervision, he needs to know, of course, never to go off with strangers. Your explanation should help him be sufficiently cautious without being unduly afraid. What he is told should be true as far as it goes; but, hopefully, some such explanation as this will suffice: "Most people are kind and honest, but some are not. So you must never go away with someone whom you do not know. In any case, if you want to go farther away than this side of the street [or whatever your child's play boundaries are], you need to consult me first."

Fear of the dark. What is called "fear of the dark" often involves fear of something more specific and concrete than "the dark." So far as you can, you need to find out what, specifically, your child fears about the dark and how he came to develop his fear. Perhaps it is burglars, or some bad creature lying in wait for him—the "boogieman," or "bears," or "wolves."

How you go about reassuring your child, of course, depends on what he is afraid of, the circumstances under which he developed his fear, his developmental level, and facts about whatever is feared.

Since nightfall accentuates these fears, your child needs such support as having you cheerfully go with him to turn on lights and having you carry him cozily and matter-of-factly to bed. If he spontaneously feels that having a hall light on would be a great comfort, let him have it, but do not get a light started at bedtime unless it is his idea. Once you start, you are likely to have to keep it up, and sometimes it interferes with going to sleep.

Other nighttime fears. In discussing sleep, I have already talked of bedtime evasions, real anxiety at bedtime, mild bedtime fears, and troubles and wakefulness during the night. Therefore, here I simply refer you to these sections (pp. 232–37).

Fear of the house burning down. If your child has experienced a bad fire, firsthand or vicariously on television, he may be haunted by fear of fire. A sound procedure in this case is to reassure him in terms of its improbability, to educate him in fire prevention, and to instruct him what to do in case of fire.

Fear of water. Around 3, many children go through a stage of wariness about going into the water, even when they have felt at ease about it earlier. It is a good idea to accept this attitude without making great efforts to change it. Let your child enjoy shore activities.

When the time comes to learn to swim, try to have this take place under optimal conditions—that is, in calm water, under the competent instruction of someone who not only knows how to teach swimming, but who understands children and gears what is expected of them to their abilities and to their attitude toward the water.

Fear reactions which have resulted from changes in living conditions. Young children, particularly children in the neighborhood of 2, may be thoroughly upset by pronounced changes in living conditions. If such changes are going to occur, it is important to minimize them by maintaining a familiar framework for life. This can be done by adhering to a child's old pattern in business activities and in play, and by giving him access to familiar playthings. If his environment is being radically changed, he will probably show increased dependence on his parents; you should expect this and provide a secure link between the new and the old by your presence. As he is becoming accustomed to a new way of life, help him out by being understanding of his need for you; do not, for example, combine moving into a brand-new house with disappearing at once for an evening out, leaving him in the hands of a strange sitter. But with understanding parents working for a "life as usual" atmosphere, he will probably not take long to become acclimatized, perhaps no longer than a week. If it is parents' absence on a trip which has upset him, much the same pattern of reassurance is needed.

Upsetness at the prospect of parents leaving. Here is an example. A mother lived alone with her two young children, one of whom, Howard, was then just a month under 4. When it had been necessary for her to be away overnight, she had obtained a sitter whom she had thought to be reliable. As it turned out, the sitter entertained a friend, stayed up very late, apparently had a lot to drink, and when morning came, just went on sleeping, despite the fact that the children called out and finally wept with alarm as they kept waiting to get up, having been taught to stay in bed until a grownup greeted them in the morning. The result of this experience was that Howard became anxious about his mother's whereabouts at night. Over a period of months, he got out of bed so many times each evening to come see his mother that he habitually was late in going to sleep.

On hearing this account of Howard's behavior, Mrs. A thought that sociability, as well as genuine uneasiness about his mother's whereabouts, might be involved in these frequent checkups. Accordingly, Mrs. A suggested to his mother that she modify her guidance by 1) telling Howard that she did not have plans to be out in the evening, and that if she were going out, she would always tell him beforehand; and 2) telling him that if he really felt the need to get up and see that she was there, all right—however, this would mean that the next night, he would have to go to bed earlier, because he was missing a lot of rest by getting up. Howard's mother followed this advice. When he did get up, his mother adhered to what she had said: instead of reading a story after supper the next night, she popped him in bed.

Her aim was twofold: to permit him to get up to check on her whereabouts if he felt really anxious; to encourage him, on the other hand, if he felt reasonably assured about her whereabouts, to stay in bed and enjoy a full measure of sociability the next night before bedtime came. Over a period of time under this new program, he resumed staying in bed, once put there, as he had done before his frightening experience.

When a child seems upset at the prospect of his parents leaving, they need to try to figure out how intense his feelings are. I am not suggesting, however, that whenever a child protests at the prospect of his parents' departure, they should stay home to keep him company. What is he feeling? That is the question. If it is genuine fear, you need to estimate how strong it is to see what guidance is necessary. Being left in the hands of a kind, competent, familiar sitter, with some such measure taken as receiving a little "surprise," well wrapped, to be opened only after parents depart, as I have said earlier, may be enough to turn apprehension or sorrow into acceptance and even enthusiasm. It is sound to avoid departure just at bedtime, as I have also mentioned.

But what if your child is going through a period of real anxiety about your whereabouts? If his disturbance is severe, you should stay at home. When the disturbance lessens, and to prepare your still somewhat fearful child for staying alone with the sitter, have her come a few times when you are home. Let her join in some pleasant activity with your child and you, without acting as if she is trying to come between mother and child. This may seem extravagant, but here we are talking of helping a child adjust who has formerly been deeply disturbed. You will need to play by ear the number of such occasions necessary for the child to feel reasonably at ease with the sitter, and you will be well advised to absent yourself for only a short time the first time you leave him. Play it safe.

Suppose, however, that your child's feelings seem to be much more anger than fear. Then, indeed, a competent, friendly sitter and some interesting things for your child to do are just the ticket. When actual departure time comes, your job is, with cheerful assurance, to tell him goodbye and to leave with dispatch. A lingering or hesitant departure would be likely to produce or prolong an emotional outburst.

If you were to let his angry protests cause you to abandon your evening out, not only would you be deprived of recreation (I am assuming you have it coming to you, and give your child the companionship he needs), you would also be encouraging him to use angry outbursts to gain what he wants.

Fear of masks. Fear of masks often originates at Halloween in much the same way as that described for 2½-year-old Johnny (p. 276). The guidance his parents devised illustrates how to help a child overcome such a fear. They talked about Halloween and explained that it happened just once in a very long time. Johnny was bought a non-scary mask which he enjoyed using, and the next Halloween, when he was 3½, his parents made sure that he was well briefed about what was likely to happen and that one of them was with him throughout the time when costumed children might come to the door. Also, dressed up and masked, he made some calls on friendly neighbors.

Fear of bodily injury. We adults need to remember that children have no background of statistical knowledge to help them appraise the likelihood of the occurrence of various events. Until Donna was reassured to the contrary, she had no reason not to believe that a blister could develop into a loss of limbs. So, David, on hearing of death from tetanus of someone he knew, had no background of information to assure him that death from tetanus is not only rare but wholly unnecessary (pp. 17–18). The chances are that his fear of poisonous things had resulted from an overreaction to warnings.

Many times, then, acquainting children with facts is all the reassurance needed. Sometimes, however, what is called for is learning skills of adequate withdrawal, such as safety rules for pedestrians to follow.

According to Freudian theory, a boy fears loss of his penis (castration complex). Noting the anatomical difference between boys and girls may contribute to this fear, the theory goes. I have not seen evidence of a castration complex in the children I have known, nor has it been reported to me by parents. I have been interested that a friend of mine, a clinical psychologist, psychoanalytically oriented, told me that she kept watching for signs of such a complex in her two sons, but (to her disappointment) she found no evidence for it. Many Freudians do, however, find substantiation of their theory about the castration complex in their work with children. This is not surprising since the very process of therapy for a child by a psychoanalyst may lead to what the psychoanalyst expects. Children are suggestible.

I think, nonetheless, that it is sound to take into account the possibility of such feelings on the part of a child (of girl children, too, lest their shape make them feel cheated—see p. 305 for further suggestions in this regard). Make sure that a little child has opportunities to see what children or babies of the opposite sex are shaped like, long before curiosity is evinced. This will come about without arrangement if your family includes children of different sexes who are not far apart in age. Otherwise, give your child the opportunity to see the anatomical appearance of children of the opposite sex when he is quite small. This may happen in the natural course of events, though opportunity for observation is likely to be rather fleeting. Better still, therefore, is watching a baby of the opposite sex being given a bath. The point is to let a child see anatomical differences between boys and girls when he is so small that these differences do not come as a surprise. If by any chance, a child should indicate that he thinks some part of a girl is missing, one can assure the child that little girls are shaped that way, just as little boys are shaped another way. One observation is not enough, of course. A child needs to keep having opportunities to see small children of the opposite sex during his preschool years, so that he comes to take their anatomical shape for granted as something "always" known rather than something suddenly discovered.

Fear of death. During the preschool years, children meet the concept of death, in one form or another. I know a 4-year-old who remarked one day, apropos of nothing his mother could connect it to, "Mommy, I hope I won't die when I'm a boy. There are so many words to learn."

She assured him that usually, nowadays, people live a long time; that finally, the time came for them to die when their bodies were old and tired. Later, when he again mentioned death, she talked of what is done to help people live a long time—in terms of shots, of accident prevention, and of medical care—making these measures intelligible to him through reference to experiences he had had.

What you tell your child about death depends, of course, upon the circumstances under which your child meets the concept of death and upon what you believe. As always, it is important to be honest about your own feelings and beliefs and about the facts of the case. It is not just old people who die. Whether you are talking with him about death as a remote eventuality, or groping to communicate with him because tragedy has struck your immediate family, you may find helpful a pamphlet written by Anna W. M. Wolf, published by the Child Study Association of America, entitled *Helping Your Child to Understand Death*.

Jealousy

Jealousy is an emotion involving both anger and fear. A person who is jealous has approach feelings which are threatened. He wants to maintain a personal relationship; he wants that relationship to be secure. But someone else seems to be jeopardizing it. He shrinks; he has a real feeling of withdrawal from the threat of losing this relationship which means so much to him. Remember these components both of approach and of withdrawal if one of your children is jealous of another or jealous of one parent.

Suppose an older child shows jealousy of a new baby by hitting the baby, and you respond with anger, indicating what a monster you think he is: "Everybody loves helpless little babies. We all need to take good care of our baby and love him." Where does that leave him? It simply confirms him in his uneasiness that he is being supplanted by this little object, and probably also makes him feel guilty about his attitude toward the baby. Thus, such a response on your part intensifies his fear. So much for what not to do. I shall make positive suggestions for guidance of children when they show jealousy, when I discuss relationships in the family (pp. 321–23).

Tensional outlets

By "tensional outlets" I mean certain kinds of behavior which, sometimes at least, seem to be a way in which a child finds relief from his feelings, or an outlet for tension of some sort. Specifically what I have in mind is stuttering, nail biting, thumb sucking, handling the genitals.

STUTTERING

Many children go through periods of stuttering in their preschool years. I am thinking now of a child who showed this pattern well before he was 2. One way of interpreting his stutter was that his language could not keep up with his ideas. Accordingly, his parents tried to reduce the stimulation of life around him whenever he went through a phase of stuttering. Because he was an alert little boy, he absorbed a lot without any stimulation on their part. When he was going through a stage of stuttering, they deliberately gave him a chance to consolidate his experiences, without adding to them. For example, out for a walk, they would refrain from the kind of remarks which spring so easily to grownup lips: "See the bird, there on the tree. Hear the train?" and so forth. When a child is going through a period of stuttering, relax life for him and reduce the tension. I do not mean to scrap the pattern to his day, or to cater to his whims as opposed to his needs. But be understanding and sympathetic, and try to arrange that life is satisfying without being overstimulating. Emphatically, do not tackle stuttering directly— by telling a child to slow down, for example, or to speak clearly. If he becomes trapped in repeating a sound, help him out in a gentle way by responding to his conversation, if you can, from the context of his remarks. And take it easy yourself; relax and remember how normal it is for children to go through phases of stuttering.

NAIL BITING

Guidance in regard to nail biting is much like that for stuttering. You need to deal with causes, not symptoms. The chances are that some kind of tension is finding an outlet in nail biting. Children are notorious imitators, of course. Perhaps your child imitated someone else when he first bit his nails, but probably he would not persist in nail biting unless it has become a tensional outlet for him. So look over his life to see where you can relieve pressure, just as you would if he were stuttering. Keep his nails short and smooth; refrain from nagging about biting them.

THUMB SUCKING

Babies seem to differ greatly in the strength of their sucking drive. I have been struck for a long time with the importance of seeing to it that babies have plenty of chances to suck, right from birth, when the drive is strongest, and when their ability to get a thumb or finger in their mouths to satisfy their sucking urge may be undeveloped.

As regards thumb sucking beyond babyhood, your attitude is important, as in all other types of tensional outlets. It is curious that thumb sucking seems to bother parents to such an extent. Of course, they worry lest it produce protruding teeth, but most doctors and dentists agree that if a child stops sucking before his permanent teeth have appeared, no lasting damage will result. I am convinced that attempts to deal directly with thumb sucking in preschool children only intensify the habit.

I know an ardent finger sucker, who sucked his fingers so vigorously when going to sleep that he could be heard anywhere in a two-story house. His parents suffered in silence, annoyed with themselves that the sucking bothered them. Then, when this child was just over 4, they put on an intensive campaign to "keep your hands away from your face." Ten days later, he no longer sucked his fingers. But he had taken to sucking his tongue. Still later, it turned out that this child was a "reverse swallower." Every time he swallowed, he thrust his tongue against his upper teeth, and pushed out against them. It is not unlikely that the "successful" campaign against finger sucking produced this result.

Or here is another child, just under 3, whose parents were understanding about his thumb sucking, but whose grandparents, when they came to visit for a few days, talked a great deal about his sucking. He kept on sucking, though now often with a furtive look. Soon, in addition, he took to handling his genitals. I cannot say that this was cause and effect, but it is a fact that this child found a second tensional outlet after grownup attention was focussed on his thumb sucking.

Is the idea then to relax and remind oneself that few of one's acquaintances suck their thumbs at the age of 20? Not just this, but hold on to that thought. It helps. Examine the total picture; appraise your child's life to figure out the satisfactions and dissatisfactions he is experiencing. (For suggestions for doing this, see pp. 114–16.) Try to discover unsatisfied needs, the feelings which led him to turn to his thumb for solace. You will have to look back into the past, since thumb sucking does not necessarily denote a present lack of security in a child. It may often stem from earlier insecurity, or from delay in feeding, and persist into the present merely because it is pleasurable. However, do not assume that the reasons are rooted in the past.

Next, after your appraisal of his life, take careful note of when sucking occurs. When he is fatigued, hungry, bored, thwarted? Deal with conditions which lead to thumb sucking, not directly with thumb sucking itself.

Here is an example in which thumb sucking proved to be related to fatigue:

A 3-year-old, who shared a room with an older sister, used to suck her thumb frequently. Since her older sister tended to keep her awake at bedtime and to wake her early in the morning, it seemed that fatigue might play a part in her desire to suck. Her parents, therefore, had one of the children go to bed in the parents' room, to be transferred later into her own bed. Though this helped, unfortunately the 3-year-old was still fatigued; she needed even more sleep. A rest during the morning was not the answer, for, if she lay down, she tended to fall asleep, and then wake for lunch and fail to take the long nap she clearly profited from in the afternoon. So whenever she started sucking her thumb in the morning, a grownup picked her up and said, "Are you feeling tired? Let's find something that might be fun for a tired person to do." Since she was a very musical little girl, she was often given a chance to use musical instruments which encouraged the use of both hands (and, therefore, discouraged thumb sucking). Note here, no reference whatsoever to the thumb sucking. Guidance was entirely indirect.

Suppose thumb sucking occurs when a child is put to bed. Relax. That is par. But make sure that you key bedtime to your child's sleep needs, so that you are not putting him there unreasonably early.

If you think hunger is producing thumb sucking, augment your child's midmorning (or midafternoon) snack, or see that mealtimes come somewhat earlier. What about boredom? The answer is obvious. You simply need to have your child's play surroundings stimulating. What about lack of pleasant companionship? If there is a good nursery school in your community, this may be part of the answer. Is your child experiencing unnecessary thwarting, perhaps being teased, or, on his own, aiming unreasonably high in what he would like to do? Then think in terms of the obstacles he is encountering (pp. 266–67). Sometimes I have seen children who have discovered that thumb sucking is a weapon to be employed when annoyed with parents. I know a child who, when told not to do something by her father, deliberately placed herself in his full view, thrust her thumb into her mouth and sucked lustily, casting a malicious glance in his direction. If her father showed his annoyance, he would only strengthen her arsenal. She held all the aces.

HANDLING THE GENITALS

Sooner or later children discover that handling the genitals produces pleasurable sensations. It is important not to make them feel guilty about it.

When you notice that your young child is handling his genitals (I remind you that "he" stands for both boys and girls throughout this book), find out in a casual way whether too small underpants or some local irritation is prompting it. If not, then relax. Without watching your child like a hawk, see whether he continues.

In any case, try to arrange your child's life so as to reduce the number of occasions on which he may take to handling his genitals. For instance, when you change your baby's diapers, give him something interesting to play with. And with an older child, arrange that bedtime occurs when he is likely to feel sleepy—I have already given many reasons for this procedure, but another is that a bored child may turn to masturbation for something to do. Suppose your child habitually takes an hour to fall asleep at night. Some children simply have this kind of sleep pattern. Do not have masturbation on your mind if your child does not fall asleep the minute he hits the bed. But if he does change his sleep pattern, so that instead of going to sleep pretty promptly he lies awake for a long time, then avoiding circumstances likely to invite handling the genitals is one of the many reasons for revising his bedtime to fit his sleeping needs. It is also another reason for not using bed as a punishment or as a safe, out-of-the-way place to park a child.

Although there are many other reasons for providing your child with an interesting play environment and congenial companionship, one is so that he does not turn to handling his genitals through boredom. Again, avoidance of any invitation to handle the genitals is only one among many reasons for not requiring your child to sit over a toilet a long time in the hope that he will function.

For the rest, guidance should proceed along the lines just described for thumb sucking. Of course, if a child of preschool age takes to habitual and prolonged masturbation (prolonged in the sense of continuous time spent masturbating), you would probably do well to seek competent professional advice. But be sure that you consult someone who realizes how natural it is for children to handle their genitals and who is likely to be astute in judging whether or not there is really cause for concern.

OTHER TENSIONAL OUTLETS

There are many other tensional outlets which children may turn to —for instance, rocking in bed, pulling on a strand of hair, combining thumb sucking with stroking the upper lip with fingers or with plucking fuzz from a blanket. The general principle of guidance for these tensional outlets is identical with that for the behavior we have already discussed: try to appraise a child's whole life in order to understand why he seeks this kind of outlet; deal with causes, not symptoms.

Guidance of sexuality

YOUR OWN ATTITUDES AND YOUR WHOLE PATTERN OF GUIDANCE AFFECT YOUR CHILD'S FEELINGS ABOUT SEXUALITY

Parents sometimes confuse the giving of sex information with guidance of sexuality. Certainly, giving your child information about sex is part of the guidance of sexuality, but only part. The shaping of attitudes toward sexuality is going on in many experiences which make up your child's life, with or without your awareness—from remarks and actions of contemporaries and of adults, from tones of voice, from facial expression, from animal behavior, from the emotional atmosphere in which he lives.

Basic feelings on your part which may influence your child's attitudes toward sexuality begin before he is born—for instance, in your hopes that your baby will be a boy or a girl. What is important if parents' desires are disappointed is almost too obvious to mention: that a child's sex not be held against him and that a child of one sex not be encouraged to play the role of the opposite sex.

The evaluation each of his parents makes of the sex he (or she) belongs to also influences a child's feelings about sexuality. Suppose a mother feels, by and large, that being a woman is rewarding. Then some of this attitude is likely to be passed on to her daughter. But if a growing girl senses, and hears, from her mother what a hard lot women have, she is very apt to be affected by this viewpoint.

Similarly, the attitude of each of his parents toward the other, both as representatives of the opposite sex and as individuals, will affect a child's conception of manhood and of womanhood, and influence the feelings he has about his own sex. If one parent is continually derogating the opposite sex ("Isn't that just like a woman—what else could anyone expect," and so forth), children are bound to be affected. If, on the other hand, children are lucky enough to be growing up in a home where mutual esteem and affection underlie the relationship between parents, then these children may perpetuate this attitude in their own lives.

I hope, then, that your child is growing up in a home where his parents accept the fact of his sex, without persisting disappointment, where each of his parents is content with the role in life which his sex has determined for him, where each parent respects members of the opposite sex in general, and where both boys and girls are valued—neither is catered to merely because of the sex he happens to be. You will notice I did not say that I hope boys and girls would be treated in the same way. After all, as adults, they need to have different attitudes in many respects in order to accept and perform effectively, and reasonably contentedly, the roles demanded of them in our kind of social order.

The chances are that, even as small babies, boys and girls will be treated somewhat differently. Boy babies are likely to come in for rather more boisterous handling in play than are girl babies. This is one reflection of a difference in concept on the part of adults as to what boys and girls are like.

But as boy and girl babies grow into the preschool years, I hope that in many respects they are treated alike. I am in favor of much the same kind of play environment for both sexes. Little boys, like little girls, spend much of their time in these early years in a domestic situation. They may want to dramatize it by playing house, by playing with dolls. This is natural and wholesome. It would be a pity if grownups belittled such play by a boy as sissy, "girlish" activity. (What a derogatory note that term "girlish" introduces in this context!) But see to it that the play equipment available for dramatic play also includes materials which lead to acting out not only a feminine, but also a masculine role—for instance, a make-believe razor, a man's hat, perhaps a doctor's kit or a brief case.

Or your boy may want to help in cooking. Fine. Do not think he ought to be sparring with a punching bag. (Besides, many a man asserts that the best chefs are men.) But provide, too, play materials for boisterous, outdoor activity and the development of physical skills. Girls as well as boys need this. If a father is eager to play ball with his son, he should not overdo it by expecting a boy to perform beyond his capacity or by showing a sustained interest in ball playing before his son is developmentally ready—that is, before he has left his preschool years behind. Needless to say, girls may enjoy ball playing, too.

In short, in arranging your child's play environment, emphasize provision of interesting, constructive, varied occupation, as already discussed (pp. 81–112).

These suggestions do not lead to the development of girlish boys and boyish girls. Rather, they lead to the development of varied interests and skills based on what appeals to individual children. It is simply a fact that boys and girls enjoy much the same play materials during these preschool years. However, watch for opportunities to help your child be glad he is the sex he is. When a little girl is interested in clothes or feminine activities, capitalize on her interest, her enjoyment of femininity. But do not rush her. Many a girl has persisted in tomboyish ways until the brink of adolescence, when she then makes up for lost time in her pursuit of femininity. Similarly, watch for opportunities to have a little boy enjoy masculine attire and pursuits, without forcing either of these.

Leaving the matter of play activities and attire, let us turn to possible differences in the way you guide emotional upsets for boys and for girls. When your son is upset, do not encourage him to be stalwart just because he is a boy. "Crying just like a girl," I have heard a parent say in a disgusted tone to a small son who had banged his head painfully. In the long run, it is true, in our culture breaking into tears fairly readily is condoned in women and not in men. But your child will pick up this attitude soon enough without your pushing him into it. The preschool years are not the time for it. You already know that I believe you should help children scale the extent of their upsetness to the degree of their hurt or frustration (pp. 282–83). If a child tends to overreact emotionally, the guidance I recommend does not differ on account of the sex of the child.

Again, it is not advisable in these preschool years to defer to the sex of a child as a reason for preferential treatment. Chivalry can wait. If Jimmy starts using the wagon first, or is ready to go through a door before Mary, he is entitled to.

INFLUENCE OF GUIDANCE OF ELIMINATION
ON ATTITUDES TOWARD SEXUALITY

Your attitude toward your child's elimination may carry over to his attitude toward sexuality. This is another reason for not showing disgust or displeasure with his eliminative functioning.

GUIDANCE OF A CHILD'S AWARENESS OF
ANATOMICAL DIFFERENCES

I talked earlier of how to guide a little girl making an attempt to urinate standing up (p. 252). You will notice that she is not told, "You don't have a penis"; the emphasis is positive—on "being made differently." The reasoning behind this phrasing rests on the Freudian view that girls may feel deprived because of lacking a penis. Bearing this possibility in mind, it is a good idea, by the time a little girl hears how a baby grows inside a woman, for her to learn that there is a special place where the baby grows, and to hear about this in scientific terms. Then she knows that girls, too, have a "special" kind of construction, even though it cannot be seen.

I talked in some detail of providing opportunities for children to see the anatomical differences between boys and girls at such an early age that they would feel as if they had always known this difference. I spoke, too, of the importance of continuing to have these opportunities throughout the preschool years (p. 295).

This reminds me of a boy who did not have such opportunities. It was late in his preschool years when he saw a girl cousin in the bathtub. His cousin was a versatile young lady; she could wiggle her ears and roll her tongue. When this boy saw her in the tub, he thought she was just performing another of her conjuring tricks. He spent some time trying to see if he could pose so that his penis was similarly out of sight, for he assumed that all people had penises, until finally a grownup enlightened him. This episode should serve to remind us that many of the things adults take for granted do not have logic on their side at all, merely experience. I know a child, for example, who thought that the dog and the cat were members of the same family, the dog was the male, the cat the female. I know another child who thought spontaneously that his parents would get younger, as he grew older, which was revealed when he remarked to his mother, "When I'm older than you are . . ." I cite this to remind you that sex is not the only aspect of life which presents complexities.

To go on with guidance of sexuality, if there is a new baby boy in your family who has been circumcised, it is wise not to expose a little child to the sight of the baby's penis until it is healed. This can be easily managed, without being furtive, if your older child is only 2 or 3 (and hence cannot readily see when the baby is being cared for on a surface as high up as a bathinette).

Further, right from the start, use scientific names for sexual and eliminative organs. If you use some general term which applies to both male and female, like the old-fashioned "private parts," you fail to underline the difference between male and female, which is helpful when children need further sex information.

HANDLING THE GENITALS

In the section on tensional outlets I talked about children's handling the genitals, and guidance when this occurs (pp. 300–301). Let me supplement this discussion with two examples of guidance which I do not advocate.

The first concerns a 3-year-old boy who, according to his mother's report, masturbated regularly when put to bed, keeping himself awake for a long time. She informed us that she had told him that if he handled his penis, it would turn black. When her warning did not deter him at all, one afternoon after he had fallen asleep she proceeded to put ink on his penis, without awakening him. When he woke up, and was being helped to dress, he noticed his penis, and remarked, "Aw, that's just ink." In my view, all the honors in this engagement go to the young man, especially for recognizing that ink is ink. As for Mother, she was baffled. Unfortunately, she only sought advice after this episode rather than before.

The second case involves a 4½-year-old girl who had learned to shinny up a pole and discovered, in sliding down a slanted support, that she received pleasurable sensations in the genital area. She confided this pleasure to her mother, who responded by telling her she must never do that. If she did, her mother continued, when she grew up, she would not be able to have children—a statement, incidentally, which her mother believed. The little girl reacted to this warning by being afraid to wipe herself after a bowel movement, although she had previously done this competently. This is a good example of how instilling fear may result in a withdrawal reaction. It is important in guiding children in regard to sexuality to avoid causing fear, lest this interfere with a positive attitude toward sexuality in adulthood. As always, there is a fine line between an attitude of reasonable withdrawal (or postponement, or caution) and the stronger withdrawal attitude that is fear.

QUESTIONS ABOUT SEX

As is the case with all the questions a child asks, the parents' job is to try to figure out what the child is wondering about, so that the answer given provides the information sought. If you are perplexed as to the intent of your child's question, you may get a clue by asking, "Tell me some more about what you are wondering. Could you say it in a different way?" I believe firmly that what you tell your child in reply to any question should be true as far as it goes and so serve as a basis for more complex information when he is ready for it. I also believe that the amount of information you give should be scaled to what the child is seeking and, of course, that any explanations presented be in a form suited to developmental level.

There is one aspect of imparting sex information which is particularly perplexing to most parents. This results from the fact that families differ widely as to what children should be told and at what age. Even if the families of your child's friends have different views, I think that as soon as it is clear that your child is wondering about a particular aspect of sexuality, he is ready for an honest answer. However, tell him that every family likes to decide how and when questions like this are answered, so it is better to talk about these matters just at home; that some parents wait until children are older to tell them about these things. But holding one's tongue is very hard in the preschool years. Therefore, if your child talks, do not censure him severely. Just remind him how other parents feel.

Another aspect of imparting information about sexuality which may be perplexing is the circumstance in which your child asks a question. Prepare yourself to be taken by surprise. Envisage the possibility of his asking questions about sex long before you think it is likely. Then you will not be evasively groping for words. In this connection, as well as for the other content presented, I recommend an excellent publication of the Child Study Association of America entitled *What to Tell Your Children about Sex.*

What kind of questions are preschoolers likely to ask about sex? Many and varied ones. I shall mention only a few. Questions about anatomical differences, for instance. I have already discussed this, and you know I believe in using scientific names for genital and eliminative organs.

What about questions as to where babies come from? They are likely to occur in these preschool years. If they do not, you should find an appropriate occasion to tell your child how a baby grows in a special place in his mother's body called the uterus (*not* in his mother's stomach) until he is old enough to be born. If a friend is having a baby, or if your cat is having kittens, this is a good time to impart the information. What if your child is adopted? In the first place, I would make a point of having one of the first stories an adopted child hears be the story of how his parents wanted him, and how he came to be their child—a story he should hear often enough when he is little to feel that he has "always" known it. It might be a story like this: Daddy and Mommy wanted a baby very much, but a baby did not grow inside Mommy, so after a while Daddy and Mommy went to a particular place (if it is an agency, call it by name), and told the people there all about it. And after a while, they let Daddy and Mommy know that their baby was ready. So Daddy and Mommy drove to (wherever the place was) and there was Jimmy in a little bassinet. And they all went home together.

When it comes time to tell an adopted child how babies develop, it is helpful to bear in mind the distinction made by some adoptive agencies between spiritual parenthood and natural parenthood. According to this viewpoint an adoptive parent is entitled to think of himself as a parent in a very real sense. True, he has not given his child physical existence, but he is nevertheless the child's parent, for that is a spiritual, or if you prefer a social, relationship. In telling an adopted child how a baby grows, I would say that a baby grows inside a lady (rather than "inside its mother"). When an adopted child wonders why he was available for adoption, I think some such honest statement as the following is in order: his Mommy and Daddy do not know, but it must have been a hard thing to do, done for his sake because it was best for him. Babies need a home and two parents, and the lady inside of whom he grew must not have been able to take care of him and give him the kind of home a baby needs.

Once a child is well aware of the fact that he is adopted, there is no need to keep referring to it. If one does, it is apt to make him wonder what is so unusual about being adopted. But he should hear of the fact of his adoption often enough when he is small so that he does not forget it.

So far, in answering a child's questions about where babies come from, I have been suggesting answers in terms of growing inside a special place, called the uterus, in a woman's body, with details adapted to being part of a family either by birth or by adoption.

Eventually children wonder how a baby begins growing inside a woman's body. Though this query usually does not come in preschool years, it may—particularly if a child has heard some remark that has set him wondering. It is well, therefore, to be prepared. As with all the questions a child asks, your job is to try to figure out exactly what your child is wondering about and to answer him truthfully, without overwhelming him with information he does not want and will not understand. A child may be content with the statement that a father starts the growing of a baby inside a mother. But even in the preschool years, he may pursue the topic to its logical conclusion, so that the only honest answer is one which gives some idea of the fact of sexual intercourse. If your child does pursue the topic to this point, do not be evasive. Some such statement as the following can serve as a basis to be built on as a child gets older: He knows that when people are fond of each other, when they love each other, they like to be with each other. They like to be close. Sometimes a father and mother have a very special kind of closeness together, when the father's penis fits into a place in the mother's body called the vagina. When this happens a tiny sperm from the father can join an ovum in the mother, and from this joining of sperm and ovum, a baby grows.

You probably hope that during your child's preschool years his questions will not reach as far as this. But remember, he may be on the receiving end of some account which has left him confused and wondering. So, in answering his question, you may be not so much imparting brand-new information about sex as helping him begin to understand something he has already heard. Remember, too, that such an explanation as the one I suggested is only a beginning and needs to be amplified as your child progresses in questioning and in understanding.

SEX PLAY

What about experimentation? Does accurate sex information lead to sex play? According to members of the staff of the Child Study Association of America, "specialists in child behavior agree that when sex information is wisely given by parents a child trusts, there is less likelihood of unwholesome sex experiments. A certain amount of sex play seems to be a normal part of growing up."

I certainly know of cases in which withholding information did not prevent sex play. I recall, for instance, a mother who phoned me in consternation on discovering her daughter, just 5, and a 5-year-old boy were carrying on sex play, and I can still hear her wail over the phone, "I've never told her anything."

You know already that I think the play of children of preschool age should be supervised. If you discover sex play going on, redirect the play. Help children find something else interesting to do. Certainly tell the children firmly that this is not the way to play, but do not overdo your reaction and so create undue guilt. Continue to keep an eye on the kind of play going on. You should, in any case, for many reasons.

"DIRTY" WORDS AND "BATHROOM TALK"

I include discussion of "dirty" words and "bathroom talk" here because they often have emotional overtones which link them closely with sexuality. Use of "dirty" words and "bathroom talk" seems to be a normal part of growing up. Let us consider first "dirty" words, which refer to some aspect of sexual behavior. If your child is going in for this sort of talk, what do you think are his feelings about it? Does he do it to get a rise out of the grownups, to create a stir among his contemporaries (giggles and sidelong glances), to show what a clever person he is? In short, what purpose is the talk serving in his life? And what about your reaction? A marked emotional reaction on your part only defeats your end, if that is to have your youngster take this sort of thing in stride without dwelling on it. If you indicate that his behavior is beyond the pale, you are likely to drive his talk underground, to give it all the more status as a titillating utterance to be whispered into somebody's ear. What do you do, then—just grin and bear it? When a child first utters an expression you do not like, ignore it. Do not emphasize it in his mind by talking about it. If it does recur—suppose it is one of the Anglo-Saxon monosyllables—then tell your child that it is not considered the way to talk. Actually, he may not have any idea of the meaning of the term. He may have just caught its emotional overtone. But if he keeps using it and if he already has some facts which provide him with a background for understanding aspects of sexuality (so that his introduction to these facts will not be in a context of "dirty" words), then go ahead and talk of the meaning of the word. Suppose the word is "fuck," and he has some idea of the fact of sexual intercourse already. He uses the term "fuck" every once in a while. It has not dropped out. Then ask him, does he know what it means? You can explain that it is a word some people use to talk about mating— the kind of mating animals do. It does not take into account the kind of close relationship a mother and father have who love each other and want sometimes to be very close together.

One of the reasons for seeing to it that your child has some background knowledge about the complexities of adult sex life is precisely in order to avoid having him introduced to the fact of sexual intercourse in a context of innuendo and "gutter talk." Of course, each parent will handle this sort of thing in his own way. That goes without saying. But, however you deal with this kind of talk, I suggest that you avoid putting a premium on "dirty" words by a marked emotional reaction to them.

Suppose your child uses a lot of bathroom talk. I have known many children who have done so, for one, a 4-year-old girl who frequently introduced "B.M." talk into her play ("The sofa is made of B.M."—giggle, giggle, and so forth). As always, the grownup's job is to figure out what gives this talk special importance. Does it reflect concern with the process of bowel functioning? If so, the child needs guidance so as to accept movement of the bowels as a natural process. Many times, the appeal of such talk seems to lie in the fact that it is a sure-fire attention getter among contemporaries. I think the best thing to do in this case is to wait to see whether it will die a natural death. If it does not, tell your child, "People are just tired of hearing about B.M.s. If you want to talk about them, do it by yourself as much as you like." If he keeps on, isolate him and again encourage him to "talk about B.M.s as much as he likes."

Now, suppose, on the other hand, you have a child visitor who starts this kind of talk and keeps it up. Your child has not been involved. There is no reason to treat the talk differently from the way you would handle any other kind of undesirable behavior. What would you do if the visitor started hammering on a newly painted fence? You would redirect him, wouldn't you? Do the same thing about toilet talk. Say, as the talk keeps on, "Everybody's heard that now. How about talking about something else? It gets tiresome to keep hearing the same thing," and suggest some interesting alternatives for play.

As your child grows older, beyond his preschool years, he will encounter some of the many aspects of sex, and some of the many moods in which it may be approached. I hope he will continue to turn to you for information and clarification, and that you will continue to be honest with him. One of the most important influences on his attitude toward sexuality will remain the emotional tone in his own family—an emotional tone which is influenced by the sexual relationship which exists between his parents and by the attitude of each of them toward sexual behavior generally.

SUMMARY

In this chapter on guiding your child's feelings, first we dealt with guiding your child when he is angry and when he is fearful; then certain tensional outlets were discussed; finally we concluded with a discussion of guidance of sexuality.

Now we move on to still another aspect of a child's life in which you continue to try to base guidance on an estimation of your child's motivation: getting on with other people.

10

Getting On with Other People

THE THESIS OF THIS BOOK is that effective guidance furthers a cordial relationship between you and your child, whereas the nagging and inconsistency which are likely to accompany ineffective guidance tend to produce irritation for all concerned. The kind of guidance I have been advocating encourages maximum freedom for children within a framework of consideration for other people's rights, parents included. In Chapter 3, What Do You Want Your Child to Learn?, I indicated various specific learnings which contribute to getting on with other people, including the important matter of developing inner resources and a sense of one's own competence, and an attitude of willingness to accept the consequences of one's behavior (pp. 57–64, p. 66). But actually the whole book bears on the kinds of relationships your child has with others. If you are carrying out the guidance advocated, you are already going a long way toward helping your child have satisfactory relationships with the people who make up his life. However, I shall supplement what has already been said by discussing your child's relationships with particular individuals or groups of people.

The immediate family

PARENTS

Let us begin with the first-born child's relations with his parents, before the birth of other children. I hope there are plenty of chances to do things together that are fun for all concerned, a chance to do things not only as a family group of three, but as twosomes, mother and child, and father and child, not to mention a chance for a mother and father to step out together on their own. What is fun for adults depends, of course, on individual preferences; I cannot speak for you. As for what is enjoyable for children, since I have already suggested many kinds of play activities (pp. 83–112), and various ways in which parents may contribute to play (pp. 188–92), I refer you to that discussion. Here, as I am concentrating on activities that parent and child may share, I suggest that most small children enjoy walks; a chance, in parents' company, to look (at their own pace) at the wonders of the world; not too boisterous romping; piggyback rides; rides in the car; "helping" in the kitchen or in the garden; being read to; looking at pictures with parents; hearing songs and, in due course, singing them; listening or moving to music, or being held while a parent dances; the added fillip to life provided by seasonal celebration (a Halloween jack-o'-lantern, for example, and colored napkins for special occasions); picnics; guessing games suited to a child's ability. These are just a few of the ways one or both parents may be companionable with a child. I hope you are on the lookout for ways to have fun with your child, fun which takes everyone's needs and interests into account.

To move on to another point, parents should expect that a child will sometimes show a preference for one parent over the other. I hope that the unfavored parent of the moment will be mature about his child's preferences and not be hurt or put out. Mothers are often the favored parent when children are little, or when they are hurt or ill. As in the case of all feelings, it is unsound to try to talk or shame a child out of his emotions. It is much sounder to acknowledge them. Suppose, when a young child wakes in the night crying, Father comes to help. "I want Mommy," the child sobs. "Yes, I can see how you feel," a wise father may answer. "But Mommy is asleep, so I'm glad to help as much as I can." Fathers may be comforted to know that the light of approval may well shine on them when children are older, and Mother may come in for her share of the shade. I hope that neither parent exploits the child's feelings or courts favoritism. Instead, try to work out and present a united adult front in regulating the child's behavior.

Sometimes a child shows unmistakable jealousy of a particular parent. Of course, according to Freudian theory, a child inevitably considers the parent of the same sex as himself a rival. While this may be an exaggeration, it is nevertheless a good idea for parents to try to arrange life so that the arrival home of one parent is not the cue for the immediate unavailability of the other parent, whose company the child has been enjoying up to this point. It is also sound, as I have already indicated, for a child to have a chance to enjoy not only the company of both parents together, but also that of one parent at a time, so that sometimes he has each parent's full attention. Remember that a child may feel left out because of the very fact of adult companionship, that is, his parents' enjoyment of each other; an only child may feel particularly isolated, since he is entirely dependent upon grownups for companionship within the family. This reminds me of a 4-year-old girl, an alert, appealing child who used to listen to her father's detailed account of some matter he was reporting to his wife, the complexities of which she could not possibly follow, but who would remark in a pause in the conversation, "You're talking to both of us, aren't you, Daddy?"

Little things can make a lot of difference. I know a pair of parents who, if surprised by their small child as they were putting their arms around each other, would say at once, "Come have a hug, too," and enlarge the circle to include the child.

As is always the case, prevention is better than cure, and this applies to a child's jealousy of a parent. If unmistakable jealousy does occur, acknowledge it frankly and take steps to foster a happy relationship with both parents.

THE NEW BABY

The advent of a new baby usually effects an enormous change for a child who, up until this time, has been the one and only. Even when it has happened before in a family, a new baby always means a great deal of change. Tact, sympathy, and intelligent planning can facilitate an older child's adjustment to an increase in the family.

First, there is the question of when to tell the older child of the new baby. If the older child is in a here-and-now stage of psychological development, it may be inadvisable for him to hear of the baby long in advance. But since the last thing you want is to have him sense furtive preparations, tell him before he feels something in the air which is being hidden from him. Help him understand how little a newborn baby is. Otherwise he may visualize someone he can play with right away. You can explain that the baby will sleep most of the time, "just the way you did when you were little." Once he knows of the baby, it is fine to have him help in preparations. Remember, he is likely to drop things, so do not commission him to undertake activities which will lead to irritation or frustration on your part if accidents occur.

An obvious aim, in facilitating a child's adjustment to the new baby, is to maintain the security and pattern of his life, so far as possible, after the baby comes. Therefore, institute necessary changes in his living arrangements long enough ahead so that a child is used to them before the advent of the baby. If the location of his bed is going to be changed, make the change well before the baby is due. While managing to be honest, explain the new arrangement on other grounds than those of making way for the baby. Make a change from crib to bed at the optimum time for the older child, rather than shifting him merely in order to have the crib available when the baby is ready for it (p. 231).

It also helps maintain the continuity of life if your child already knows and likes the person who will look after him while Mother is away. Since the helper should be informed about his accustomed way of life, a notebook to indicate what happens when, and how it is carried on, is a boon to child and helper alike. What if a father is to be in complete charge at home, with no helping hand, synchronizing a vacation from work with the arrival of the baby? Before this plan is adopted, think realistically about whether this is best for all concerned. Will the father take it in stride, or will he find the job of trying to run home and child worrisome and vexing? If the latter is likely, then how about a compromise (finances permitting) so that someone else helps with household and child care, but Father has some extra time for visits with his wife and companionship with the older child?

It is a good idea to have an alternate plan in mind for emergency care for your older child, in case your baby fools you and arrives early. Perhaps you can make an arrangement with a friend to help out until your regular arrangement can go into effect. This is to avoid a period of such marked confusion that it might be frightening to a little child.

In case a mother leaves unexpectedly during the night, a brief, cheerful note can mean a lot to the older child, to be read to him when he wakes, so he knows his mother was thinking about him.

When his mother is returning home with the new baby, it is a good idea if the older child can be happily occupied elsewhere, so that by the time he is reunited with her, both mother and baby are comfortably settled. Then he can receive her full attention at their reunion, rather than feeling shunted off while concern is still focussed on the new baby. There are other ways of helping the older child have a happy reunion with his mother. I know a mother who was called for at the hospital by her husband, her own mother, and her older child. Grandmother sat in the back seat of the family car, holding the baby. The older child sat in front with his mother and father, in the manner in which he was accustomed to ride.

Once home, it is sound to keep the older child from feeling that baby care is the be-all and end-all of existence. For instance, there is a lot to be said for reserving a feeding time alone for mother and baby. If you agree, this can be done without making the older child feel excluded. Work things out so that he is already used to some interesting activity during many of the occasions for intensive baby care. A good deal depends, of course, on when the baby is hungry. Suppose the baby is fed early in the morning before the older child gets up. Then, once helped up, he has a chance to visit with his mother. While he has outdoor play, or visits at a friend's home, baby care is going on. During the older child's afternoon rest, again the baby is likely to be cared for. Perhaps the next feeding is the one best suited to having the company of the older child. But if the mother is nursing her baby, it may be well to postpone having the older child present because the closeness of the nursing relationship is particularly likely to make him feel jealous. Once the child is somewhat used to the new baby, this is another aspect of life he can become accustomed to.

The arrival of a new baby is a good occasion for providing an older preschool child with a baby doll, be he boy or girl, and some "baby" equipment, which he can be encouraged to use alongside Mother when she is looking after the baby.

When the older child is present during baby care, encourage him to feel that the baby is his, too. Even if he is just 2, you can ask, "Would you like to hold the baby?" Then, have him sit cross-legged on the floor and put the baby in his arms; but support his arms, too, for he may let go. If he likes to, it is fine to have him do things for the baby (fetch a diaper, for example), but do not burden him with jobs. With a new baby in the house, tell him what he was like when he was a tiny baby. This is a good time to bring out snapshots. If he wants to play baby, let him; hold him like a baby, and go along with the game.

See to it, however, that he finds satisfactions in being the age he is. You do not need to blow a trumpet about this, but keep on the lookout to see that deprivation and a bleak series of days do not coincide with the baby's birth, that happy, interesting experiences do occur. Thoughtless friends sometimes concentrate so much on the baby that the older child feels neglected. Therefore, have a supply of trinkets and playthings on hand. If life seems to be perpetual Christmas for the baby, produce some presents for the older child, too.

As I talk of giving special attention to your older child's early experiences with the baby, you can probably guess that I am mindful of the part which conditioning may play in the formation of attitudes.

Gradually accustom your older child to the presence of the baby during more and more of the family day. The nature of a tiny baby and the care he needs lend themselves to a gradual introduction to round-the-clock life with baby.

When some activity which your older child enjoys has to be terminated in order for you to look after the baby, explain the change on other grounds than baby care. Suppose you are out for an afternoon stroll with your older child, and you need to go back to check the baby. If your older child enjoys his juice, "Time for juice, now," you tell him. "Home we go." You produce it, perhaps preparing some for the baby, too, and then go ahead with baby tending. How different this is from the treatment received by a child I know, who was terribly eager for a new doll. "We can't afford it now that we have a new baby," she was told. I am not saying the child should have had the doll. Certainly not, if it was beyond the family means. But an explanation can be couched in honest terms and still not point an accusing finger at the baby.

What about nursery school as a solution to an interesting life for an older child with a new baby in the family? You can probably guess here, too, what my answer will be. By all means, send your child, if he is ready for nursery school, if a good one is available, and if you can manage this financially. But see to it that he enters in time to be well adjusted to the school before the baby's arrival, or else put off entrance until he is accustomed to the change at home. Avoid having him feel he is being shipped off to school while the baby takes over at home.

If your older child reverts to behavior of younger days, be cheerful and understanding. Even with the best of parental management, acquiring a brother or sister is a great adjustment. Symptoms of the adjustment may take many forms—getting wet, bowel lapses, a return to thumb sucking, emotional upsets. If so, relax; put your emphasis on trying to make life satisfying for your older child. This advice is in keeping with everything I have already said about guiding your child's feelings. By no means indicate that "he is too big to act that way." From where he sits, it may seem that it is babies who have a place in the sun; such talk would only confirm your child in his opinion.

Let us move on now from the advent of a new baby in the family to consider other kinds of guidance for brothers and sisters.

BROTHERS AND SISTERS

Jealousy of brother or sister. Now, let us suppose that despite your efforts, your older child shows unmistakable signs of jealousy. I have already referred briefly to jealousy in Chapter 9, Guiding Your Child's Feelings. The point I made was that jealousy involves both anger and fear. A jealous child has approach feelings toward someone (say, his mother) which he believes someone else is blocking. Toward this obstacle (the baby) he therefore feels anger. He also feels fear, lest his relationship with his mother be disrupted.

Sometimes jealousy takes the form of hurting the baby. You have to get there fast to protect him. Pick up your older child, while you acknowledge his feelings. "Lots of brothers and sisters feel cross with each other sometimes," you might tell him. "But I can't let you hurt the baby. If you feel like hitting, come on, hit your baby doll," as you carry the child to the doll and give it some smacks yourself. "And if you feel cross with the baby, it's fine to tell me about it, too. I always like to know how you're feeling." You are trying to give him a substitute activity to let out his thwarted approach feelings, his anger. And look for opportunities to reassure him in regard to thwarted withdrawal, his fear—to reassure him through the warmth of your relationship. Show him that you love him.

Suppose your child puts his feelings into words. I know a child, a few months over 3, who viewed her new baby brother with coolness, and then suggested, "Let's take him back to the hospital." Here again, acknowledge that you understand and sympathize with such feelings. "I can see how you feel," you might say. "Lots of times boys or girls do feel that way about a new baby and I'm glad you told me. The baby does stay here because he's our baby, but let's see what we can do to make life nice and interesting for all of us." But these words will do little good unless you make life really satisfying for the older child.

Arrange that a jealous child (and for that matter, each child in the family) has a cozy time just for himself with one or both parents—"a big-boy storytime," for instance, when a younger child is out of the picture. Watch for an opportunity in this cozy interlude to help a child express his feelings and to encourage him to think and say what makes him feel cross, when this is appropriate.

Watch, too, for opportunities to talk over with a child how to gain his ends (within reason) without being unpleasant to another child in the family.

Remember, especially if your child's jealousy worries you, that the very fact that there are adjustments to make has positive aspects for a child; in the long run, he is likely to emerge as a more adaptable person in his relationships with other people because he is not an only child. If there were no adjustments to make to brothers and sisters, there would be little to learn from living with them.

Sometimes an older child seems to take easily to a new baby when he arrives, but, as the baby begins to emerge as a personality in his own right, jealousy shows up. I am thinking of a boy who showed every sign of easy adjustment to his baby sister, but who regarded her with less and less favor once she was walking and talking. When he was almost 4 and she was slightly less than two years younger, he remarked, "I wish there wasn't any Nora." His mother replied in the way I have suggested, then went on to say, "Tell me the things Nora does that you don't like." This led to an extended discussion, ferreting out, as far as possible, the trouble spots so as to do something about them, while being fair to both children. At the end of the conversation his mother said, "You know, one good thing about having Nora for a sister is that there are more things to play with because there are two of you."

When the baby has learned to navigate around under his own steam, it is important to protect the older child's constructivity from interference; otherwise there are often good reasons for an older child to feel intensified resentment of a younger one.

It is important for parents to realize that very likely they will have different feelings toward the different children in their family, and not to cherish the notion that they ought to feel the same way about a first child, a second child, and so on. They should recognize, too, that the position held by each parent in his own family constellation, as he was growing up—younger, middle, or older—probably predisposes him to understand one of his children better than the others, and, perhaps, to identify with that child. A parent needs to keep his eyes open to be fair to all the children, despite such a predisposition.

Before I leave the subject of jealousy between brothers and sisters, I shall mention a technique which may help produce congenial feelings when children are little. When one child has a birthday, how about a present for each non-birthday child as well, to promote an attitude of general rejoicing? Of course, attention is focussed on the birthday child, but great pleasure may be given to non-birthday family members through this device. It does not have to be kept up forever. Certainly, by the time the youngest child in the family is of kindergarten age, an announcement a year ahead that henceforth presents will be limited to the birthday boy or girl should be accepted with reasonably good grace.

Play at home with brothers and sisters. The way you arrange your children's surroundings (pp. 74–112) and the kind of guidance you give in play have a pronounced effect on the kind of relationship which develops between brothers and sisters. The discussion in Chapter 7, Guidance in Play, under the headings shown below is a description of ways to help your children get on together on a live-and-let-live basis (pp. 192–204).

> *Settling conflicts over play materials*
>> *Playpen rights*
>> *Private possessions*
>> *Joint play materials and equipment*
>>> *"Sharing" and "taking turns"*
>>>> *Let the right to use something depend on who got it first*
>>>> *The idea of "right"*
> *Play with other children*
>> *Helping children to be willing to play together*
>> *Oversociability and nonconstructive activity*
>> *Duplicate play materials*

Consolidate duplicate materials when you no longer need two sources of supply

Helping to parcel out one adequate supply of a play material between two or more children

Preventing and dealing with one child's disturbing or spoiling another child's constructions

I shall augment in what follows the points made on the subject of helping children to be willing to play together.

Children of the same family are much more likely to enjoy each other's company if they are free to play apart from one another when they want to. Granted, one of two children may be disappointed when the other wants to play by himself. But enforcement of joint play is simply an invitation to ill will. I do not mean that a child should be allowed to monopolize joint play equipment. If he wants to play by himself, he should be helped to find something interesting to do which he may legitimately reserve for himself. Suppose your two children are in the sandbox. One is starting a particular undertaking. The other joins in, to be met with protests. If the box is of the size I advised for two children (4 by 8 feet) you might suggest, "Jenny, if you want to have a place just for yourself, let's put a plank across the middle as a marker. Roger, see, it is fine to use the sand on this side of the plank." Suppose Jenny wants the whole sandbox to herself. To my mind, that is unreasonable. "That just doesn't work, Jenny, when you are both outdoors together. If you want to use the sandbox all alone, I'll remind you about it some time when Roger is not outside. Right now, if you want to play by yourself, let's look around and see what is all right for you to use."

What about visitors? I think it is a good idea as a general rule to arrange that when one of the children in a family has a visitor, the second child has one too. If this does not work out, do not force play by a threesome. Instead, help the child without companionship to find interesting occupation.

Quarreling between brothers and sisters. If children are close in age, with similar interests, there is going to be quarreling. So far as possible, therefore, arrange home life to prevent conflicts of interest.

One of the difficulties about dealing with quarreling is that often a parent is not aware of trouble until it is full-blown. If Mother is at the stove, "stirring constantly until the mixture thickens," and hears angry wails, screams, and thuds in another part of the house, what is she to do? There are three alternatives: do nothing, bellow to the children, go where they are. Difficult as it may be for the cook, I favor the latter. But this is no time for a relaxed, judicial investigation. Cooking matters as well as children. Perhaps she will say, "I don't know what has happened, but since there is trouble, you'll just have to come in the kitchen with me" (or, "take turns being in the kitchen"). "When I can, we'll talk about the trouble." Then, having returned with the children to the kitchen, "You'll have to sit over there, Roger, at that end of the room, and Jenny, you sit at the other end till I get this finished. I have to be able to pay attention to cooking."

You will notice that Mother did not assume she knew what had happened; she did not place the blame on either child, even though she may have felt almost sure in her own mind which of the children had started the trouble. It is important, in dealing with quarrels, not to make assumptions about unknowns, but to arrange life subsequently so that one *does* know what has happened.

When there is time, a conversation about what caused all the trouble is in order. If it gets nowhere, then everything I have said about settling conflicts over play materials (pp. 192–97), and particularly about the idea of "right," is relevant here.

I hope your children reach the stage in which it is effective for you to say, "Let's see if you can work out the trouble. If you can't, tell me, and I'll try to help you both decide what to do." By the time your children are, say, 3 and 5, this may be possible a good deal of the time. But a 2-year-old cannot even begin to handle this sort of solution.

Remember always, it takes two to make a quarrel, or to make teasing effective. In any episode like the one above, where the mother was busy in the kitchen, either both children should be brought in to cool their heels (and their heads) apart from each other, or else each should be given a turn at this. In this way, one child is not the gainer, the other the loser in the guidance given by the grownup.

FAMILY CONFERENCES TO TALK OVER FAMILY CONCERNS

I know parents and children who have found "family conferences" helpful in promoting congenial home life. The idea is that any member of the family may request an all-family conference, to be held when convenient for everyone, with ample time for each member of the family to say what is on his mind. By the time a child is 3 he is probably ready for this. If a child does not want to attend a conference, all right, but then he has no grounds for objecting to decisions that grow out of it. Perhaps a conference as often as once a week is desired; perhaps weeks or even months may go by without one, but always with the possibility of one occurring if anyone wants it.

Such conferences can deal with any matters of concern, pleasant or unpleasant, to anyone in the family. I am in favor of getting across to children the idea that objections and protests are fine, providing they are raised at such a conference. Mother and Father are making no promises. But the point is not just for children to air opinions and then for parents to forget what has been said; rather, the aim is to make plans and follow them up with action— maybe a family picnic, maybe a fastening on a child's door at his request to give him privacy, maybe something more important.

The family conference is a democratic idea. If you do not like the notion, it would be a mistake to pay lip service to it. If you like it, do not run the plan into the ground. Hold conferences infrequently enough so that they really are desired, and be sure they accomplish something. Of course, though decisions can sometimes be reached on the spot, sometimes parents will have to talk matters over and give a verdict later.

Contemporaries outside the family

As you already know, I recommend that from time to time you appraise the life of each of your children to see what are the satisfactions and dissatisfactions he is experiencing. Such an appraisal involves thinking through his relationships with other people. During these preschool years you are often able to arrange that the relationships he has outside the family supplement in-family relationships in a satisfactory way.

Suppose you have two children, two years apart. Suppose the younger one shows unmistakable signs of feeling less competent than the older. Then, you will want to arrange for the younger child —as a complement to the relationship he has at home—play with a group of peers, or of younger children if necessary, among whom his abilities place him at the competent end of the scale. What about the older child? If he is beginning to think of himself as the Lord of All Creation, one hopes he will have opportunities to play with sufficiently capable children—children who will help him find out that other people, too, have plenty of ideas and can do things well.

Hopefully, you have a chance to see your children interact with others. Keep your eyes open for congenial play combinations which foster your child's development and enjoyment.

Not infrequently, however, it is easier for parents to find pleasant companionship for their children than to control unwanted, unsought visitation from children who, the parents feel, are not good companions for their own child. But before you discourage any companionship which a child enjoys, try to figure out both what appeals to your child in his friend and why you object to him. Your own childhood experiences go deep. If you look objectively at your child's play companion and find that your objections are rooted in your own past, try to overcome your prejudice.

If, however, on an objective basis, the children seem not good for each other, then give an honest explanation to them, and probably also to the other child's parents. "Grant and Sam get too excited when they play together," or "They seem to have nothing to do as soon as they are together" (or whatever is the trouble), "so they'd just better be apart." Then seek other companionship for your child which leads to enjoyable, constructive activity.

Sometimes neighborhood difficulties arise because parents differ in regard to how much supervision children need. This is no simple matter. I hope that neighboring parents can agree sufficiently so as to take turns at adequate supervision. If this is impossible, then the alternative is importation of congenial child visitors from outside the immediate neighborhood and, I hope, exchange visits under adequate supervision at the other end. Then there is the possibility, of course, of nursery-school attendance.

Nursery school for your child

I am not suggesting, by my last remark, that nursery school is to be sought only if there are neighborhood problems in play companionship, but such problems might well increase the desirability of nursery-school attendance.

WHAT A GOOD NURSERY SCHOOL HAS TO OFFER

A good nursery school offers your child the companionship of peers in an interesting environment, where he has a chance to develop a variety of interests and abilities under the supervision of teachers fitted for their work through their training and their characteristics as human beings.

I emphasize a chance to play with peers, because this is an opportunity which many neighborhoods do not offer, even though a number of children live in the same locality. And as for home, child companionship there is likely to involve a fairly crystallized kind of relationship as regards capabilities and domination and submission, since the children represent different developmental levels. Play with approximate equals is the best way to learn a give-and-take relationship. Also, it is important to balance the kind of relationships a child has inside his family with relationships outside the family. A good nursery school will be interested in helping you do this.

HOW TO TELL WHETHER A NURSERY SCHOOL IS A GOOD ONE

Without going into an extensive discussion of the characteristics of a good nursery school, here are some points to look for:

Health and safety precautions. Health and safety precautions should be maintained both in the physical plant and through the school procedures. Does the school require examination by a physician before children join the group? Does it take necessary care each day to see that the children in attendance are healthy? Its program should be geared to the physical and psychological needs of children, with adequate opportunities for boisterous and for quiet play, for rest, and for nourishment. The play equipment and the plant should be so designed as to facilitate supervision and safety in use.

Space. Adequate space, indoors and out, is important for health reasons, but there is more to it than that. As you survey the nursery-school scene, pay attention to the space allotted for the children. Do they have room to carry on activities not only without physical crowding, but also without what I might call "psychological crowding"? Psychological crowding may occur if activities are carried on so close together that children are distracted from their play by the very proximity of another activity. Such might well be the case, for example, if a block-building area were located so close to a track for tricycles and wagons that locomotor activity continually distracted the attention of block builders.

Visitors. A good nursery school will welcome visitors—by appointment at convenient times (not, for instance, when new children are adjusting to nursery school). Allow yourself adequate time to make an appraisal of the school, preferably a view of an entire school day, if the school is willing. Avoid leaping to hasty conclusions on the basis of isolated incidents.

Staff. Both the training and the personality of staff members of a nursery school are important. What are their professional qualifications? What is their manner in dealing with the children? What are the children likely to learn from the guidance they receive? Observe grownups and children interacting, without a stereotype in your mind of the way a staff member should act. Important qualities may not be readily apparent through casual observation. (Some adults, for example, have a real warmth of attitude toward children without wearing their feelings on their sleeves.) Are staff members alert to what is going on? Are they aware of the needs of the group as a whole, even as they focus attention on the needs of individual children? (Since this entire book has to do with child guidance, you can infer the kind of guidance I would look for in a nursery school.)

What is the ratio of staff members to children? There is no magic formula, but certainly at least one staff member to every eight or ten children for 4-year-olds is necessary; a somewhat higher proportion of adults is needed with younger children. Each separate group of children should have at least two staff members available, not necessarily active with the children all the time; one adult, for instance, can be available for emergencies in two different groups.

Size of the group. Of course, you must consider the size of the group in relationship to the space and layout of the school and grounds, as well as to the number of staff members. Nonetheless, I am in favor of fairly small groups, although sufficiently large to offer a number of opportunities for companionship at the developmental levels represented by the children in attendance. I dislike having to be specific about size, since the number of children that works out well in a group situation depends upon many variables, including the characteristics of the individual children; but since my term "fairly small" has little meaning, I will go ahead and say that a group of sixteen 4-year-olds is a good size. This is absolutely the outside limit for 3-year-olds. I favor a smaller group of 2-year-olds, say eight or ten. As I write this, I am mindful that people tend to like what they are used to, and I am no exception. Nonetheless, when groups of children of preschool age get much larger than the sizes I have suggested, I feel that one of two things happens; either social stimulation becomes high, too high for some children, and the tempo of life speeds up too much, or else measures to counteract these tendencies have to be taken which sometimes limit freedom more than I, for one, would like.

Developmental level of children within a group. How wide a developmental range is represented by the children who play together?

I have worked with groups which include 2- to 5-year-olds, and with groups in which much narrower ranges of developmental level are represented—for example, 2-year-old groups, 3-year-old groups, or 4-year-old groups. I prefer the latter setup, because the pace of life of the younger children is a great deal slower than that of 4-year-olds. I have seen young 3-year-olds and 2-year-olds in widely mixed age groups seek sanctuary in swings and sandboxes from the hurly-burly tempo of the older children. I have seen a smaller child gravitate toward a tricycle, with the evident intent of using it, only to be outstripped by a 4-year-old. When asked by a grownup, "Would you like to use the bike?" the little child shook his head and returned to a sandbox. The staff member felt this was not a free choice; it was unduly influenced by the dashing assurance of the 4-year-old, but she had done what she could. A mixed age group hampers the older children as well; they have to curtail their activities. For example, the slant of slides must be adjusted to the needs of the littlest children, so that the 4-year-olds' chance to try out their powers is sacrificed to some extent. This is just the kind of limitation of activity which is likely to occur at home for adventurous 4-year-olds if there are younger children in the family. In short, other things being equal, I favor fairly narrow developmental levels for nursery-school play groups. Peer companionship is one of the unique and important opportunities which a nursery school can offer.

Children's apparent reaction to nursery school. As you visit a nursery school, what signs do you see of the children's feelings about it? But remember, a happy, interested child does not necessarily wear a smile. Furthermore, upsets are bound to occur. Here again, allow plenty of time to draw your conclusions. By and large, do the children find activities which interest them? Do they have access during a nursery-school morning to a variety of activity, so that they have a chance to work off energies and develop finer skills, too? What about music and stories? When difficulties arise between children, when children become upset or unhappy, are adults alert to it? Do children and adults have a friendly relationship?

The school's plan for the adjustment of new children. What is the school's plan for the adjustment of new children? Is there planning on an individual basis, keyed to the needs of each child? Nursery schools that have ease of adjustment in mind wish a parent to come into the school setting, certainly the first day of a child's attendance if he is 2 or 3 in almost all cases; thereafter, the plan for the parent is likely to be played by ear. The aim is to have a parent present as long as is really necessary, but to dispense with his presence before a child comes to count on the parent as a permanent fixture in the school setting. Plans for the adjustment of 4-year-olds to nursery school need to be worked out on an individual basis, too, but most 4-year-olds do not need the support of a visiting parent the first day of school.

Is there a chance for parent-staff conferences? Staff members of a good nursery school hope to report on a child's development in school, hear about behavior at home, and to confer about guidance in both settings.

DECIDING WHETHER YOUR CHILD IS READY
FOR NURSERY SCHOOL

Whether or not a nursery school gives thoughtful consideration to a child's readiness for group experience is one more test of a good school. But at this point I shall leave further discussion of criteria for appraising nursery schools, and ask you instead to think over the question of your child's readiness to attend nursery school.

Before considering *his* readiness, you need to be honest about yours. Your feelings matter, too. Suppose you feel, "I love having him around home; I really dread sending him off for the whole morning. Compulsory school attendance will come soon enough." Pay attention to such feelings, but be sufficiently objective about your child's needs to take them into account, too. He profits by the chance to play alongside other children long before he is 3. By that time, if he does not have congenial companionship, then you owe it to him. Whatever you do, make peace with yourself in regard to what you really want. Do not expect a nursery school to make up your mind for you.

Suppose, on the other hand, your feelings are, "I can't wait to get him out of the house." Then you need to lean over backwards to make sure he is really ready for the experience.

This requires particularly thoughtful consideration if your child is 2. Some 2-year-olds are ready for and profit by nursery school; others need to have more living at home and close experiences with their mother before joining a group. How can you be sure your child is ready? You cannot, but you can think through some indications of readiness and talk over the question with the nursery-school director.

Of course, the particular kind of group experience that a school offers is knit into your query about your child's readiness for school experience. Is the school under consideration really geared to 2-year-olds? Think over what you know about 2-year-olds in general and your child in particular. In a large mixed age group, a busy, even though well-intentioned, staff may tend to think of 2-year-olds as inefficient 4-year-olds in the making. Staff members need to gear themselves psychologically to 2-year-olds, to give them plenty of chance to move at their own pace in activities which they enjoy, to help them learn to perform necessary business activities without rushing. Although two well-trained staff members can supervise a group of about twelve 2-year-olds and young 3-year-olds, a more homogeneous age group of smaller size is really better.

Here are some questions to ask yourself in regard to your child's readiness for nursery-school experience: How does he feel in the company of other children his age? Is he interested in being active, or does he seem to crawl into a shell, hover near, or hang onto you? (You will observe that the question is not how does he *interact* with children his age, for if he is close to 24 months of age, interaction is not to be expected—as you know—but rather individual and parallel play.) Then, how does your child feel about your leaving him? Do not worry over a temporary protest, including a short period of crying, if it is soon followed by contented activity. Prolonged anxiety about your whereabouts, on the other hand, probably indicates that this is not the time for nursery school.

Now finally, I shall expose my prejudices about just-2-year-olds. If they are living in a beneficent home environment, nursery school can best wait till later; but by the time they are 2¾ or 3, the chances are high that they will enjoy and profit by attendance. A child who has to wait until 4 for companionship his own age is at a great disadvantage in learning how to get on with his contemporaries.

HELPING YOUR CHILD ADJUST TO
NURSERY SCHOOL

Follow the suggestions of the school your child is attending, of course. Provided the school agrees, here are points to bear in mind:

Suppose your child makes a brief, initial visit to school with a few other new children. Let him proceed at his own pace. Many children need to look the scene over. Stay in the background yourself. Do not expect him to play actively on this first visit.

Once home, avoid talking about school in glowing terms. If you paint a picture in too rosy hues as to what a splendid time he will have, he may find the reality disappointing, or suspect there must be something wrong with a place which is being sold so enthusiastically.

If you are to come into the school setting, do so unobtrusively; stay in the background, preferably with some occupation of your own such as knitting or reading. Avoid watching your child's every move as if you were at a tennis match. You want to avoid having him overconscious of your presence.

When the time comes for you to leave, say goodbye, and be forthright about departure. If your child is upset, trust the school to handle the upsetness, rather than lingering there yourself and so prolonging it. Feel free to talk the whole matter over from day to day with the staff, but do so out of the hearing and presence of your child.

Later, when your child is left on arrival, if he finds parting from Mother still a bit hard, is there a chance his father can bring him? In any case, time your loving farewell earlier than the moment when you deposit him at school. He might have a hug and kiss in the car, then a ride in your arms up the school walk, where you hand him over to the friendly, familiar staff member who is waiting for him.

If your child cries when you leave, a good school will tell you honestly how long he was upset, and will want to plan with you the best way to handle your departure.

Do not expect adjustment to school and departure from you to be accomplished with no signs of sadness. Here again, consult with the school about your child's degree of upsetness.

Do not be surprised, if your child is having some difficulty in leaving you, to find that his upsetness backs up in time, first occurring on the way to school, then perhaps before leaving home. This shows he is growing up and anticipating events. Talk the whole matter over with the school as to the best way to handle it.

Finally, when your child returns home from nursery school, eager though you may be to hear news each day, do not ply him with questions. And do not conclude that he is not enjoying himself if he does not talk spontaneously about school. Certainly, show your natural interest when he does share experiences with you, but let him have a life of his own. This may be hard for you; up until now you may have been in a position to see and hear almost everything he did. But it is healthy for him to have you respect his growing independence, and much more likely to lead to willing communication on his part than is a daily cross-examination. By all means, of course, satisfy your curiosity by consultations with staff members and by observing, if and when the school welcomes visits.

So much for the question of nursery-school attendance. Let us now consider a very different kind of group experience.

Parties for children of preschool age

At parties for young children it is easy to have what was intended as a happy time for everyone turn into an occasion which leaves in its wake jangled nerves for grownups and overexcitement or tears of fatigue for the child host and guests alike. Here are a few ways to foster enjoyment for all concerned:

SIZE

Keep the party small. A good procedure is to have as many guests as a child is years old. Now, of course, one needs to take into account broken hearts ("I'm not going to ask you to my party"), and sometimes a compromise is necessary between advisable size and the feelings of one's child's playmates. If you tip off the mothers of invited guests to wait until the party day to tell their children about it, discussion will be kept to a minimum. Children are far less likely to talk about a party after it has happened than before, and the pangs of the uninvited are milder if the affair is already over when they first hear of it.

DURATION

Keep the time set for the party short. A party from eleven o'clock to one for preschool children makes a convenient and pleasant arrangement, for reasons I explain below.

ACTIVITIES

When giving a party for children of preschool age, it is important that grownups have up their sleeves a sufficient number of organized activities to keep life interesting and moving in a controlled way, along with opportunities for self-initiated everyday play activities if children enjoy them. How can you arrange this? Well, suppose a child is celebrating his fourth birthday. Four guests are invited for eleven o'clock, but you will need an activity which lends itself to occupying children who arrive at slightly different times. One such is to offer each child on arrival a string which he winds up on a clothespin and follows here and there until it finally leads him to a favor he can use to occupy himself, perhaps in conjunction with the regular family play equipment, until all the children have arrived. Once all have found the treasures at the end of their strings, and have had a chance to play with them, it may be time for another organized game. Even with only five or six children, having two adults on hand to keep things running smoothly is a good idea. Let us say that more organized games are interspersed with self-initiated activity for the children. Around noon, it is time for lunch—lunch rather than dinner because it is much easier to serve. (Most young children do not consume vast quantities at parties, anyway.) Sitting down to eat provides a change in activity, and also gives children some nutritious food to anchor down the inevitable cake and ice cream. Suppose you serve two kinds of substantial sandwiches, raw vegetables (which most children like), cake and ice cream. If you happen to have two of the kind of children's tables I recommended (pp. 80–81), you can put them end-to-end and decorate them with a paper (nonflammable) tablecloth and with flowers or whatever. Provide party hats, napkins, and individual baskets (with animal crackers rather than candy, if you are mindful of tooth decay). Possibly your child guests can each bring a chair from home to sit on; otherwise wooden boxes of the right height will do.

After the festivities of lunch, arrange another organized occupation: read a story to the children, or perhaps provide a favor for each, say a ball or a balloon (with more balloons in reserve to replace those popped), or bottled soap-bubble material, so that these playthings may occupy the children happily till time to go home. You may find it convenient to deliver your child guests to their homes at the end of the party rather than having to wait for them to be called for—at different times, despite the wording of your invitation.

You will notice no mention of prizes. This is in keeping with what I have said about competition during the preschool years. Favors, yes, for each guest—to be presented at the completion of a game, but not as awards for expertness.

Here is a letter dictated by a little boy two days after his fifth birthday party, which closely followed the lines I have suggested. Do you think he enjoyed it?

> Dear Granny and Granddaddy:
> Here is the party that I had just a little while ago, and here are the people that came. The people are Len White, Alice Wood, Jim West, David West, Neil Winter, and George Smith [the birthday child's own brother]. We played "winding up." Each person had a string and they wound and they wound and they wound. And then I'll bet you'll never guess what happened. They came to a paper bag, and I'll bet you'll never guess what was in it, but I'll tell you. Well, there was a pail. Then we played "spoon." Each person had a spoon and a potato. And they ran where they were going and at the end Daddy gave them a shovel. And then we played

"pin the tail." You have a donkey with no tail at all—what a poor donkey!—and then you take a tail and you put a blindfold on so you can't see, and then you pin the tail. But usually, do you know what happens? The tail goes on the wrong place and everybody laughs. But you try to put it in the right place. And Len White almost got it where it belongs. The tail, I mean, when I said "it."

That's the end. Goodbye.

Love,

Johnny

Grandparents

What I have to say about getting on with grandparents relates mainly to the relationship between parents and grandparents rather than child and grandparents. The child will be the gainer if there is a harmonious relationship between these two older generations.

Grandparents and parents are likely to have different points of view about child upbringing. And if I am right in thinking that growing up in our culture almost inevitably engenders some hostility between children and their parents, some vestiges of this and other childhood attitudes may color the relationship between the two sets of parents.

The relationship of grandparents and parents is one which requires tact and understanding on both sides. It is helpful if both older generations approach the subject of child upbringing with the expectation that their views will be different; all the better if they are pleasantly surprised at times by agreement.

Tactful grandparents will accede willingly to the parents of a grandchild the right to rear him as they see fit. If grandparents' advice is sought, they will offer it, but not brandish it freely. And they will try to fit their behavior into whatever plan of upbringing the child's parents prefer. Just as a parent of a young child should not make him have to fight for his independence, so grandparents should not make their grownup children feel they have to fight for their right to raise their child as they wish. It is bad for the child concerned if he becomes a pawn in a power struggle. I hope that grandparents will confer with parents (out of the child's hearing) to get clearance for any activities they plan for the child, just as the child's two parents, in their turn, should talk over his guidance and reach agreement at the action level about what is to happen, even though their own viewpoints differ.

Parents, for their part, should also try to be flexible, to be willing to sacrifice unimportant details about child upbringing for the sake of something more important, a happy relationship between grandparents and grandchild. On the other hand, they should not hesitate to take a stand in opposition to grandparents on matters of real substance.

Two more points. I think it is sound if parents and grandparents pay each other the courtesy of operating on a come-when-you-are-invited or could-we-stop-by-to-see-you basis, rather than just dropping in whenever the spirit moves them, unless perpetual open house is explicitly agreed on.

Also, parents should not assume that grandparents are charmed to act as baby sitters. After all, the grandparents have already raised at least one child. Perhaps they are glad to have child-tending days behind them. However, if grandparents really enjoy baby sitting, this is a different matter. It is sound for both parties to be sufficiently honest with each other so that whatever is done is genuinely agreeable to all concerned, rather than to get started on a basis that either or both sets of parents find onerous or undesirable.

To sum up, I hope that shared activities carried on by parents, grandparents, and the child in the family reflect the degree of warmth in the relationship which exists among all these people, so that everybody is reasonably comfortable. In some families, of course, the relationship between a child's parents and his grandparents (on one or both sides) is much more harmonious than the one I seem to be assuming. If this is true in your case, you are lucky. But even so, when one is grown, the relationships with in-laws and one's own parents are sufficiently complex to warrant careful thought and effort to establish them on a footing which can be maintained without undue strain. This may require compromises, which, like all compromises, satisfy no one completely.

The sitter

How can you help your child take in his stride being left with a sitter? For one thing, by giving him adequate companionship with you, his parents. For another, by helping him become acquainted with the sitter under auspicious circumstances. What are these?

First, find a sitter with a pleasant personality, who likes children and who also has sufficient *savoir-faire* and force of character to be able to control them when necessary.

Next, inform the sitter sufficiently about your child's way of life so that play and business can go on in much the usual fashion when you leave him. A notebook with important points set forth briefly is useful for both parents and sitter.

When a sitter is to take over, give some thought in advance to activities your child will enjoy with the sitter in charge—unless the sitter is so brimming with ideas that you do not have to bother. If your absence includes mealtime, see that the menu is one your child particularly likes.

We have already considered guidance of a child who is deeply anxious about his parents' whereabouts, and discussed how a sitter may help a still somewhat fearful child adjust to his parents' absence (pp. 291–94). Also remember my suggestion for a child who is mildly disturbed at the thought of parents leaving: provide him with an attractively wrapped little plaything, to be opened only after Mother and Father have left.

SUMMARY

In this chapter, Getting On with Other People, I have supplemented what has been said on this topic in other parts of this book by discussing your child's relationship with the particular individuals or groups of people who make up his life: parents, a new baby, brothers and sisters, contemporaries outside the family, children and adults in a nursery school, parties for children of preschool age, grandparents, and, finally, a sitter.

Now, in the final chapter, I shall focus attention on parents instead of children, and consider what you would like your life to be like.

11

What Do You Want Your Life to Be Like?

YOU MAY HAVE FELT as you read this book that I have fallen into the very error I criticized in other books for parents: an emphasis upon satisfactions for children to such an extent that parents are overlooked. It is true that I have talked a great deal about children, but the theme underlying all of this talk is that effective guidance is a help to you, to your enjoyment of life, to your sense of adequacy. Of course, I have not suggested that effective guidance eliminates the abundance of supervision which small children need. Sometimes you may be able to delegate supervision, but this is no period in life for Mother to write the great American novel. It is a period to enjoy for what it is, this time when your children's lives are so closely bound to yours. Make the most of it, for children grow up fast. But nonetheless you need not feel, if you are the woman in the family, that life has nothing to offer you but child care.

At various points and in various connections, I have suggested that you appraise your child's life, size up the satisfactions and dissatisfactions which he is experiencing. Now, do this for yourself, each of you parents. And do it within a realistic framework. I am not suggesting that just because you happened to have had the lead in a high school operetta you should scrap home and family and set out on a professional concert career. But in less drastic ways, how can you put more satisfactions into life? What is the source of some of the dissatisfactions? What, if anything, can be done about them?

Let us look briefly at satisfactions first and, in the main, leave child guidance out of the picture. Do husband and wife sometimes give themselves a chance to enjoy each other's company, to do something pleasant together, just for the fun of it? How about lining up an adequate sitter and making use of her often enough to have some life together which does not include children, perhaps one evening a week on a regular basis?

What about interests which go beyond child rearing? A father, leaving his home each day for work, is apt to be involved in more interesting activities outside his home than is the mother of young children. I would like to focus on her in the remainder of this chapter because of the rather paradoxical role that an educated woman with a husband, a home, and small children is likely to find herself playing. I will address myself to the woman in the family, though what I say greatly concerns the man—in the way his wife feels about her life and in the relationships which exist among all members of the family.

If you are a mother of young children, life may seem something like this: You love your husband, your children; you enjoy your home. You would not trade lots with your unmarried friends for anything. But, at the same time, life is not adding up to what you hoped for. It is very probable, if you have young children, that you are tired, dead tired, at the end of the day. To be sure, you have a lot of labor-saving devices—they help—but you are the one who runs them. You look after everything. You are the indispensable woman in a two-generation home.

A remedy which may occur to you, if you can afford it, is a paid household worker. The trouble is, this is likely to be a remedy in theory only, for household workers are scarce. So, even though you would like to employ full- or part-time household help, you may not be able to. If you cannot, the solution to your fatigue problem will have to come from being realistic about where it is most important to put your energies, and will depend a great deal on your efficiency in getting done what needs doing, without waste effort. This includes efficient child guidance.

But let us suppose that it is not fatigue which bothers you as much as it is the clutter inhabiting your mind. There is not much room for more than the baby formulas, the shopping lists, the cleaning chores, the recipes, the chauffeuring that fill your life. When your husband comes home at night, you feel you do not have anything very interesting to say. Contrary to what the ads would have you believe, it does not send you both into raptures to have him hear that his family has the whitest laundry in the whole block. No. You feel you are not bringing to your marriage what the kind of person you were before you were married seemed to promise. You feel a need to put some varied interests back in life.

Putting varied interests into her life is not simple for an indispensable woman in a home with young children. It takes a lot of planning and resolution. But it can be done—if you want to enough and your husband agrees.

First of all, remember that to have outside interests you do not necessarily have to go outside your home. One way to develop them is through making time for yourself. If you have read Anne Morrow Lindbergh's *Gift from the Sea*, you know how important she thinks it is for a woman to have some solitude. Time to yourself can help you if you have the kind of interest or talent which you can carry on alone—writing, sculpture, painting, or reading, for that matter. Freeing some time for solitude is one solution for a woman with young children. Released time requires adequate help in child care, of course, perhaps through children's attendance at a good nursery school, perhaps through sharing child care with a friend who has children of similar ages and a similar desire for time to herself. Or perhaps the answer is that vanishing American, the daytime baby sitter or household worker, one who is competent and kindly in child supervision.

This remedy to the all-day, every-day absorption in home and family will not be a remedy unless it is carried on consistently as a pattern of living you can count on. Under the best of circumstances, the pattern will sometimes be interrupted. Children get sick. Crises arise. But if you and your husband agree that time to yourself is important, you can make it work. Having this free time will allow you to develop refreshing interests to share with your husband, and bring you a deepened enjoyment of your children's company because you are not immersed in it all day, seven days a week.

Another way of putting outside interests into your home-centered life is through volunteer work. If you have felt lonely and cut off from grownup contact, you may get real satisfaction even out of routine tasks (addressing envelopes, for example) if they bring with them a chance to be with other people. But as you move up the scale of volunteer jobs, from those requiring little responsibility to those which require a lot, you will find, if you do not know it already, that these volunteer jobs assume more and more the characteristics of paid occupation. First, they require you to put in time which can be counted on by the organization concerned, not dropped on short notice when life becomes pressing; second, they require the skill that comes from sustained effort along one line of endeavor. Very probably, though, the more responsible the volunteer job is, the more satisfaction it brings an able woman in search of a way to use her energies and talents outside her home.

If I am right in saying that the more responsibility a volunteer job carries, the more it resembles paid employment, then we are ready to think over some of the patterns of employment which married women may follow. These patterns apply to responsible volunteer work, too.

Usually in thinking of employment for women, people distinguish between "full-" and "part-time" work. The number of work hours is obviously important—there are just so many hours in the day. But the amount of flexibility a job permits, whether full- or part-time, is equally important. For example, I know two women, both of whom have what is fair to call "full-time" jobs. One works in an office from nine to five. The other is also an office worker, but since she helps her husband in the administration of a small manufacturing company, she has considerable latitude as to when and where she works. Furthermore, there is a variation in the intensity of her work, since busy periods alternate with slack ones. At the other end of the scale is a woman who acts as a substitute teacher. When work is offered, she can say, "Not this time. Try me again, please." This is obviously a minimal job which provides maximum flexibility. In between, there are various degrees of flexibility. For instance, full-time teaching allows more flexibility than full-time office work. Even within the teaching profession, there are degrees of flexibility. Though college teaching is likely to offer more flexibility than teaching at lower levels, all teachers have an option with respect to the time they use to grade papers and prepare for classes.

The amount of flexibility as to when and where work may be done is of crucial importance to a working mother. One way of achieving this—if the nature of the job does not offer built-in flexibility—might be the sharing of one full-time job by two women. This possibility may develop—if employers can be educated to the idea and if women are conscientious and take advantage neither of their employer nor of each other. Two women holding one job could spell each other when unlooked-for household emergencies or important family activities came along. Granted, this arrangement has potential hazards, but in the hands of the right women it might prove satisfactory for all concerned.

A third important consideration, in addition to total hours of work and their flexibility, for a mother contemplating a job is, of course, her children's age, since that will determine child-care requirements while she is working.

Let us look more closely at the arrangements necessary if a mother is working full-time. The older the children, of course, the smaller the problem, though even school-age children need someone to come home to; and they share with children of younger ages a need for adequate supervision available on short notice when they are ill. But in good health, they will be provided for at school from at least nine until three. Arrangements for younger children are a different story. A good nursery school may be part of the answer, but a mother must not be tempted into an easy assumption that her child is ready for group experience merely because she wants to work. Nor should she assume that all places which call themselves nursery schools offer beneficial experiences for children. You already know some of the qualities I think a good nursery school should possess (pp. 328–32). In all probability, even if a good nursery school is available, a preschool child with a mother working full-time will also need at least a part-time mother substitute at home. And as the demands of the mother's job increase, there will come a point at which the only way she can carry on, without grave disservice to her children, is with a full-time mother substitute. Such a mother substitute would have to be permanent, so as to provide continuity in care and affection throughout the early years, and indeed virtually replace the actual mother in the lives of her children. Care by a changing shift of helpers is detrimental to children's well-being.

Obviously such a paragon is not easy to find. But is an arrangement of this kind desirable even when practicable? I feel a mother would miss something irreplaceable, which she could never recover later. Of course, you can hear contrary views. Recently, for example, at a conference on women's education, I heard an "expert" say to a group of college students, "Just because mothers are the ones to bear children is no reason to think that they are the people who have to give them the care they need when they are young. Have children. Go ahead with a full-time career."

I profoundly disagree with this blithe generalization for the reasons I have just given. However, by the time children reach school age, what is generally regarded as full-time work—that is, work which makes heavy and steady demands on a woman's time—begins to be feasible, but only if she has either dependable household help or a husband who is wholeheartedly in favor of his wife's employment and who shares home responsibilities ungrudgingly. If he does not feel this way, his wife's employment can be a source of controversy, or a source of exhaustion for a woman trying to accomplish more than one person can do.

To summarize, I believe that only under the most unusual circumstances, is full-time work advisable for women with young children. Part-time work is quite another matter. I have been insisting first on the importance of a mother's deep involvement in the care of her small child, but, second, on the idea that she does not need to spend all day, every day, at it. Indeed, all day every day is not desirable. Children actually profit from happy, constructive occupation under someone else's supervision. Hence, a mother who plans well can to a large extent have her cake and eat it, too. That, of course, is one of the main points of all the guidance that is recommended in this book.

Let us get back, therefore, to the question of part-time work. For instance, what does a young mother who makes herself available as a substitute teacher gain from this part-time employment of her particular skill? Three things: 1) an interest outside her home; 2) a chance to keep her hand in at a profession she might possibly want to go back to later when her child is older; 3) an increase in family income (about $25 a day at the going rate in my community) to contribute to family needs or pleasures.

Part-time work will be easier for a woman who has acquired a skill before marriage. I realize, even as I say this, that in many occupations a skill acquired before marriage, put on ice or used only occasionally while children are growing to school age, then picked up once more may have become not only rusty but outdated. Therefore, the skill which a woman acquires before marriage needs to be carefully chosen. Many young women do not think about this problem realistically when they are being educated. They fail to discover a congenial occupation which lends itself to the needs of a woman with children.

Teaching works well, but is not universally appealing as a profession. Suppose a young woman is interested in working in the business world. Then I would hope that before she is married, certainly before she has children, she develops the skills (by training in a graduate program for instance) which will help her to find congenial full- or part-time occupation.

Before marriage is not the only time to gain a skill, but by and large it is much easier to do so then than after acquiring a home and children of one's own. I know a woman with four children, ranging in age from 10 to 4, who has just completed two years of technical training, commuting from her home to a professional school, more than an hour's drive each way five days a week. Would you like to know what time in the morning she and her husband got up for two years to make this possible? Quarter of five, Monday through Friday. This is the way she acquired a skill after marriage. How much easier it might have been to do it earlier! But she is putting her new skill to use now, working part-time, and thoroughly enjoying it.

Why should I be voicing here these ideas about the soundness for a woman of acquiring an occupational skill before marriage? If you are reading this book, the chances are that you are already married, with one or more children. But children grow up surprisingly quickly. Almost before you know it, your preschool daughter will be old enough for college. You, as a parent, may be interested in helping her think along these lines.

To get back to you, even if you did acquire a skill before marriage, it may be that you will need additional training to bring you up-to-date before you are ready to start work again (though remember, in this connection, that I favor a woman's keeping her hand in an occupation by part-time work when children are little). Or, perhaps you simply want to continue your general education. In either case, you may just happen to live in a locality where the education you are looking for is available. There is, at the present time, a growing interest in fostering continuing education for women, education planned to be fitted into the complexities of family living. In fact, centers for continuing education are being established at such a rate that it is difficult to keep informed about them. Explore the possibilities in your community. (Three pioneer centers for continuing education are those at the University of Minnesota, at Radcliffe, and at Sarah Lawrence. Other well-known programs include those at Oakland University in Rochester, at Syracuse University, and at the University of Wisconsin. A center has recently been established at the Claremont Colleges.) Yet, despite such possibilities of continuing education, I will stand by my previously stated bias in favor of a woman's gaining an employable skill before marriage.

Until now, in thinking of ways to put some varied interests into the life of a woman with children, I have stressed the advantages of employment for married women. It is only honest to look at disadvantages, too. If a married woman works, there will be times when her husband wants her to do something and she cannot. There will be times when she wants to do things with or for her children and she will not be able to. There will be times when she is tired, when she feels there are not enough hours in the day and night to get everything done that needs doing. But there will be other times, too, when the rewards of being a person in her own right, with outside interests that have not been allowed to lie fallow, will make it seem well worth the effort and planning involved in being a working wife and mother. At these times she will be able to look at her children with the kind of perspective which can only come from having something besides these children to occupy her.

My intent, in everything I have said so far, is to emphasize the importance for a mother of having interests outside her home to round out the satisfactions she is gaining from life, including the very real satisfaction of doing something worthwhile for someone other than herself or her immediate family. If I seem to have stressed one kind of outside interest—the kind for which people are paid—it is mainly because the demands of paid employment require more planning than do most other outside interests. Also, it is sound for a woman to possess a skill which she can market if necessary: knowing that she has it contributes all along to her sense of adequacy; and that skill may be invaluable to the welfare of her family if some disaster should make it necessary for her to become a wage earner.

Now perhaps as you have been reading what I have to say about outside interests for a wife and mother, your thinking has paralleled that of a friend of mine, who wrote me recently. (She did not know my mind was working in the directions you have seen.) This mother of two school-age children and a kindergartener wrote, "I'm sick of being made to feel guilty because I find my life completely to my liking, just the way it is. Why should people like me be made to feel that they ought to want to do something more than look after a husband and children and enjoy it?" If you agree with her, then you must feel that you have no problem to solve.

Certainly no woman should feel guilty if she finds that being a full-time wife and mother bring her all the satisfactions she wants. But are you sure that you will continue to be content? And is it best in the long run for your husband and for your children? I find it hard to believe, if you are a capable woman, that you will always be satisfied with a life that involves only being a good housewife. If you have an active mind, you will want to use it.

Next, as regards your children. Children have a way of growing up fast. (That point keeps cropping up in this chapter.) Of course, they continue to need their parents, but they need them, as they grow older, in a different way from the all-day, every-day supervision which really young children require. A mother who keeps all her energies and interests focussed on these growing children can make them restive, even resentful, of her highly concentrated absorption in their affairs. Far from basking in the sun of Mother's full-time devotion, they can find the perpetual high noon of her absorption uncomfortably warm.

What is more, if a mother is all-absorbed in her children, she may devote so much of herself to them that she grows apart from her husband in the process. Then, when children leave home for good, she may find herself quite lost, alone and lonely, with a husband who has learned to lead his life with interests of his own which largely leave her out. She was always busy with the children. And now that they are gone, it may be hard for her to weave herself back into his life.

Therefore, I suggest, a mother can actually do both her children and her marriage a disservice if she devotes too much of herself to them alone. This will certainly be the case if she is always so available for all the cooking, cleaning, shopping, and family errands that growing children never have to lend a hand to keep a household running. Perhaps it is rather healthy, in a democracy such as ours, that servants are disappearing. It means that the family itself has to perform the necessary household chores. If children have practice in helping to keep a household going as they busy themselves with school and friends, they are in an advantageous position when their turn comes to marry. But if mothers turn themselves into servants, their children will not learn how to adjust to a servantless world— will not learn how to manage home and outside interests, too. Then, suppose that two such well-looked-after young people, one of them a child of yours, get married. Suddenly, with no experience at all, they have to cope with all these unaccustomed jobs. How much easier for them if they had had an apprenticeship as they were growing up.

In this chapter, I have been urging you, each parent, to consider the question, "What do you want your life to be like?" You know already that I have a good deal of faith in the ability of many people to use their intelligence, at least some of the time, in everyday living. This is what I hope you will do. You need to remember how quickly the years pass. You need to look ahead, for your own sake, for the sake of wife or husband, for the sake of children, to help each member of the family be ready for the changes which lie ahead.

What comes to my mind as I write these words, is a small girl in our nursery school, not yet 3, in her first few days of school. She was painting a picture with gusto, poised in front of an easel taller than she was, when she turned to me, paint dripping down her brush as she held it up, to say, "When I grow up, I'm going to be a Mommy-painter."

There you have it! Marriage, children, outside interests, perhaps a career. She has started planning already and she is less than 3.

You do some planning, too. It is not too late.

References Cited and Readings Suggested

The number in parentheses following a listing indicates the page in *Guiding Your Child from 2 to 5* on which the book or article is referred to.

ASSOCIATION FOR CHILDHOOD EDUCATION INTERNATIONAL (3615 Wisconsin Ave., N.W., Washington, D.C. 20016). *Bibliography of Books for Children.* Revised 1965.

CHILD STUDY ASSOCIATION OF AMERICA (9 East 89th Street, New York, N.Y. 10028). *Books of the Year 1960, 1961, 1962, 1963, 1964, 1965.*
> Each of these annual guides contains two lists: one of books for parents and professionals; one of books for children.

CHILD STUDY ASSOCIATION OF AMERICA. *The Children's Bookshelf: A Guide to Books For and About Children.* Revised 1965. Bantam.
> This, too, contains two types of lists: one of readings for parents and professionals; one of books for children.

CHILD STUDY ASSOCIATION OF AMERICA. *Children's Books of the Year 1966.*

CHILD STUDY ASSOCIATION OF AMERICA. *What to Tell Your Children about Sex.* Revised edition. (Duell) Meredith, 1964. (Also available in a paperback Pocket Books reprint of a 1954 edition.)
> An excellent little book about guidance of sexuality from the early years into adolescence. The passage I have quoted appears on p. 39 in the 1964 edition (308).

COLEMAN, SATIS N., and THORN, ALICE G. *Singing Time.* John Day, 1929.
> Short, simple, tuneful songs for small children (109).

353

FLETCHER, MARGARET I., and DENISON, MARGARET CONBOY. The New High Road of Song for Nursery Schools and Kindergartens. W. J. Gage, 1960.
A delightful collection of songs, singing games, and "playlets" (the latter being a series of related songs woven around a central theme) with unusually pleasant piano accompaniment (111).

FRANKLIN, ADELE. Home Play and Play Equipment for Young Children. Children's Bureau Publication No. 238, U.S. Department of Health, Education, and Welfare, 1960.
A brief discussion of play is followed by directions for a few items of homemade play equipment, including a sandbox. Readers are reminded that the directions will have to be modified if a sandbox 8 feet long is built, as I have recommended, instead of the one shown, which is only 6 feet in length (85).

GESELL, ARNOLD, and ILG, FRANCES L. Infant and Child in the Culture of Today. Harper, 1943.
The descriptions of various stages of infancy and early childhood up to age 6 in this well-known book are more helpful than are the suggestions for guidance.

GRUENBERG, SIDONIE M., and KRECH, HILDA S. The Many Lives of Modern Woman. Doubleday, 1952.
These authors discuss some of the complexities in the lives of modern women with children and make suggestions for utilization of women's talents.

HARTLEY, RUTH E., and GOLDENSON, ROBERT M. The Complete Book of Children's Play. Revised edition. Thomas Y. Crowell, 1963.
Excellent play suggestions for children, starting with babyhood and going into the teens, with a useful appendix which includes suggestions for children's books, magazines, and records; directions for making play equipment; readings for parents; and various other sources of helpful information (101, 111).

JOHNSON, WENDELL. Stuttering and What You Can Do About It. University of Minnesota Press, 1961. (Also available in a paperback reprint: Interstate, 1966.)
Advice from a well-known speech specialist.

JONES, MARY COVER. "The Elimination of Children's Fears," Journal of Experimental Psychology, 1924, 7, 383–90.
This is a report of the experiment in which the little boy, Peter, unlearned his fear of a white rabbit (24).

LINDBERGH, ANNE MORROW. Gift from the Sea. Pantheon, 1955. (Paperback reprints: Pantheon and Vintage.)
Mrs. Lindbergh considers the role of woman and the contribution which some real solitude may make to her life (343).

MAC CARTENEY, LAURA PENDLETON. *Songs for the Nursery School.* The Willis Music Co., 1937.
Songs for children of all preschool ages   (111).

PARENTS' MAGAZINE.
Articles on a variety of topics related to parents, children, and the home.

SHEEHY, EMMA DICKSON. *There's Music in Children.* Revised edition. Henry Holt, 1956.
Suggestions for children's enjoyment of sounds, of instruments, of singing, of dance, and of listening to music   (111).

SPOCK, BENJAMIN. *Baby and Child Care.* Revised edition. Pocket Books, 1957.
Dr. Spock needs neither introduction nor recommendation to anyone, anywhere   (211).

WATSON, JOHN B., and RAYNER, R. "Studies in Infant Psychology." *Scientific Monthly,* 1921, 13, 511, 512.
This is the report of the conditioning experiment in which an 11-month-old boy learned to fear a white rat   (20).

WOLF, ANNA W. M. *Helping Your Child to Understand Death.* Child Study Association of America, 1958. A pamphlet.
Helpful suggestions on the subject   (296).

WOLF, ANNA W. M. *The Parents' Manual: A Guide to the Emotional Development of Young Children.* Second revised edition. Ungar, 1962.
An interesting book, first appearing in 1943, built around the theme that "what parents are matters more than what they do." The sentence I have quoted appears on p. 139 of The Parents' Manual (60).

WOMEN'S EDUCATION. (Published by the American Association of University Women Educational Foundation, 2401 Virginia Ave., N.W., Washington, D.C. 20037.)
This quarterly provides information about opportunities for continuing education for women.

Index

Adaptability, 54, 57, 322
Adequacy, sense of, 59–63
Adopted child, sex information for, 308–309
Affection
  disapproval and, 49
  in motivation, 43–45, 51
Anatomical differences
  chances to observe important, 295, 305
  in elimination, 252
  and fears, 294–295
  4-year-olds, interest in, 18
  and sexuality, 305–306
  3-year-olds, interest in, 13
Anger, 262–274
  analyze situations causing, 268–269
  appraise whole life of child, 268–269
  guidance for, 265–274
  jealousy and, 296, 321
  in learning situations, 264
  preventing, 266–267, 269
  venting, 274
  when it occurs, 262–263
  when parents leave, 293–294
Antagonism
  in guidance, 118–119
  in learning, 72, 74
  toward adults, 47
  toward parents, 23–24, 37, 44
Appetite, see Eating
Appraisal of whole life of child, 49–52,
    114–115, 146, 158, 171, 199,
    267–269, 274–275, 299, 326
Approval
  in elimination training, 245, 253
  expressing, 44, 46–49, 62, 130

  in motivation, 46–48, 51
  when merited, 47–48, 51, 160
  wholesale, 62–63

Baby
  new in the family, 317–322
  play materials for, 84–85
  playpen rights, 193, 323
  private possessions, 193, 323
Baby sitters, 100, 235, 292–293, 317,
    339, 340, 342, 343
Behavior
  accepting consequences of, 56, 66,
    115, 175
  immature, 142–143, 320
  influences on, 1
  modifying, 37, 40, 71–72, 262
  negativistic, 9–11, 145–147, 157–
    171
  on-the-way, 117–118
  records of, 176
  standards of, 69–70, 114, 135–136,
    181, 219, 261, 267
Birthdays, 90, 323; see also Parties
Books, 58, 101–109, 190–192
  aims of, 103
  daily experience with, 192
  encouraging use of, 101, 190–192
  fostering imagination, 101, 103, 105
  fostering intellectual development,
    192
  illustrations in, 103–105
  joining child with, 191–192
  language development, 192
  lists of, 104–109
  make-believe in, 101–103

Books (cont.)
  poems, 102
  story-telling, 102, 105
Bowel movements, see Elimination
Brothers and sisters, see Family
Business activities, 210–261; see also
    individual activities
  dispatch in doing, 65, 210, 256, 268
  dressing, 255–258
  eating, 211–227
  elimination, 241–255
  4-year-olds, 16, 179
  guidance for, 134–136, 162, 210–
    261
  learning aims for, 65, 210, 265
  motivations for, 210–211, 261
  parental attitudes toward, 215–216,
    220, 245, 247–248, 252
  physiological needs, 40, 210–211
  sleep, 228–241
  tidying up, 260–261
  washing, 258–260

Caution, learning, 79, 287, 288–289
  in attempting physical feats, 289–
    290
  toward animals, 289
  toward matches, 290
  toward traffic, 289
Christmas, 90, 97–98
Clothes
  designed for self-help, 256
  dress-up, 96, 303
  feminine and masculine, 304
Clothes consciousness, 15
Competence, sense of, 59–61, 184,
    314
Competition
  adult-sponsored, 63
  emphasis on enjoyment, 63
  evenly matched, 64
  group, 63–65
  prizes, 337
Concentration ability
  3-year-olds, 11
  2-year-olds, 8, 144–146
Conditioning in learning, 19–26, 62
  consideration and, 46

definition, 20
eating, 23, 223
elimination, 23, 247
fears, 277
guidance for, 24–26, 319
reactions, 22
stimuli, 20
timing, 24
unlearning, 24, 277
Conflicts
  4-year-olds, 15–16
  over play materials, 192–197, 323–
    324, 325
  3-year-olds, 11
  2-year-olds, 8
Consequences, learning by, 2, 26–52,
    54, 77, 113, 176–177, 231, 264
  acceptance of, 56, 66, 115, 175, 314
  alternative, 169, 173–177, 273
  appraise whole life of child, 49–52,
    114–115, 146, 158, 171, 199,
    268–269, 274–275, 299, 326
  awareness and, 32–35
  consideration and, 46
  consistent, 29–31, 37–38, 77, 136,
    163, 206
  feelings in, 47–48
  maturity necessary, 43
  motivation in, 27–29, 31–32, 35–
    38, 40–52, 116, 167
  relevant, 31, 49, 77, 163, 167, 169,
    206, 269
  satisfactory, 27–29, 31–32, 35–37,
    42, 50–51, 74, 115–116, 121,
    136, 167, 269
  spanking, 38, 163
  summaries, 32, 51–52
  timing in, 37, 39–40
  unsatisfactory, 28–29, 32, 36, 41,
    43, 46, 48, 136, 167
Consideration of others
  conditioning and, 46
  motivation in, 41, 45–46, 51
  play experiences, 184, 204, 207
  security and, 56
Consistency
  in consequences, 29–31, 37–38, 77,
    136, 163, 206

in guidance, 119–120, 135, 159–
   161, 265
Coordination
   promotion of, 83
   3-year-olds, 11

Decision making, 56, 66, 115, 136–
   137, 144, 175, 181
Development, levels of, 7, 18, 62, 69,
   113, 143, 206–207, 266–267, 328,
   330–331
Dirty words, see Sexuality
Disapproval
   expressing, 44, 46–49, 62, 131–132
   when merited, 47–48, 51, 131
   and motivation, 46–48, 51
   wholesale, 62
Discipline
   security and, 39, 62
   spanking, 38, 163
Dressing, 255–258
   encourage child in, 257
   guidance in, 255–258
   how to help, 256
   independence drives and, 257
   playing while, 257–258
   responsibility, child's, 256
   undressing, 258
   with dispatch, 256

Easter, 99
Eating, 211–227
   additional servings, 214, 216, 221
   appetite fluctuations, 225–226
   conditioning process in, 23, 223
   desserts, 217–218
   disliked foods, 221–224
   distractions during, 213, 225
   equipment, 213–214
   guidance in, 211–227
   health of child, 212
   helping child, 220–221
   introducing new foods, 224
   length of meal, 219–220
   manners, 218–219
   milk, 221, 223–224
   pattern of day, 212
   playing while, 224–225

regular hours for meals, 212
relaxed parental attitude, 215–216,
   220
responsibility, child's, 215–216
serving food, 214–219
set good example, 226
summary, 226–227
surroundings, 213–214, 215
variety of foods, 211, 215–216
Elimination, 241–255
   anatomical differences, 252
   appreciation of achievement, 245,
      253
   attitude, sexuality and, 305
   attitudes toward, 243
   bowel movements, 246–249
   conditioning process in, 23, 247
   dry at night, staying, 253–254
   fears of, 243
   guidance in, 241–255
   historical perspective on, 241–242
   independence drives and, 243, 250
   lapses, reassure child about, 246, 254
   painful, 244
   physical conditions and, 243–244
   program, conditions for starting,
      244–245
   readiness for training, 247, 249
   record, keep a, 245, 246–247, 249
   relaxed parental attitude, 245, 247–
      248, 252
   responsibility for, 242–243
   simultaneous bowel and bladder
      training, 245
   summary, 254–255
   surroundings, 245
   toilet flushing, 243, 247, 248–249,
      253
   toilet seat, 245–246
   training pants, 248, 250
   urination, 249–254
   use scientific names, 306, 308
Emotions, see Feelings and specific
   emotions such as Anger, Fear

Family
   brothers and sisters, 321–325
   conferences, 326

Family (cont.)
  new baby in, 317–322
  planning home for, 2, 75–78
  play, 323–325
  relationships, 315–326
Fathers, see also Parents
  outside interests, 342, 350
  working wife and, 346, 348
Fears, 274–296
  analyze and control situations of,
    275–277
  of animals, 287–288
  appraise whole life of child, 274–
    275
  of bad people, 290
  at bedtime, 235
  of bodily injury, 294–295
  from changes in living condition,
    291–292
  conditioned, 277
  coping with, 277–279
  of the dark, 290–291
  of death, 295–296
  in elimination training, 243
  4-year-olds, 17–18
  of getting shots, 280–281
  of going to the dentist, 280
  of going to the doctor, 279
  guidance for, 274–296
  of hospitalization, 283–284
  of house burning down, 291
  jealousy and, 296
  learning caution, 287, 288–289
  learning situations and, 264
  of loud noises, 286–287
  of masks, 294
  nighttime, 291
  of an operation, 284–286
  at prospect of parents leaving, 292–
    294
  sexuality and, 307
  of taking medicine, 281–282
  3-year-olds, 13
  of water, 291
  when hurt, 282–283
  when they occur, 262–263, 274
Feelings, 7, 262–302
  basic to guidance, 116, 262, 267

complex, 279
controlling, 56, 66–67, 115, 271–
  272
expressing, 56, 66–67, 115, 159,
  271–272
in learning by consequences, 47–48
negativistic, 9
relief from, 297–302, 320
and sleep, 236
unreasonable, 279
Food, see Eating
Foundation, sound, for life, 67
4-year-olds
  books for, 104–109
  generalizations about, 14–18, 178–
    179
  guidance for, 171–183; see also
    Guidance techniques for 4-year-
    olds
  play materials for, 91–96, 99–100
  relationships with others, 334
Friendships
  with grownups outside family, 64
  with children, see Play, guidance in,
    and Nursery school

Genitals, handling, 300–301, 306–307
Grandparents
  advice, giving when sought, 338
  as baby sitters, 339
  differing views about upbringing,
    338
Gratification of wants, 8, 12
Groups, see Relationships with others
Guidance, preparation for, 113–121
  appraise whole life of child, 49–52,
    114–115, 146, 158, 171, 199,
    267–269, 274–275, 299
  basic feelings, importance of, 116
  consistency necessary, 119–120, 135
  formulate workable plan, 118–119
  ineffective, 119, 314
  instructions, give minimum, 120–
    121
  parental agreement on aims, 71,
    316, 339
  recognize behavior-on-the-way, 117–
    118

relaxed parental attitude, 116–117
requirements, have minimum, 119
self-appraisal by parents, 71–72, 114
summary, 121
Guidance technique, 123–141
approval and disapproval, 130–132
attention, gaining, 124–125, 133
avoid flat prohibitions, 128
be positive, 125–126
be reasonable, 132, 135
behavior standards, 135–136
business activities and, 134–136,
162, 201–261
conditioning and, 24–26
discretion in talk, 133–134
independent thinking, 134–137
indicate responsibility of child, 129
instructions, how to give, 124–129
one thing at a time, 127
problem solving, 58, 66, 83, 134–
139, 188, 264–268, 269–270
relaxed parental attitude, 116–117,
123–124, 132, 215–216, 247–
248, 252, 297, 320
substitute activity, 139
summary, 139–141
Guidance techniques for 4-year-olds,
178–182
balance responsibilities with satisfactions, 181
foster pleasant friendships, 180
guide child's assertiveness, 180–181
relax tempo of life, 179
summary, 181–182
Guidance techniques for negativistic
phase, 145–147, 157–171
assume he will respond to you, 162–
163, 168–169
attention of parents, 160
avoid rushing child, 161
be consistent, 159–161
be positive when ending an activity,
165
be tactful, 164–165
change situation he protests, 166,
170
choosing between consequences, 169

explain what you want, 165–167
forewarn child of coming activity,
165
ignore noisy protest, 169–170
independence drive and, 161–162
instructions, giving, 161, 163
investigate causes, 158
motivation for behavior, 158, 162,
167, 170
permissive atmosphere, create, 159,
161
relaxed parental attitude, 168
requirements, have minimum, 159–
160, 164, 166
summaries, 163–164, 167, 171
timing interruptions, 161
variety of interests, 160
Guidance techniques for 3- or 4-year-
olds, 171–178
assume he will respond to you, 172
avoid flat prohibitions, 171–172
be positive, 172–173
child appraisal by parents, 171
choosing between consequences,
174–176
dealing with refusals, 173–177
record, keep a, 176
requirements, have minimum, 171–
172, 175
speak simply and sparingly, 172
summary, 177–178
Guidance techniques for 2-year-olds,
143–157
assume he will respond to you, 155
avoid flat prohibitions, 146
be positive, 155–156
child appraisal by parents, 146
relaxed parental attitude, 155–156
speak simply and sparingly, 147–155
summary, 156–157

Halloween, 294
Holiday activities
Christmas, 97–98
Easter, 99
May Day, 99
Valentine's Day, 98–99

Honesty with children, 286, 296, 307–309, 312
Hospitalization, 283–284

Imagination
    books and, 101, 103, 105
    4-year-olds, 17–18
    play and, 58, 83
    3-year-olds, 12–13
    2-year-olds, 9
Immediate aims in learning, 54
    for business activities, 65
    for daily activities, 72–73
    play materials and, 57–58
    varied interests, 58–61
Inabilities, acceptance of, 55, 60
Independence drives
    in dressing, 257
    in elimination training, 243, 250
    in 4-year-olds, 17
    in guidance, 119, 124, 134–137, 144
    in negativism, 10, 159, 161–162
    in 3-year-olds, 13
    in 2-year-olds, 145–146
Initiative, learning to take, 57, 74, 112, 114, 137, 184, 186
Instructions to children
    attention, gain, 124–125, 133
    avoid flat prohibitions, 128, 146, 171–172
    be impersonal, 129
    be positive, 125–126, 128, 155–156, 163, 172–173
    be reasonable, 132
    be relaxed, 123–124, 132, 155–156
    minimize, 120–121, 124, 126–127, 134
    one person at a time, 127, 161
    one thing at a time, 127
    speak simply and sparingly, 147–155, 172
    while playing, 204–206, 207
Intellectual development, 67–69
    beneficent environment, 68–69
    books and, 192
    judicious comments, 68

language experience, 68
unforced stimulation, 68
Interests, variety of, 55, 58–59, 61, 77–78, 82, 114, 160, 184, 304, 328

Jealousy
    anger and fear in, 296, 321
    brothers and sisters, 322–323
    of one parent, 316
    toward new baby, 321–322

Language
    development, 68, 192
    of 4-year-old, 14, 16
    of 3-year-old, 12
    of 2-year-old, 8, 147
Learning, 113
    by conditioning, 19–26, 62
    by consequences, 26–52, 54, 74, 77
    immediate aims, 54, 57–61, 65, 72–73, 113
    long-range aims, 54–69, 73, 113
    summary, 73
Long-range aims in learning, 54–69, 73
    accepting consequences, 66
    adaptability, 54, 57, 322
    development of potentialities, 54, 55
    express and control feelings, 66–67
    intellectual development, 67–69
    making decisions, 66
    security, 55–56
    sound foundation for life, 67
    thinking independently, 65–66
Love
    acceptance of child, 63, 130
    and jealousy, 321
    in motivation, 44
    of parents, 2, 44, 116
    and security, 45, 62

Masturbation, see Genitals, handling
Maturity
    in learning by consequences, 43
    progress toward, 142–143
May Day, 99
Mothers, see also Parents
    education of, 347–348

employment
 flexibility of, 344–345
 full, 344–348
 part-time, 344–348
 fatigue problem, 342–343
 outside and varied interests, 342–351
 solitude, 343–344
 teach child to help in home, 350
 too absorbed in child, 350
 volunteer work, 344
Motivation
 and achievement, 135
 and affection, 43–45, 51
 and approval or disapproval, 46–48, 51
 in business activities, 210–211, 261
 and consideration, 45–46, 51
 in guidance, 143, 158, 162, 167, 170
 in learning, 27–29, 31–32, 35–38, 40–52, 113, 116, 167, 262
 relevancy in, 40–43, 52, 77, 206, 211
Music, 58, 109–111
 parents' singing, 109–111
 records, 111
 song books, 109, 111

Nail biting, 297–298
Naps, see Sleep
Negativism
 between 2 and 3, 1, 9–11
 guidance for, 145–147, 157–171; see
  also Guidance techniques for negativistic phase
Nightmares, see Sleep
Nursery school, 328–335
 child's reaction to, 331
 companionship of peers, 198–199, 328, 331
 develops interests and abilities, 328
 free time for mothers, 343, 345
 health and safety precautions, 329
 helping child adjust to, 334–335
 new baby and, 320
 parent conferences, 199, 332, 335
 plan for new child, 332

qualities of good, 328–332, 345–346
 readiness for, 332–334
 size and developmental levels of group, 330–331
 space, 329
 staff, 328–335
 visitors welcome?, 329, 335

Operations, 284–286
Oversociability and nonconstructive activities, 14, 178–180, 199–201, 323

Parents
 acceptance of child, 63, 130
 agreement on guidance aims, 71, 316, 339
 annoyance of, 47, 132, 162–163, 273
 business activities, attitude toward, 215–216, 243, 245, 247–248, 252
 child's jealousy of one, 316
 child's preference for one, 315–316
 demands on time, 133, 207
 expectations of, 62, 69–71, 120, 135–136, 267
 favoritism of, 322–323
 guidance attitudes, 1, 7, 116–117, 123–124, 132, 155–156, 168, 179, 297
 instructions, giving, 120–121, 123–129, 132, 134, 147, 155–156, 161, 163, 172–173
 love, 2, 44, 116
 perspective on child, 48, 115–116
 play, joining child in, 188–190, 315
 satisfactions of, 2, 341–342
 self-appraisal by, 71–72, 114, 341
 sense of adequacy, 2, 341, 349
 sexuality, attitude toward, 302–313
 sharing activities, 315
 3-year-olds, attitude toward, 13
 2-year-olds, attitude toward, 9
 when leaving child, 292–294, 333, 334–335, 340
Parties
 activities, 336–338
 duration of, 336

Parties (cont.)
  favors, 336, 337
  luncheon, 336–337
  prizes, 337
  size of, 335–336
Pattern of child's day
  in business activities, 40, 210, 212, 228, 232, 238
  in guidance, 72–73, 120, 297
  new baby and, 317
  in play, 189
Play, see also Play, guidance in; Play materials; Surroundings for children
  4-year-olds, 14
  freedom to use own ideas in, 74, 185, 186, 207
  group, 11, 197–204
  housekeeping, 8, 11, 58
  parallel, 8, 12, 333
  quiet, 8, 14, 329
  solitary, 8, 12, 185, 324
  strenuous, 8, 14, 78, 228, 329
  3-year-olds, 11
  2-year-olds, 8
Play, guidance in, 184–192, 197–201
  achievements, comments on, 185–186
  books, encouraging, 101, 190–192
  consideration of others, 184, 204, 207, 322, 324
  excluded child, 198–199
  group, 11, 193–204
  how to make suggestions, 66, 128, 136–139, 144, 186, 188, 197–198, 200, 265
  instructions during, 204–206, 207
  joining child in, 188–190, 315
  nonconstructive activities, 199–201, 323
  pattern of day, 189
  sexuality and, 303–304
  solitary, interference in, 185
  summary, 206–209
  sustained activities, 186–187
  tidying-up process, 187–188, 260–261
  visiting child, 199–201, 324, 327

Play materials, 81–96, 192–197, 201–205
  arrangement of, 91
  art materials, 87–88, 93–96
  for babies, 84–85
  conflicts over, 192–197, 323–324, 325
  conservation of, 205
  constructive, 57–58, 81–83, 88
  cost of, 82–84
  duplicate, 201–202, 323–324
  fostering imagination, 58, 83
  housekeeping equipment, 83, 87
  joint equipment, 194, 323
  military toys, 83
  new, spread out distribution, 90
  playpen rights, 193, 323
  private possessions, 193, 323
  problem solving with, 83, 265
  promote physical coordination, 83
  rights, in conflicts, 195–197, 323
  rotating, 88–89
  safety of, 81–82, 204–205, 329
  scrap, 91
  sharing, 194–195, 323
  sufficient variety of, 58–59, 81–83, 331
  for toddlers and 2-year-olds, 85–88
Poems, 102
  lists of, 104–105, 108
Potentialities, development of, 2, 54, 55, 62, 184
  intellectual, 67–69
Praise, see Approval
Problem solving, 66, 83, 134–139, 188, 264–268, 269–270

Quarreling, 324–325
Questions
  4-year-olds and, 16
  about sex, 307–310

Reaction, conditioned, 22–25
Reality
  4-year-olds and, 17
  3-year-olds and, 12–13
Relationships with others, 2, 6, 114–115, 184, 314–340

brothers and sisters, 321–325
competition in, 63–65
contemporaries, 326–328
excluded child, 198–199
4-year-olds, 14–16, 178–181, 334
grandparents, 338–339
guidance in play activities, 193–204
immediate family, 315–326
new baby, 317–322
nursery school, 328–335
oversociability, 178–180, 199, 323
parents, 315
parties, 335–338
quarreling, 324–325
security in, 55–56, 59–61
summary, 340
3-year-olds, 11, 15
visitors, 199–201
Relaxed parental attitudes important,
    116–117, 123–124, 155–156, 168,
    215–216, 247–248, 252, 297
Resources, inner, 55, 314
Responsibility, sense of, 56, 65, 129,
    135, 181
  in dressing, 256
  in eating, 215–216
  in elimination training, 242–243
  in washing, 259
Rewards and punishments, irrelevant,
    41, 51
Rights
  respecting others, 61, 184, 194–195,
    203–204, 268, 314, 322, 323, 325
  standing up for his own, 61, 184,
    194–195, 203–204, 268, 269,
    323, 325

Safety measures
  in home, 78–79, 258
  in nursery school, 329
  with play materials, 81–82, 204–
    205
Security
  consistency important in, 120
  dependent, 55
  discipline and, 39, 62
  interdependent, 55–56, 58, 60, 66,
    175, 181

love and, 45, 62
new baby and, 317
in 2-year-olds, 9
Self-confidence, 55, 57
Sexuality, 302–313
  adopted child and sex information,
    308–309
  awareness of anatomical differences
    and, 305–306
  bathroom talk, 311–312
  dirty words, 311–312
  elimination attitude and, 305
  fear and, 307
  guidance of, 302–313
  parental attitudes toward, 302–313
  play environment and, 303–304
  sex play, 310
  sex questions, 307–310
  use scientific names, 306, 308
Skills, variety of, 55, 58–59, 61, 82,
    114, 184, 267, 289, 304, 328, 331
Sleep, 228–241
  aims, 228
  anxiety at bedtime, 233–234, 235,
    291
  baby sitter, 235
  bed for punishment, 228
  bed is place for, 228, 229
  bedtime evasions, 232, 233, 235,
    291
  bedtime ritual, 231–232
  before-bedtime activities, 229–231
  crib *vs.* bed, 231
  day, 232
  fears at bedtime, 235, 291
  feelings and, 236
  guidance for, 228–241
  how much?, 228
  illness and, 229–230
  naps, 238–240
  night, 229
  nightmares, 237
  in parents' bed, 236
  pattern of day, 228, 232, 238
  quiet, in morning, 237–238
  regular hours for, 228
  summary, 241

Sleep (cont.)
surroundings, 229–230, 232, 238
wakefulness, 236, 291
Sociability, *see* Relationships with
others
Spanking as a consequence, 38, 163
Stimuli in conditioning process, 20–25,
26
Story-telling, 102, 105
Stuttering, 297
Suggestions, how to make, 66, 128,
136–139, 144, 186, 188, 197–
198, 200, 265–266, 268
Supervision, adult, 8, 78, 201, 327–
329, 341, 345
Surroundings for children, 51, 68, 73–
112, 113, 145
for business activities, 213–215,
229–230, 232, 238, 245–246
home setting, 35, 74–80
intellectual development and, 68–69
play activities, 35, 58, 74–78, 80–
81, 91, 120, 184, 323
safety measures, 78–79
summary, 112

Television, 101, 111
detrimental effects of, 112
fears and, 277
Tension
outlets for, 297–302
reducing, 4, 116–117, 123, 297–298
Thinking independently, 65–66, 119,
124, 134–137, 144, 186, 264–
265, 267
3-year-olds
books for, 104–109
generalizations about, 11–13
guidance for, 171–178; *see* also

Guidance techniques for 3-year-
olds
and nursery school, 198, 333–334
play materials for, 91–96, 99–100
Thumb sucking, 298–300
Tidying up, 260–261
guidance in, 187–188, 260–261
helping child, 260–261
motivation for, 261
as a regular activity, 230, 261
standard of behavior for, 261
sustained activities and, 260
Timidity, 267
Timing
in conditioning, 24
in guidance, 161
in learning by consequences, 37, 39–
40
Toys, *see* Play materials
2-year-olds
books for, 104–109
generalizations about, 7–9, 143–146
guidance for, 146–157; *see* also
Guidance techniques for 2-year-
olds
and nursery school, 333–334
play materials for, 85–88, 99–100

Urination, *see* Elimination

Valentine's Day, 98, 99
Visiting child, 199–201, 324, 327

Washing, 258–260
baths, 260
guidance in, 258–260
responsibility, child's, 259
safety and, 258
Worth, sense of, 55, 60, 62, 64, 184